The Development
of a Professional Self

The Development of a Professional Self

Teaching and Learning in Professional Helping Processes Selected Writings, 1930-1968

by
Virginia P. Robinson

AMS PRESS
New York

FIRST AMS PRESS EDITION: 1978

Library of Congress Cataloging in Publication Data

Robinson, Virginia Pollard, 1883-1977.
    The development of a professional self.

    Includes bibliographies and index.
    1. Social case work—Addresses, essays, lec-
tures.   2. Social work education—Addresses,
essays, lectures.   3. Supervision of social work—
workers—Addresses, essays, lectures.   I. Title.
HV43.R588   361.3   77-78322
ISBN 0-404-16015-8
ISBN 0-404-16016-6 pbk.

Contents

INTRODUCTION BY THE EDITORIAL COMMITTEE iii

THE DEVELOPMENT OF SOCIAL WORK FROM A SOCIOLOGICAL TO A PSYCHOLOGICAL STAGE

I. THE INFLUENCE OF RANK IN SOCIAL WORK– A JOURNEY INTO A PAST 3

II. A CHANGING PSYCHOLOGY IN SOCIAL CASEWORK . 31

Part One. Social Casework Before 1920: The Emergence of the Individual

1. Early Backgrounds 33
2. Influences from Sociology and Psychology 41
3. The Stimulus of Psychiatry 49
4. Early Psychoanalytic Influences 52
5. "Social Diagnosis" 55
6. After "Social Diagnosis" 65

Part Two. Social Casework, 1920-1930: The Emergence of Relationship

7. The Emergence of a Common Casework Field 76
8. Working Psychologies of Social Casework, 1920-1930 82
9. The Social Case History 91
10. Treatment in Social Casework 98
11. The Problem of Relationship 104
12. The Social Casework Relationship 112
13. History-Taking and Relationship 118
14. Attitudes and Techniques 127
15. The Worker and Her Preparation 137
16. Conclusion 147

III. PSYCHOANALYTIC CONTRIBUTIONS TO SOCIAL
     CASEWORK TREATMENT 153

IV. THE MEANING OF SKILL 169

THE DEVELOPMENT OF A PROFESSIONAL SELF:
DIFFERENTIATION BETWEEN ACADEMIC THEORY
AND ITS PRACTICE IN RELATIONSHIP

V. SUPERVISION IN SOCIAL CASEWORK–A PROBLEM
   IN PROFESSIONAL EDUCATION 195

       Part One. The Dynamics of the Self in Learning

1. A Definition of Learning 196
2. The Dynamics of the Self in Early Experience 199
3. The Development of a Professional Self in
   Social Casework Training 209

       Part Two. The Learning Process in Supervision

7. The Student's Utilization of the Learning Experience 226

VI. THE DYNAMICS OF SUPERVISION UNDER
    FUNCTIONAL CONTROLS 247

       Part One. The Nature of Social Casework

1. The Development of Social Casework from a Personal
   to a Professional Service 249
2. Functional Social Casework 257

   Part Two. Supervision as Teaching Method in Social Casework

3. The Development of Supervision in Social Casework 265
4. The Supervisory Relationship: Its Personal Sources and
   Functional Controls 271

     Part Three. The Supervisory Process as Determined by the
                 Structures of the Professional School

5. The Differentiation of Roles between Supervisory
   and Student 281

6. The Supervisor's Responsibility for Bringing out the Negative
   Elements in the Student's Early Reaction to Supervision . . 286
7. Helping the Student to Find a Beginning in His
   Contact with the Client 294
8. The Turning Point in the Process 305
9. Evaluation at the End of First Semester 312
10. The Second Semester 318
11. The Second Year of Training 321
12. The Thesis as the Ending Phase of the Two-Year
    Training Process 339
13. The Essential Basis for Supervisory Skill 342

**VII. THE DYNAMICS OF PSYCHOLOGICAL CHANGE
       IN THE IMPULSE-WILL BALANCE IN THE SELF** 349

1. Attitudes—Their Capacity for and Accessibility to Change . 352
2. The Concern of Social Work and Social Work Education
   with Change in the Will Organization 357
3. The Beginning Phase of Student Movement—Positive and
   Negative Aspects of the Admissions and Placement Process . 363
4. The Movement Toward Change in the Self 366
5. The Relation of Time Structure to Change and Growth . . . 393
6. Conclusion 395

NOTES 399

SELECTED BIBLIOGRAPHIES 421

INDEX 433

Introduction

Virginia P. Robinson was one of a few outstanding figures in social work at the time it began to emerge, some fifty years ago, from its sociological orientation to the more psychological one with which her name is so closely associated. This new edition of her writings represents the realization of a plan to bring together a substantial part of her work, making it readily accessible to new generations of social workers and others in the helping professions. The project was undertaken in the fall of 1973 by The Otto Rank Association, of which Miss Robinson was co-founder and president, and arose out of its desire to honor her on the occasion of her ninetieth birthday. Ahead of their time, these writings come through with surprising modernity, opening new perspectives even now.

Dr. Robinson spent thirty-two years of her professional life (from 1918 to 1950, the year of her retirement) in a position of leadership as teacher in a school of social work. While the title of "teacher" is in one sense accurate since she always taught classes of students until her retirement, nevertheless the word is a limited one, because during all these years she was—in association with her lifelong friend and colleague Dr. Jessie Taft, and along with an able faculty—continuously at work with faculty, supervisors, caseworkers and students in a process of developing theory and practice which came to be known as the functional process.

It is noteworthy that, while she held the same post throughout this long span of years, her point of view, method of teaching, and curriculum content were never static or fixed, but continuously in the process of change, her work always marked by fresh insights, new experience, and deepening understanding. At the time of her retirement Miss Robinson was Professor of Casework and Vice-Dean. After her retirement as Emeritus Professor, she was awarded an Honorary Degree of Doctor of Science by the University of Pennsylvania. During this span of fifty years, the name of the School (which always remained an autonomous graduate unit) changed from Pennsylvania School of Social and Health Work, to Pennsylvania School of Social Work, and finally, when it became an integral part of the University, to University of Pennsylvania School of Social Work.

The sequence of the writings in this anthology, while for the most part chronological, was arranged in part to show this continuity. The first article, entitled "The Influence of Rank in Social Work—A Journey into a Past" orients the reader to the sources of the psychology rooted in the work of Otto Rank. The last article, "The Dynamics of Psychological Change," is the definitive statement by Miss Robinson concerning the universal process that underlies all learning, no matter what the content.

The title of the present collection is Miss Robinson's own: "The Development of a Professional Self." This, like the subtitle, "Teaching and Learning in Professional Helping Processes," suggested itself to her during the early stages of planning for this book:

> Rereading my published books and accumulated writings, with selection in mind for republication, I am struck by one aspect that pervades this material—a sense of discovery, of new creation. My writing seems to me to be both exploratory as new problems present themselves, at the same time it became singularly authoritative when a new base or a partial solution was reached. It has a curious single-mindedness, and read as a whole from a first paper presented to a meeting of the Association of Schools of Social Work in 1920 to a paper written in 1961, it gives a sense of continuity. Looking back over these decades, I see that a single focus has dominated my writing, namely, my interest in the development of the professional self.

This "single-minded" focus of interest in the development of the professional self, and the teaching process through which this objective is accomplished, can thrive in the larger professional realm only where focus is upon the individual—how he changes, how he grows, how he develops the skill demanded of him if he is to offer help to others. Characteristically, the history of social work shows clear swings from periods when the dominant interest has been on the environment, on social reform, on resources and mass movements—to periods centering around the psychological processes of inner growth and change. Interest in the external forces in life experience has dominated the field now for the past twenty years or more. Yet today we are witnessing a return to the psychological, with evidence of an urgent need on the part of individual practitioners—students, caseworkers, supervisors—to find the channel through which they may deepen their understanding of themselves, of their clients, and of the process by which help can be effectively given. Hence the timeliness of this book. No matter how adequate the offer of resources—money grants, housing, medical care services of whatever diversity—the fact nevertheless remains that the individual for whose benefit they are designed must himself choose to use them effectively and responsibly.

Those who have experienced this training process remember it as a period of creativity, of accelerated life, of inner growth and development. It has become part of ourselves, never to be lost. Familiar as these writings are, we find, unfailingly, freshness and vitality as we reread and edit for this new edition.

The process of teaching and learning described in the pages that follow is not intended to be a description of the current curriculum structure at the University of Pennsylvania School of Social Work, which has changed and is changing in line with changes in the field of social work and social work education. But the issues explored in this book remain vital ones that continue to engage the attention of the field.

The prefatory notes introducing each section were prepared by Dr. Anita J. Faatz, formerly of the faculty of the University of Pennsylvania School of Social Work.

For further reading we refer the reader to the book edited by Miss Robinson entitled *Jessie Taft, Therapist and Social Work Educator, A Professional Biography;* to the book written by Dr. Jessie Taft (during the years just before her death in 1960) entitled *Otto Rank, A Biographical Study;* and to the address entitled "History of the Pennsylvania School of Social Work," delivered by Miss Robinson on the occasion of the fiftieth anniversary of the School and later published in the *Journal of Social Work Process* (Vol. II, 1960).

The Editorial Committee,
The Otto Rank Association: Assisted by:
    Jacob Hechler, Chairman   Blanche Cirker
    Anita J. Faatz   Clara Rabinowitz
    Pauline M. Shereshefsky   Eva Salomon
    Ruth E. Smalley

Acknowledgments

Grateful acknowledgment is made to the publishers below who have granted permission to reprint material and who reserve all rights in the selections appearing in this volume.

"The Influence of Rank in Social Work—A Journey into a Past," *Journal of the Otto Rank Association*, Vol. 3, No. 2 (December, 1968), pp. 5-41.

A Changing Psychology in Social Casework. Chapel Hill: The University of North Carolina Press, 1930.

"Psychoanalytic Contributions to Social Casework Treatment," *Mental Hygiene*, Vol. XV, No. 3 (July, 1931), pp. 487-503.

"The Meaning of Skill," From *The Journal of Social Work Process*, edited by Virginia P. Robinson; overall title: *Training for Skill in Social Case Work*, series prepared by the Pennsylvania School of Social Work and published by the University of Pennsylvania Press, 1942.

Supervision in Social Casework—A Problem in Professional Education. Chapel Hill: The University of North Carolina Press, 1936.

The Dynamics of Supervision under Functional Controls: A Professional Process in Social Casework. Philadelphia: The University of Pennsylvania Press, 1949.

"The Dynamics of Psychological Change in the Impulse-Will Balance in the Organization of the Self," *Journal of the Otto Rank Association*, Vol. 10, No. 2 (Winter 1975-76), pp. 1-52.

The Development of Social Work
from a Sociological to a
Psychological Stage

I

The Influence of Rank
in Social Work

A JOURNEY INTO A PAST

In the era of swift moving dramatic change in which we live to-day buffeted by violent forces operating in every direction, we long for and seek peace while realistically we know that what we seek is control, if not of external circumstances, at any rate of our own reaction. We seek an anchor against attack and destruction, for stability in ourselves that can weather threat and confusion. The word *control* is in every mind, voiced continually on TV and radio. What can we hope to control and how? These are the persistent questions. Neither science nor sociology provides the answers. Answers will come only by experiment in imaginative thinking and responsible action in the long slow process of time.

Underneath the word *control* as we examine it the word *influence* comes to mind to challenge thought as it resists understanding and definition in its usage throughout history. One thing only stands out clearly, the sense of power it conveys. In primitive times this power was believed to emanate from the stars to men and could be all-powerful and pervasive while it remained magical and inexplicable. In present usage of the word this power is more direct, from man to man, from group to group. It may be good or evil but it remains inexplicable as in primitive times. We have not learned how to direct it or control it.

Among the questions that arise are how does one person influence another or a group; is it conscious and planned or does it occur only in natural association; when is it brief or sustained, can it be carried from its original source in one person to create a movement extending beyond itself as waves follow the stone thrown in a pond. Freud's influence is of this nature still powerful today in the technical magazines of psychoanalysis, effective as well in political, social and literary thought. In psychoanalytic theory and practice many differing groups have branched out, some called by the name of a leader in its practice. Two men in Freud's group and related to his brilliant discoveries were the earliest "defectors" from Freud's leadership and their names continue into the present to distinguish their followers. Jung and Adler of Freud's generation may be said to have established their difference perpetuated since in their names, Adler in the American Society of Adlerian Psychology and the *Journal of Individual Psychology,* Jung in the C. G. Jung Foundation. The main stream that emanated from Freud's genius is well described in *Psychoanalytic Pioneers,* its final chapter bringing this movement in the United States into the present era.

When Rank was forced to leave the "Ring" group around Freud with the publication of his *Trauma of Birth* in 1924 his activity as a therapist continued in America and later to some extent in Paris. His differentiation from Freud found expression in two books written as he has said simultaneously, *Genetic Psychology* and *Technique of Psychoanalysis.* These contained the essence of what Rank, the youngest member of the Freudian group, had learned as a practitioner of psychoanalysis. It went far beyond and beneath Freud's theory in his understanding of the individual and his description of the creative, neurotic and average types. More important than this, he created a new form for the therapeutic process out of his comprehension of the dynamics of the positive and negative will with a brilliant use of time in an ending process that differed for each individual. His influence on social work began at the time when he left Vienna, established his residence in Paris and began to lecture at the New York School of Social Work, the Pennsylvania School of Social Work, the Graduate School for Jewish Social Work and to take patients in New York and Philadelphia.

Among his patients in 1926-27 were two social workers whose relationship to him was an important factor in sustaining and carrying on his point of view. To describe this I must write autobiographically from my own memories still vivid and accessible to me today and from Jessie Taft's memories as she made use of them in 1959 in her book, *Otto Rank, A Biographical Study.*

At first it may seem an impossible task to disentangle the thread of a single individual born before the First World War from the tremendous world-wide changes that have brought us into the era of the Vietnamese War. One must differentiate among one's memories in order to focus on and find the turning points where influence can be said to determine choice and direction.

Born, raised and educated through high school in Louisville, Kentucky, my memories of childhood are of happy and uneventful school days and vacations shadowed only by the usual accidents and illnesses. Nature provided the forces to which a child could react with fear—flooding when the rivers rose, the Charleston hurricane, a tornado that devastated a section of the city. But even then, so it seems to me in retrospect, fear was not generalized but projected on a small experience as content, on a question that took the form, "would I be equal to it; would I get where I was going." I think of the society in which I lived as stratified by class, the upper social class distinguished by the family tree behind them. The middle class was the only one familiar to me, where education through high school was important, and a sense of security was derived from family background. Money was of less importance.

High schools were segregated as a matter of course by sex, not color, although Negroes lived in special sections of the city, had their own schools and were segregated in use of transportation and other services. This was taken for granted without discussion that I remember. Religious differences were much more important than color difference, the Catholic church bearing much negative projection. The Jewish families in this community were the distinguished families, among them Flexners, Brandeises, Dreyfuses. The Flexners were my playmates on my street and when I was older I visited in the family of "Uncle Louis" Brandeis when Mrs. Brandeis was president of the Women's Club and one of the girls was, like myself, getting ready for college. The only factor of difference that I was aware of as I grew up was between North and South. To be born north of the Mason and Dixon line or to talk like a "Yankee" was to be in some curious way inferior. I became conscious of this attitude as prejudice and reacted against it. I know that I felt my difference from the girls I knew in high school who were already going to parties with boys and looking forward to marriage. This sense of difference was balanced happily by the fact that my aunt who lived in our family was librarian of the only library in town (it was long before the days of Carnegie libraries) and I had the run not only of its books and beautiful garden close where tuberoses grew but a summer job when I was old enough to be useful.

I enjoyed school as I enjoyed this library and it was no surprise to me or to my classmates, I think, when I was offered the valedictorian scholarship to the University of Chicago. There seemed to be a tacit assumption on the part of my teachers that I would go to college but surprise when I refused the scholarship and made application to a small woman's college in the East, Bryn Mawr College, where standards were high and I was not sufficiently prepared to meet all its requirements. I needed help in making up enough credit to be considered by this college and an alumna who was a teacher of English in a private school who read Ovid with me once a week in the summer before college opened gave me something I had not found before among my teachers, an ego ideal, a standard, a distinguished personal quality, and a dedication to the content that she taught. Much older than I, she became a friend who carried my projection as long as she lived.

Four years in this eastern college followed by a fifth with a master's degree in philosophy and psychology gave me new experience and great personal satisfaction in my contacts with others whose interests were like my own, but no sense of dedication to scholarship or to any particular career or profession. It was taken for granted in that era and particularly in that college that a college education, so rare for girls in the South, should lead to a career. My sense of *career* had always been teaching where my interest and opportunity for employment lay. Social work was unknown to me. Without experience or training in teaching I struggled through a year of not unsuccessful teaching in the girls' high school in my home town. Relationships with faculty, young and old, who, like myself, were baffled and absorbed by problems of teaching and administering a high school held me for a year.

It seems to me in retrospect more chance than choice that led me to enroll in the summer school of the University of Chicago in 1909, a decision that provided the dynamic that was to change the shape and direction of my *"career"* for the rest of my life. When I chose the small woman's college in 1902 I must have been guided by some inner wisdom away from the big university until I was ready to make use of it and what was being taught there.

This was a brilliant era in the University of Chicago. Dewey's influence still permeated its thinking; after he had left to go to Columbia, Tufts, Mead, and Angell were still active in the departments of philosophy and psychology. Even in summer school I was able to get classes with outstanding professors; one with Angell in psychology, one with W. I. Thomas, well-known for his work on *The Polish Peasant*. The house I lived in was rented to a graduate student for the summer use of a small number of graduate students by its owner, Dr. James Tufts. So I was surrounded by the sense of these creative men, the atmosphere of university life and the dynamic point of view that permeated it. *Pragmatism* was the word that identified it, used first by William Pierce and carried to popular knowledge by William James. It assailed everything I had been taught in college work in philosophy and psychology and the standbys I had built for myself or taken for granted in a conventional Protestant home and Quaker college.

Surely it was chance that brought together in the small group of graduate students in Dr. Tufts' house that summer two students as unlike in externals as Jessie Taft and I, she from the Middle West, I from the South. Writing of her to a college friend I said, "I've never met such frankness in a mortal being. She is so frank and sincere and free from conventionality that she compels you to a like frankness and you find yourself telling her things in the most natural matter of course manner." Underneath the external differences we were drawn together by our interest in the courses we were taking and by a common dislike of the person in charge of the house. This likeness was to grow into a relationship life-long, determinative for our professional and personal development.

At the end of summer school I returned to my teaching position more interesting now in a smaller branch high school and with content I loved to teach, grammar and literature. Challenging too was an invitation from a small group of older professional women to teach them something about psychology. I used the abridged psychology of James that I had worn out in college courses and learned more, I expect, than my responsive students.

There must have been more protests against the management on the part of teachers in those days than I was aware of. Any interest in social or political problems of the times seems to have been completely lacking in me. Woman suffrage was the only movement in which I became involved when I was asked to become president of a newly formed College Association for Woman Suffrage in the city. I learned to argue and speak in public for this cause that seemed important and inevitable but I was never moved by it as were its leaders, Mrs. Park of England, Sarah Anthony, Anna Howard Shaw, Mrs. Car-

rie Chapman Catt and others. It was their dedication and their quality
that influenced me, not the cause itself. I marched in the suffrage
parade in New York City because I was there and friends were march-
ing but my feeling was not engaged as presumably it is engaged today in those who march in the civil rights marches.

After our summer together in Chicago, Jessie Taft had found an
anchorage and a goal in the University of Chicago in a program leading to a doctor's degree, but I was growing increasingly dissatisfied
with the limitations in my experience and in the realization that,
though teaching was what I wanted to do, I did not have the secret
that would engage my high school students in a learning process. In
letters that Jessie Taft and I exchanged we were expressing our desire to know "people," to get away from the academic atmosphere
of school, college or university. When the person who was head of
Dr. Tufts' house in the summer of 1909, who evidently had a confidence in us that we did not return, recommended us to Katharine
Bement Davis, head of the New York State Reformatory for Women
at Bedford Hills and the Laboratory of Social Hygiene, a research
center, we agreed to come for a spring-summer trial experience. Here
was the new experience we longed for, with people and problems
utterly unfamiliar to us. Jessie Taft found in the job that Miss Davis
offered her as assistant superintendent the opportunity to use herself
with people that went beyond her expectations. As sociologist in the
Laboratory of Social Hygiene I was a learner in a new undefined field
offering all kinds of experience for me.

Of the greatest importance to both of us was the contact with
the members of the board of the Laboratory of Social Hygiene who
met at times with Miss Davis and her staff to hear reports and to advise on future steps.

These men were psychiatrists, some trained in Europe, all doing
creative work with the mentally ill in institutions or clinics, Campbell, Hoch, Adolph Meyer, Salmon to name a few of them. In them
we found the stimulus that led to the next step in what was now our
own self-directed education. When we left the Bedford Reformatory
after Miss Davis resigned to become Commissioner of Charities and
Corrections of New York City, we had to find jobs to support ourselves but we knew with what we wanted to be associated. It was not
social work as represented by Mary Richmond of the Russell Sage
Foundation who had developed social casework, but what seemed to
us a more creative dynamic approach to human problems. We spared

no pains in examining this field while we each got work on a temporary basis until we could find where we belonged. We had found
assurance in ourselves and the opportunities ahead for this field
that we now knew as *mental hygiene*. Jessie Taft described this movement as "epoch making" in a paper called *The Relation of Psychiatry to Social Work* and tells of her part in it at a meeting of the New
York City Conference of Charities and Corrections in 1926. By this
time she had found a specific job with the Mental Hygiene Committee of the State Charities Aid Association of New York where she
had many speaking opportunities, a chance to experiment with a
small school for difficult children and experience in helping adoles-
cents in the Cornell Clinic of Psychopathology.

Meanwhile I spent a year with a small group of teachers from
the Public Education Association in New York engaged in defining a
function for home and school visitors later known as school counselors. Following this year, I accepted a position in Philadelphia
where a well-endowed new institution was to be built for orphan
children. It seemed to have much to offer but I found that in a paper
planning stage it had no function to engage me and when the board
of the Pennsylvania School of Social Work asked me to take over
the direction and activities of the school whose small staff had gone
to war, I accepted with alacrity. Jessie Taft had many offers of positions in Philadelphia and chose one that involved the opening of a
new Department of Child Study in The Children's Bureau. This developed into the first mental hygiene work in Philadelphia. It gave us
the opportunity we sought to be together, to teach and practice and
use what we had to give. By this time we knew through reading something about what Freud was doing in Vienna. It was focused for social workers by William Alanson White in his books, *The Family Ro-
mance, The Meaning of Disease, Mechanisms of Character Formation*
and his editorship of a great progressive journal, *The Psychoanalytic
Quarterly*. We incorporated what we could use into our thinking,
adding material we did not have from science, from Cannon, Herrick,
Child, Kempf. My ignorance of social work meant that I had everything to learn about social agencies and resources in a community
strange to me in order to help students in their field work assignments with family agencies and child placement agencies. Underneath
the practical problems there was always the more fundamental problem I felt in the student in his need of help of some kind for himself
as well as the client of the agency. We knew that these problems could

not be understood by visiting in the homes of the clients of social agencies or giving financial aid to the poor or finding a home for a child. We were accepted for what we knew about behavior that was new and different and our conviction and our relation to people asking for what we knew gave us recognition and authority in the community. Jessie Taft had added to her equipment six months of supervised training in mental testing in order to have a tool for use in interview contact with individual children. She began to use her title of Doctor and her papers of this period describe what she could do in interview contact with the individual child, not only the children in placement agencies but with children of troubled parents in the community.

Education for social work was in a very early stage in this era and little was known as common knowledge by the few schools that existed when I became Associate Director of the Pennsylvania School of Social Work in 1920. The New York School, the Boston School, the Philadelphia School were among the first schools in existence; the Smith College School for Psychiatric Work developed in relation to the war experience as a summer school. Financial and organization problems were important to these schools as were relationships with sponsoring universities or colleges. Fundamental for all of us were the questions that concerned the individual student, supervisor and teacher, from selection of students through the learning-teaching process to accreditation. After several years of experiment with one or another part-time director, the Pennsylvania School was fortunate in obtaining a full time director in Kenneth L. M. Pray, a recognized leader in community social services. For him, too, the development of education for social work in the Pennsylvania School became a lifelong job until his death in 1948.

This was the school where the impact of Rank's point of view was most directly felt and where his influence was sustained throughout his life.

These early years in Philadelphia with Jessie Taft at work in the Children's Aid Society and I in the Pennsylvania School of Social Work in retrospect seem the most active years of our lives. Were we impelled by our so recently acquired knowledge of mental hygiene with its promise of help for troubled children or by our pressing need to learn more for ourselves? Whatever this drive might have been, circumstances shaped themselves to fit our need in ways that seem to me now little short of miraculous. Soon after we came to Philadelphia while visiting a friend on the staff of Carson College for Orphan Girls in Flourtown, Pennsylvania, we did no more than look at the old stone house across a picket fence from her house when the aged owner died, the house was up for sale and we bought it on "Building and Loan" and borrowed money. These two houses stood alone on a road running from the Bethlehem Pike through country occupied only by cornfields and a railroad track carrying freight and two passenger trains a day from Ambler to Philadelphia. The house lacked water, electricity and heat and was in need of general renovation. We named it *The Pocket* for once inside of it the problems of getting out would be all absorbing. It asked all the strength and ingenuity we possessed but we did not grudge this expenditure of ourselves. House and garden thrived. I do not think our jobs suffered, for both of us continued to be involved in the problems of children and child placement. When the house had been made habitable our good friend Sophie Theis in the Child Placement Department of the New York State Charities Aid Association suggested we take a child to board on a trial basis for a year. She described to us an interesting gifted boy seven years old whose mother had died and whose father had remarried. The year's trial as a boarding home led to adoption. A year later we took a second child, a girl of five, both of whose parents had died.

The house adjusted to a second child by the addition of dormer windows and a housekeeper. This constituted our family through thick and thin over the years until the boy was in college and the girl had completed her training as a dietitian at Drexel. We could not have done this without the help of unusual schools, Germantown Friends for the boy, Sunnyside Day School and public school for the girl and two wonderful women in succession as housekeepers. Good child-placing practice today would not have approved this placement of two children with two professional women but I think we survived this experience without harm to any of us. Grown up now, the boy with a good marriage and three children of his own, the girl with a responsible job as chief dietitian in a big hospital, would not repudiate their unorthodox childhood experiences nor did we as adopting parents ever regret our experience in living with children we loved whose problems of growing up became our own to learn from, to help with as best we could.

Jessie Taft describes her first meeting with Rank in the foreword to her book, *Otto Rank: A Biographical Study* (page ix to xii):

My first contact with Otto Rank occurred on June 3, 1924, at a meeting of the American Psychoanalytic Association in Atlantic City where he was to give a paper in English on *The Trauma of Birth*, the title of his book recently published in German. As a clinical psychologist from Philadelphia working chiefly with children, I had no official right to participate in a psychoanalytic conference, but I was interested in psychoanalysis as a further training measure for myself in the future and I wanted to see who these analysts were and what they were like. An acquaintance who had worked in Vienna with both Freud and Rank had told me of something new and different in Rank's theory as well as in his therapeutic technique that had aroused immediate interest, although I had known nothing of Rank previously except his name and a title, *The Myth of the Birth of the Hero*.

I do not remember how I got to the meeting nor what was said there, but I still retain a vivid impression regarding the quality of the several speakers. With one exception all seemed to me unimpressive, if not actually dull, until the slight, boyish figure of Rank appeared beside the speaker's desk. He was the very image of my idea of the scholarly German student and he spoke so quietly, so directly and simply, without circumlocution or apology, that despite the strong German accent I was able to follow his argument and I thought to myself, "Here is a man one could trust."

It took two years, with letters and a single interview, before I finally pinned myself down to a definite date for analysis with Rank in New York in the fall of 1926. Meantime, I had been saved from myself and my attempt to escape by engaging a substitute analyst, through the latter's untimely death. Later I was able to appreciate what a fateful accident it had been for me, as I remembered the two application interviews with their portent for the future of the analysis. The first man, in spite of his frank doubts of my suitability in terms of age and my limited time allowance, had ended by accepting me, but only after I had remarked, with full awareness of its possible influence on a man who had himself been analyzed by Rank, that Dr. Rank had previously agreed to take me. I left that interview knowing in my heart that I was the stronger of the two and had conquered in the first round.

In contrast, my meeting with Rank had been quiet, brief,

without controversy. No doubts were expressed by him, no fear of my age, no interest in my life history, nor was there any contest regarding my rigid time limit. He did not promise anything. He merely agreed to try, on the basis of the time at my disposal. I can recall only one remark from that interview in response to something I had presented about myself. 'Perhaps the problem lies there.' And that was all, but on that one sentence I began to make myself over before anyone else should have the chance.

Coming to the point of being willing to subject myself to anything as strange as was psychoanalysis in the United States at this time was not due to any conscious personal need nor to lack of professional success, but to the deep awareness of being stopped in professional development. I knew that I had not the basis for helping other people, however deep my desire. Psychological testing of children was useful but, as I knew only too well, it was not therapeutic. Failure with the few neurotic adults who had been referred to me had filled me with guilt and fear. Psychoanalysis seemed to be the only resource, however fearful.

When I finally came to my first hour with Rank, while consciously submissive, afraid, and fully aware of my ignorance of psychoanalysis, my underlying attitude was far from humble. I was, after all, a psychologist. I had some knowledge of myself and my problems. I had achieved a point of view, psychologically. If there was anything in my unconscious in terms of buried memories, I would have to be shown. And so the battle was joined; but I soon found that it was a battle with myself. I was deprived of a foe. It took only two weeks for me to yield to a new kind of relationship, in the experiencing of which the nature of my own therapeutic failures became suddenly clear. No verbal explanation was ever needed; my first experience of taking help for a need that had been denied was enough to give a basis for the years of learning to follow.

At this time I had no idea of Rank's growing difference from Freud or of his alienation from the Vienna group. In cheerful ignorance, I combined with my daily hour a weekly evening lecture given by Rank for the New York School of Social Work, another by Ferenczi for the New School of Social Research, a regular seminar for social work students with a Rankian analyst, and still a third evening lecture course, by whom I do not recall. To this extreme activity on my part Rank offered no objection, but turned my naïve daily reports to good account in terms of their meaning for me in the therapeutic process. Never did I sense on Rank's part the bitterness or resentment that he might well have been feeling at a time when Ferenczi, who had but recently been his friend and collaborator, was refusing to speak to him. I did not try to account for the look of pain and constraint that characterized his appearance at the evening lectures, except by recognizing the hardship of reading such difficult material in English to a group no better prepared than myself to understand, and by projecting upon him my own exquisite embarrassment at these revelations of the secrets of the analytic hour.

At the end of an eight or nine week period—the time altered just enough to undo my original intent to control it—I returned to Philadelphia overflowing with emotion engendered by a vital experience, at that point quite innocent of theory of any kind, but eager to give to others the kind of help that had been given to me. It was not long before I realized that emotion and intuition were not enough. I had to earn a point of view by my own efforts, had to face Freudian difference, painful as it was, not merely through Rank but in my own thinking, reading, and use of the therapeutic relationship.

I turn now from Jessie Taft's account to my first contact with Rank in June 1924 when he was in the United States for the first time and came at the invitation of the Pennsylvania School of Social Work to be its commencement speaker. I was too responsible for the arrangements for that occasion, too involved in holding an audience which crowded the auditorium of the Social Service Building at 311 S. Juniper Street on a hot night while they waited an hour for his arrival delayed by the confusion in the change from Standard to Daylight time, to be able to listen to what he said but my impression of the importance of what he had to say, of the depth and significance of his thinking, of the quality of his conviction is unforgettable. Vivid too in memory is the impression of the intentness of his listening audience as they laid aside their discomfort and irritation with the heat and delay to try to the best of their capacity to hear and to understand something of what he was saying.[1] I had more freedom to listen the second time I heard him speak from the lecture platform of the New York School of Social Work in the fall of 1926. Again the sense of the tremendous significance of his thinking took precedence over the impression of his youth, his lack of freedom with the English language and the sense of his loneliness, his "difference" as he faced this strange, alien audience. The content of the lectures he read there and of those he was later to give in a lecture series at the

Pennsylvania School of Social Work in the fall of 1927 came straight from the books he had written as his thinking began to differentiate itself from Freud's in his *Genetic Psychology* and *The Technique of Psychoanalysis*. This was formidable material and perhaps the very effort required to get any foothold in it was an additional stimulus in our struggle to find the meanings we could sense were embedded in every word he uttered. These lectures as he delivered them in English were multigraphed and distributed to the members of his audience. Later they were remultigraphed and bound for the use of students in the Pennsylvania School Library. In this form they were used by faculty and students in the School and are the only English translation of *Genetic Psychology* available.[2] Happily, Jessie Taft's knowledge of German and her willingness to spare neither time nor effort in her struggle to comprehend the meaning of his *Technique of Psychoanalysis* resulted in translations, which, published by Knopf in 1936 under the titles of *Will Therapy* and *Truth and Reality*, made accessible to social workers the individual psychology in which they were interested.

When I applied for therapy in the fall of 1927, Rank accepted me within the framework of my position and my responsibility as head of the casework department of the Pennsylvania School of Social Work, without question for what use I could make of him in the analytic relationship. My picture of analysis was a naïve mixture of what was current in the social work community, especially in New York where friends had been analyzed and of what I had experienced through Jessie Taft's analysis as I spent weekends with her either in New York or our home near Philadelphia. My own analysis was completely different from anything I had heard from others. I began in the first hour with a description of my family where no problem existed for me and continued with family history until my interest flagged—as did Rank's. Dreams interested him and served me well to take me into the fundamental problems of relationship, the problems he was working on in his lecture series. These were problems of denial, identification and projection to show how the self builds itself up through likeness and difference in a search for its own identity. Figures in my current professional and living situations appeared in dreams for this purpose rather than figures from the past. I realize today more vividly than at the time how brilliantly and considerately Rank made use of these to show me my "patterns" in relationship. I remember today the sense of illumination when he said, "perhaps what the self really seeks is identity; does it ever accept difference?" And the exhilaration when in response to a dream he said, "Perhaps you are really ready to leave. It would be the shortest analysis I have ever had."

How little I realized when I applied for "therapy" with Rank in 1927 that the experience which was to follow of one hour a day for six weeks, a time-limited, internal process, could possibly be the basis, the raw material, as it were, for an understanding of the problem of relationship, of self and other, professional as well as personal relationships. That it can be so remains always beyond explanation, often beyond belief, and certainly beyond proof when one approaches it intellectually or scientifically.

Dr. Taft recognizes and speaks to this dilemma in her article entitled "The Function of the Personality Course in the Practice Unit":[3]

> Those few social workers who experienced something quite unlike classical psychoanalysis in their contact with Rank were saved in part from the tendency to put into practice with clients what they themselves had found helpful, by the fact that they were not at all sure what technique had been used with them. It was not anything they could grasp and formulate intellectually. Difference they had certainly experienced and were still experiencing, but they were unable to pin it down to anything definite enough to be used on their clients. They had learned that help comes from something more than intellectual knowing, that it goes beyond the facts or even the traumas of a life history, that it is a dynamic, present, swift-moving experience with an ending; but what to do with it in casework could not be determined so easily.

Our need, in truth our necessity, to get hold of something we could use in our understanding of the process of change that we had experienced in ourselves and of its applicability to our efforts to help our clients proved to be a powerful dynamic. But what Rank offered to an audience in his early lectures at the New York School and the Pennsylvania School of Social Work presented us with the barrier of his profound and difficult thinking complicated by his lack of ease in expressing himself in English.

My first opportunity to use what I had learned from Rank in addition to what I gave to students in classes grew out of a decision made earlier to work for a doctorate in the University of Pennsylvania department of sociology on a part time basis over the minimum acceptable time span of seven years. The faculty of the University of Pennsylvania were glad to have a closer connection with the School of Social Work that was associated with it and individual members could not have been more helpful in suggesting courses and planning a program for me. Nevertheless this period stands out as one of the most miserable periods of my life. All my interest remained in my students and my teaching and University courses got only the left-over crumbs of my time and energy. I did a minimum of required reading and went to classes feeling unprepared. But when it came time to write a dissertation I knew what I would do. Using the Proceedings of the National Conference of Social Work as content, I surveyed the development of social casework giving my own evaluation of its changing theories and practice from Mary Richmond's *Social Diagnosis* to the period of the thirties in which we were living and working. This was not research in the terms in which the University defined and expected it but the generous thesis committee accepted it and the University of North Carolina published it under the title of *A Changing Psychology in Social Case Work.* It contained the best of what I knew and what I hoped for in direction for this field. Its sale was unprecedented for a thesis in this field but it went beyond what practice in the field had attained and made enemies as well as friends for the School of Social Work and Rank's influence in it.

As I look back over thirty years in this effort to clarify my own comprehension of Rank's effect on social work, and as I follow Dr. Taft's account of the development of Rank's thinking, I realize in a new way that, at this critical time in the history of social work when social caseworkers were so eagerly and hungrily turning to psychoanalysis for some answers to the problems of helping individuals in need, Rank had already explored the problems of individual psychology and therapeutic processes to the bottom and reached his own solutions both in personal experience and in theory. His therapeutic gift remained for his use but he did not need further experience with therapy to enlighten him on the "Organization of the Self" or the problems of "Growth, Learning, and Change in the Development of the Individual," the title of two of the lecture courses that Dr. Taft organized at the Pennsylvania School of Social Work in 1936 and 1937 in which Rank participated and which she has described in Part III of her biography of Rank. Dr. Taft's account of his classes in the Pennsylvania School and Rank's letters to her during this period need nothing added to show the responsible nature of his relation to the field of social work, his responsiveness to the problems presented to him by social workers, his ability to share his experience and his thinking with them especially after he came to this country to live in 1935 when his own greater freedom with himself and his easier use of English permitted his spontaneous relation to a group to be manifest. However, even after he had an appointment on the faculty of the Pennsylvania School and took this appointment in all seriousness, he never thought of himself as a teacher in this field. In a class of caseworkers bringing their own cases as content for discussion, he lent himself fully and intently to the problems involved without at any time taking responsibility for the case from the worker to whom it belonged. It would have been utterly foreign to him to have supervised a worker on a case, as he might have supervised a therapist in a controlled analysis. But his slightest comment, spontaneous as it was, could touch an area of process the worker had failed to see, illuminating the case under discussion with his deep and penetrating comprehension of the dynamics involved.

> It is interesting and characteristic of Rank's own understanding of differentiation in growth processes, that when the powerful influence which emanated from his therapy, direct personal teaching and writings began to be assimilated by the faculty and supervisors in the Pennsylvania School of Social Work where his relation to social casework was most fully expressed, there was no tendency to introduce into casework or supervision any imitation or adaptation of the therapeutic form or method of treatment. On the other hand, there began to appear a sharper sense of focus and responsibility developing around specific services or functions of agencies and deeper sensitivity to the feelings and movements of the clients in using those services.[4]

This development in social casework soon found a name for itself, functional social casework, under which all distinctive casework processes could be described. One book, *The Nature of Choice in Casework Process* by Anita J. Faatz, has traced this development from Rankian psychology to the authentic process of giving help in social casework. I turn to it now for two quotations which contain the precise recognition of what it is that carries the continuity. Recognizing the discovery of *function* by Dr. Taft and her definition of it in the first volume of *The Journal of Social Work Process,* as its authentic definition, Miss Faatz traces the continuity between this development of an authentic professional process which can be described in the different fields of casework, in supervision and in teaching, and the understanding of Rank's will psychology and helping processes.

In the chapter entitled "The Discovery of Function" she writes:

> But first, in order to give the focus and approach by which this development unfolds, I should like to state the thesis which constitutes, in these pages, the single strand of development to which all detail and factual content are related. It is this: that the important change, above all others, which functional casework embodies, is the shift of the dynamic center for the source of therapeutic results from the helper to the one being helped. From this all other detail of concept, method, process, and content flows. By this statement we do not intend to imply any denial of the determinative role played by the skill of the helper or lack of it: nor of the crucial importance of the helping process in affecting release of these vital elements in the self. But the quality of this skill does not arise from the caseworker's understanding of the facts and the problem, or from the competence of the diagnosis, or the control by the caseworker of the level upon which the self uses help; nor does it rest upon the accurate delineation of steps of treatment. It arises, instead, out of a primary acknowledgment that the source of understanding is within the self; that here, internally, is located the original upspringing of the impulse towards life, and here lies the control of change and growth.[5]

In the chapter on "The Search for the Therapeutic Factor" she adds to the statement quoted above the following:

> The problem in 1930 was one of discovering where the control of the process lay: what distinguished casework from psychotherapy. In 1930 it was still believed that the caseworker somehow controlled the client's use of help and the extent and quality of the internal change which he experienced. The importance of the external reality factors of agency and client problem was fully acknowledged but not yet with clear understanding of where the significance of the outer reality lay. From this awareness of problem, explored and worked upon in the teaching process, in the supervisory process, in casework process in school and agency, it at last became clear that form bears a fundamental relation to the process; that the concrete reality

of the helping situation carries the true projection of the deepest conflict of the self; and that help upon a practical, tangible life problem affords the potentiality for help which touches the core of the self and sets in motion an authentic process of growth.[6]

In addition to the historical development of functional casework which Miss Faatz's book follows with penetrating understanding of its continuity, the main body of the book authenticates her profound understanding of Rank's psychology by a description of the processes of giving and taking help that she practiced in her teaching and supervision of students.

Other references to the earlier literature of functional casework should include *The Journal of Social Work Process*, the first one of which, mentioned above, contains the definition of function in the article entitled "The Relation of Function to Process in Social Case Work." Other *Journals* which followed edited by Dr. Taft and other members of the faculty described the use of function in different casework fields, with illustrative articles and cases from the practice of the field work agencies of the Pennsylvania School of Social Work; also Dr. Taft's article published in the *Newsletter of the American Association of Psychiatric Social Work*, 1939, "Function as the Basis of Development in Social Work Processes"; "Conception of the Growth Process Underlying Social Casework Practice," published in Social Casework, 1950; and my own books, *A Changing Psychology in Social Casework*, 1930, *Supervision in Social Case Work*, 1936, *Training for Skill in Social Case Work*, 1942, and *The Dynamics of Supervision Under Functional Controls*, 1942.

As the use of the word *Functional* gained meaning in the field of social casework characterizing the practice of the Pennsylvania School of Social Work and its training agencies, Rank himself reacted against the use of the word as Dr. Taft describes quoting his letter of February 28 in which he says: "As to function I get more and more suspicious of words (or terms). It seems that besides clarifying something, they contain (or create) a new problem. I am afraid you will have to tell me whether I am function or 'need' (and which of the two Freud is)." Dr. Taft goes on to say that "Rank was the last person to understand function as used by the social agency . . . the only function he understood was a professional one but in his case self oriented and self maintained. Its importance as a support for the social worker was hard for him to realize or to conceive of as allow-ing for a truly helpful relation to the client." "At any rate," Dr. Taft says, "Rank should not be held responsible for the functional approach in social work which has been a bone of contention in social work discussions and often identified with the Rankian influence on the Pennsylvania School."[7] True as this statement is, I would add to it that the functional school of casework grew out of what to it had been experienced and learned from Rank and that its differentiation and growth were inevitable, never just expedient, as Ira Progoff suggests in his book *The Death and Rebirth of Psychology*. The concept of "limits" and the search for authentic limits in function and in the social agency service and structure which became the focus of the misinterpretations and hostility directed against functional casework grew out of the experience and discovery of limits in the self in a growth process and of the "voluntaristic acceptance of the inevitable" to use Rank's term.

Under the banner of the name *Functional* or *Rankian,* students in the Pennsylvania School waged war for what they were learning in their casework classes and field practice against the students from the Smith School and the New York School whose theory and practice stemmed from Freud and was beginning to be identified as *Diagnostic.* Nor were the arguments over point of view and practice confined to students. For the first time in its brief history, the field of social casework found itself no longer united by one approach and purpose, to do good to people in need, but divided by basically different approaches in its understanding of need and of how to help those who sought its services.

By 1947 the controversy between the two schools of casework in philosophy, principles and practice became particularly disturbing in the field of family casework to the point where the Family Service Association of America decided to sponsor a committee to study the differences between the two orientations, calling it a "perplexing professional problem." Under the leadership of Eleanor Sheldon for the functional group and Patricia Sacks for the diagnostic group using case illustrations of practice,the committee worked faithfully over a two-year period, examining the differences in respect to concepts of personality theory, of methods of helping and of responsibility undertaken. They agreed in finding:

> "widely divergent points of view in basic concepts," "opposing methods of appraising a client's need and of extending help" and "opposite views about the nature of responsibility undertaken in extending professional help."[8]

The report states in conclusion: "Because of the nature and profundity of the differences in philosophy, purpose, and method, the committee is in agreement in believing that these two orientations cannot be effectively reconciled or combined."[9]

In 1947, the year in which the Family Service Association of America initiated its study of difference in the casework field, the National Conference of Social Work took notice of this controversy and it was Kenneth L. M. Pray who, with "apologies for the fact that he was not a caseworker and never had been one" undertook to present to the section on casework a paper entitled, "A Restatement of the Generic Principles of Social Casework Practice." Mr. Pray was not only Director of the Pennsylvania School of Social Work, where admittedly the predominant emphasis of the faculty was on casework, but he was also regarded as the dean of social work, a man related to every field of practice. His dedication to the field of social welfare, both public and private, was known to be lifelong; his experience in teaching, board membership, committee work, with assignments on a national as well as a social level, as chairman of the Philadelphia chapter of the National Association of Social Workers, as President of the National Conference of Social Work, etc., had involved him constantly in a search for his own attitudes on the pressing problems of professional practice and of organization and education for social work. While he was always open to what was new in practice or theory, he took nothing from another point of view superficially or facilely, engaging only with what was pertinent to his own focus of inquiry where it had meaning for him until he could find use for it in his own thought organization. It is interesting to remember how responsive he was to Rank's philosophy, how much he enjoyed a personal contact with him without any impulse to seek therapy for himself. His ability to accept the new point of view that his faculty were introducing into casework and to deal with the criticisms of it that were projected on him in his contacts with other schools of social work was amazing, understandable only in terms of a wholeness and integration in himself and an undeviating respect for the other person, a balance rarely found. As he struggled with the problem which occupied his mature life, the problem of finding the limits within which professional helping could develop, he made distinctive and important contributions to the literature of functional social work, notably an article on "The Agency's Role in Service."[10]

His paper before the National Conference of Social Work on

"Generic Principles of Social Casework Practice" was eagerly awaited and accepted as a definitive statement of functional casework in its difference from the diagnostic school by his casework faculty and by practitioners in the field. I quote from the end of this paper where, speaking of the difference he has described and which on the whole he regards as promising for the future of social work, he closes with "a word of warning."

> It is not, and cannot be, a matter of indifference either to the individual or to the profession, what choice is made among these alternatives. . . . Either choice, any choice of basic concepts of professional practice, involves giving up something of oneself, of one's own accustomed and comfortable patterns of thought and feeling and action. Especially, perhaps—I am free to admit—does the functional point of view demand this kind of change. For the individual, the old personal freedom of professional purpose and achievement must yield to the limits of a defined and controlled function and to the realization that the determination of the outcome is within the power of another. This is not easy to accept and to make truly one's own. It involves a discipline of the self which is probably unique among all professions, in its demands upon the worker, both in training and in later professional practice.[11]

In this paragraph just quoted lies the most personal statement of the internal source of his philosophy that to my knowledge Mr. Pray ever made. Inherent in this statement is the recognition of the moment of internal change in the self in relation to "the other" and realization of the discipline of the self which follows. This is a precise description of what functional caseworkers experienced in the development which followed the impact with Rank's psychology.

Mr. Pray's death in March 1948 following this major speech at the National Conference of Social Work, the retirement in 1950 of the two oldest members of the faculty, Dr. Taft and myself, was the occasion for major changes in the University of Pennsylvania School of Social Work. The New York School of Social Work had become Freudian or diagnostic in its psychological orientation. The Graduate School for Jewish Social Work, where Rank's influence through Dr. and Mrs. Karpf was important, had ceased to exist. Rank's psychological point of view was carried into other schools of social work, notably the North Carolina School of Social Work and as far west as the University of Southern California where Rose Green, formerly of the Philadelphia Child Guidance Clinic and a patient of Rank's, held an important position on the faculty.

When the Pennsylvania School of Social Work found a new center of gravity in its relation to the University under the able Deanship of Ruth Smalley, undoubtedly the influence of Rank continued to prevail and individual graduates have carried the meaning of that influence into their practice. There is no way of assessing the extent of, and depth of that influence except through what comes back to those of us who represent the Otto Rank Association and edit its journals.

Rank preserved folders among his papers for every class or lecture he had given, containing notes usually on scraps of paper and often illegible, about some case or question presented by the group or class members; sometimes a complete outline of a lecture on a topic which he had prepared in advance for a particular meeting. Sometimes the choice of a topic was left entirely to him as was the case in an invitation from the New York School of Social Work Student Organization on November 16, 1935. An all day meeting of the conference was scheduled, the morning session to be on a philosophy of social casework with a paper and several discussions prepared by students. Rank was to be the afternoon speaker and though he was not expected to make any connection between his speech and the morning session, copies of the students' papers were sent to him in advance. His blue-penciled marks in the margin of the papers indicate how thoughtfully he read them. He entitled his own paper, "Psychology and Psychologies" speaking very simply and directly to the point of the changing character of psychology saying:

> That is the one idea I would like to impress upon you, psychology is not and never can be, purely scientific, i.e., absolute, in as much as it has to be human and not the experimental and laboratory kind. Theories of psychology are just as much a product of their civilizations as everything else, they not only change like fashions, I might almost say, but they have to change in order to be applicable to the understanding of the existing type of man.

This was the theme of his opening address to the Psychological Center in Paris, in the summer of 1934[12] perhaps his one attempt to use his influence directly to gather a group of professional workers from various fields, psychiatrists, psychologists, child guidance workers and general counselors who might come together to discuss the problems of counseling and helping under his leadership. This opening address was very important to him as evidenced by the number of copies he preserved, handwritten and typed, indicating various stages of rewriting before it satisfied him for delivery to the group that was finally assembled in Paris, its membership indicating the widespread extent of his leadership in the United States at that time. This interest in "changing psychologies" was his own, expressed in his *Seelenglaube und Psychologie* (written in 1930) and *Art and Artist* of the same period. *Beyond Psychology* which was to carry on this line of thinking was already beginning to formulate itself in his mind at the same time.

The focus of the problems that were of concern to social workers in the decade of 1930-40 and where they turned to psychoanalysts for enlightenment can be read in an outline of a series of six lectures which Rank prepared for the Graduate School for Jewish Social Work with the help of Dr. and Mrs. Karpf, at that time director and faculty member of the School, to be given in the spring of 1935. The outline was divided as follows:

> Three lectures on theory:
> 1) Activity vs. Passivity
> 2) Denial vs. Repression
> 3) Will as a Dynamic Factor
> Three lectures on therapy:
> 1) Time limit and the ending phase
> 2) The role of the analyst as a type
> 3) Illness and healing

The first topic was one of the most controversial issues in social casework at that time and Rank brought to it his own experience with the question of activity and passivity of the analyst in psychotherapy. He evidently discussed this topic in different groups of social workers and two rough copies of a lecture on this subject were saved among his papers. In this paper he gave a brief account of the changes he had seen in the attitude of the analysts towards their activity in the psychoanalytic process leading to "a movement in the past fifteen years towards a more active, more direct and more effective approach than orthodox analysis had to offer," beginning with his own separation of theory from therapy in 1921. Of his own attitude he says:

> I allowed the patient a much more active part not only in the analytic situation but also in life by putting the whole em-

phasis of the process on an emotional, instead of an intellectual experience. . . . I introduced the setting of a time limit to the analytic process on the basis of a philosophy of life in which the principle of separation plays the most important role. In this way the whole emphasis was shifted from the investigation of the cause to the present emotional situation in the analytic situation . . . analysts criticizing this approach as 'suggestion' overlooked the fact that this dynamic activity called forth in the client an intense reaction—equally active— which left less room for suggestion than the analysts' explanation. . . . Their own reaction was due to fear, fear of suggesting something to the patient which had to be explained to him anyway and fear of his reaction, that is fear of his activity.

This fear was less or even non-existent in social work which was basically more active by its very nature and so could easily adopt the more active approach of the new therapeutic movement. This was first and foremost achieved by the Philadelphia School, the leaders of which were by virtue of their own approach attracted to my philosophy. But what they accepted from it was not only a confirmation of their own activity as social workers but the more essential and deeper meaning of the therapeutic process as an active, almost creative experience, on the patient's part. And because they try to permit the client to work out his own salvation, with their help to be sure, their approach was characterized as 'passive' from the worker's point of view whereas it is 'active' from the point of view of the client, that is, purely therapeutically speaking.

This point around passivity and activity in social casework has been confused by the same fundamental error which led Freud to the mixing up of theory and therapy. The whole psychoanalytic approach is centered around the therapist who is doing the research and the explaining on the basis of what he knows; while real therapy has to be centered around the client, his difficulties, his needs, his activities. It seems to me irrelevant whether the worker is active or passive as long as the client can be made active in a constructive way.[13]

Again and again in answer to the question which never failed to present itself in any audience of social caseworkers as to the nature of therapy, he made the point that therapy could not be based on causality but can only be based on spontaneity; that it was by its very nature anti-causal, "an assertion of the individual against causality, that is creative."

The following statement which I take from his notes on this

subject can stand today as a brief definition of therapy as he understood and practiced it.

Therapy, then, in its broadest sense is a process in which the individual is taught to accept limitations, an acceptance which ordinarily is brought about by the living experience in reality. Hence therapy, as said before, should be nothing else but a conscious and purposeful utilization of the normal growth in every existing relationship. Thus adjustment, which cannot be forced anyway, becomes acceptance, which, on the other hand, can only be internally achieved by a reevaluation of one's own past experiences.

From self-acceptance, which is the biggest change from self-denial, follows acceptance of others, the world at large, that is of life. Therefore acceptance starts with the individual's own limitations within himself, limitations which his imagination tries to override. (Ideal, etc.). This is necessary and helpful as long as he does not try to carry out his imagination beyond his own capacity. In other words, the imaginary expansion of one's own self has to be kept apart from real life inasmuch as it is impossible to carry it into life.

The danger in therapy is due to the same imaginative jumping beyond one's own self, because this leads to a vicarious living beyond one's own limitations in the other, the therapist, a phenomenon which has been described as identification or idealization. On the other hand, the more a therapist or a teacher is himself, that is, has accepted and remains within his own limitations, the more effectively will he enable his client or pupil to accept limitations in himself instead of projecting them and fighting them outside himself. This typical resistance of analytic therapy can be easily avoided if one does not demand more of one's client than oneself was or is able to achieve. As long as we do that we are just as much neurotic as is the other and are bound to accept all the other's projections and identifications. In other words, this kind of therapy becomes mutually vicarious instead of independent growth which finds its own limitations automatically in the individual himself.

Human relationship, common to all situations in all times and in all places, is the one basic element which forms the basis of social psychology as it is the sum and substance of so-called individual psychology which is in truth a relationship psychology. The only real individual psychology is a laboratory psychology in method and a biological psychology in content. Everything beyond that like emotion, intellect, language, etc. is relationship psychology which leads to social psychology of a new kind. The use one individual makes of the other in every relationship situation is the real subject of social psychology. So far only the relationship between doctor and patient has been made use of therapeutically until we discovered that every human relationship is therapeutic in essence, the parent-child relationship, the teacher-pupil relationship, marriage, friendship, love. The difference between therapy as a specially utilized relationship and other human relationships which operate therapeutically is then that in life the other becomes not only a part of the situation but of the other self as well.[14]

Rank carried this psychology to the many places in the United States where he was asked to speak in this period of his greatest popularity. Often the invitation came from a university, from faculty members and therapists, or from a school of social work. In Hartford, Connecticut, it originated in a clinic whose psychiatrist and chief social worker were present at the Psychological Center in Paris and here he gave what amounted to a continuous class or institute. At the University of Buffalo it was a weekend seminar organized by its faculty members. In Cleveland the enrollment for his lecture from both social workers and psychiatrists was so large that the group was divided into two parts. There were other lectures on his way west of which there is no record except a newspaper clipping. In California on the invitation of Dr. Lovel Langstroth he gave a weekend seminar of four lectures, one at Stanford University. Dr. Langstroth's interest in Rank's point of view stimulated a book of his own entitled *Structure of the Ego*.

California became Rank's goal as a place to find a new life for himself.

In the fall of 1938 Dr. Taft was in the hospital with pneumonia, too sick to know that Rank had been to see her in the hospital. His letters have much to tell her of his ups and downs in writing, of his own illnesses, of his *Beyond Psychology*. During the two weeks he spent with us in our summer cabin in Vermont in 1939 he was absorbed in writing his *Beyond Psychology*—always cheerful, full of good humor in spite of bad weather. He was planning to go to California as soon as Estelle Buel, then his secretary, returned from Europe.

The divorce from his first wife, Beata, long planned, came through in August 1939 and released him to marry Estelle Buel. His letters, though he is not well, are full of his plans to settle his affairs in New York and move to California as soon as possible. His letter to me October 22, 1939, expresses his farewell to the School. He died nine days later in Polyclinic Hospital, New York, of a sudden, undiagnosed infection.

October 22, 1939

Dear Virginia,

It was a real pleasure to receive such a good letter from you, especially at a time when I was beginning to feel a little better.

Though I was only a couple of days in the hospital—for the removal of the stone—I was still or two weeks afterwards pretty much 'hospitalized' but at least at home. The picking up is still rather slow and I am taking things easy.

It seems to me the right time to go out West, not because I am not feeling quite well but because I want and need a different kind of life. This also applies to my relation to the School. I was glad to hear that things look so much better this year and I am sure the School has a unique function to fulfill. I am naturally proud of whatever I may have contributed to its present status and future significance.

At the same time I feel that that's all I had to give, not because I don't feel so strong at the moment but because my interests are decidedly narrowing down to some problems of which there is little use in either therapy or social work. I have to come to some peace within myself and with the world at large, which is a purely personal matter. Not that others may not benefit therefrom but it is not primarily meant for that.

Yet, it is still nice to hear that the help I could give to some people has borne fruit.

I shall certainly make it a point to come to Flourtown before going West and probably wouldn't come anyway without Mrs. Rank and Spooky. I'll let you know in time.

With best wishes to both of you
Your
Rank

This paper comes to an end while influence continues for wherever there is life as in Rank's contribution it can spring up anew in unexpected places. In working on these problems I have been newly impressed with the dynamic power of Rank's thought and the wholeness it achieved in expression in his short life from his first book,

Der Künstler, to *Art and Artist* and *Beyond Psychology.* As time goes on evaluations of Rank will depend almost wholly upon his work without the biographical facts that his reticence concealed. His letters to Jessie Taft and his relation to Anaïs Nin as described in her diary are frankness itself without factual detail and a revelation of an outstanding and unusual quality of this man of genius. Like other men of genius—I think particularly of D. H. Lawrence, with whom Rank has been compared—his dynamic personality operated as a magnet to draw others to him. But unlike other men of genius his necessity to express himself creatively was finely balanced by a sensitivity to the other person. The discipline he exercised upon his expression of his own creativity eventuated in an understanding of relationship and of relationship psychology that remains his greatest contribution to psychology and to therapy.

II

A Changing Psychology
in Social Casework

*The preceding article, "The Influence of Rank in Social Work—
A Journey Into a Past," was placed first in this new edition of the
writings of Virginia P. Robinson (even though it is the last to have
been written) for two important reasons: first, because it serves as an
introduction by the author herself, but also because the narrative written as a "journey into a past" is essential to an understanding of all
that follows. The development of the professional self, as it evolves
in these pages, is rooted in an undeviating philosophy and psychology which grows with the years, every experience serving to enrich
and deepen the insights which come to a dramatic conclusion in
the final article in this volume, "The Dynamics of Psychological
Change."*

*The dates in this early sequence are noteworthy: toward the end
of the year 1927, Miss Robinson applied to Otto Rank for therapy.
She writes, "Rank accepted me within the framework of my position and my responsibility as head of the casework department of
the Pennsylvania School of Social Work. . . ." At some date within
this same period, she applied to and was accepted as a doctoral can-
didate in the sociology department of the University of Pennsylvania
as she continued with her teaching program. Her doctorate was con-
ferred in June, 1931; in the fall of 1930 her doctoral dissertation*
"A Changing Psychology in Social Case Work," *was published by the
University of North Carolina Press. In the Preface she writes, "This
study was undertaken as a fulfillment of the thesis requirement for
a doctorate. As the problem evolved in my mind the study ceased to
have any external character and became the organization and expression of my own thought and philosophy in the casework field. This
philosophy has been taking shape over the twenty-year period of my
association with social work. While the following pages have been*

31

written solely out of the necessity to organize my own thinking and not from any consideration of the needs of the casework field, in publishing this book I have had in mind an audience of teachers, supervisors, and caseworkers who are occupied, as I am, with these problems of relationship." On the flyleaf of her own first copy of this book, she wrote: "First Copy, November 1930."

The whole of A Changing Psychology in Social Case Work *(excepting the Preface and Introduction) is published in the pages that follow. There can be no doubt that it was written in the heightened excitement, awareness, and evolving clarity of the fresh psychology which was emerging during her work with Rank. The book is divided into two parts: Part I is historical—brief but clear and complete for what she calls "The Emergence of the Individual—Social Casework Before 1920," and Part II, "The Emergence of Relationship" is indeed a "changing psychology." She does not write about Rank or attempt to present his point of view. Only an occasional footnote refers to his work.*

This is an all-important point to be observed regarding the "human-professional" experience of influence. The reader may observe here the process by which a new idea is assimilated into the self, emerging finally as a new creation of the writer because the new has become an integral part of the self and is changed and recreated in the new expression.

Among the reviews which appeared following the publication of A Changing Psychology *was one written by Bertha Reynolds, a teacher and leader in the field of social work, who wrote "Some books sink into the pool of oblivion without a ripple. . . . Some are like earthquakes, felt but not comprehended at the time and producing no one knows what changes. One only knows that after their coming nothing is the same again.* A Changing Psychology in Social Case Work *bears the mark of such a book." She adds, "It produces fear, consternation, wonder, deep delight. It cannot be dismissed lightly even though one's fundamental disagreement prompts one to set it aside."*

PART ONE. SOCIAL CASEWORK BEFORE 1920: THE EMERGENCE OF THE INDIVIDUAL

1. EARLY BACKGROUNDS

Search for an understanding of the problems and conflicts in modern social casework must take us back to its origins in a movement animated by a very different drive. "Charity," "Philanthropy," "Relief," "Correction," were the first watchwords of social work in America. By the year 1840 there were over thirty private relief-giving societies in the city of New York, associations instituted "on the principle of providing for particular classes of the indigent, which united moral objects with the relief of physical want."[1] From the first, giving was tied up with the problem of restraint in giving, since along with the community's concern for suffering and poverty and its desire to relieve itself of the pain of this burden, went a fear as great that relief of poverty would contribute to its increase. This fear had far-reaching roots in the English treatment of its serious problem of poverty leading up to the Poor Law Reforms of 1834 for the protection of the community against the demands and impositions of its poor. The reports of the charitable societies of the nineteenth century show clearly the origin of the philanthropic motive in the desire to rid the community of the unpleasantness of having to live with its poor, and, at the same time, the necessity to restrain and to punish to avoid spoiling the poor. Since relief had to be given, it had to be administered in such a way as to carry with it a measure of discipline, a measure of warning, and a measure of reform. This point of view stands out in the 1818 report of The Society for the Preventon of Pauperism which Devine quotes as giving the most positive enunciation of the modern idea of that period:

> Let the moral sense be awakened and the moral influence be established in the minds of the improvident, the unfortunate, and the depraved. Let them be approached with kindness and an ingenuous concern for their welfare; inspire them with self-respect and encourage their industry and economy; in short, enlighten their minds and teach them to take care of themselves. Those are the methods of doing them real and perma-

nent good and relieving the community from the pecuniary exactions, the multiplied exactions and threatening dangers of
which they are the authors.[2]

The fear and impatience of the last sentence cannot be missed: "To
relieve the community from exactions and threatening dangers."

A new regard for the individual rather than pity or disgust or
fear for his poverty appears in a critical reaction against the work of
these earlier societies and the inauguration of a new movement, The
New York Association for Improving the Condition of the Poor, in
1842. Its aims were expressed in the following statement:

> It was primarily and directly to discountenance indiscriminate
> alms-giving; to visit the poor at their homes, to give them coun-
> sel, to assist them when practicable in obtaining employment,
> to inspire them with self-respect and self-reliance, to inculcate
> habits of economy, industry and temperance, and whenever
> absolutely necessary, to provide such relief as should be suit-
> able to their wants.[3]

Several societies modeled on the New York one were founded in
other cities with their primary object the improvement of the condition of the poor rather than the giving of relief. They tended, however, to become purely relief societies, and the evils of indiscriminate
giving, begging, and pauperism continued to increase until the charity
organization movement became established in this country.

Strongly impressed with the necessity for reducing pauperism,
overlapping of relief, and the activities of impostors as this organized
movement was, nevertheless from the beginning there was a new consideration of the family in need, and appreciation for the individuality of the disadvantaged that went beyond pity and even beyond a
sense of moral responsibility, some real feeling of the value of social
relationships to the philanthropist as well as to the client, some
dawning understanding of the treatment value of this relationship
apart from any material changes it effected.

The first Charity Organization Society in this country, organized
in Buffalo in 1877, grew out of serious conditions there, a report of
the Poor Department in 1877 showing the expenditure of $147,000
for official relief during the year and an estimate of as much more
given away by the relief associations, churches, private societies, and
individuals. The first report of the Council of the Charity Organization Society of Buffalo in 1879 states, "It was believed that nearly

one in seven of our population was wholly or in part supported by charity, and that one-half of the enormous sum distributed to them was thrown away on impostors and the undeserving, either through lack of thorough investigation or from want of organized cooperation."[4] In the first ten years a saving of half a million in poor relief was claimed. But much more interesting for the development of casework was the attitude towards its clients which marked this society from the start. This attitude is described in the report of 1879 as follows:

> Now the first thing we did was to lay it down as a rule that the District Office should be near the center of the district, in order to be easy of access to the poor, and that, if practicable, it should be in the dwelling house of the paid Agent who was to have charge of the district, so that there should be no hint of officialism about our work, but that the poor might come to a real home, with home surroundings, and thus be, perhaps unconsciously, bettered by the contact.[5]

The motto adopted by the society was the motto of the Boston Society inspired by Octavia Hill, "Not alms but a friend."

It will not be possible or necessary to trace in detail the development of the charity organization movement in this country, a task already well done by Dr. Watson.[6] It is sufficient to show the growth of its point of view towards the individual in his social relationships developing out of the contacts between visitors and the poor. This development can be observed in the papers given under the section on the Charity Organization Society, later known as the section on the Family in the *Proceedings of the National Conference of Social Work.*

In 1880, the first report of the charity organization movement was given before the National Conference.[7] In its statement of objectives, two different emphases were apparent, on the one hand, the old concern for pauperism and its control and, on the other, the new interest in the individuals revealed to the visitors. Papers with the first object in mind discussed relief-giving, how to distinguish between worthy and unworthy. A different note was struck in an article in 1885 on "The Personal Element in Charity," which called attention to the "personal and peculiar need of all manner of impotent folk," and continued, "the ultimate object of this organized movement is to reach the individual. While for purposes of investigation and control of causes it deals with classes, yet its thought is to reach the individual man ... thus its broad object is restoration not detection of impostors, not relief."[8] Buzelle in 1886 discussing "Individuality in the Work of Charity," made an even stronger statement—"Classifications of our fellow men are apt to prove unsatisfactory under the tests of experience and acquaintance with the individual. The poor, and those in trouble worse than poverty, have not in common any type of physical, intellectual or moral development which would warrant an attempt to group them as a class."[9]

Here is the enunciation of the principle of individualization, the foundation of modern casework. This principle of individualization, at first most vague and undefined, began to gain content in terms of certain types of families singled out for special study, for instance, drunkards' families and poor widows with dependent children. The analysis of the situations under these classifications was very general and superficial, and treatment was dogmatic and stereotyped. As late as 1895, a National Conference speaker offered three headings under which all cases known to the Associated Charities could be classified: cases of "degradation, destitution, and of conditions requiring special work for children."[10] That sociology had not progressed much further in analysis of types is evident from Professor Giddings' paper before the National Conference in 1895, "Is the Term Social Classes a Scientific Category?" in which he named four scientific categories under which society could be classified, "social, non-social, pseudo-social, and anti-social."[11]

The children's sections during these years indicated the same effort to find types with stereotyped treatment for each, such as delinquent, crippled, and deformed children. But the realization of the need of more knowledge of families and individuals before classifications can be made forced itself occasionally into the discussions of investigation as, for example, when Devine pointed out that the wood yard or work test cannot be a substitute for knowledge as some claim "since investigation should afford knowledge of conditions."[12] Also, we must assume that from the first the friendly visitor, and there were six hundred in Boston alone in 1884, achieved her success with her families through a rare individualization of each one, even though her understanding was intuitive only, and her methods, as laid down in the Hand-Book for Friendly Visitors of the New York Society,[13] were advice, persuasion, and exhortation.

Mary Richmond in her book *Friendly Visiting Among the Poor*, published first in 1899 and reprinted as late as 1910, made an interesting statement of the relationship of the friendly visitor to her family. "Friendly visiting means intimate and continuous knowledge of and sympathy with a poor family's joys, sorrows, opinions, feelings, and entire outlook upon life. The visitor that has this is unlikely to blunder either about relief or any detail; without it he is almost certain, in any charitable relations with members of the family to blunder seriously."[14] Here is a recognition of the casework relationship itself as the most fundamental and important factor in treatment.

In 1900, William Smallwood of Minneapolis emphasized the importance of considering man rather than his condition and urged combining ethics, psychology, and economics with practical work.[15] But psychology and sociology were not advanced beyond casework in their knowledge of the individual and the motive forces of behavior. The following quotation from C. R. Henderson of the University of Chicago, Department of Sociology, and president of the National Conference in 1899, speaking on child-saving, will serve to indicate how far we have to go before anything like our modern understanding of children and their adjustments is reached:

> For the most part the task is simple and hopeful; the homeless child is taken to a childless home, or to family care where love makes room for one more object of mercy and hope. Where a good home has been discovered, philanthropy has no further duty; the ordinary social forces take charge of the case. The old sad history is forgotten; with a new home begin new memories and a new career. But child saving is complicated by the intrusion of the incapable and the degenerate and perverted. Just as we were singing the triumph of environment over heredity, the stormy straits of adolescence had to be crossed, and some vicious ancestral trait burst through the weak film of acquired habit.[16]

While the knowledge of psychology was still undeveloped in 1900 and therefore individualization both in understanding and treatment was still on a superficial, intuitive basis, real development has taken place in family case work in analyzing social relationships and responsibilities. In the decade between 1890 and 1900, the family had emerged out of its covering of pauperism, though a needy family to be sure, and this family was being placed in relation to its community. Miss Richmond, then of the Philadelphia Society for Organizing Charity, in a paper presented in 1901[17] drew a chart to show the forces by which the family is surrounded, family forces, personal forces, and public charity forces. In this chart the relation of community forces to the family was skilfully analyzed, but of the relationships within the family itself little was said or known.

In the period from 1900 to 1910, the social conscience was stirred to a sense of many wrongs in the social order other than poverty. Attention passed from the more obvious problems of poverty, defectiveness, and delinquency to a consideration of the improvement of living conditions for all members of the community. The National Conference meetings were full of discussions of neighborhood and civic improvement, working men's insurance, old age pensions, child labor, the promotion of health in home, school and factory. The emphasis on causes, the trend towards preventive work were marked in this decade. Statistics were discovered by social workers in the early years of the century and records analyzed to reveal the causes of dependency. In 1903, the following simple questionnaire to study causes was sent out by Edmond J. Butler of New York, chairman of the section on Needy Families in their Homes:

> 1. What are the general or specific causes which make for the pauperizing of the poor families in your state or community?
>
> 2. What remedies are applied to these causes and what new means or extensions of existing means would you recommend for making more effective the efforts of charity workers and the uplifting of destitute poor families?[18]

Devine, in his presidential address before the Philadelphia Conference in 1906, defined the social task of the age, to be "that the social causes of dependence shall be destroyed." He charged the charity organization movement with having failed to appreciate the importance of environmental causes of distress, with having fixed attention too much on personal weaknesses and accidents.[19] Dr. Lee Frankel in the same Conference, as chairman of the Committee on Needy Families, reported, "The committee offers the alluring proposition that poverty, the sordid, grinding poverty which eventually spells dependency, is eradicable and preventable." The causes of poverty he found to be four: (1) ignorance, (2) industrial inefficiency, (3) exploitation of labor, and (4) defects in government supervision of the welfare of citizens.[20]

Along with this effort to analyze and control the causes of poverty on the environmental side went an effort to analyze the causes within the individual, less successful because of the inadequate psychology of that period. W. H. McClain, then with the St. Louis Provident Society, in an article on "Relations Existing Between Defective Character and Dependency,"[21] classified the defects of character which are factors in dependency, under seven headings: (1) inefficiency, (2) improvidence, (3) immorality, (4) stupidity, (5) intemperance, (6) shiftlessness, (7) ignorance. There is little analysis of these qualities. Shiftlessness was defined as "that defect in character which leads men and women to be careless in performing duties which they assume." One other quotation to show the naïveté of the psychological viewpoint of this period may be added from Edmond J. Butler in 1903:

> From the foregoing we arrive at the logical conclusion that the greatest and noblest labor which may claim our attention is the preservation of the normal unity of the family. In no way can this be more effectively done than by a study of the needs of the family for its proper well being, by ascertaining the causes which make for its proper well being, by ascertaining the causes which make for its destruction and the means necessary to avert them, and by the application of these means. . . .
>
> The positive direct causes of poverty show us at a glance the fact that they exist because of deficiencies in the development of the individual. Man's nature is threefold in character, physical, mental, and moral, and for the proper fulfillment of his duties it is necessary that his whole nature should be developed. If his physical nature be fully developed by habits of regular living, cleanliness of person, good food, temperance in eating and drinking and a sufficient amount of exercise or labor, he will develop a manly vigor that will require little stimulation and repel all tendencies to shiftlessness, indolence and habits of laziness. If his mental nature be fully developed by proper training of the mind, not only in matters commonly termed education but also on the lines of industrial and domestic knowledge, his will be an intellect that will forestall the evils which follow improvidence, lack of thrift, bad management and other variations of the common cause of ignorance. If his moral nature be fully developed by the proper training of nature's guide, the conscience, his physical, mental and moral forces will be so directed that all of his actions will tend to raise him above the base desires which lead him to intemperance, crime, vice, desertion of family and all other disregard of duty.

In this analysis of man's nature and the means necessary for attaining his end we find a forcible warning to all persons who undertake to deal with positive causes of poverty. We are forced to realize the fact that if we hope to accomplish any good of a lasting or permanent character, our study and preventive work will have to be based upon a complete regard for man's entire nature and that any such study or work which ignores this demand can but result in confusion and failure.[22]

By 1910, the end of the first decade of the century, many national movements had been organized for preventive work, i.e., the National Association for the Study and Prevention of Tuberculosis in 1904, the National Desertion Bureau in 1911, the National Mental Hygiene Society in 1909. Various other agencies attacking some phase of prevention in the field of poverty were active locally, such as agencies for housing reform, for legal aid, for health care.

At the thirty-seventh annual conference in 1911, Homer Folks, president, discussed the rate of progress, stating: "Of the six standing committees of the conference of 1881, five dealt with institutions or relief, the sixth with immigration. Of the nine standing committees of this conference, four dealt with institutions or relief, while five, having to do with the improvement of living conditions, have been added."[23] He reviewed these movements and concluded that while the rate of progress had been erratic, it need not be slow and that social reform of social conditions was really within reach.

In this same year, 1911, Porter R. Lee, now director of the New York School of Social Work, defined the social function of casework as an "attempt to split up a large problem into units and to deal with those units efficiently and comprehensively,"[24] claiming for casework, therefore, a permanent function as an essential method in dealing with social problems.

By this time, the charity organization movement was well established in most cities and had a national organization as well. It had thought its way through several stages from mere almsgiving, through the organization of community sources for relief, to casework or treatment of the family as a whole that used relief only as a tool for family rehabilitation.

In the next decade, from 1910 to 1920, we are to see the introduction of new influences giving new content to the understanding and treatment of family and individual problems. These influences emanate from psychology and psychiatry but not from the academic

psychology of the college classroom and laboratory, or from the institutionalized psychiatry of the hospitals for the insane. Both psychology and psychiatry had to come under the pressure of the practical
problem of social workers, "What is to be done with this badly be-
haved individual in his home and community environment?" before
they evolved the dynamic point of view of behavior commonly referred to as the "New Psychology" today. Looking back over the
past fifteen years, we can see this point of view being forged out
through the efforts to understand and deal with the recalcitrant individuals who would not stay put in community or institution, and to
whose behavior already existing psychological and sociological categories did not apply.

The effect of this emphasis on the individual and on the motive forces of his behavior is profound and far reaching. Once the
safe and sure controls of the social order, established institutions,
and moral standards were loosened, the social worker found himself
confronted with the blind forces of individual striving and maladapt-
ive behavior, which must be understood before they could be controlled. The passion to understand the meaning of these forces carried
the social worker over into active contact with other fields of knowledge which were studying and interpreting behavior.

2. INFLUENCES FROM SOCIOLOGY AND PSYCHOLOGY

The choice of the year 1910 as a time to evaluate sociological
and psychological contributions to the development of social casework may be somewhat arbitrary, but the date has significance for
both fields by virtue of an abortive effort to relate them at this time
in the organization of a national child welfare conference on which
G. Stanley Hall, the president, comments:

> We desired that the new bureau at Washington . . . should
> be made the organic center of all child-study activities and
> should make it one of its chief functions to bring together work-
> ers in all fields, representatives of each of which, as there was
> abundant evidence to prove, often knew very little of the work
> of others, and so pool both knowledge and interest. The orga-
> nization we here effected, however, made little appeal to those
> intent chiefly on the immediate practical work of mitigating
> abuses and ameliorating the conditions of childhood, so that
> research and welfare again showed their incompatibility and it

was realized that the latter had little interest in the former, and the two drifted apart. Hence this organization proved to be ineffective and soon lapsed.[1]

Child study had been an active interest of G. Stanley Hall from 1883 on. Through the stimulation of Clark University the questionnaire method of studying children's minds, activities, and interests was carried far over the country. It called the attention of parents, teachers, and social workers to the adjustment difficulties of the living, active child as legitimate psychological problems and resulted in the accumulation of a large amount of observations and autobiographical material of real interest though not all of it was of scientific value. The most impressive publication from this period was G. Stanley Hall's book, *Adolescence*.[2] Other books on child psychology, such as A. S. Tanner's *The Child*, show a modern interest in behavior and growth but a limited capacity to interpret these problems.

Two other developments related to the child-study movement of far reaching importance for psychology and social casework should be noted, first, the recognition of sex as a factor in behavior, and, second, the elaboration of the mental testing technique as a method of studying individual differences.

The first introduction to the problems of sex as a legitimate field for scientific exploration came through the works of Krafft-Ebing, Forel, Moll, and Ellis, the latter probably with more influence upon the thinking of case workers. Ellis' *Studies in the Psychology of Sex* began to appear in 1897, the sixth and final volume, *Sex and Society*, having been published in 1910. In Volume I, Ellis proclaimed his interest in this field which led him through the tremendous work resulting in his six volumes: "I regard sex as the central problem of life. And now that the problem of religion has practically been settled, and that the problem of labor has at least been placed on a practical foundation, the question of sex—with the racial questions that rest on it—stands before the coming generations as the chief problem for solution. Sex lies at the root of life, and we can never learn to reverence life until we know how to understand sex."[3]

For years the six volumes gathered dust upon the closed shelves of the libraries that had the courage to buy them. Of the taboo on this subject even in the scientific field G. Stanley Hall says: "Up to and even during the great war psychological orthodoxy, especially in this country and England, almost entirely ignored this subject, and in our journals and on the programmes of our meetings it was rarely touched. Nor had it received much more attention in child-study circles."[4] Hall traces the change in attitude towards the significance of the sex factor to Freud's contribution from psychoanalytic studies.[5] But this influence was indirect and devious in its effect upon casework and must be traced through secondary influences later.

While the present decade is concentrating on the entire emotional life including the sex needs in understanding behavior, in the decade preceding, 1910-1920, the intellectual factor and its importance in determining individual difference and behavior was exaggerated. The interest in feeble-mindedness in relation to behavior and social problems dates back to Dugdale and his study of the Jukes of New York State reported to the National Conference of Social Work in 1877, but there was no consistent pursuit of this field of research until the working out of the Binet-Simon scale of measuring intelligence in 1905-1911 which offered a tool for studying this factor. It was seized upon with avidity by groups of workers who were balked by behavior problems, chiefly in the courts, and in feeble-minded, penal, and reformatory institutions. Later the scale and its various modifications found extended use in schools and colleges, in industry and the army. Some of the leaders in this group brought this point of view before the National Conference of Charities and Correction in 1911, Healy, Goddard, and Frank Moore, under a section called "Lawbreakers," giving papers on methods of studying the offender. Dr. Frank Moore of the New Jersey Reformatory for Boys pointed out the limitations of the emphasis on feeble-mindedness in this study but also felt that it constituted a valuable point of attack even though it was only one aspect of the problem and that the whole approach was a significant step in advance, "in that delinquency had come to be regarded as a disease to be treated instead of an offense to be punished."[6]

Many institutions developed research stations for studying the human material committed to their care. In the reformatory group, the interest and initiative of several very powerful and able women workers, Katherine B. Davis of the New York Reformatory for Women, Mrs. Martha Falconer of Sleighton Farms, Pennsylvania, Mrs. Jessie Hodder of Sherbourne Prison, Massachusetts, Maude and Stella Minor of Waverly House, New York, carried this movement very far. The first publications of the work of this group appeared in 1914, one based on a five-years' study to discover the causes of feeble-mindedness among the children in Vineland, New Jersey, by Dr. Henry

Goddard,[7] the second, the result of five years' work with juvenile offenders in the Juvenile Court of Chicago, by Dr. William Healy.[8]

The resulting emphasis on the intellectual factor in individual difference and behavior dominated social casework interpretations for some time. Feeble-mindedness was found to be a useful explanation for much anti-social, unmodifiable behavior and back of feeble-mindedness lay a final hereditary cause. Adequate treatment for so static and unmodifiable a factor lay outside of social casework method in segregation, sterilization, and other social and legal measures, so that the constant effect of the psychological emphasis of this period was to separate diagnosis and treatment. The caseworker felt it to be an essential part of good casework procedure to have mental tests for any doubtful individuals in her family, but only in rare instances did the diagnosis lead to effective social treatment. Usually the individual remained in the community in spite of the diagnosis of his I.Q. as 60 or 70. The social worker must struggle with the consequences of his bad behavior as best she might.

While Healy's first studies of delinquents emphasized the individual's make-up chiefly in terms of intellectual ability in its relation to social behavior, other laboratories connected with reformatories and feeble-minded institutions interested themselves in family backgrounds following the method described by Dugdale in his study of the Jukes reported on to the National Conference in 1877.[9] The Eugenic Research Station at Cold Spring Harbor and any number of other institutions, were collecting elaborate histories of family backgrounds. These workers had usually no other training in gathering social data than that supplied by a summer's course at Cold Spring Harbor. On the basis of these data, rough-and-ready but final diagnoses of character and personality were made. Feeble-mindedness, insanity, epilepsy, alcoholism, and some strange trait known as *SX* on the chart were inferred from the neighbors' or relatives' accounts of an individual's behavior and the application of Mendelian laws to the inheritance of these traits was discussed. Superficial and unscientific as the eugenic movement was, however, it made its contribution towards a social program for the treatment and control of the burden of feeble-mindedness. It achieved one particularly valuable point, without realizing its full implications, in the development of methods of studying individuals whose behavior constituted social problems, in calling attention to the social nature of feeble-mindedness and mental disease.

The interpretations of these research stations based on an emphasis on the intellectual factor were upset by observations of the behavior of individuals under institution conditions and on parole, where it was clear that the individual's adjustment capacity did not necessarily correlate definitely with intelligence. The recognition of the importance of emotional factors in the treatment of the feebleminded was presented to the National Conference of Social Work in 1918 in a paper by Dr. Jessie Taft in which she suggested analysis of the feeble-minded into adjustment types, a study of the problem to determine how far anti-social behavior may be the result of prolonged maladjustment due to defective intellect, emotional and impulsive make-up complicated by bad environment and training. "May it not be possible that even in the field of intellectual defect, the insight of modern psychiatry as to the mental mechanisms which produce maladjustments in the intellectually normal may have a bearing?"[10]

From this time on there is increasing concentration on the study of emotional factors in the behavior of delinquent and defective individuals. Psychiatrists were appointed on the staff of the research stations in institutions. The Reformatory for Women at Bedford Hills, New York, for instance, erected a Psychopathic Hospital for the purpose of more intensive study of its difficult behavior problems.[11] Laboratory psychology in its emphasis on intellect, tests, diagnosis, and classifications was found increasingly sterile by those whose necessity and whose passion was the understanding of human behavior and relationship, while psychiatry steadily assumed greater leadership in the discussion of the crucial problems of behavior and adjustment. To this new leadership caseworkers turned eagerly for light on the problems which psychology had failed to solve.

The early work of Dr. William Healy with juvenile delinquents reveals most clearly the growing strength of the drive to understand behavior and the refinement in the tools at its command as developed by sociology, psychology, and psychiatry. Healy began to publish in 1914 results of the five years' study of the Juvenile Psychopathic Institute in Chicago of which he was director. *The Individual Delinquent* in 1915 was rich in case histories and more thorough in its method of study, more penetrating in its insight in behavior and motive, than any other work from this field of this date. The outstanding points in Healy's contribution may be summed up as follows: first, Healy cut through the social problem of crime to its dynamic

center in the individual offender,[12] and located the explanation of
delinquent behavior in the mental life;[13] and second, he described
treatment following from this localization of cause in the mental life
as taking place in resolution of the mental conflict.[14]

He qualified this emphasis on mental life as the source of conflict
by a recognition of the necessity for investigation of other factors:

> Notwithstanding all this, I fully realize that there are many
> cases in which sole dependence on the psychological standpoint
> would be a grave mistake. Repeatedly I have asserted the opin-
> ion, still held, that it is very difficult to decide which is in gen-
> eral the most important investigatory vantage ground—social,
> medical or psychological. The point is clear, however, that one
> can most surely and safely arrive at remedial measures through
> investigation of the mental factors.[15]

The diagnostic measures described include a careful physical, intelligence, and social study in addition to the psychoanalytic study
which is Healy's peculiar contribution. The name "psychoanalytic"
is a misnomer, however, and is replaced later by the term mental analysis for, however much he may have gained in his original point of
view and approach to this problem from the psychoanalytic school,
he soon became independent of its influence and developed his technique without reference to analytic procedure. His original emphasis
on the importance of the emotional and unconscious factors in personality and behavior soon narrowed to an emphasis on "the mental
conflict" involved in sex repression and usually associated in delinquent careers with stealing as a symptom. "Since nothing, by the
innermost nature of animate beings, so stirs emotion as the affairs
of sex life, taking this term in its broadest sense, it is to be presup-
posed that we should find most cases of mental conflict to be about
hidden sex thoughts or imageries, and inner or environmental sex experiences."[16]

Mental Conflicts and Misconduct, the third book to follow *The
Individual Delinquent,* gives the clearest account of Healy's original
theory and method. His debt to the psychoanalytic school was clearly recognized in this book, which appeared in 1917, and the distinction between psychoanalysis and his own theory and method was
carefully defined. The Preface thus explicitly states his independence,
"I would have it thoroughly understood that our studies are tied to
no one psychological school. The efforts at mental analysis which

are here represented have been stimulated more by uncovering facts than by any theories, although I gratefully acknowledge the help to appreciation of principles which has been derived from various writers on psychoanalysis and kindred topics. It has been no small aid to scientific conviction that many others, even though working in separate fields, clearly discern that often there are covert mental mechanisms basically affecting attitudes and conduct."[17] In this book he definitely distinguished between the method of his own "mental analysis, the method of using the memory to penetrate into the former experiences of mental life,"[18] and the much more prolonged explorations of psychoanalysis. He went on to explain the Freudian concepts of the complex and repression as of primary importance in the explanation of delinquent behavior. "The complex has energy producing powers: by reason of this it may be, and often is, a great determiner of thoughts and actions."[19] A part of this complex may become cut off by the process of repression and "continues to have its own existence as a separate unassimilated entity and to be possessed of a special energy."[20]

In the cases of young delinquents with whom he worked, Healy believed that the complex might lie very near the surface and that a slight exploration would often bring the entire conflict to light. Though qualifying this by the statement, "I am far from believing that our studies have explored the deepest mechanisms conceivably at the roots of misconduct,"[21] nevertheless he reiterated, "At present, however, it is clear that mental conflict does often stand in causal relationship to misconduct and that the vital fact may be brought out by even a moderate amount of analysis."[22] Relief, often cure, followed the unearthing of the complex. "The solution of the problem and the cure of the trouble mainly lies in developing the individual's own cognizance of the essential association of facts. The task, thus, is the synthetic, conscious establishment of reality within the mental life."[23]

He described the method of unearthing this conflict to be based first on an attitude on the part of the observer which never condemns or judges, whose approach is sympathetic and patient and gives the impression that the inquiry "is born of the desire to help."[24] The inquiry as a short cut to the complex may press for the recall of the delinquent's earliest knowledge of social offenses. Indirect inquiry in regard to playmates, the source of sex knowledge, of bad words . . . may assist in reviving memories leading to the complex.[25] He discarded the use of artificial association tests, dreams, and symbolic interpretations of objects in vogue with other analysts, but did not, however, discard the inquiry into environmental factors so important to the social worker nor . . . the importance of treatment in the environment.[26]

Stimulating and illuminating as Healy's use of the concept of the mental conflict in diagnosis and treatment proved to be, it found its limitations shortly, in that it carried the investigation no further into a deeper level of understanding. Search for a particular sex trauma, as an objective fact, with corroboration from other sources of information, continued as an essential part of the Healy method. The confusion between psychological fact or the meaning of experience to the individual, and actual fact was never cleared up. There was need of such a distinction with a logic of psychological fact and a centering of interest on the entire personality instead of on its sporadic behavior and its underlying mental complexes before a satisfactory science of criminology could be recognized. That Healy made the first and the most outstanding contribution to this science cannot be denied.

A limitation of Healy's work in 1917, which operated to some extent destructively on casework, was the effort to establish conduct classifications and diagnostic terms. It is to Healy that we owe the inhibitory effect of the term "the constitutionally inferior" personality which figured so glibly in the casework records, and which Healy referred to as a "peculiar type of abnormality" showing a "strange lack of ability to adjust to the demands of society" but "who is by tests neither mentally defective nor insane."[27] The extent of this classification interest finds its clearest expression in a paper on "The Bearing of Psychology on Social Case Work" read before the National Conference of Social Work in Pittsburgh in 1917 where he says, "From psychology the social worker can learn the types of disability and peculiarity which are defined as entities, and I would insist that knowledge of these to the extent of comprehending how mental life is through these abnormalities in general affected and what their social implications are should be part of the basic equipment of all who in social work deal with human beings." There follows a presentation of his classification of mental abnormalities into (1) mental defect, (2) mental dullness from physical conditions, (3) constitutional inferiority, (4) mental aberrations (insanities, psychoses, psychopathics), (5) mental peculiarities.[28] The effect of this emphasis on diagnostic entities led the social worker to think in terms of mental status rather than behavior pattern and so maintained for caseworkers the same kind of dependence on the psychiatrist as existed with the psychologist and physician. The final key to understanding the individual in any aspect, his physical make-up, his mental capacity, or his personality equipment lay in the hands of another professional group, to be secured only through another scientific training which the case worker could not hope to acquire. Educational as these dependent alliances were, their inhibitory effect on independent organized thinking remains active to this day in the caseworker's timidity in the interpretation of her own material.

3. THE STIMULUS OF PSYCHIATRY

Psychiatry, far more than psychology, was to mold the point of view and approach of social casework from the year 1910. It was in this year that Dr. Adolf Meyer went from the Psychiatric Institute of New York to Phipps Psychiatric Clinic at Johns Hopkins, and Dr. August Hoch succeeded Dr. Meyer as director of the Institute transferred at that time to Ward's Island. These two men, leaders in the development of modern psychiatry, and those associated with them in the Institute, Phipps, and similar psychiatric hospitals and clinics, were to bring to social work from their studies of disordered mental functioning a more comprehensive and dynamic psychology and a new understanding of personality.

Psychiatry, itself, had only recently advanced from its old-time concern with custodial care of the "insane" to an interest in research and treatment. In 1850, treatment of the insane was dominated by Benjamin Rush (1745-1831) of the University of Pennsylvania Medical School, whose point of view can be inferred from the following statements: "The first object of a physician when he enters a cell or chamber of the average person should be to catch his eye and look him out of countenance. * * * If these means prove ineffectual to establish a government over deranged persons, recourse should be had to certain methods of coercion. * * * Among these methods are the straight waistcoat, the tranquilizing chair, the deprivation of customary pleasant food, and pouring cold water under the coat sleeve so that it may descend to the armpits." If these methods failed, Rush regarded it as proper to resort to the "fear of Death."[1]

In England and other countries, care of the insane had developed without the use of restraint and observation of the amenable behavior of the inmates of English institutions led finally to the abolition of restraint in the better hospitals of this country by 1890. With the disappearance of restraint, new attitudes and relationships on the part of doctors and nurses were necessitated, and in response to these new attitudes, there appeared new and greater variety of behavior on the part of the patients. At the same time, the trend in medical treatment was away from the strenuous, depleting measures of Rush (blood-letting, emetics, cathartics), in favor of "supporting" treatment (baths, rest, etc.). With the growth of a more human approach on the part of the doctors and a more individualized response on the part of the patients, the emphasis in work for the insane began to shift from custodial care to an interest in study and treatment. The first scientific efforts in this direction were directed at organic and physiological causes, Dr. Meyer and Dr. Hoch both starting in pathological laboratories (Meyer at Kankakee, Illinois, in 1885, Hoch at McLean, Massachusetts, in 1895). The psychiatric hospitals and clinics beginning with the establishment of the Pathological Institute of the New York State Hospitals in New York in 1896, represented a further step towards scientific study and treatment, in that acute cases were separated from the chronic and given the best and most intensive study and treatment. It was in the observation of these acute cases, close to their everyday living situations in the environment and soon to be returned to them, that analysis of the psychological and social factors in mental disorders went forward rapidly.

It was not long before the significance of this movement was seized upon by other workers engaged in the study of personality disorders and behavior difficulties. The research stations in reformatory institutions previously referred to turned to psychiatry for help with the extreme behavior problems not amenable to any institutional regime. At the New York Reformatory for Women, for instance, where a psychiatric hospital was built in 1916 as part of the equipment of the Laboratory of Social Hygiene for the study of women offenders, and in other laboratories, there was a close association of psychiatrist, psychologist, and social worker in research work and treatment.

The contribution of the psychiatric understanding and point of view was most definitely presented to social work in the organization of the National Committee for Mental Hygiene in 1909 following the organization of the Connecticut Committee by Clifford Beers, a recovered mental patient who told a convincing story of his experiences in *A Mind that Found Itself.* While the National Mental Hygiene Committee was organized primarily for the prevention of insanity through the control of some of the known causes of insanity, such as alcohol and venereal disease, the association with this movement by Clifford Beers, able to use his own experience in describing the transition from sanity to insanity and back again, called popular attention to the functional type of disorder. This was of sufficient significance for social work to receive attention in a presidential address before the National Conference in 1910, in St. Louis, when Jane Addams pointed to two cases in hospitals for the insane "where reassurance and removal of dread were factors in the cure of that type of disordered mind which alienists define as 'due to conflict through poor adaptation'."[2]

In 1911, Dr. Adolf Meyer, of Phipps Psychiatric Institute in Baltimore, appeared on the program of the National Conference. The effect of his understanding of the depth and complexity of human problems, his conviction of the "endurance of the human organism and its capacity for adaptation,"[3] combined with his acceptance of social work as legitimately concerned in this field, had a far reaching influence.

The 1914 and 1915 conferences revealed the real sweep of the interest of psychiatry and psychology in social behavior and its control, with papers by such people as Dr. Meyer of Baltimore, Dr. Southard of Boston, Dr. Owen Copp of Philadelphia, Dr. Edith Spaulding of New York, Dr. Walter Fernald of Boston, Dr. Mabel Fernald of New York, and Dr. Goddard of New Jersey. Many of these papers were reports of research work done in studying individuals under custodial or institutional care, but throughout all the studies the borderline types that refused to stay institutionalized, baffling understanding and treatment, the high grade feeble-minded and the psychopathic delinquent, received most attention. Psychology and psychiatry combined in an effort to throw some light on the make-up of the psychopathic offender creating disorder in reformatories and correctional institutions. In 1918, a sharper contact with psychiatry came about as a result of the war and the interest of psychiatrists in the readjustment problems of soldiers. The Smith College Training School for Psychiatric Social Work was organized in 1918 and psychiatry swept the National Conference of Social Work at Atlantic City in 1919. Salmon, Southard, Glueck, Campbell, Dunham, Williams and White contributed advice and guidance, from their psychiatric knowledge and experience, to the tremendous task recognized as a social casework job, of adjusting the mentally disabled to peace conditions. From this time on this contact has grown steadily closer, leading to the Child Guidance Clinics and Institutes for Child Guidance of the present day in which psychiatrist, psychologist, and social worker explore and treat together the problems of the child's adjustment.

4. EARLY PSYCHOANALYTIC INFLUENCES

It is important to examine the extent of influence of the psychology of the psychoanalytic movement in America at this point though the more significant effect of this psychology on social casework is to come much later. The first contact with the founder of this movement we owe to G. Stanley Hall since he brought Freud to this country to speak in 1910 and in his lectures and his writings presented the salient points of that theory, so revolutionary at that time. Translations of Freud's writings began to appear shortly after and were followed by the first popularizations and applications of this psychology to personality and behavior problems. Healy in 1917 cites a list of about half a dozen titles in this field.[1] Several other titles should be added.[2] *The Psychoanalytic Review,* edited by White and Jeliffe, began publication in 1913.

Wilfred Lay, in *Man's Unconscious Conflict,* published in 1917, included a list of the available books on the subject in English, twenty-one titles in all.[3] While these lists are not necessarily absolutely exhaustive of the literature of that time they are complete enough to give a picture of the extent of our contact with the psychoanalytic movement in 1917.

William A. White in his enthusiastic and brilliant presentation of the Freudian psychology in 1916 describes it as "a psychology which has opened the door to the understanding of man and as such I believe is the psychology which will prove of the greatest pragmatic advantage."[4] This presentation of Dr. White's is known to practically all caseworkers and has formed a very real part of their working psychology.

Much of the detail of psychoanalytic theory and method could be lightly disregarded by caseworkers in 1916 as immaterial to their purposes since psychoanalysis was then concerned with the treatment of the mentally ill and had developed a technique so elaborate and expensive that no relation to the caseworker's technique was obvious. But in the psychology which soon began to be set forth as the working basis for the analytic therapy, social casework found at once a stimulating dynamic point of view which was to prove more fertile than the intellectualism of the psychological school just preceding.

Three points particularly were seized upon from the psychoanalytic psychology and made a permanent part of the caseworker's psychology. All of these points, it will be recognized, have other origins in other fields than psychoanalysis, indeed have become so prevalent in general scientific thought by now that it may seem unfair to ascribe them to any one source. However, though no doubt casework absorbed from the prevailing scientific concepts, it seems clear that psychoanalysis had a more direct influence at this point through the interpretations of such men as Dr. White and Dr. Glueck who were peculiarly influential in casework. The first, which it has taken casework some years to assimilate, is the concept of determinism in psychic life. Generalized and philosophic recognition of the application of this principle in psychology may have been granted by many sociologists and psychologists but it is Freud's distinction to have shown for the first time a concrete working out of this principle in experience. In the words of Dr. White:

> Freud, for the first time, formulated an hypothesis which considered that each psychic event had a history and which has led to the same recognition of the value of the past of the psyche which has been for so long accorded to the past of the body in the science of embryology and comparative anatomy. ... In the sphere of the psyche it is but natural that a definite deterministic and genetic method should be long delayed as we are not only dealing with phenomena which are so complex as to be too long a way from concretely expressed laws for us to see any possibilities of explanation but, too, we have been dominated for generations by the theory that psychic events, many of them at least, are brought about "at will" in some mysterious way which precludes the necessity of even attempting to bring them under the operation of natural laws.

> A reaction from this crude conception of mental phenomena, from this hit and miss type of explanation which explains

mental facts by the most obvious superficial causes and relegates many of them to the category of accidental or chance occurrences, has come about in recent years as the result of a clearer understanding of the reasons of certain types of mental reactions, with a result that the theory of determinism has definitely taken its place in the field of psychology, a place that it has long occupied in the biological sciences.[5]

A second revolutionary concept which casework seized upon from Freudian psychology was an emphasis on the need basis of behavior as opposed to the intellectual factor. Whatever in Freud's early concept of the unconscious may have been metaphysical, unscientific and crude, it gave dramatic revelation of unsuspected meanings of experience to the individual, of reaction, of continued affect and attitude and even character formation in terms of hidden, subtle, unsuspected, "unconscious" motives. Here was the clue to an understanding of much that had been obscure in the reactions and behavior of patients and clients. Casework now began a search for the individual's needs as a first step in diagnosis, not from the old sociologic approach which accepted the need of all human beings for food, shelter, clothing and certain human associations but with a much more painstaking effort to find the concrete symbols in which these needs had expressed themselves in each individual. Through the Freudian psychology, sex was thrown open to exploration as a human need and the caseworker's treatment of sex behavior grew increasingly tolerant and understanding.

Edwin B. Holt has given a clear statement of this aspect of Freud's contribution in his book entitled *The Freudian Wish,* written in 1915. He states:

> It is this "wish" which transforms the principal doctrines of psychology and recasts the science; much as the "atomic theory" and later the "ionic theory," have reshaped earlier conceptions of chemistry. This so-called "wish" becomes the unit of psychology, replacing the older unit commonly called "sensation"; which latter, it is to be noted, was a content of consciousness unit, whereas the "wish" is a more dynamic affair.[6]

The third contribution from psychoanalytic research to social casework lay in the light thrown upon the knowledge of family relationships and their effect on individual development. Flügel in *The*

Psychoanalytic Study of the Family summarized this contribution up to 1921. Economic and sociological thinking which dominated the casework approach in its earlier days had emphasized community factors in individual and family life. The emphasis from the new psychology pointed out the small family group as the first and most important pressure in conditioning attitudes. Here attitudes, behavior patterns, and the personality of the child were primarily determined. From this point of view, later environmental pressures and obstacles became less and less significant and important. The problem of family relationships and their effect on the development of the child proved to be stimulating to study and research in many fields so that the accumulation of knowledge now at the disposal of students in technical and popular literature has gone far beyond its psychoanalytic origins.

These early contributions from psychoanalytic psychology were so truly assimilated by casework that they have continued to operate with their own independent drive in this field. Continued and sharper contacts between the two fields have produced new developments which will be discussed in Part Two.

5. "SOCIAL DIAGNOSIS"

In a National Conference paper in 1917, under the title of "The Social Worker's Task," Miss Richmond, for years a leader in the casework movement, defined the psychological basis for social casework. New skills and new aims are developing, she says, (1) "skill in discovering the social relationships by which a given personality has been shaped; (2) ability to get at the central core of difficulty in these relationships, and (3) power to utilize the direct action of mind upon mind in their adjustment."[1]

In spite of this statement of the psychological basis of casework, however, it is the sociological rather than the psychological basis which organizes and gives unity to her presentation in *Social Diagnosis*,[2] published in the same year as her paper before the National Conference. This offers the only definite formulation in book form of the point of view and method of social casework. It represents the assimilation of many years of experience, the answers to problems set herself fifteen years before the publication of the book, and six years of actual research work. More than this, as the work of a scholar, and a deliberative able mind, it reflects the finest thinking of the period. Law, Medicine, Psychology, History, Philosophy, Sociology, and Social Work each contributed a vital part in the synthesis which this book presents.

Representing as it does, an assimilation and organization going on over a period of fifteen years, its central focus of interpretation is to be found in a point of view antedating 1916, its publication date. More was being discovered and introduced to this country about the science of "characterology" than Miss Richmond believed, as has been pointed out in the preceding chapter. The references to psychiatrists in her volume, limited to references to Paul Dubois, W. E. Fernald, William Healy, Adolf Meyer, S. Weir Mitchell, Irwin H. Neff, and James J. Putnam, will indicate the extent of Miss Richmond's recognition of this point of view. She is very familiar with Healy's *Individual Delinquent* and uses it frequently for illustration of methods of interviewing. His emphasis on the symptomatic nature of delinquent behavior requiring "a search for the physical, mental, and social facts behind that symptom before a cure can be effected"[3] is identical with her own approach to social problems. Healy's *Mental Conflicts,* with its more complete statement of his psychology, its emphasis on psychological fact, had not yet appeared. There is no reference in Miss Richmond's book to Freud or to William A. White's *Mechanisms of Character Formation* which appeared in 1916.[4]

The book sets out for itself a broad definition of purpose; the effort to formulate the elements of social diagnosis which "should constitute a part of the ground which all social caseworkers could occupy in common, and that it should become possible in time to take for granted, in every social practitioner, a knowledge and mastery of those elements, and of the modifications in them which each decade of practice would surely bring."[5] It is her belief that casework is advancing to a point where its work is becoming standardized in a professional way.

"It soon became apparent, however, that no methods or aims were peculiarly and solely adapted to the treatment of the families that found their way to a charity organization society; that, in essentials, the methods and aims of social casework were or should be the same in every type of service. . . . The things that most needed to be said about social casework were the things that were common to all."[6] It carries out this purpose in a careful detailed description of the processes which lead up to social diagnosis and to the shaping of a plan for social treatment. There is no attempt to discuss the treatment processes.

Through all the detailed discussion of process and procedure the underlying conception and philosophy of social casework is consistent. Its keynote is stated in a quotation from Dr. James J. Putnam which introduces the book: "One of the most striking facts with regard to the conscious life of any human being is that it is interwoven with the lives of others. It is in each man's social relations that his mental history is mainly written, and it is in his social relations likewise that the causes of the disorders that threaten his happiness and his effectiveness and the means for securing his recovery are to be mainly sought."[7]

This concept of the social nature of the self is elaborated fully in Chapter 19 entitled "Underlying Philosophy." While emphasizing the importance of the recognition of individuality which Miss Richmond considers fundamental to social casework effort, perhaps even more significant to her mind is the less obvious concept of the "wider self." In clarifying this concept, Miss Richmond quotes from Bosanquet, the following quotation: "The soul literally is, or is built up of, all its experience; and such part of this experience, or soul life, as is active at any given time or for any given purpose constitutes the self at that time and for that purpose. We know how the soul enlarges and expands as we enter upon new duties, acquire new interests, contract new ties of friendship; we know how it is mutilated when some sphere of activity is cut off, or some near friend snatched away by death. It is literally, and not metaphorically a part of *ourselves* which we have lost."[8] Quoting again from Miss Richmond: "a man really is the company he keeps plus the company that his ancestors kept. . . . Many of the more thoughtful caseworkers of today are learning to study the relations of individual men in the light of this concept of the wider self—of the expanding self, as they like to believe. In so doing, they are allying themselves with the things that 'move, touch, teach'; for where disorders within or without threaten a man's happiness, his social relations must continue to be the chief means of his recovery."[9]

While Miss Richmond states that the relation of diagnosis to the practical end of treatment cannot be too much insisted on, actually in the discussion social evidence is for the sake of diagnosis, "the attempt to arrive at as exact a definition as possible of the social situation and personality of a given client."[10] "Investigation, or the gathering of evidence, begins the process, the critical examination and comparison of evidence follow and last comes its interpretation and the definition of the social difficulty."[11] This discussion of investigation, the gathering, weighing, and interpretation of evidence, the main theme of the book, is developed in the best light that can be thrown upon it from logic, law, psychology, medicine, common sense, and casework practice, the contributions from the other specialized fields being well assimilated into a philosophy and practice that are perhaps distinctive and unique to social casework. Reading it in 1930, in the light of the deepened knowledge of human motives which a decade's advance in psychology, psychiatry, and social casework has brought about, caseworkers are too apt to discard the whole conception and procedure as inadequate to their purposes. In this case we need to remind ourselves that the concepts on which we are working today are no where as yet formulated with sufficient definiteness to afford comparison with the concepts of *Social Diagnosis*. Evidences of the changes which have unquestionably taken place can only be inferred from brief articles and casework practice itself. The formulation of the psychological basis on which casework practice rests today will no doubt be met with as much criticism and divergence of opinion as is the formulation of the sociological basis of casework of 1917 which Miss Richmond expressed. However much we have departed from the social point of view of *Social Diagnosis* we have not yet achieved any articulation comparable to this work in unity and organization which we may venture to believe was truly inclusive and expressive of the best thinking and practice of social casework of that period.

Miss Richmond's conception of social evidence and its reliability must be built up through her own statements:

> Social evidence may be defined as consisting of any and all facts as to personal or family history which, taken together, indicate the nature of a given client's social difficulties . . . and the means to their solution.[12] . . . The initial difficulty in case work is always that of getting at facts which are ample and pertinent.[13] . . . Fact is not limited to the tangible. Thoughts and events are facts. The question whether a thing be fact or not is the question of whether or not it can be affirmed with certainty.[14] . . . The gathering of facts in any field of interest is made difficult first by faulty recollection or by inexpert or prejudiced observation on the part of persons giving testimony,

and second by a confusion between the facts themselves and inferences drawn from them on the part either of witnesses, or,
in the special realm of our study, of social workers.[15]
Thus at the threshold of our consideration of social evidence,
the duty confronts us of making sure what are facts in a client's situation. Evidence which is reliable and which is sufficient in amount and cogency is the first requisite for searching
diagnosis; the second is clear reasoning to inferences that shall
further our purpose.[16] . . . In social diagnosis, the kinds of evidence available, being largely testimonial in character, can of
course never show a probative value equal to that of facts in
the exact sciences. All that is possible for us is to obtain proof
that amounts to a reasonable certainty. Social treatment is
even more lacking in precision than the treatment of disease,
of which Dr. Meltzer says that every treatment is an experiment. This is true partly because social work has as yet amassed
but a small body of experience, partly because its treatment demands for success an understanding of "characterology" for
which no satisfactory body of data yet exists, but most of all
because, for the social case worker, the facts having a possible
bearing upon diagnosis and treatment are so numerous that he
can never be sure that some fact which he has failed to get
would not alter the whole face of a situation. He can, however,
partially offset these handicaps by being on the lookout for
the special liability to error characteristic of each type of evidence used in his investigations.[17]

In discussing the reliability of evidence, competence and bias are emphasized with the factors affecting each pointed out:—attention,
memory, suggestibility as affecting competence, racial or national or
environmental factors and self-interest as affecting bias.[18]

In the above quotations we have a clear definition of social fact
and social evidence on which sound social diagnosis and treatment
must rest. Succeeding chapters lay out the concrete steps through
which social histories may be obtained, in interviews with relatives,
employers, schools, churches, hospitals, neighbors, and other members of the community.

Treatment, also, is seen to involve contacts with many of the
client's relations in the environment in his behalf with a fairly clear
picture in the worker's mind of what his situation should be. While
there is explicit warning against too inelastic a conviction about family life, nevertheless the family as a whole is the usual unit of treatment in family work and in other fields as well. It is stated that "as

society is now organized, we can neither doctor people nor educate them, launch them into industry nor rescue them from long dependence, and do these things in a truly social way without taking their families into account."[19] "One who has learned in the details of a first interview, to keep the 'combined physical and moral qualities,' the whole man, in view, will appreciate the importance of applying this same view to the family. The family life has a history of its own. . . . What will help to reveal this trend? What external circumstances over which the family had no apparent control, and what characteristics of its members—physical, mental, temperamental—seem to have determined the main drift?"[20] "With reference to their power of cohesion, we shall find that families range themselves along a scale, with the degenerate family at one end and the best type of united family at the other. Whatever eccentricities a family may develop, the trait of family solidarity, of hanging together through thick and thin, is an asset for the social worker, and one that he should use to the uttermost."[21]

The discussion of the Ames Case in *Social Diagnosis* will serve to illustrate the point of view and method of diagnosis at that time. Though the record opens in 1909 it may be considered as representative of the type of work which was being done at the time *Social Diagnosis* was written. It offers a clear presentation of Miss Richmond's point of view that a family situation or an individual can only be understood as it is understood in its social setting through the eyes of the various social contacts with which it has been associated. The picture of the family is built up only by information from these various sources with the family's own point of view as one element in the total picture. Relatives, friends, neighbors, employers, schools, and churches contribute their opinion of the situation and all of these factors are again called upon in treatment by the agency "interested in coordinating the social service of the community" in behalf of the family in need.[22]

The Ames family was called to the attention of the society by a charitable woman on account of the sickness of the man who had been advised to apply for admission to the State Tuberculosis Sanitorium but felt that he could not leave his family. The first interview gives the facts of Mr. Ames' employment, his health, of Mrs. Ames' health, their financial situation, their resources. Of the relatives it is said that Mrs. Ames feels rather bitterly about her husband's people, that none of the relatives are in a position to do any more for them, that they did not want us to see the relatives. Mr. Ames, on the other hand, says he understands our position in the matter and thinks they ought to furnish us with their addresses. Mr. Ames says that it is impossible for him to go away, that he is very hopeful of being able to go to work soon though he is not quite sure he has the strength to walk around the streets.

The investigation begins at this point, covering the tuberculosis dispensary, Mrs. Ames' two sisters, the church and the employer. The dispensary gives definite information about his health which is more serious than was supposed and sanitorium treatment is found to be necessary. The interviews with relatives confine themselves to getting a picture of the man and the wife from the health, financial, and character angles. The character interest goes no deeper than the following remarks of relatives indicate, "He has always been a good man, never made big wages but was kind to his family, hard working." "Mrs. Ames has always to have things like a lady and if it weren't for that she might have saved something for a rainy day." The doctor says the family have always paid their way and have an excellent reputation and the school principal speaks pleasantly of the people. One relative offers an important clue to treatment when she says that it is Mrs. Ames who is holding her husband back. Mrs. Ames is seen and agrees to try to let her husband go away when she understands the seriousness of his situation. Mr. Ames' health situation is solved through sanitorium treatment, help from the employer and the church and a job later with the old firm. Mrs. Ames develops an incipient case while Mr. Ames is receiving all this attention but is treated in time to prevent serious consequences. We might infer that the relationships between the relatives on the husband's side and Mrs. Ames might have been slightly benefited by the interest which the worker took in the situation but nothing was consciously done to effect this.

A simple case, Miss Richmond comments, but perhaps the simplicity lies in the attitude and understanding of the caseworker rather than in the situation itself. At any rate it affords a good illustration of a health and economic adjustment at least temporarily successful made on the basis of social data collected from all the sources of information in the environment. Of the individuals chiefly concerned and their attitudes towards health and disease, towards each other and towards life in general we know little.

It seems then, that *Social Diagnosis* is concerned entirely with the situation aspects of a family problem.

> In talking with our client, the whole man, for any diagnosis that deserves to be called social, must concern us. We must be alert to every possible clue to his personality, or, in other words, we must note the current of events in his life as well as his social relationships. What has been the main drift of that current? Who are the people and what are the social situations that have most influenced him?[23]

His own life and personality described as a "drift," the understanding of this drift referred to previously as "characterology for which no satisfactory body of data as yet exists," the facts from which this drift is to be inferred, the social situation diagnosed, regarded as so numerous that "he can never be sure that some fact which he has failed to get would not alter the whole face of a situation;"[24] —these possibilities offer but a feeble foundation for a procedure which it is hoped to make scientific and professional. Some laws determining drift or trend, some principles of relationship between a man's personality trend and its expression in his social relationships, will have to be in mind before there can be any basis for predictability in treatment.

Actually there was no basis of predictability for treatment of the individual and actually no prediction in treatment at that time. All things were possible to social casework which had so recently discovered the individual and his thrilling possibilities for regeneration. Since all individuals coming to a casework agency had been deprived, there was always room for the hope that under more satisfying conditions they might change their behavior. Treatment consisted therefore in supplying environmental opportunity often in stereotyped prescriptions, such as employment for men, recreation for children standardized by scout and settlement movements, etc., and health examinations and treatment for all. Obdurate and persistent refusal to respond to these efforts was the only sufficient reason for giving up treatment and in such cases the closing entry read: "Case closed. Family will not cooperate," without any effort to analyze the basis for lack of cooperation or to wonder if there were any factors in the known trends of the individuals' personalities which might have led us sooner to this conclusion.

Miss Richmond makes an effort to put the diagnosis of the social situation on a more scientific and logical basis in the diagnostic summary[25] where the situation is analyzed into "Difficulties Defined: Causal Factors: Assets and Liabilities." This analysis offers a basis for social treatment in specific terms but the reliability of this diagnosis is dependent entirely on the reliability of the evidence or facts behind it and the fineness of analysis of the individual concerned. This type of analysis could not go far in its usefulness until there was greater development in the science of "characterology." As a matter of fact one finds in actual practice little use made of the diagnostic summary in case records today.

Of the social casework relationship, of "contact," little is said directly in *Social Diagnosis,* probably because Miss Richmond assumed that contact was more likely to be good and investigation, history and diagnosis, poor. Enough of Miss Richmond's attitude however can be inferrred to give us a sense of a very real and rare human kindliness entering into her conception of this relationship. In spite of all the development that has taken place since her day in making the casework relationship more conscious and more effective, I doubt if we could frame any more satisfactory expression of the caseworker's attitude in interviewing than Miss Richmond's description: "To be really interested, to be able to convey this fact without protestations, to be sincere and direct and open-minded—these are the best keys to fruitful intercourse."[26] Critically examined, the relationship between caseworker and client is on a friendly, naïve, unanalyzed basis. In the first interview it is important to establish a good contact "to give the client a fair and patient hearing,"[27] but the worker must never lose sight of her object "to get below the present symptoms to a broad basis of knowledge"[28] and "a slow, steady, gentle pressure toward that goal"[29] must be exerted. "Giving the client all the time he wants often leads to that fuller self-revelation which saves our time and his in the long run."[30] It is important in this first interview to gain clues to other sources of information and "to begin even at this early stage the slow process of developing self-help and self-reliance, though only by the tonic influence which an understanding spirit always exerts, and with the realization that later the client's own level of endeavor will have to be sought, found, and respected."[31]

The effect of the pressure for history on the relationship is obvious:

> We must have succeeded in getting enough of the client's story and of the clues to other insights to build our treatment solidly upon fact; and we must have achieved this, if possible, without damage to our future relations, and with a good beginning made in the direction of mutual understanding.[33] Economy of means marks the skilled worker; he asks no useless questions, he gets fewer misleading replies.[33]

While it is recognized that history without contact is not enough, that "interviews that have covered every item of past history and present situation with accuracy and care can be total failures"[34] nevertheless it is clear that an interview lacking in history would be a more serious failure. Great optimism is expressed that, in this drive for history, even though "we may have had to ask some embarrassing questions and touch a nerve that is sore,"[35] the relationship may be sustained on a friendly, helpful level. Therefore, "It is most important, . . . that in the last five or ten minutes of the interview we dwell upon hopeful and cheerful things, and leave in the mind of the client an impression not only of friendly interest but of a new and energizing force, a clear mind and a willing hand at his service."[36]

This chapter has attempted first, to trace the sources of Miss Richmond's philosophy and method in social casework to her concept of history and treatment as social and her search for the logic and science on which intelligent diagnosis and planful treatment could be based to a belief that in the successive events of an individual's life could be found the key to his difficulties, the clue to indicated treatment. Second, it has pointed out the acceptance of the family group as the unit of study and the unit in which reconstruction must precede. Third, the concept of the professional caseworking relationship has been discussed as a friendly helpful one dominated especially in the early stages by the pressure for knowledge which to Miss Richmond is inseparable from history.

The hope held out of finding a logical sequence in the elusive material of every day human experience and in the caseworker's hitherto trial-and-error methods of trying to render that experience more profitable for some individuals, proved enormously stimulating to the casework field. The methods detailed so painstakingly and thoroughly afforded immediately usable tools for the refinement and standardization of procedures, all too rough and variable at that time, and laid down a basis for training invaluable to the schools of social work. Finally, the importance attached to detailed history was stimulating to deeper and deeper search for facts and for principles of interpretation other than social. As has been pointed out in the preceding chapter, it was Miss Richmond herself who, in a National Conference paper of 1917 a month after the appearance of her book, when pressed for a definition of "social," brought out the individual and psychological factors involved and pointed out the psychological task of casework in such a way as to stimulate a new interest in getting beneath the purely situational aspects of an individual's problem;—"the criterion of the social, its indispensable element, always is the influence of mind upon mind."[37] How to get at "the central core of difficulty" in the social relationships by which "a given personality had been shaped"[38] remained the alluring task which Miss Richmond set for her followers—unsolved but possible of solution.

6. AFTER "SOCIAL DIAGNOSIS"

The entrance of the United States into the war in 1918 brought new and upsetting influences to bear on a philosophy and procedures which might otherwise have crystallized around the organization and point of departure which *Social Diagnosis* offered. The sudden appearance of a new group of clients, the families of the soldiers and sailors, not previously known to any social agency, not accustomed to asking or receiving assistance; the large group of Red Cross workers, recruited some from the ranks of trained Charity Organization Society workers, others untrained and inexperienced—these raised new problems of approach, of contact, of training. A Red Cross worker pointed out to a National Conference meeting in 1918 the growth of a newer type of service with families, "case work above the poverty line." "The people who come to us of their own free will" force us to reconsider our approach and to recognize that "case work above the poverty line is absolutely dependent for its existence on the satisfaction of its clients. . . . The average family has overcome whatever dislike it may have had for investigation before making any appeal. And there is a real temptation to the busy worker to go ahead with the steps of her investigation without the close cooperation that ought to be present."[1] Here, then, from the angle of consideration for the client's attitude is the beginning of a criticism of the "investigation" procedure so recently set up in definite form by Miss Richmond.

To the war experience was due also the close contact with modern psychiatry, so fruitful in developing more knowledge of the mechanisms of behavior and character formation, a science which Miss Richmond felt to possess no "satisfactory body of data." Wartime neuroses, behavior developed in the effort to adjust to war, precipitated new problems, the understanding and treatment of which proved enormously stimulating to psychiatrists and social workers. The inadequacy of social work to meet this emergency was clearly recognized. New workers were needed in numbers and a new training must be devised. Distinguished psychiatrists, among them Dr. Adolf Meyer, Dr. Bernard Glueck, Dr. C. Macfie Campbell, Dr. Thomas Salmon, Dr. Ernest Southard, all generously shared their knowledge of human behavior and its motivation with social workers and new recruits to casework in the school for psychiatric social work organized at Smith College in the summer of 1918, in the department of mental hygiene at the New York School of Social Work, and in the course in social psychiatry at the Pennsylvania School of Social and Health Work. So rapid was the spread of this interest, that by the time of the Atlantic City Conference in 1919, psychiatric social work commanded the center of attention. Social workers crowded a hall to overflowing to hear Mary Jarrett, Jessie Taft, Dr. Spaulding, and Dr. Glueck talk on the psychiatric worker and her preparation. And at that meeting the famous issue, a bone of contention at many succeeding meetings, was raised as to whether this work is to be emphasized as a specialty with specialized training or as the essential approach to any casework with individuals. The swing of opinion then, as later, seemed to be in favor of accepting the psychiatric point of view as the basis of all social casework. Miss Jarrett made a clear statement of this point which we quote in full. It may be taken I think as an adequate description of the working psychology of that period in use by psychology, psychiatry, and social casework:

> Inasmuch as the adaptation of an individual to his environment, in the last analysis, depends upon the mental make-up, the study of the mental life is fundamental to any activity having for its object the better adjustment of the individual.

The special function of social case work is the adjustment of individuals with social difficulties. It is the art of bringing an individual who is in a condition of social disorder into the best possible relation with all parts of his environment. It is the special skill of the social case worker to study the complex of relationships that constitute the life of an individual and to construct as sound a life as possible out of the elements found both in the individual and in his environment. Our relations to our environment are caused by mental, physical, and economic factors existing in our own experience and in the experience of other persons. It is no matter which of these three classes of factors is considered of *primary* importance since they are all of *fundamental* importance in dealing with a case of social disorder.[2]

This is not essentially different from Miss Richmond's point of view in *Social Diagnosis* except that in Miss Jarrett's statement, as in the whole spirit of the 1919 Conference, there was an emphasis on the individual and on the mental factors and a new conviction that we know something about these factors. Another quotation from Miss Jarrett may seem naïve in its optimism at the extent of this knowledge and its confidence that objective and subjective observation can be so easily separated:

Another product of the psychiatric point of view is the habit of objective observation—the study of an individual as he really is, not as we feel that we should be in his place or as he himself tells us that he is. In social case work we need to know as accurately as possible the nature of our client. We do him an injustice if we form a conception of him in terms of our own experience. His own account, though honestly meant, may not be accurate. Through observation of his behavior and reports of other observers upon his conduct, the best account of his character is to be obtained. When we come to the point of trying to understand him, we must necessarily think in terms of our own experience, but the objective study should precede the interpretation. We should first find out what an individual is like, and then think how we should feel and act if we were like that. ... Not only is understanding of the individual a requisite of good case work, but also the individuals with whom we are dealing are apt to feel the difference between genuine and assumed sympathy; so that any gain in better understanding is of great value in securing their confidence. ... One by-product of the psychiatric point of view is worth consideration in these

days of overworked social workers, that is, the greater ease in
work that it gives the social worker. The strain of dealing with
unknown quantities is perhaps the greatest cause of fatigue in
our work. The better we understand our cases the more readily
and confidently we work. More exact knowledge of the personalities with which we are dealing, not only saves the worker
worry and strain but also releases energy which can be applied
to treatment. Besides we know that the more our clients realize that we understand them the more we can do for them.
Another result of understanding the natural causes of vexa-
tious conditions is that impatience is almost entirely eliminated. No time is wasted upon annoyance or indignation with
the uncooperative housewife, the persistent liar, the repeatedly
delinquent girl. A small dose of reproof may be administered
occasionally for therapeutic purposes, but as a rule no variety
of impatience is of value in social treatment.[3]

Again we would point out in this quotation that there is no difference in the conception of psychological and social fact from that
found in Miss Richmond. Simply a new interest in the psychological,
a new zeal to understand it.

Southard contributed to this interest in the psychological by
pleading at the 1919 Conference as he had done before for the individual rather than the family as the unit of casework.[4] In 1919, he
pointed to the dominance of psychopathic figures in many family
situations—"all family situations whatever will benefit by individual
analysis as to what I call the family handle or the dominant figure."[5] Mr. Lee answered this argument in 1919 in his paper on "The
Fabric of the Family" making the point that the individual can no
more be treated as individual without reference to the family of
which he is a member than can the family be treated without treating its individual members. "No individual is wholly an individual.
He is himself plus every other person whose interests and his touch.
. . . The family organization gives to each member of the group the
right to demand certain things of other members. Treatment that
considers one member alone irrespective of these demands and the
obligations which go with them is inadequate. No more puzzling
problem arises in social case work than that which is due to the conflict of interests between the family group and some one of its members. . . . But, neither, I submit, is there possible in the treatment of
individuals as individuals alone any such success as could be gained if
it were related to the conditions of the family life as a whole."[6] But

in spite of the effort on the part of the family workers to keep a well-balanced point of view of the family unit, the emphasis on the individual gained steadily.

In agencies where the individual was the unit of treatment as in child placement agencies, study of the "mental factors" in the child's problem had progressed rapidly. Such agencies and departments as the Iowa Child Welfare Research Station established in 1917, The Department of Child Study, Seybert Institution, Philadelphia, organized in 1919 (later continued under the Children's Aid Society of Pennsylvania), the State Charities Aid of New York, the New England Home for Little Wanderers, the Boston Church Home Society—all using psychiatric and psychological assistance in understanding the material with which they were dealing—pointed to the value of this understanding in the practical problem of child placing.

However, the true import of the emphasis on the individual and his psychological fact did not begin to be comprehended at this time. The first statement I find in National Conference discussion which brings out this significance is a paper by Dr. C. Macfie Campbell presented to the 1920 Conference. In discussing the relation of the doctor and the patient he says:

> The patient is more than a group of symptoms, more than a collection of interesting juices; he is a living individual with a most complicated pattern of reactions, and the physician who overlooks this pattern may find the symptoms untractable, the disease unintelligible. Headache may be a reaction to eye-strain, but it may also be a reaction to a mother-in-law. . . . The extent to which a man is disabled depends partly on the nature of his disease, but perhaps more on the way he reacts to it. Trudeau, tubercular, withdraws to the Adirondacks to establish the scientific treatment of tuberculosis, R. L. Stevenson continues his literary labors to the last; Helen Keller astounds the world by her demonstrations of what personality can do to overcome physical handicaps.
>
> Not symptoms, not diseases but sick and handicapped people are what the physician has to deal with. He has to study man's ways of getting along in the face of the tests of life, and if the failure in one case shows itself by a convulsion, in another by a theft, the analysis of the factors involved to a large extent follows the same lines. It is in both cases a problem of human conduct, and a study of the underlying forces. Human conduct is the reaction of the individual to the environment;

that reaction depends on the conditions of the bodily organs
and systems, on factors such as fatigue, sleeplessness, pain, etc.,
on the constitutional equipment of the individual, and on its
modification by previous experiences. Each man has his own
innate endowment—intellectual, emotional, dynamic—and the
reaction of today is determined in part by the reactions of all
the series of yesterdays. In face of the same situation, different
men behave differently; danger threatens, one man faints, another is struck dumb, a third is paralyzed, a fourth trembles
violently. To some are given at birth stout hearts; some have always stomach for a fight; others are continually weak-kneed.[7]

Here is true recognition of the individual and the primary importance of his own reaction patterns, built up in reaction to the environment it is true, expressing themselves again and again in behavior
in relation to environment, but to be comprehended only as a pattern of reaction. How to isolate this pattern for study and control
remains a problem the key to which we have not yet found. Dr.
Campbell, in his elaboration of the amount of psychological and psychiatric knowledge necessary to an understanding of the individual's
reaction patterns would believe that the key must forever remain beyond the social worker's reach. She must be familiar with the facts
"which are the product of the labor of the consulting room,"[8] but
she cannot develop any independent interpretations out of her own
thinking about her material since she lacks a first-hand knowledge of
physiology and medicine.

Dr. Salmon, speaking on the same program as Dr. Campbell, presents the same point of view of the individual and his reaction pattern as the center of the problem and at the same time sets no boundaries to the explorations and efforts of social caseworkers in this field.

There are two special tasks of mental hygiene organization
which overshadow all others. The first of these tasks is to direct attention first, last, and all the time to the importance of
the individual in any well founded efforts to deal with mental
factors in health and disease; and the second is to insist that
mental hygiene is not an independent activity sometimes of interest and of value to social workers, but is, itself, as much a
phase of social work as it is of preventive medicine.

Securing better adaptations in society—whether of one
group of persons to another group of persons, an individual to
a group, or one individual to another—depends upon the knowing and making use of mechanisms by which the adaptations

of one human being are made. It is impossible to understand, much less to direct, group adaptations without understanding individual adaptations or to understand individual adaptations without taking into consideration the processes that govern mental life. Every living thing continues to exist only through its power of adaptation, and in man important adaptations are largely or wholly mental. In these adaptations intelligence or the lack of it plays an important part, but a smaller part than factors which operate in the emotional field. There has been a change of direction in social studies, which "after playing upon scenery, and chorus, the audience, and the orchestra finally cause the spotlight to rest upon the individual actor." Such a change is highly inconvenient because nothing approaches in economy of effort and quickness of results the group method of dealing with problems. Nevertheless, we must be prepared to train a great many people for individual work or else admit that mental hygiene is a field of effort too difficult for human beings to undertake. When we consider the enormous cost in human happiness of not only that group of mental diseases to which we have applied the term "insanity" but the psycho-neuroses, psychoneurotic reactions toward critical affairs of life, mismanagement of mental deficiency, disorders of conduct and interference with the fulness and usefulness of life through development of unfavorable mental habits, such a confession of unwillingness to cope with a situation on account of its difficulty is unworthy of the spirit which lies behind all preventive work in the world today.

Assuming that such an effort is justified and will be undertaken, I urge that the practical application of psychiatric information to social work be not brought about by creating a liaison between general social work and mental hygiene work but by putting mental hygiene into social work—a little in all fields and a lot in some.[9]

From this point on, the psychological nature of the social caseworker's task emerges with clearer and clearer distinctness. The only real deviation from it occurred in a line of development rooted in the philosophy of *Social Diagnosis,* which attempted to establish diagnosis on a social basis. This effort to further scientific social diagnosis found its most earnest exponent in Mrs. Ada Sheffield of the Research Bureau of Social Case Work in Boston who published several articles describing her point of view in a pamphlet entitled *Case-Study Possibilities. A Forecast,* in 1922.[10] Mrs. Sheffield's plea was for a scientific analysis of cases covering the individual's heredity, his physical and mental make-up, and the interplay between this native endowment and his social milieu, including his relation with his family and their neighborhood setting, his sexual life, et cetera. She proposed to analyze these social facts in terms of "relational groupings"[11] a proposal based on a conception of personality as a "web-like creation of a self interacting with other selves in a succession of situations."[12]

> The ultimate units for the analysis of social situations are not personalities thought of as free agents set over against circumstances; they are rather this or that person's socially conditioned habits—established modes of activity—within which personality and circumstances are inseparable terms.[13]

From this point of view she conceived it possible to study the "fact-items" in any case history in a more logical relevant way. Records should be written "analytically" using such familiar categories of analysis as "family, recreation, occupation and so on."[14] An analysis of three cases of unmarried mothers from this point of view clarifies the conception. From these, it is apparent that there are certain norms of sentiment, feeling, relationships, in family life which dominate the analysis, determine the choice of "clue aspects," and influence the selection of diagnostic terms. For instance, take the first situation, in which the father is a sober man but habitually ugly and abusive at home, rousing fear in wife and children, the wife untidy making no effort to cope with husband or children, the girl remembering no affection from either parent. From these facts elaborated Mrs. Sheffield concludes that the important clue aspects are, "socially irrelevant anger" and "deficient parental joy" and that "each of these represents an impairing of the function of a sentiment which contributes to right living."[15]

The diagnostic conclusions in these cases depend entirely upon the assumption of vague, undefined social norms, and upon a psychology of "sentiments" equally vague and confused. The logic of the diagnosis lies neither in the social situation nor in the individual's response but in some undefined middle territory. These limitations Mrs. Sheffield herself recognizes but feels that through the analysis and interpretation of many histories on the same general plan, the diagnostic terms will begin to take on explicitness:

Meanwhile even the vague terms used in the beginning will have the effect of leading workers to observe with more discrimination and to note more alertly the significant indications of interplay between endowment and milieu. Such improved terms as socially irrelevant anger, affectionate parental monopoly do at least this; they supply a worker with a set of expectations as to the possibilities within a case. And she is testing her observations by ideas destined to count in a science of society.[16]

That this method of diagnosis found few followers in social casework was due to some of the obvious difficulties in the method which Mrs. Sheffield points out—the difficulties of getting accurate objective fact-items. But these all rest upon the underlying difficulty of which Mrs. Sheffield is not apparently aware, that the diagnostic interpretations she suggests, "in phrases of from one to three carefully chosen words"—"filial distrust," "maternal-sexual conflict," "affectional parental monopoly"—believed to be explicit, precise, scientific, are no less subjective than the descriptive terms, "self-centered, obedient, truthful, lazy, middle-class" which Mrs. Sheffield deplores. In either case the term loses sight of, obscures, and confuses the behavior behind the term and must do so unless the basis for the interpretative general term can be made absolutely clear and objective. Social caseworkers had not yet developed the capacity to observe and record clearly enough the concrete behavior facts in a situation to be ready to trust themselves in such crystallizations of observation and interpretations as diagnoses enforce.

Happily there was no crystallization at this level of development in social casework. The workers continued to amass facts often far beyond their capacity to interpret or their need for treatment; but this refusal to accept classifications prematurely was the saving grace of social casework in that it preserved its identification with the moving changing flow of its human living material until that content became rich enough to risk some tentative classifications. The use of a term such as "affectionate parental monopoly" may serve to facilitate comparison in a variety of case histories if any two caseworkers could agree on the fact-items which should lead up to such a diagnosis but just in proportion as it selects certain items, and focuses upon their related aspects, it ignores others and fails to see other relationships. Casework thinking, like other scientific thinking, must become selective and interpretative, it must learn to see and compare the "typical" but it must do this on the basis of a logic yet to be found in the material and not in the individual worker's mind. Mrs. Sheffield comes close to seeing this weakness of her system and, almost to the discovery of its remedy:

> The traditions and training of the observer more or less condition the *nature* of the fact-items that make their appearance. Two visitors who know the same girl may, through their different personalities, *bring* out and become cognizant of quite different facts in her experience. In this sense the subject matter of much social study is unstable. Not only do two students perceive different facts, they actually in a measure make different facts to be perceived.[17]

One other attempt to offer a scheme for sociological diagnosis was offered in *The Kingdom of Evils* written by Dr. Southard before his death in 1920 but not published until later in 1922 when it was edited and presented by Miss Jarrett. The book is more noteworthy for the rich case material, the play of comment and interpretation from Dr. Southard's wide psychiatric and social work experience and knowledge, than for the brilliant, interesting and highly individual analysis it offers of a fivefold classification of the Kingdom of Evils into Morbi, Errores, Vitia, Litigia, and Pennuriae. Since analysis has had little effect on thinking or practice in social casework, we shall attempt no further exposition of its application.

To summarize—in the period immediately following the publication of *Social Diagnosis* we have found an effort to establish social diagnosis on a scientific basis following the philosophy laid down by Miss Richmond. A new and more dynamic trend of development as well has been pointed out as due to the war and the new class of clients and problems and the contact with psychiatry which followed. Fresh appreciation of the individual and a drive to understand and work with his problem were the outstanding developments of the social casework movement in this period.

Summary

In the preceding chapters we have attempted to indicate some of the backgrounds and influences affecting the development of social casework in the decade 1910-1920. The most important trend has seemed to us to be one leading out of an economic, sociological, and philanthropic movement to one with distinctly psychological interests predominating. There has been distinct progress in this period in analyzing and distributing the burden of poverty among state and community agencies. Greater responsibility on the part of the public schools for adult as well as primary education, of the state for widowhood and industrial accident, of state and private health agencies for the health of the community, has left social casework more free to develop the newer psychological task, understanding and treatment of personality. This trend in development parallels a trend in scientific development, and popular thought as well as casework has advanced with this general movement in constant interaction with it. There has been no time to show in detail this influence from other scientific fields and we have chosen rather to limit this review to influences from psychology, psychiatry, and psychoanalysis. The decade has produced the finest presentation of the sociological basis of casework in *Social Diagnosis* but, as we have seen, this is rather an analysis and summary of the bases upon which social casework was operating up to that time. These motives still continue into the present decade but there can be no doubt that the interest in the individual and his psychological problems has revolutionized the casework movement of the country. Perhaps never before nor since have caseworkers been more inspired than in the 1929 conference by the realization of the magnitude and subtleties of their problem of understanding the individual and his mechanisms as it was presented by psychiatrists and a few social workers who had accepted this point of view. The absorption and assimilation of this understanding of the individual has been the great achievement of casework in the decade just coming to a close.

PART TWO. SOCIAL CASEWORK, 1920-1930:
THE EMERGENCE OF RELATIONSHIP

7. THE EMERGENCE OF A COMMON
CASEWORK FIELD

Social Diagnosis offered a unified basis of point of view and procedure to all fields of social casework. The only book in the field which attempted a complete statement of philosophy and method, it became the authoritative text for workers. All schools of social work based their casework courses on it and no new apprentice was admitted to training in any good agency without a copy of *Social Diagnosis* by her side to resort to in every situation. It maintained this prestige in spite of the extent to which casework at that time was broken up into specialized fields with differences of approach and method sharply emphasized. The tendency to specialization, well established in the family and child welfare fields, was perhaps greatly increased by the psychiatric influence we have been tracing in previous chapters. As certain social workers in contact with psychiatric clinics gained more rapidly the knowledge of behavior mechanisms, the conviction spread that this was a highly specialized field of casework into which one could gain entrance only by longer and more advanced training. Medical social work, a much later development like psychiatric work,[1] also achieved a special knowledge through its contacts with the medical sciences. By 1920, these four fields were thought of as distinguished by specialized knowledge and specialized techniques. The family field was generally assumed to be fundamental and training and experience here commonly held to be preparatory for other fields. In 1920, the important schools of social work were advertising four specializations of social casework. The New York School in this year announced eight departments each said to represent a specialization for which distinctive training was necessary. Four of the eight were in the casework field—Case Work, Child Welfare, Medical Social Service, and Mental Hygiene.[2] In 1919-20, the Pennsylvania School, previously offering a general course in social work, was reorganized on a departmentalized basis carrying in its announcement the following statement:

> In order to develop the most satisfactory correlation between lectures and field work and to keep the students from the first in touch with successful workers and employers in the field which they will enter later, training has been grouped under nine departments. All departments have certain fundamental courses in common but differ in specialized vocational courses.[3]

Five of these departments were in social casework: Family Welfare, Child Welfare, Educational Guidance, Social Work in Hospitals, and Psychiatric Social Work.

This tendency to specialize has been stimulating, perhaps, and productive of clearer definitions of purpose and method. It has drawn together homogeneous groups of workers for study and analysis of common problems and furthered the growth of a professional consciousness in these groups. On the other hand, it has set up false barriers and defenses within the larger field of casework and maintained alliances with other fields inimical to the development of research interest and professional spirit in casework itself. In the medical social field particularly, this alliance with the older, surer, more secure field of medicine, and the necessity of fitting in with the highly institutionalized hospital demands has operated to set medical workers apart with a sense of their problems as unique to the medical field rather than common to all casework. There has been an insistence upon medical knowledge and a drive for method and technique which would fit into the doctor's problem and hospital requirements.[4] In the psychiatric social work field as well, a similar attractive alliance with an older, well established profession offered itself, with the attendant risk of accepting the definitions of the problems as determined by psychiatrists. Casework then would have developed as a tool of psychiatry subject to the limitations imposed by hospital and clinic procedures. In some situations where the psychiatry has been of a more conventional, highly professionalized type and casework has been immature and dependent, this has been the development.

In general, however, casework has not remained dependent and subservient in its alliance with psychiatry; rather, it has been constantly stimulated to new definitions of its essential problems.[5] One obvious reason for this reaction lies in the common character of the available material, the problems, and the methods in psychiatric work and social casework with individuals. Psychiatric knowledge of the mechanisms of behavior built up in hospital experience with the mentally sick shed new light upon the problems of the behavior of the client in any casework agency. This insight was eagerly sought after by caseworkers from all fields in a spirit at first largely subservient. Truant children, drinking husbands, deserting mothers, so called "behavior problems" of all kinds, were brought into a psychiatric clinic for the revelations which a psychiatric study might produce into the causes of their behavior and for the magic which contact with the psychiatrist might work in character and conduct. This expectation with which caseworkers approached psychiatry in 1920 has not everywhere and altogether been destroyed in 1930. Undoubtedly it has been modified as casework has become more competent and as psychiatry, in its clinical study of human behavior, has become more aware of the complexities of the problems presented and the lack of any ready made solutions. The psychiatrists who have had the courage to leave the comparatively well known field of hospital work, where classifications of mental disease and even treatment, such as it is, are laid down, for the unclassified problems which pour in and out of a clinic for children or a juvenile court, were animated by an experimental research attitude. Many have been willing to accept the social worker as having an equal stake with the psychiatrist in the problem of the individual. This joint responsibility for treatment has had a very stimulating effect upon caseworkers and psychiatrists as well whenever they have been associated. Furthermore, this attitude on the part of the psychiatrist of expecting the caseworker to be responsible for her social problems has had a very tonic effect upon caseworkers from all fields bringing their problems to the psychiatrist for advice. No magical solution but a deeper appreciation of the problem in its more subtle and complex factors has been the response of the psychiatric clinic to caseworkers seeking help.

At the present time, then, we see the effect of this increasing recognition of the psychological nature of casework problems and the direct influence of psychiatry upon all fields accepting this definition, operating to obliterate the distinction among specialized fields in favor of the recognition of one common basis for all casework. The grounds for this belief in a common field lie in the recognition of the nature of the problem as fundamentally one of human nature and its adjustments and a belief that in working with it there are certain attitudes, certain approaches, certain techniques, as yet to be defined, which are essentially casework attitudes, methods, techniques whether they are used by court worker, clinic worker, or visitor in a family society.

In the last few years the catalogues of several of the larger schools indicate this tendency towards the giving up of specialized departments in favor of the recognition of a common ground of all casework. In 1922-1923, the Pennsylvania School of Social and Health Work, three years after the departmentalization undertaken in 1919-1920, reorganized its five casework departments under one general social casework department, interpreting this change as follows:

> Social case work is employed in the field of human relationships with the objective of bringing about better adjustments between individuals and their social environments. Whatever its point of departure, or the institution with which it is associated, or the particular kind of maladjustment it is specialized to treat, all work in this field proceeds from a common point of view and has developed some common technique. For this reason, the department of social case work offers a required group of courses covering the common knowledge and technique for all students in the department and another group of courses required for the students in training for each specialized field.
>
> Five fields of work are included under this department—Family Case Work, Child Welfare, Educational and Vocational Guidance, Medical Social Work, Psychiatric Social Work.

The New York School of Social Work also has abandoned its departmental divisions by 1930 and indicates in its sequence of courses and its second-year seminars an increasing effort to recognize and emphasize the common ground of all casework.

An admirable statement of this growing acceptance of a common foundation in the casework field is given in Porter Lee's Introduction to the series of vocational pamphlets on casework published by the American Association of Social Workers:

> It is true that, until recent years, the differences among the various forms of social case work have seemed to be more significant than their common foundation. The most important evidence, however, that social case work is achieving a professional status is the fact that the scientific and technical foundation common to its various forms has steadily increased. At the present time, the differences between the various forms of social case work are more largely administrative than professional. That is to say, the different forms of social case work are handled by different agencies chiefly to permit more economical

and more efficient organization of service. Whatever may be the future development, it is at present more efficient, in the larger communities, at any rate, to maintain separate organizations for different types of social case work even though fundamentally the objectives and the fundamental characteristics of these different forms of social case work are much the same. This differentiation of organization permits a concentration upon particular forms of human difficulty, such as the need for foster homes, probation, the development of self-maintenance in families, mental problems, and so forth. Furthermore, to a considerable extent social case work is now practiced in association with other professional services. It is a part of the medical program of a hospital; it is a part of the service of a psychiatric clinic; it is incorporated into the program of the school; it may be an important part of the work of a court. These are specialized forms of social case work as it is administered; but they present fundamentally the same general purpose and technique.[6]

That this common basis of casework should remain theoretical and even contentious for many years to come is inevitable. The psychiatric social worker endeavoring to cooperate with a less well-equipped worker in a family agency feels a differentiating sense of her own knowledge and skill. It is important to her to distinguish between family work with an environmental approach and psychiatric work with personality factors. That the problem in either case is fundamentally a personality problem and that up-to-date social workers are so considering it is pointed out by Miss Myrick in her presidential address before the annual meeting of the American Association of Hospital Social Service Workers in 1928 at Memphis. But she qualifies, "The fact remains, however, that the vast majority of social workers are not as yet so equipped" (to practice casework from the angle of development of personality) "even though they may have enough theory to discuss their work from this angle. It is this discrepancy between abstract knowledge and ability to apply it which at present largely prevents these workers from doing work similar to that of the psychiatric social workers. It will take a long time for the approach, the objectives, and the philosophy of mental hygiene as indicated above to permeate and displace the present primarily economic, legal, or health approach of the average non-psychiatric social case worker."[7]

Miss Dawley, of the Philadelphia Child Guidance clinic, speaking at the same conference on "The Essential Similarities in All Fields of Case Work," goes further than Miss Myrick in accepting understanding of personality and behavior as the basis for all casework. She ponts out that her discussion is concerned with the most progressive trends and objectives in each field of casework rather than with the necessary practice in many communities at this time. From this point of view then, she makes the following statement:

> The first basis of similarity in all case work is the human material with which we are working. All social case work is concerned with individuals or families who have been unable to conduct their lives without seeking assistance. All social case work is concerned with assisting these individuals to become as mature and adequate and self-sustaining as it is possible for them to be. It is not possible so to assist these persons without understanding the basis of their dependence as it lies in the early network of subtle and intricate family relationships by which they were molded and from which they have developed. The necessary equipment for the understanding of this background is becoming increasingly a common foundation for the training of all case workers in the schools of social work. Out of this understanding the direction in which the case worker will participate depends somewhat, at the outset, upon the predicament for which the individual has sought assistance and the field of casework to which he has come. The direction soon rights itself, however, after the initial reasons for seeking aid have been successfully met and as the basic needs which made it necessary to seek that aid have been uncovered. Case work, both in theory and in practice, owes a great debt to modern psychology for the emphasis in recent years on the common bases of human behavior, regardless of whether it is found in a state hospital, an orphanage, a banking institution, or a National Conference of Social Work. Each field of case work has developed and will develop in the future to the extent that it recognizes and utilizes this understanding of human behavior as the essential part of its job.[8]

The Milford Conference report may be quoted as affording final authority for the belief in a common casework field. Published in 1929, under the title of *Social Case Work Generic and Specific*, it represents the work of a committee of caseworkers from different fields in defining generic social casework, of which it states:

> Social case work is a definite entity. It has a field increasingly
> well defined, it has all of the aspects of the beginnings of a sci-
> ence in its practice and it has conscious professional standards
> for its practitioners. The various separate designations (chil-
> dren's case worker, family case worker, probation officer, visit-
> ing teacher, psychiatric social worker, medical social worker,
> etc.) by which its practitioners are known tend to have no more
> than a descriptive significance in terms of the type of problem
> with which they respectively deal. They have relatively less sig-
> nificance all the time in terms of the professional equipment
> which they connote in comparison with the generic term "so-
> cial case work." . . . The outstanding fact is that the problems
> of social case work and the equipment of the social case work-
> er are fundamentally the same for all fields.[9]

In conclusion, we find the significant movement in the decade
1920-1930 to be the emergence of a common casework field in which
the individual, his adjustment and development, is accepted as the
essential problem. Specialization may perhaps continue indefinitely
as a practical and administrative necessity but is superficial and irrelevant to the fundamental problem of the social casework job wherever it is practiced. The discussion that follows will concern itself
with this common casework job. It will be occupied with the efforts
of casework first, to define its understanding of its material and secondly, to describe its treatment processes in dealing with it.

8. WORKING PSYCHOLOGIES OF SOCIAL CASEWORK, 1920-1930

Understanding and treatment of the adjustment problems of the
individual must rest upon a substantial genetic and social psychology.
This psychological basis is constantly being enlarged and modified
by contributions from psychology and psychiatry and social casework remains receptive to every new point of view from these sources.
It is obvious from the book reviews in the *Survey, The Family,* and
Mental Hygiene that caseworkers read extensively in the literature of
these other fields. The published articles from caseworkers themselves
in these journals indicate a ready use of one or another psychological
or psychiatric point of view. But these various and often conflicting

or psychiatric point of view. But these various and often conflicting viewpoints are frequently used indiscriminately and nowhere has there been any attempt by a caseworker to organize or originate any psychological principles of interpretation. A group of caseworkers in one city is exceedingly stimulated by Dewey's psychology of experience. Another year the same group may be interpreting their material through psychoanalytic concepts. In one section of the country Overstreet's *Influencing Human Behavior* has great vogue; in another, White's *Mechanisms of Character Formation.* Ernest Groves's efforts to simplify and popularize mental hygiene for parents are included on the same reading lists as the original sources. This popular literature offering interpretations of character and behavior has grown beyond the bounds of review in the past few years, and caseworkers take from it whatever seems illuminating to a case problem without much discrimination.

Mr. Bruno sees in this characteristic of social casework "to grow independently of any theoretical discipline" a wholesome growth tendency. "The whole history of our movement," he says, "is one of refusal to pay much attention to theory of whatever nature; and rigorous insistence upon experimentation in social facts. This, however, does not mean that we have not had our theories. It means that no one of them has dominated the field." Later in the article he is critical as well of this lack of theory:

> Of theory they haven't even a vestige which is their own and is generally accepted. Yet as a profession they should be producing contributions to the knowledge of facts—which they are doing; and also to their interpretation in terms of larger and new syntheses—which they are not doing.[1]

Undoubtedly this unwillingness to be held to any set theory, this hesitancy in attempting formulations of its interpretations has had both advantages and disadvantages in the development of casework. At the present time, it seems that the disadvantages are more serious and that a formulation of the psychology on which casework is operating would do much to clarify its thinking and procedures. Such a formulation would have to be made here and there by likeminded groups of caseworkers active on common problems and each formulation should be recognized as tentative only, subject to modification, criticism, rejection by other groups. One effort in this direction has been made by Mr. Harry K. Lurie in his introduction to the study of the interview by a committee of the Chicago chapter of the American Association of Social Workers;[2] another appears in *Reconstructing Behavior in Youth*, by Dr. Healy and his collaborators. Dr. Healy's attempt to ascribe credit to the sources of the "new psychology" in which he names certain psychological and psychiatric concepts, with illustrations of their application to foster home care—under the headings: 1. The Behavioristic School, 2. Thomas's View, 3. The Adlerian School, 4. The Freudian School, 5. The Jung School[3]—reveals the hodgepodge of theory on which much casework practice is based.

Though we may feel disturbed by this indiscriminate interest in any new psychological theory on the part of caseworkers, by their lack of a clearly organized psychological point of view, by their slowness in formulating new interpretations from their own experience, on the other hand, there is encouraging evidence in the whole trend of casework thinking, as revealed in its articles, its records, and the expressed opinions of caseworkers, of a movement towards more careful concrete analysis of psychological fact, towards more dynamic theories of behavior and treatment processes, and towards a more organized point of view.

Two dominant schools of thought may be recognized as differentiating casework approach and treatment at the present time; behavioristic psychology[4] and psychiatric interpretation. The former emphasizes habit training, conditioning and reconditioning in treatment and sees the interview as a stimulus-response situation where the behavior of the interviewer sets the response of interviewee. Illustrations of a partial use of this psychology in treatment are abundant in any casework field. Particularly in dealing with the problems of the preschool child, while interpretation may be on the basis of emotional factors, treatment may be in terms of modifying certain stimuli in the situation and so conditioning a new response. For the sleep problem, the mother is given routine procedures; for the feeding problem, diet changes as well as many more subtle modifications of the food situation can be suggested. These suggestions, with the weight of authority behind them, often operate as prescriptions and a change of the behavior symptom may be effected. For a more satisfying explanation of the dynamic processes on which such changes in behavior take place, however, the caseworker must go beyond behavioristic psychology. It is impossible to find case records where the casework has been limited consistently to behavioristic interpretations and methods of treatment. A conscientious effort to approach the study of the interview on this basis has been undertaken at times, notably by the Kansas Chapter of the American Association of Social Workers and the Sociological Department of the University of Kansas reported on by Dr. Queen before the American Sociological Society.[5] Nothing more clearly indicates the limitations of this point of view which deals with such external and descriptive factors as "gestures," "dialogue," "thought processes," to explain a process of interaction between two people where the significance lies in feeling and emotional factors. Alluring as the behavioristic approach may be in its offer of objective measures, definite procedures, and more assured controls, it fails for these very reasons to satisfy the needs of the caseworker confronted with the problem of understanding a deep-laid pattern of emotional response and guiding a process in which her own patterns of interacting play a constant part.

Psychiatric interpretations are of many breeds but we may assume with some allowance for slight variations of point of view that there is an agreement on fundamental principles in the psychology which is taught in the leading schools of social work in the East.[6] These schools, since the war, have given an important place in the curriculum to such courses as "Human Behavior," "Development of Personality," "Social Psychiatry," "Psychopathology," etc., developed by such psychiatrists as Dr. Glueck, Dr. Williams, Dr. Campbell, Dr. Meyerson and Dr. Kenworthy. In a majority of the schools such courses are still taught by psychiatrists. The clearest formulation of this point of view in its application to social casework is to be found in Dr. Kenworthy's elucidation of her ego-libido method of case analysis presented to the National Conference of Social Work in Cleveland in 1926 in a paper entitled "Psychoanalytic Concepts in Mental Hygiene."[7] A more recent and simpler formulation of her point of view and the content of her courses in the New York School of Social Work appears in *Mental Hygiene and Social Work.*[8]

A distinction should be drawn between the ego-libido method of case analysis and the psychological point of view upon which this method of procedure rests. The point of view is in fairly common use and is generally accepted by the schools mentioned and the students and workers in the communities in contact with these schools. The use of the method is much more limited to Dr. Kenworthy's own students. The psychological point of view rests upon the well-established psychiatric principle of determinism in mental life, a belief in cause-and-effect relationships in the behavior of individuals.

From this it follows that behavior is regarded as "a symptomatic response to the needs and strivings induced in the individual as a result of life experience."[9] It is treated no longer per se as the primary disease issue but as an effect rather than the cause.

This psychology is at the opposite pole from Behaviorism as it approaches behavior always with the intent to find its meaning for the individual. What problem is the individual trying to solve through this specific behavior, what value does it have for him, what effect does a particular environmental pressure have in releasing or inhibiting the individual's desires, his strivings, his purposes—these are the questions which this psychiatric psychology brings to the analysis of an individual's behavior and history. As to the nature and genesis of these needs and drives, there is great confusion of terminology and thinking among the psychiatrists, some starting from an instinctual psychology, others from a greater emphasis on the effect of the conditioning process in determining the individual's specific needs, interests and purposes. Much of the confusion can be laid to a careless terminology and a substantial agreement found in an hypothesis of a fundamental striving to preserve life. In Dr. Kenworthy's point of view (which she at this point ascribes to Freud) this striving is described as dividing into two streams, "libido" and "ego" "instincts."[10] The primary determinant of the movement of this life force she, again following Freud, calls the "Pleasure Principle."[11] Positive and negative are the terms used to denote the values which experience has for the child in terms of the pleasure principle, whether pleasure-giving, satisfying, to be desired, or unsatisfying, not to be desired.

At this point Dr. Kenworthy sets up a new principle, essentially normative. Experiences are classified not only as positive and negative but also as constructive and destructive. The constructive experience possesses a progressive or constructive growth opportunity leading towards integration and maturity. . . . The destructive experiences then become identified with those trends in the daily contacts which tend to interfere with progress and integration. . . . Our ideal for growth represents the continuous progress towards stable adult integration. Any experiences which tend to assist in this integrative process, whether conscious or unconscious, are constructive.[12] Biological growth is used as an analogy to warrant this assumption in the following statement:

> Since nothing in the organic world remains fixed and static if an experience does not lead to a constructive growth process,

it is bound to produce, relatively speaking, a destructive or disintegrating force, which interferes with the continuous growth
of the organism. This fact is a biologically accepted one in
terms of psychical growth and structure and can be paralleled
by the dynamic impulse in integration, or the obvious destructive lack of integration, and finally towards disintegration.[13]

Experience in an individual's history may now be subjected to
this threefold classification; first, in respect to level of activity (ego
or libido), second, in respect to the pleasure-giving quality of experience (positive or negative), third, in respect to the growth-producing
quality of experience (constructive or destructive).

The intrauterine experience, a universal beginning pattern is described as a "stage of complete omnipotence" in which we see the
embryo "surrounded by the protective body of the mother, furnished through her circulation the warmth, the nutritional products,
and oxygen components for organic growth and comfort without
struggle or effort of any kind. A pattern as complete and pleasurable
as this product of a sensory experience in utero must needs be recognized as a strong determinant for future strivings."[14] Later experiences of early childhood are described with emphasis always upon
this principle:

in order to make possible the continuous progressive growth
and integration of the personality, there must be a predominance of constructive satisfaction, both on the level of the ego
and libido. In other words, to wean the growing child into re-
linquishing the infantile sources of satisfaction on both the
love and self-evaluating sides of his personality, the growing-up
process on the feeling or emotional level must contain positive
values and satisfactions for him. An overemphasis of the destructive infantile values, through the prolongation of the too
highly charged and satisfying baby sources of comfort and pleasure, is bound to interfere with progressive growth, as will the
predominance of negative unsatisfying denial of the infantile
period tend to warp and interfere with progress.[15]

The article goes on to apply the same method to the evaluation
of behavior as has been applied to the environmental and experien-
tial contacts of the individual. Behavior regarded as the "symptomatic outcropping of the expression of the individual's needs"[16] is
examined to determine whether his symptomatic responses are constructive or destructive and whether they are satisfying or unsatisfying to him. This leads into a further elucidation of the mechanisms

of human behavior based on the terminology and point of view of Freud. "Introjective reactions" described as leading the individual to withdraw and turn in for the solution of his problem are well understood through the contributions of analytic study of the neuroses and later of the psychoses, while the "projective " types of response "which lead to a discharge of the irritations against the offending objects or their substitutes" depend for their understanding on the future progress of "social psychiatric study of the overt, explosive types of behavior, found in the asocial, predelinquent, delinquent and criminal careers."[17] These two types of response can again be subdivided into four sub-orders, protective, substitutive, compensatory, and defensive mechanisms, a classification which describes purpose and use in one.[18]

The dependence of such a "purposive" diagnostic method on "sufficient study of cause and effect relationsips in the whole of the life experience of the individual and his reactions to these life contacts in terms of behavior"[19] is obvious. The value of such a method Dr. Kenworthy points out, is apparent,

> if we compare the possibilities of treatment planning, in these cases where we have established a knowledge of the cause and effect elements and evaluated them as already suggested, with the old time method of diagnosis of a "neurotic child," "psychopathic personality," "constitutional inferiority" and "moral imbecile." ... Treatment processes must take into consideration the factors which determine behavior, and then we will save ourselves time and unnecessary effort in trying to treat symptoms.[20]

This method of diagnosis based on a study of cause-and-effect relationships seems to hold out, therefore, the hope of a long-sought control of personality development and reeducation. It is possible to pick out on the ego-libido chart the causative factors of undesirable development in destructive experience and to balance these with constructive satisfying experience. With this chart in mind the worker can proceed with much greater sureness to seek constructive and satisfying opportunity for her patient.

In the discussion of treatment the article makes one reference to the treatment relationship called "positive transference" in which the patient becomes willing to follow the advice of the worker. This paragraph must be quoted in full:

In the handling of individuals, the fact that it is possible to create in our relationship with our patients a kind of positive feeling which leads them to be willing to follow our advice needs
also to be understood in the simple analytic terminology of
positive transference. Social workers, teachers, ministers, and
physicians would do well to gain a clearer understanding of this
phenomenon. Psychological interpretation of this so-called
transference phenomenon indicates that through the medium
of the positive feeling that the patient develops, there is a recreation to a degree at least of the sense of security and emotional dependency of the childhood period. As long as the
worker or psychiatrist furnishes additional opportunities for
this kind of unproductive and unprogressive satisfaction the
patient will remain receptive. Unless then the worker or physician learns to use this positive transference as a medium through
which constructive progressive opportunities are gained, and
emancipation from the physician or worker (as the parent) is
made possible, the results of treatment will be limited.[21]

To recapitulate, this social pyschiatry set forth by Dr. Kenworthy is seen to rest upon a conception of causality in mental life
and dynamic interaction between experience and behavior with experience as a prior cause of behavior. Conscious control of the development of personality becomes possible through the assumption of
a norm of personality growth in the light of which certain facts in
experience and certain types of reaction patterns can be reckoned as
constructive and others as destructive. Treatment takes place through
the medium of the dynamic relationship of patient to worker when
the worker can use this relationship to offer constructive progressive
opportunities and a final emancipation from the dependence upon
the relationship itself.

The value of this psychiatry for the casework field in this decade cannot be overestimated. Dr. Kenworthy's formulation, particularly, with its definite application to social casework analysis and
treatment delivers over to the caseworker a new essential tool of her
job. The ego-libido method of analyzing a case history penetrates
below the sociological generalities of Miss Richmond's diagnostic
summary into concrete psychological fact and necessitates constant
refinement of understanding in analyzing the relation between experience and its meaning to the individual. Like all forms of standardizations, however, this ego-libido outline has a tendency to crystal-

lize with routine use. In assigning items to their place on the chart too definite a causality between single items of experience and behavior reactions appears. No chart is flexible enough to indicate the complexity and relativity of interaction between the individual and his experience. Furthermore, the hypothesis of a norm of personality growth by which certain factors in experience and certain behavior patterns can be adjudged as constructive and others destructive in the total personality, is an assumption for which there is no warrant in science or therapy.

Nowhere in psychiatric literature are the bases for this norm described clearly. Such terms as "adult," "mature," "adequate," "adjusted," are used but their actual content is not apparent. "Mature" states a belief in a growth principle which we understand concretely, it is true, in biology and physiology in the difference between a seed and a mature flowering plant, between a newborn animal and the adult of the species. But we do not know so concretely the distinction between the immature or infantile and the mature or adult personality. The more we analyze personalities with this distinction in mind the more hesitant do we become in regard to "maturity" as a finished product. We may more readily sense a growth process but this does not provide the final norm for which the theory seems to contend. The terms "adequate" and "adjusted" imply a relationship to something outside the personality in terms of which the norm may be described. Is it adequacy and adjustment to social conditions, to the demands of the environment? Here we strike the root of the problem of social casework treatment at the present time which we shall have occasion to discuss later, a problem that centers around this difficulty—"Is the norm of personality to which we seek to adjust individuals to be sought in some criteria of performance and relationship or in a balance of functioning within the individual himself?" Theoretically and philosophically it may be possible to find a synthesis on which the issue will disappear, to argue that a more balanced functioning within the individual will result in more satisfactory performance from a social point of view. Practically, however, in social casework, a radical difference is defined by emphasizing one or the other of these factors as the goal of treatment.

Since this vagueness in the definition of personality norms is so apparent we may well feel a reservation about the optimism expressed in the possibilities of conscious definite control of the treatment by psychiatrist or caseworker. The relationship between worker and patient as the medium of treatment is suggestive but not sufficiently defined in this article to offer a basis for criticism. This relationship medium however is a topic which needs much discussion and will be treated as a separate chapter.

We will leave the theory at this point and turn to the consideration of the effect of this psychology on casework practice.

9. THE SOCIAL CASE HISTORY

A layman, with no knowledge of social work, who might read a record from the files of any family agency kept during the period 1920-1930, and compare it with a representative record from the period, 1910-1920, would be struck by the great difference in subject matter, in emphasis, and in method, in these two histories. The major influence in this change, undoubtedly, is the increasing prevalence of the psychological point of view outlined in the previous chapter over the earlier interest in sociologic and economic fact of Miss Richmond's day. The layman on a first reading will probably be struck by the increase in detail concerning behavior and attitude and possibly by a decrease in sociologic and economic fact. Secondly, he may be impressed by the greater brevity and system in the older record and may find the newer record more humanly interesting.

Let us examine these differences from a more technical point of view. In *Social Diagnosis,* as we have seen, a case history was a study of a social situation, i.e. "all the facts as to a personal or family history which taken together indicate the nature of a given client's social difficulties and the means to their solution."[1] We have seen, too, how definitely the procedures for collecting these facts were outlined in a process termed investigation covering evidence from documentary sources, relatives, employers, neighbors, and friends. The diagnosis reached through such a study was of the social difficulty and the treatment aimed at some improvement in the social situation.

With the change pointed out in the preceding chapter from emphasis on sociologic to psychologic fact, from environmental circumstances per se to their value and meaning as individual experiences, the entire organization of the social history is altered. A family case history becomes rather an analysis of the individual members in their interaction to each other and in their social setting rather than a history of a social situation. The unit of study has shifted to the individual, although in family casework the family is still assumed to be the treatment unit.

The content of the record today is much richer and fuller consequently in detail of behavior, attitudes, and relationships. Every child in the family frequently stands out well characterized in its own individual difference from other members of the family with their interacting attitudes carefully defined. This tendency appears in striking contrast to the older tendency to "lump" the children under such characterizations as,—"the two school children in this family look undernourished," "the younger children seem well and happy." A record of 1928 describes five children in the family all with as much detail as the following picture of Sarah, the third in the family:

> Sarah born 7-24-24. While Mrs. C. was pregnant with Sarah Mr. C. was ill and in the Navy. During this period the family often had to go for a day or so at a time with nothing to eat. Mrs. C. could get no one to help her and Mr. C. was not earning enough to support them. Sarah was more than full time so the birth had to be forced. She was breast fed for six weeks and after that time fed with a bottle because her mother was no longer able to nurse her. She walked at two years and still does not talk plainly. Had rickets, whooping cough and measles.
>
> Sarah has occasional enuresis both at night and during the day. She has a habit of rocking back and forth whenever she is disturbed or angry and also at night she likes to rock and sing herself to sleep and then she keeps on after she has gone to sleep. She frequently sings and mumbles to herself. She also eats irregularly and gets too little sleep. Once when she was very tiny she had to go for four days with absolutely nothing to eat. Sarah likes to play by herself and although she has many toys she will not play with any except her dolls. Mrs. C. lets the children use the front room as a play room and often sits down to play with Sarah herself, but as soon as her mother goes away Sarah drops her toys. When she goes out of doors the children tease her so she either stands in a corner and rocks more than ever or hits children younger than herself. She frequently wets herself when she is being teased. When she is asked to play she becomes angry if she cannot be the leader. She enjoys playing with the boys rather than with other girls. She is particularly unkind to her younger brother, always taking his toys and often slapping him until she makes him cry. Mrs. C. is afraid to let them be together when she is not watching them for fear Sarah will seriously injure her brother.

Sarah is usually very unresponsive when people attempt to make friends with her or when her parents speak to her. She often does just the opposite of what she is told. Although she is not noticeably untruthful in other ways, she usually blames her older sisters for anything naughty she has done. When she has overcome her shyness with anyone who comes to the house she is constantly trying to engage that person's whole attention by showing her dolls, or throwing her arms around the visitor.

This detail has become expanded particularly in relation to early childhood experiences. To get a really complete picture of an individual's history and development sufficient to interpret his behavior patterns and character in terms of it as indicated by the ego-libido analysis demands finer and finer detail of early experience. As the caseworker's understanding of this psychology has deepened, her capacity to analyze this type of fact has grown increasingly. As an illustration, take the nursing situation which entered the case history of a child first as a health item, of importance only in a medical record and then discriminated only as "breast fed" or "bottle fed" with the time of weaning given. Very recently it has become an important situation in the child's experience with significant influences and indications. An effort is made to describe the child's nursing experience in its emotional aspects in terms of the mother's attitude towards the child, towards nursing, the child's response in gain in weight, in general nutrition, in total satisfaction and dissatisfaction. The time and method of weaning, the mother's attitude and the child's response and reaction to new food objects, is as finely determined as possible.

The interest in this type of history drives the worker with deeper and more searching inquiry into her material, but it does away to a large extent with much of the process of investigation described in *Social Diagnosis*. Only the individual himself can reveal the true meaning of his experiences. Therefore the individual's own story is the first and most significant evidence in the history. This may be supplemented by observations from other members of the immediate family group, by mother or father, by brothers and sisters. Outside of this immediate family group, however, there is seldom enough knowledge or insight into the experiences and behavior of another to make it worth while to inquire. Where a behavior picture is desired, observations of others, particularly of the school or the employer, are of importance. What is obtained from neighbors, friends, tradespeople, or in-laws is usually more revealing of their attitudes than of the characters of the clients they describe and of course may be of value when treatment of the situation is attempted. Verification of a fact in the old sense is seldom called for. The caseworker's major interest now is in the individual's dynamic, propelling attitudes and the use these make of objects, people, and situations—in other words, in the individual's own reality. Frequently it is essential to know how this reality relates to the reality of another. The inquiry at this point is a search for two realities, or the different meanings of the same situation to two individuals, not a search for an independent objective fact. For instance, a child is convinced his father hates him and prefers a younger child; he describes various situations in which he is slighted and ignored. To understand this attitude and to attempt to alleviate the boy's conflict it is necessary to know how the father feels about the two children and how he treats them from his point of view, rather than to get a description of his behavior from a third person.[2]

A striking illustration of the decreasing use of sources other than the client himself and his immediate family may be found in the children's field in the study of a family applying for a child. In 1920 this study had to conform to standardized procedures which included interviews with the foster parents applying and references given by the family, and from two to six so-called independent references.[3] Today in the practice of one of the largest child-placing agencies, the use of independent references not offered by the family has been completely abandoned and the whole practice of interviewing references is considered a waste of time, perhaps soon to be set aside in favor of spending more time in learning to know from the foster parents themselves—who alone can tell—their attitudes, relationship, and motives in seeking a child.[4] Elizabeth McCord, writing on the value of the psychiatric approach for all children's caseworkers in 1928, stated:

> It is the inside, and not the outside, story which we care most about learning. Our shift in the records of foster homes from a gathering of references to a real understanding of the family relationships is another evidence of this change.[5]

A justifiable criticism of this newer type of history relates to its bulk and poor organization. As the interest in personality problems has grown and pressure for this kind of fact both from the psychiatric clinic and her own interest has driven the caseworker to collect more and more descriptive detail of behavior and personality and more background material, interviews quickly doubled in length. In this new field the caseworker had no compass to lead her to the significant nor will she ever achieve one as long as she is simply preparing a history for a psychiatrist in a mental hygiene clinic who will provide the interpretive key to her material. Only as she organizes her own psychological point of view and becomes responsible for the interpretation as well as the collecting and assembling of the material, will her choice of facts possess a true relevancy and her organization logic and meaning. The question of objectivity in the record or the influence of worker's impressions, prejudices, and judgments will probably be raised at this point. This discussion of objectivity will have more meaning later after the question of the treatment relationship has been opened up, but we may say here that, in the judgment of the writer, objectivity of material that is not affected by the point of view of the person collecting that material is a false and impossible goal of achievement. The relevant and significant detail of social interaction in any situation involving even as few as two people is too great to be completely taken in by any one observer. This material undergoes a selective and organizing process under the observer's interest just as detail in the visual field is organized into wholes determined in the last analysis by the attitude of the observer. The caseworker's point of view, her emphases in interpretation, the growing changing reach of her own capacity for identification and understanding, are legitimate factors affecting individual choice and use of material in history taking. The more personal factors of individual prejudice or bias, of change of mood or attitude, may be considered truly subjective, as defects in approach rather than necessary and legitimate factors of difference.

It is possible to watch in a record the growth of a worker's point of view from an interest in a single factor of interpretation such as the popular "inferiority complex" of a few years ago or an "attention-getting mechanism" to the building up of a substantial understanding of complex and interrelated factors in personality determination.

For the most logical organization of material revealing the real content of the social case history we must turn to an agency which aims to make a complete study before entering upon treatment. In a children's agency, for instance, a comprehensive study of the child and its background must be undertaken in order to make a permanent plan for its care, and analysis of the foster home must be carried through to a point where it can serve as an adequate basis for a decision as to whether to place a child in that home. In the same way, a child guidance clinic history attempts to present a full picture of the situation and the child before treatment is attempted.[6] An agency administering mother's pension funds must complete a study of the mother applying before her application is accepted. Histories from such agencies show clearly the type of material considered necessary, follow a definite organization in ordering this material, and indicate the sources from which it is obtained. Forms showing the content of a social history in the Bureau of Children's Guidance, New York, are appended to the volume previously cited entitled *Mental Hygiene and Social Work* by Lee and Kenworthy.[7]

In the record of such agencies as family societies, on the other hand, no such necessity for decision and consequently for completing history for diagnosis exists. Here the contrast with the history advocated by Miss Richmond in *Social Diagnosis* is seen more strikingly. It may be that the history is never summarized but must be gathered here and there through the long interviews of a treatment process. Only if the case is to be referred to a psychiatric clinic or other social agency or to be reviewed by "committee" may a summary of history and contact appear in the record although in some agencies a "diagnostic" summary may be routinely entered at a certain point in the development of a case. In these long involved histories of families we may sometimes read for pages without learning the man's work references, or the name of the family doctor, or the location of the relatives, or any of the items which were thought to be essential for a good first interview in the teaching of *Social Diagnosis*.

The Milford Conference report presents a skeleton for the social case history intended to include all of the data now regarded as relevant by the various fields of social casework. The committee says of this history:

> Nowhere in our analysis of social case work does its essential unity appear more strikingly than in the comparison of the range of social history which is considered important by the different specific fields. ... The most striking fact regarding this compilation of data is its complete relevancy for each field of social case work, however much variation there may be at

present in the social history outlines which the different fields use. The organizations in the field of social case work attach different degrees of emphasis to the same items in the list. There is no item, however, which would be regarded as of no significance by any one field.[8]

There can be no doubt as to the accuracy of this statement that no field of casework would question the relevancy of any item in the history as outlined but this relevancy is theoretical only.[9] Theoretically it is interesting to gather a complete personal and social history of an individual but practically very little of this history has relevancy in treatment. The latest records of any good treatment agency indicate strikingly the influence of some factor more powerful than logic and training which is skewing the well-rounded history out of its established form and shape.

The more one reads records from a competent family agency, the more convinced one becomes that it is not just indifference to history, or carelessness in organization which explains this loose arrangement, but that there must be some other pressure or purpose active, which is more important to the worker than history. There is no reason to believe that the worker in the family agency brings any less interest in history or skill in obtaining it than does the children's worker or the psychiatric worker. Some other difference must operate. An obvious difference is the pressure for treatment which the more emergent nature of the family problem may put upon the worker. The problem is brought to a psychiatric or children's agency with more expectation that some study will have to be undertaken and a plan made before any helpful action can be taken. Active help is frequently expected of a family society, however, on a first visit. This willingness to help, characteristic of every agency, immediately involves the worker, whether she be from a children's agency, a psychiatric clinic, or a family society, in a treatment relationship which from the moment of its initiation may be the determining factor in the progress of the history and treatment. The family record shows this more clearly than the work of other agencies since its history is not organized as to content but develops only in the process of the relationship. But evidences can also be observed in all agencies working with personality problems that this relationship is rapidly becoming the focus of the casework job. Changes in history-taking and treatment can only be understood as this relationship itself and the caseworker's changing orientation to and awareness of it is studied.

The discussion of the social case history will be interrupted at this point to be resumed again in certain details on which a discussion of the treatment relationship will throw light. Three points may be made in a cursory summmary: first, the social case history of this decade is rich in psychological fact; second, this psychological fact is growing finer and more concrete in quality and there are signs that it is based on a progressively better organized and more substantial point of view of the cause-and-effect relationships in development; third, histories from all agencies tend to favor the individual's own story and the observation of the worker in preference to outside sources of information; and finally, while the content of the history is determined by the desire for a sound treatment plan in terms of an understanding of the meaning of an individual's experience, we recognize another factor which may at times cut into content and operate as a decisive control of method and procedure in the history taking process itself. This factor, which we are calling the treatment relationship, will be our problem for discussion in the following chapters.

10. TREATMENT IN SOCIAL CASEWORK

When we approach the subject of treatment in social casework we are on new and uncharted territory, in a field where much has been done courageously, often helpfully, but where little has been analyzed or described. *Social Diagnosis* came to a close with a discussion of the necessity of treatment based on sound social diagnosis, but the second volume describing the treatment process itself has never been written. Mr. de Schweinitz has much that is interesting and suggestive to say concerning treatment in *The Art of Helping People Out of Trouble,*[1] but it is written for a lay audience and so leaves unanalyzed the basic underlying principles important for the professional worker to think through. Dr Healy, from the days of his pioneer work in the Juvenile Court of Chicago, to his latest publication in 1929[2] has contributed franker and more detailed accounts of his treatment methods than any other worker. But his work with problem children while it aims at personal and social readjustment is distinctively Dr. Healy's and cannot be claimed by social casework. Even his latest publication (in which two social caseworkers collaborate) cannot be considered an account of social casework adjustments.

The Commonwealth Fund Publications, *Three Problem Children,*

The Problem Child in School, and *The Problem Child at Home,* give interesting but popularized reports of treatment plans with clinic children.[3] Recently another publication has been added to this group by the Commonwealth Fund, *Mental Hygiene and Social Work,* which gives a more technical consideration of the work of a child guidance clinic.[4] Miss Marcus's study of relief cases in the New York Charity Organization Society offers a penetrating analysis of some of the problems involved in treatment through relief giving.[5] The American Association of Social Workers publication of *Interviews,* the work of a committee of the Chicago Chapter of Social Workers, is a real contribution to analysis of treatment processes in the interview.[6] Finally, a dozen or so articles in *The Family* and *Mental Hygiene* and a few National Conference papers in the last ten years have contributed case illustrations or analyses of some phase of the treatment problem.

This list constitutes a very meagre output in expression for ten years in which the casework movement has seemed to show signs of great strength and vigor. Case records, case committees, the standards of agencies, the personal expressions of caseworkers as one comes in contact with these at conferences and in a school of social work, all give evidence of more penetrating thinking about the philosophy and method of social case treatment than the published literature indicates. This hesitancy in becoming articulate about the essential core of the casework job seems to be tied up with certain fundamental conflicts inherent in casework treatment in 1930. These conflicts are felt to some extent by every student and new worker in the field, though they seldom rise to conscious articulate expression. To the writer the conflicts seem profound and far-reaching, immediately practical as well as deeply philosophical in their implications. The analysis attempted in these chapters has no solution in mind but aims merely to bring into consciousness the elements in the conflict.

Following the history of the meagre discussion of treatment back to its beginnings reveals that, in the early days of social work when the public conscience was painfully stirred by the sense of social wrongs and economic injustice, much more was said about treatment than about history. When the problem was simply perceived in its social and mass aspects rather than its psychological and individual aspects, it was easier to know what to do and how to do it. The earliest case records are of simple effective action. Families "cooperate" or "fail to cooperate," in which latter instance the case is closed.

A complete plan of treatment could be mapped out in advance for different types of problems. For the family of the inebriate, of the deserter, for the unmarried mother and her child, certain social procedures were indicated as definitely as medical treatment for tuberculosis or pneumonia. The following amusing illustration of the assurance with which treatment prescriptions were administered in earlier days comes from a National Conference speech of 1888:

> The drunkard is a criminal, because he wilfully, by his inebriation, destroys that institution which, as we have said, lies at the basis of the civil and social order. The inebriate, then, by his wilfull persistence in drunkenness, makes himself a criminal, and unfitted to care for the morals of his children; and, therefore, the general conclusion which I think we must accept as a working principle is that the children must be taken from drunken parents.[7]

With increasing insight into the psychological factors in these problems the social classifications ceased to have value and disappeared from use as treatment units. Even the famous "Inter-City Conference on Illegitimacy" which had such vogue for years, holding its separate meetings at National Conferences and organizing much thinking and effort around the problem of individual and social treatment for the mother and child, has lost its power to focus attention on this problem. The interests that once united here have broken up into efforts concerned with improvement in laws and court procedures relating to illegitimacy, and in casework interest in the mother and child. In respect to the method of study and treatment of personality and behavior, the problem presented by the unmarried mother with her child is no different in kind from the problems presented by the deserted mother or by the girl whose sex inhibitions prevent her from having a child. Everywhere separate casework agencies for the treatment of the unmarried mother have been going out of existence and the problem is being absorbed by general casework agencies, family societies, children's agencies, and medical and social service departments.

A similar development has taken place in the treatment of delinquency. A general agitation of interest around delinquency as a social problem finally culminated in the Committee for the Prevention and Treatment of Delinquency sponsored by the Commonwealth Fund. Out of this program has grown a very intensive casework interest concentrating in two types of organizations, Child Guidance Clinics and Visiting Teacher Organizations, not limited in their intake to one set of social symptoms but attempting a fundamental analysis and treatment job on any problem of personality or behavior. So, throughout, as casework has become psychological in interest, treatment classifications and stereotyped plans of solution based on social causes and environmental treatment have broken down.

In those early days the caseworker seemed to know unerringly what to do and her brief history recorded a succession of activities— "Visited family, left 5 . . . Took 1 to employment agency. Got job." "Took Mary to the hospital. Had tooth pulled. Sent Christmas basket." As interest was transferred from the activity and accomplishment of the worker to the feelings and attitudes and behavior of the client, the worker almost vanishes from the record in favor of the client. All the elaboration in case histories in the past ten years has been drawn from the client's history and behavior, not from the treatment process.[8]

This disproportion of history and behavior, over against plan and treatment in the record, is instanced by critics of the emphasis on psychological interpretation as indicative of a real lack in treatment accomplishment. From this group and from others with economic and social betterment at heart comes a plea for the evaluation of results in social casework. A few optimistic articles have appeared in *The Family* suggesting ways and means of measuring achievement.[9] Healy and Bronner's follow-up studies of their cases,[10] Miss Theis' study of *How Foster Children Turn Out*,[11] interesting as they are, point out how simple and crude must be the standard selected for measurement. A searching and critical analysis of the difficulties involved in measurement of social treatment is contributed by Miss Claghorn in her review of Healy and Bronner's study, *Delinquents and Criminals*.[12] And Mr. Bruno speaking at a National Conference meeting in 1926 leaves little to stand on for those who hope for objective tests in casework. He finds our evaluations subjective and qualitative and the caseworker's share in accomplishments in any situation difficult to determine.[13]

This effort to evaluate results would seem to be a fruitless inquiry in this stage of the casework job when we know so little of the material with which we are dealing and much less of what we are doing to it. All the caseworker knows for certain as she loses herself in this human experience is that something very real and very significant is happening here. At times she may feel she plays very little part in these lives that act themselves out so dramatically before her, at others she may realize that in some strange way her entrance has made a vital difference in their situation, but very seldom does she feel that she is in conscious control of the effect she is exerting upon these personalities and their reactions.

It is unnecessary to illustrate this trend in treatment in the case-work records of today. Every agency knows that many of its cases on which the most thoughtful painstaking work has been done are frequently cases in which the personalities and their relationships have been carefully analyzed but where the worker may not even know what she can attempt to accomplish in treatment much less how to go about it. The established goals of social work—restoration of family life, readjustment to environment—in abstract terms loom large before the caseworker but concretely the individual himself has caught her in an identification with his needs, which may war against the desirable social plan. The chronicle of the relationship in which the client pours out his problem to the worker often fails to show any indication of change or improvement in the social situation. The social objective of treatment is accepted without question by the Milford Conference, at the same time the relationship with the individual client is pointed to as the flesh and blood of treatment.

> The measure of the skill of the social case worker is not only the body of knowledge and method he has acquired but his ability to utilize these creatively in social case treatment which has as its objectives the social well being of the client.[14]

Social well-being implies, as the report points out, the existence and use of certain norms which have nowhere been defined. Its goals are both ultimate and proximate.

> The ultimate goal is to develop in the individual the fullest possible capacity for self-maintenance in a social group. . . . Proximate goals may involve such things as restoration of health; re-establishment of kinship ties; removal of educational handicaps; improvement of economic conditions; overcoming of delinquent tendencies. . . .
>
> We could list the treatment services given on the statistical cards used by social case work agencies but they would give merely the bare bones of what is involved in social case treat-

ment. The flesh and blood is in the dynamic relationship between social case worker and client, child, or foster parent; the
interplay of personalities through which the individual is assisted to desire and achieve the fullest possible development of
his personality. Social case treatment has to do with the way in
which the social worker counsels with human beings; at every
step it ties up with his understanding of those requiring service, with his concepts of social relationships and with his philosophy of normal standards of social life.[15]

In this statement lies the essence of the conflict inherent in treatment in 1930. The social welfare of the client versus the relationship
between the worker and the client; the one determined by an undefined but active norm varying with the worker's standards and background, the other indeterminate, dynamic, often subversive of social
norms. If the worker is chiefly animated by the desire to plan for
the social welfare of her clients, she assumes a control of the situation with her plan in which the client is permitted to participate. If
the relationship with the client has become paramount to his social
welfare and the welfare of his family, then a new factor of control
must be sought for within the relationship itself, in an understanding
of its dynamic trends and its meaning to the client.

Casework has no accurate knowledge of the dynamics of this relationship at the present time, therefore the worker is left with only
an intuitive appreciation of the value of this relationship to the client, which sweeps her beyond her satisfaction with a previously
thought out plan for his social welfare, leaving her lost, without a
guide to his development within the relationship and with no confidence in her social plan. In this dilemma, the worker may well feel
that her whole task is fruitless.

We may go all the way with the critics of "modern" casework
and agree that there is very little conscious, controlled treatment in
the casework job. This does not mean that nothing takes place as a
result of the caseworker's participation in a situation. Because what
does take place is so dynamic and as yet so unknown, so unanalyzed
and uncontrolled, there is much to be gained by giving it a name
which implies process, not result, and which will enable us at the
same time to concentrate upon it as a tangible and essential process
of the casework job capable of being subjected to study and analysis.
The word "contact," which has long-established usage, seems too
one-sided an affair and ignores the dynamic interaction which is an

essential characteristic of the process. In addition it carries a time limit in its meaning and must be modified to describe the continuing process of intensive casework. The word "participation," defined by the Milford Conference as "the method of giving to a client the fullest possible share in the process of working out an understanding of his difficulty and a desirable plan for meeting it," implies a subtle patronage of knowing what is right for the client and permitting him to help in the worker's plan.[16] The term "transfer" is too directly borrowed from psychiatric terminology and leaves the caseworker again with a dependence upon another profession and a confused sense of likeness at this point instead of forcing her to analyze her own process in its unique difference from every other professional venture.

The word "relationship" which I have chosen here implies interaction and continuity. Further than this it remains to be defined by whatever distinguishing characteristics we can find as we examine the use of this relationship on the part of the client and on the part of the caseworker.

11. THE PROBLEM OF RELATIONSHIP

Of relationship, the most incomprehensible phenomenon in human development, little has been written except specifically and descriptively of particular relationships between individuals or groups. Trotter's *Instincts of the Herd in Peace and War* brought the herd instinct into vogue for a time but recent sociology and psychology have abandoned the concept. They have pictured the individual, following many impulses, pursuing many interests, usually with others in a group of two or more individuals, and they have accepted this interaction in a social setting as the process out of which behavior patterns and personality are determined. But of this tendency to seek relationship, of the characteristic pattern with which each chooses a one-person or a group relationship, of the uses which each makes of it, of its meaning to an individual, little has been said. Relationship has been taken for granted as the fundamental background and reality of human development.

Essential background though it may be, nevertheless it may have value for us in understanding what takes place in treatment in the relationship between the client and the worker, to lift the fact of relationship out of its setting and consider it afresh, asking ourselves the question—why and for what purposes does the individual seek to relate himself to another?

At the basis of the human and psychological drive to relationship lies a deeper, biological reality of growth through union and separation of cells. To unite and to separate are equally essential growth processes. On this biological basis there develops for the human being, a psychological growth process in which the biological union with the mother in nine months of uterine experience is deeply determinative. From birth on we see the psychological development of personality, of impulses, drives, attitudes, traits, going forward in relationship situations to mother, father, sister, brother, to teacher, friend, lover, child. When we know enough we can read the individual's rhythm of growth in his relationships, in his choices of an "other," in the use he makes of the other and the way he separates from it. We can picture the entire drive of an individual starting in identity with a parent organism as a lifelong struggle to reproduce that original unity through relationship, a movement vividly pictured by psychiatrists who know it in its regressive phase so intimately. There is another equally valid and perhaps more helpful way of conceiving of the individual's career as an effort to realize his growth possibilities through relationship as the environing medium. On the basis of this latter hypothesis, separation is as natural and significant a phase of the growth process as union and identity.[1] The natural impulses of the growing organism, animal or human, carry it out of its old familiar confining environment to seek new experiences in strange contacts. These impulses are never merely the effort to repeat the original experience. There is an essential ambivalence in this movement but it is never merely repetitive; its direction is never simply backwards except in cases of profound illness. The process is a cycle without a beginning or end, the goal to be conceived at times as union, return, at times as individuation, differentiation, one dependent upon the other.

Actually, in human experience, the natural process of growth is complicated by two experiences which under conditions of twentieth-century Western civilization have become traumatic, the birth separation and the weaning separation.[2] For this reason we have no basis for knowing what balance the child would find between itself and the self of the other under the influence of a more natural growth process. What we observe instead are the problems of the relation between the self and the other in the process where traumatic separation operates to inhibit the natural growth impulses. Characteristic among these problems are dependency, possessiveness, jealousy, inferiority, narcissism, compensatory assertion of ego, denial of the other, accompanied by all the manifold expressions of guilt which denial either of self or other occasions. Complicating these problems is the fact that for the child the mother is not only the first object with which the child is identified and whom it must come to see as a different object through the separation but that she is also the alien opposing force, which acts as the inhibitor of his own impulsive self as it expresses itself in behavior.

Consequently she may be the identical object of which the child is so much a part that it can only hold on to this safety in protection for its own self which it has never known as independent; or she may be the different, unknown object, mysterious, infinitely desirable but threatening in the very power with which his desire endows her. In the latter case the child may episodically strive to overcome this difference and achieve the object, or he may accept his inadequacy and deplore his inferiority in relation to the object. As she permits him the satisfaction of his own impulses or denies them she becomes the object from whom approval is sought and blame or punishment accepted or resisted.

The sense of self which slowly emerges in this relationship is a very confused affair. The development of the child's own impulses give no satisfactory clue to it since these are encouraged and checked from the outset by the mother's "yes" and "no" responses, and since the self of the child may constantly be taking over into itself these approving and disapproving attitudes of the mother by identification. Even where the child rejects vigorously the mother's interference with its impulses and resists her definitions of the environment and his activities, the sense of self is no clearer than in the case of the child who accepts the mother, since this self is developed in opposition to her will. Concretely the situation is even more complicated, in that probably each individual child develops with a mixture of positive and negative attitudes towards the maternal prohibitions. In this complex ego structure of natural impulses, strengthened, checked, inhibited, over asserted, first in reaction to an external agent and again in reaction to attitudes set up in the ego itself, it is rare that an impulse can come through spontaneously and be accepted as a part of the real self. The question, what is the own self in its essential, unique and natural desires and ways of satisfying these desires, can seldom if ever be answered.

The consequences of this confusion between self and object are twofold: first, the accumulation within the ego of more and more conflicting and painful attitudes which it may seek to project upon the other object as they become incapable of assimilation into the ego; and, second, the persistent, insistent drive of the ego to define itself more adequately against the other object in successive relationships, to express and recognize and make right its own impulses. Relationship has therefore for the individual a double, often a contradictory meaning. It represents, on the one hand, the security of the identical self with which one can find safety, protection, and satisfaction; on the other hand, it represents the different, the unknown which may be used for projection, domination, or release according to the need.

The individual, in a lifetime of experience, will seek relationships that within the limits of these meanings will be differentiated for him in a thousand ways determined not only by his own need at the time but by the other individual with whom he relates himself. Some of these will remain on a superficial basis, will involve him only slightly and leave him but little changed. In others he will engage himself deeply and in these the structure of his ego may be greatly modified. Some may give him greater security and freedom to grow in his own individuality, while others may confuse and baffle and throw him back upon a more painful conflict among his own ego patterns. Rarely, in a relationship, the individual meets with an understanding of his conflict, an acceptance of his impulses, bad as well as good. In the measure in which this understanding is really accurate, fine, and comprehending of every shade of difference in the individual's feeling, he will tend to use this relationship on deeper and deeper levels to release his conflicts, to project his impulses, to work through his problems, and define himself as a real self in differentiation from the other.

A similar point of view of the relation of the self to the object and its efforts to define itself in relationship is developed by M. Piaget in his discussion of the development of thinking and the child's conceptions of the world about him.[8] His experiments rest on the hypothesis that the child's thinking is in the beginning egocentric, that he has no conception of a reciprocity existing between himself and the object or between different points of view and therefore cannot reason logically. He wavers between two extremes; he is either lost in "imitation" of the object in reality or he preserves his own stability by assimilating this reality to some already existing scheme in his own mind. These two processes are antagonistic since "assimilation" forms the object in reality and "imitation" deforms the self as it becomes lost in the object.

> Primitive relations are always relations between the self and things, since reality in these early stages is a confused mixture of "imitation" and "assimilation." This means that the measuring factor which is the ego intrudes upon the measured entity which is the world, and every relation given by mental experiment must originally bear the traces of these two inseparable terms. Now we have seen that the whole perspective of childhood is falsified by the fact that the child being ignorant of his own ego, takes his own point of view as absolute, and fails to establish between himself and the external world of things that reciprocity which alone would insure objectivity.

As Piaget points out, this problem in which the child is absorbed, of defining himself in relation to reality, is a problem to which science has only recently found a key in the concept of relativity which takes into consideration the factor of the measurer as well as the object measured. This concept is appearing in all fields of science and thought today as perhaps the most profoundly revolutionizing concept of this century. Not only has it revolutionized physics and the concepts of causality of the natural sciences but it has permeated the social sciences as well until the concept of fixed causality in mental and social phenomena has yielded to a conception of a functional correlation between the factors studied.[4]

This same movement towards relativity has been growing within the casework field, becoming articulate and gaining reinforcement through contact with the prevailing scientific concepts of the time as they spread through all thinking. The channel through which casework is being most directly influenced toward relativity, however, is psychoanalysis. In 1910, it was Freud's concept of determinism in mental life which gave impetus and foundation for the psychological history with its cause-and-effect relationships culminating in the ego-libido analysis with its concept of causality as located in past experiences and with its hypothesis of a norm of constructive experience in accordance with which the caseworker can modify environmental influences and behavior. In 1930, Rank's[5] concept of relativity in mental life and of dynamic interaction in the present analytic situation is profoundly affecting the understanding of the treatment relationship. Caseworkers have come in contact with Rank's point of view through three series of lectures given in 1926, 1927, and 1929 at the New York School of Social Work and at the Pennsylvania School of Social and Health Work. The developmental psychology presented in these lectures has contributed substantially to the caseworker's psychology. One hypothesis, particularly, seems to bear most intimately on the experience of the treatment relationship in casework. I refer to Rank's concept of the analytic situation as a dynamic situation in which the patient works out his own "will," his conscious desires and his unconscious and unaccepted strivings, against the attitude of the analyst.

Two conditions seem to stand out as characteristic of this situation as utilized by Rank. The first may be described as the analyst's acceptance and understanding of the patient's attitudes as they emerge as an expression of the patient's real self. This attitude of acceptance releases the patient to use the analyst simultaneously, as an identical self and glorified object, and so permits a unique sense of union with the other. Through this sense of union, earlier experiences that have had a similar feeling tone are reanimated so that the patient's impression is often of a regressive force which draws him inevitably back to the earliest origins of experience. In this movement of the libido its drive is to break up its differentiating and separating ego structures and yield to, or become absorbed in, the other. The actual process of this movement, however, on the patient's part conceived as relationship to the analyst, consists of the patient's own patterns of projection and identification, so that even in this so-called regressive phase, the self is active and creative in relation to the other object.

A second equally striking and essential characteristic of the analytic situation is secured by the patient's acceptance of this experience as a separation experience in that he must leave it daily and in the end finally. In coming to analysis he tacitly accepts this condition of the experience while the almost universal characteristic of separation experiences in the course of a lifetime from birth and weaning to death is their inevitability, their externality. "It is inflicted upon me" is the individual's feeling, whether he reacts to bear it with "Thy will be done" or fights bitterly against an unjust fate. To take over into himself the responsibility for separation without denial of the value of the other is a development so rare that it may easily not happen once in a lifetime.

These two conditions, the acceptance by the analyst of the patient's difference and the acceptance by the patient of the time limit of the experience, seem to operate as guarantees of a safety zone in which impulses may be released without too great fear of destruction. The analyst's acceptance of the patient's attitudes without personal response[6] gives a new and unique character to the patient's efforts for self-expression and self-realization in which he has been through all his life engaged, in that here for the first time all his attitudes are accepted as alike real and significant. Here he is free to feel and admit the value of his impulses to himself, since for the first time he is met with no approval or disapproval of their value for the object, as is the case in the response of parent, teacher, friend, or lover to the expression of all feelings. The analyst may help the patient to get an interpretation of the meaning of these attitudes and their relation to other attitudes but only in terms of the patient's own balance of impulses, not in terms of a social norm as "what the patient ought to want, or ought to do, or ought to be." This constitutes a new experience out of which each individual will bring a new organization of impulses, a new self, so to speak. Essential to this experience is the factor that the analyst does not do anything to the patient, to control or reorganize the patient's pattern in terms of any more desirable norm which he or society sets up.

It is valuable for our purposes to elaborate a little further the quality of the analyst's acceptance of the patient, since it is this attitude which the caseworker is attempting to apply in her treatment of the client. In her use of it, we find it frequently conceived as a passive superficial acceptance of the client upon the level on which he presents himself to her. This attitude will come up for further consideration in the chapter on the worker. Meanwhile it is important to point out the essentially active quality of the analyst's acceptance of the patient. It implies a constant search for deeper meanings which the patient may be struggling to express, rather than a passive toleration of the attitudes he may assert on the surface. Furthermore the acceptance which the patient requires of the analyst must extend to his whole growth capacity; it must understand his patterns as they define themselves in repetition and as they modify in expression in this new relationship; it must be as ready to accept the patient's impulse to leave the analysis as his impulse to stay. To achieve so active and so complete an acceptance, the analyst must be constantly alert to his own behavior and attitudes as the patient reacts to them.

To bring out the difference between this active meaning of acceptance as one experiences it in the analytic relationship and the caseworker's use of it as a passive attitude, a simple illustration may be of value. An individual is late for a set appointment and brings an excuse that everything went wrong on the way. A teacher's response to this might be, "I hope it won't happen again," which accepts the excuse but with some indication of criticism and a firm insistence on a standard for the future. The caseworker might say, "Too bad you had such a hard time." In this she accepts the excuse and leaves the explanation where the other placed it, on the "thing that was wrong." The analyst on the other hand, might ask, "Did you not want to come today?" In this question, the analyst accepts the behavior without criticism, correction, or personal irritation but sees the meaning which it expresses and the negative impulse toward himself which underlies it. The caseworker accepts the behavior and the excuse; the analyst, the behavior and the meaning of the behavior.

This illustration should not be interpreted to suggest to the caseworker that she take over wholesale the analyst's more active acceptive attitude. It is intended merely to clear up a misconception prevalent in the caseworker's understanding of analytic acceptance as passive.

To attempt any more thorough exposition of the principles upon which therapy rests in this type of analysis would carry us far beyond the scope of our present purpose, the understanding of the problems in the casework relationship.

From a very different school of psychology, not primarily interested in therapy, the Gestalt Psychology,[7] we get very suggestive confirmation of one of the principles which seem to underlie therapy in relationship. The work of this School is furnishing an experimental basis for an understanding of drives which determine the repetition of behavior in situation after situation, the striving to finish a task, to complete an experience. To quote Koffka:

> An incomplete task leaves a trace which is unstable, comparable to a non-closed figure. Such figures possess, as we know, a tendency towards closure, and we find that this tendency is also a characteristic of the trace of an incomplete act. ...
> This stress makes these traces more capable of influencing conciousness than the traces of the complete acts in which these stresses do not exist. ... Not only do they influence consciousness, they also determine action. The person works until the stresses are relieved.[8]

From this point of view we can see the individual returning again and again to certain "tasks" or problems of relationship driven by "stresses" which frustration and defeat have made more painful. The analytic situation and the casework situation, in the understanding which they offer, withdraw the obstacles present in previous relationship situations and permit the patient to work out a particular drive without opposition. Once carried through to conscious expression a drive may lose its tension.

This chapter has attempted to focus the problem of individual growth and development in the problem of relationship and to point out the various and profound meanings of relationship to all human beings. While the point of view here presented comes to me personally and to many other caseworkers through the analytic psychology of Dr. Rank, it seems only fair to point out at the same time that the very rapidity and thoroughness with which caseworkers have assimilated at least certain parts of this point of view seem to be evidence that their own thinking and experience have been moving along the same direction and find a satisfying expression in this psychology. If this is not true, if this psychology does not express the realities of the caseworker's experiences with her clients, then it will yield to a more adequate formulation. At the present time it offers the best approach I know to the obscure and subtle problems of the relationship between the worker and the client.

12. THE SOCIAL CASEWORK RELATIONSHIP

In early days the relationship between the client and the worker was accepted by the worker as a matter of simple, natural, human friendliness. "To be really interested, to be able to convey this fact without protestations, to be sincere and direct and open-minded—these are the best keys to fruitful intercourse," says Miss Richmond.[1] Dr. Southard writing in the *Kingdom of Evils* in 1922 describes the relationship as a mixture of authority and friendship in which the worker must contrive to be at the same time a personal friend and an impersonal adviser.[2] In a friendly contact the worker could express her own natural, spontaneous, best self, she could make use of her own personality, interests, and even her own problems to win the confidence of the client as she would with a friend. Miss Kempton illustrates this approach in an article in *The Family* in 1926[3] where she quotes an episode in which the worker finding her client antagonistic and reticent introduced into the conversation a personal problem of her own and thereby won the client's sympathy to a point where it was possible to have a three-hour conversation with her. This concept of a friendly contact in which the worker uses her own natural equipment spontaneously has been hard to resign. This the worker understands from her own experience. Perhaps in her experience the word friendship defines the most complete relationship possible. But the client frequently requires of the caseworker far more understanding and patience and self-discipline than one is ever called upon to exercise in the relationship of a friend.

Gradually more technical words, usually borrowed from psychoanalytic literature, are substituting for "friendly" in the caseworker's vocabulary: "transfer," "rapport," "identification." Their usage indicates an increasing and more objective concern with the meaning of relationship to the client and the worker's responsibility in this experience. They are still vague and confused in meaning and reacted to by some workers as to something unknown, fearful, and uncontrollable. The first frank use of the word "transfer" as far as I can discover was in a paper read before the National Conference at Toronto by Dr. Jessie Taft called "The Use of the Transfer in the Office Interview." The transfer was described as the emotional relationship in which the client gained sufficient security to release impulses to which fear and guilt were attached and secondly, through identification with the worker, took over ideas and interests "which during this period become dynamic through their identification with the person who suggests them, and become in time natural channels for draining off a large part of the emotion which has been going into the transfer."[4]

Dr. Kenworthy describes it as a medium of positive feeling which the patient develops through which there is a "recreation to a degree at least of the sense of security and emotional dependency of the childhood period." "As long as the worker or psychiatrist furnishes additional opportunities for this kind of unproductive and unprogressive satisfaction, the patient will remain receptive. Unless then the worker or physician learns to use this positive transference as a medium through which constructive progressive opportunities are gained, and emancipation from the physician or worker (as the parent) is made possible, the results of treatment will be limited."[5]

Dr. Lowrey, in a recent article in *Mental Hygiene,* uses the term "rapport," defining it as follows: "Whatever effects are achieved in direct contact with the child are in direct proportion to the emotional rapport between the psychiatrist and the individual. This emotional rapport has been called by the psychoanalyst 'the transfer.' What it seems to amount to in the case of children is something like this: The therapist becomes a kind of ideal or the repository of ideals which the child hopes to reach. From the emotional standpoint the child's satisfaction is achieved by inducing emotional responses in this individual (father or mother substitute.)"[6]

A last quotation may be offered from the field of group work where the same phenomenon seems to be recognized. Dr. Menninger writing of the mental hygiene aspect of the Boy Scout movement says:

> The fourth and perhaps the most powerful psychological factor in the application of the Scouting program is the transference developed by the Scout to his Scoutmaster. By transference, the writer refers to the unusual feeling, akin to affection, which the Scout develops towards his leader. The Scoutmaster figuratively becomes the idol, the hero, the originator, and the father, and the boy, the idolator, the worshiper, the follower, and the son. He responds to his leader with an unstinting devotion of time and energy to assigned tasks and loyalty to ideas and follows out the leader's suggestions to the limit.[7]

Miss Marcus has contributed the most thoroughgoing and penetrating analysis of the relationship between the worker and the client in the relief-giving agency in her study of a group of cases in the Charity Organization Society in New York City.[8] Her analysis is too complex for summarization to be possible but it may be pointed out that the relationship she describes rests upon a recognition of the tendency to seek and accept emotional dependency which Dr. Kenworthy emphasizes. Other caseworkers, notably Miss Dexter, Miss Leahy, and Miss Nichel[9] have touched upon this problem.

All the references given have one point in common; they recognize an inevitable tendency on the part of a client to seek and accept an emotional relationship to the worker under certain conditions. Such conditions are not clearly described but we may assume that fundamental among them must be an attitude of understanding and acceptance on the part of the worker. Little is said in the earlier discussions, however, of her share and responsibility in the experience. On the client's side two attitudes stand out: on the one hand, the sense of security and protection which he derives from the relationship, and on the other, his tendency to identify with the worker and take over attitudes and interests which the worker suggests.

This problem of relationship can only be clarified further by analyzing the factors in the actual present experience of caseworkers who approach this experience with much in common of point of view and attitude. Such an analysis should at least reveal the problems in the situation and be of help in defining the possibilities and the limitations of therapy in casework.

Let us begin this analysis with an illustration from casework experience.

A family down and out, the man sick and out of work, the woman in despair, the children forlorn and miserable is referred to a family society. Or, to take a situation where social and economic factors do not complicate the need, let us consider a situation where a mother in comfortable financial and socal circumstances brings to the child guidance clinic a child who has grown beyond her control. However great the differences in these two situations, in the needs involved, in the problems presented, in the resources offered, one common factor appears evident as the caseworker enters the situation. Help is asked for and the caseworker or the agency has this meaning for the applicant, whatever other meanings she may have in addition. She is the one in whom the possibility of help lies. "Help" may be variously conceived according to the immediate need. It may range from a ton of coal, to a new job, the amount of the rent bill, to help in the management of a child, but psychologically the appeal for help may be understood as having a universal meaning. To understand the significance of this coming for help as a crisis in the individual's life history, to measure its relation to other forces which fear and react against the dependency at the moment it is most desired and sought, to determine what part the caseworker can take in the struggle between these forces—this is the caseworker's first responsibility for the situation she accepts for treatment.

It will be obvious that from the moment when the applicant appears asking for help (or the caseworker offers it where the request has been made through a third person rather than through direct application of the family or individual) a dynamic relationship is set up between the worker and the client. Entered into by the client as the result of some inner pressure of psychological forces, the relationship in the first impact of these forces with the worker's attitude is charged with significance and therapeutic import for the client.

The worker's first and most essential equipment for treatment of the client's problem from this point of view must be awareness of the conflicting forces within the individual and her capacity to interpret the meaning of these as they take form and shape in the confusing guise of demands upon her for time, attention, or relief, of complaints directed upon any object handy to receive them, of resistances to her suggestions, or plan for change or improvement.

The client seeking help presents his need in as many different ways as there are individuals, but there is value for the caseworker in trying to see certain typical trends in these ways in order that she may have some clue to prognosis for the development of the relationship. In the discussions previously referrred to, as well as in general thinking and practice, there is a tendency to pick out and emphasize one type of help-seeking only. Perhaps this type is found more frequently among family agency clients. This type becomes quickly overdependent upon the worker and frequently constitutes a peculiar temptation to the worker to bestow the desired advice, approval, encouragement and support on which the dependency thrives. It is this type which Miss Marcus analyzes so skilfully in her study of relief cases. The following letter from a client after one interview with the caseworker will illustrate an extreme dependency reaction:

> My dear Miss Adams:
>
> This may seem a litttle presumptious on my part to be writing to you at this time, but I believe you to be broadminded enough to not look at it in that way. More so since you told me what you are going to do, and that gives me a sense of comfort in knowing there is someone in whom I have inspired confidence enough to do that which you are now doing.
>
> When young we were taught there was a Santa Claus, in later years we learn this is only a myth, but of late I have been led to believe there are such things existing, only in form of human beings, as such I believe you to be. In one's life there are times when friends come to light wholly unexpected and they help to change one's views on different things that are in our minds, and to help map out our future course that it may not be strewn with rocks or other obstacles, they are always in our way but hidden from view, and these friends point out stepping stones that we may not stumble on the hidden ones. This, Miss Adams, is the way I felt since you have taken an active interest in our family affair, as when the day I interviewed you, or just the opposite, things were not very pleasant in my own mind, I had very little ambition to do anything worth while,

just enough to keep on trying to do what is right, but now I have been lifted up as it were from the depths of despair with full intentions of surpassing any past performance, as before there was nothing to cause me to think that way. So to this I can only add, that I sincerely appreciate that which is being done for me and my loved ones, and I want you to know I mean this, as we can always profit by knowing what others think of us.

Respectfully,
A.B. Richards

An equally interesting and important extreme of reaction is that of the individual who says "nobody can help me but myself" and denies the worker's power to help him in every action at the same time he ostensibly asks her for assistance and advice. Experience has given the caseworker a fairly sure guide by which she can recognize these typical reaction patterns in early contacts. It may be helpful to her thinking to see in these extremes opposite expressions of the same fundamental incapacity to separate from the object. The one accepts and lives in his dependency upon the object; the other denies the object in over-protest against his feared dependency. The individual who has achieved a separation and in some measure his own freedom and independence has no need of asserting it.

The whole relationship problem may be greatly clarified for the caseworker if these two reactions are seen as opposite sides of the same fundamental difficulty in relationship and if the caseworker, instead of limiting the client's relationship to her to one of emotional dependency, conceives it rather on the deeper and more inclusive grounds of the client's effort to solve more satisfactorily his relationship to the object, the other. If dependency is stressed, the casework treatment must proceed on a divided basis: constructive opportunities for the client must be secured in spite of and to offset the sense of security and emotional dependency produced by the relationship itself. If, on the other hand, the caseworker will see in the client's very application a desire not only to depend but to solve the problem of his dependency, i.e., his relationship to the other, the treatment relationship itself becomes the constructive new environment in which he is given an opportunity to strive for a better solution. We have become too accustomed to thinking of the application for help as indicating the breakdown of the ego forces and have ignored the constructive possibility that it may also represent, the reaching out to a new relationship through which more of the individual's ego trends may be realized.

Between these two extreme forms of the relationship problem, dependency and assertion, lie all shades of capacity to accept one's self in relation to others, all kinds of ways of entering into relations with the other and of learning in that relationship. The caseworker's most difficult problems will lie in these two extremes. With some of the most extreme, the caseworker should ask herself whether the problem of relationship is not too difficult to be attempted in a casework relationship where the worker's equipment does not permit the client to go to the roots of this problem. Certainly her time is more profitably spent on less difficult clients who react quickly in relationship with independent growth.

The worker's first inquiry into the material beneath the immediate problem which the client states should be into the forces at work in the client's total psychological situation which bring him at this time for assistance, and into the problem of relationship which the client is seeking to solve. She will ask the question—what use will he make of the worker? Will the worker be able within the limitations of the casework relationship to be of sufficient value to him to justify her in embarking upon treatment?[10] Such a statement of the worker's responsibility brings us up sharply against the question of the relation of this type of inquiry to the worker's traditionally accepted responsibility for history, background and diagnosis. We will examine this problem in the next chapter.

13. HISTORY-TAKING AND RELATIONSHIP

The most generally recognized and accepted process of casework since the beginning of its history as a self-conscious discipline has been the process of history-taking. The first steps in handling any case have been to secure sufficient history, background, and knowledge of the situation to enable the worker to make an intelligent diagnosis before proceeding further in treatment. This process has always been recognized as introducing complications into initial casework contacts, but these become even more serious in import as we admit the inevitable character of the treatment relationship in the first contact. In the performance of her traditional history-taking function, the caseworker in a first or early interview must set about to inquire into the present situation and the conditioning factors behind it as fully as she can. Her understanding of the problem has been thought to depend upon the completeness of her knowledge of the factors involved in the present and of the history behind this present. This inquiry, if pursued in behalf of history for its own sake, often assumes control of the treatment relationship, introduces into it factors which confuse the client's own motives, or drives the relationship too quickly into a level too intimate for treatment.

If it be granted that therapy, not history for its own sake, is the excuse for the caseworker's intrusion into the lives of other human beings, then we must examine the first contacts from the angle of the treatment relationship which is being created there and determine each move by our judgment of its effect upon this relationship as a criterion. Evidences that this relationship is becoming more and more determinative of history-taking can be found in the recent casework records. Such records indicate that it is more and more the client's need to tell rather than the worker's pressure to extract them which is back of the long revelations of past experiences with which the records grow more encumbered usually in the later stages of contact. Frequently the worker does not precipitate these confidences, neither does she guide them in content or in quantity, and seldom does she know what to do with them. Often if she does nothing and accepts the confidence without criticism, correction, or advice, it seems to be therapeutic in effect. The worker knows this effect and frequently works for it deliberately describing her action by some such phrase as "letting the client release his guilt."[1] The therapy involved in telling one's story is, of course, more complicated than this phrase indicates. While it releases tension, it sets up new tensions in that the client, in telling has given something of himself which demands response, sometimes, also, further giving, to explain or complete his meaning. Some of this complexity is sensed by the caseworker in her reaction to the client's revelations, though not clearly enough to control her reactions. Rather, one must admit that the caseworker derives a certain satisfaction from having established a contact in which intimate history has been produced as well as the satisfaction of being in possession of a basis on which to interpret the client more adequately.[2]

Another evidence that the caseworker is modifying history-taking deliberately in terms of its effect on "contact" can be read in the use of outside sources of information discussed in Chapter 9. It is fairly general practice now in good casework agencies not to see any informants without the understanding and consent of the clients, provided of course we are working with clients who are intelligent enough to give or withhold consent. Even where significant information might be thought to be in the hands of a relative, for instance, the worker will wait to get this information until the client accepts this as a part of treatment. That information is worthless if the "contact" is spoiled in the process of securing it, is a tenet of casework teaching.

There is still great confusion between the swings of emphasis on history and contact and no sure guide to a balance between the two. Clarification will come with the caseworker's gradual acceptance of responsibility for the treatment relationship as the core of the casework job and the thinking through of all problems of history and treatment in the light of this relationship.

I should like to suggest one distinction which as far as I can discover has never been made in casework literature, in the hope that it may throw some light on the caseworker's quandary in early contacts between her need for information about the problems and her awareness of the client's necessity to develop the situation in his own way and at his own speed. It seems to me we are struggling in a confusion between *knowledge* of the present situation which carries necessary diagnostic and prognostic value and *history* of the individual's past which has value in building up our general understanding of conditioning experience but carries no meaning for treatment in the present problem. History was vital for treatment in the older conception of social casework when the worker manipulated the environment in line with her discoveries from history. For example, she might decide to move a dependent colored family South when the investigation showed that they had done well there in former years and had contacts on which they might reestablish themselves. Today a family might come to the decision that they would like to go back home and the worker might help them to see clearly their own desire and to work out a practical plan for moving, but she would do this on the basis of the attitudes and desires that were active and operative in the present situation and not on the indication from any past phase of history. Again, Mr. A's treatment of his wife is clearly a pattern of behavior built up in his relationship with a competent and severe mother. The history of his mother's treatment of him may be very interesting and enlightening to the caseworker in her understanding of the genesis and development of such patterns in general, but it will not have any influence upon her treatment attitude in the relationship between Mr. and Mrs. A. His negativistic and dependent attitudes have to be understood and dealt with in the present situation as they are directed towards his wife and the worker. Any use he still makes of his mother, long since dead, will be an active factor in the present situation and will appear as such in Mr. A's conversation.

In such a problem as that just outlined between Mr. and Mrs. A., the worker, nine chances out of ten, will be under the necessity of building up a complete picture of Mr. A's early home relationships, from Mr. A. himself, his wife, possibly from brother or sister if Mr. A. permits them to be visited. What is this necessity? First of all, it is the drive of the past ten years of interest in this process of the determination of personality pattern in interaction with experience—a drive that is far from spent as its effort reveals finer and finer relations and greater and greater complexity as it proceeds. Secondly, we may see in this absorption in history the caseworker's insecurity in the interpretation of the implications of the present situation and her fear of assuming responsibility for her part in that situation.

We can appreciate more readily the meaning which history may have for the worker if we watch a student coming into the casework field. She reads the A. record, visits Mrs. A., and reacts violently against the picture she gets of Mr. A's reactions against this capable, long-suffering woman. Her own easy sympathy and feeling of likeness with Mrs. A. rejects Mr. A. as hostile, outside. To break down this naïve negative reaction to Mr. A., the supervisor will use as teaching material Mr. A's background of experience. If the student can see those experiences and feel the interplay of Mr. A.'s reactions, can "identify" with that history in some of its moments, she can take in Mr. A. sufficiently to be able to accept his present behavior objectively instead of reacting against it judgmentally and subjectively. It requires several years of casework at the least for a student to be able to dispense with the aid which this process of living through past history offers in understanding personality and behavior. There is no substitute for the study of developmental histories in a training process. Perhaps casework needs ten years more of this identification with the experiences of its clients before it can emerge as a profession sufficiently detached to enter into a treatment relationship on the basis of analysis and understanding of the present problem.

If and when we accept this distinction, we shall be concerned, in the early contacts, with obtaining as full and complete knowledge as possible of the present situation, of each individual in his relationships with all the elements in his environment which have emotional significance for him. This will be a cross-section only, and an incomplete one from a social or economic angle. But it is a dynamic cross-section in which all the forces which determine the individual's reactions to and use of his social situation will appear. It will reveal the individual's orientation to his life problems when he comes to the caseworker's attention. If she can further accept her role purposively and intelligently as a dynamic factor of his environment at the crucial point of his coming for help, this cross-section may become a growing, changing point out of which a new orientation may develop.

If this distinction is accepted, history will not be needed to bulwark our uncertainty or to substitute for our ignorance of present reactions. History will take its place in the relationship, not in terms of the caseworker's need but as one of the client's reactions. It will come into the record at whatever time and place the client needs to make use of it, and his uses of it will be many and various as the relationship proceeds. It will usually be offered in the early contacts as the client's first gift of himself in return for the help he seeks, his first breaking down of the boundaries of separation between himself and another. But equally well it may be withheld at this time by the client who in that one move to take help, to include another, withdraws at the same time defensively to protect himself from invasion. In both cases it is not the facts of the history but the immediate present reality of the client's reaction to the worker which is important for her to recognize in the treatment relationship. Later, history may be offered again and again as an escape from present problems, as an excuse or defense, as a play for the worker's attention, or it may appear at moments of release from tension as the uncritical attitude of the worker permits the client to accept her as a part of himself and so to deposit his past upon her. Or again it may appear as an effort to think through and unify his past with the help of the understanding response of the other. The worker's response should be determined by the meaning to the client at that point in their relationship and not by her interest in the facts as presented or by her identification with the client in that past experience.

If this distinction between history of background and knowledge of the client's present reaction pattern has any meaning for casework it will lead at once to the question, how without history can the caseworker come to an understanding of the client's reaction pattern. This question, it seems to me, lies at the root of the whole approach to the casework relationship and the possibility of casework therapy. Casework has no satisfactory answer to this question in its present stage of development. Casework records give us knowledge of a client's reaction pattern built up by history of his past experiences and history of the worker's trial-and-error contacts with him. Very rarely is there sufficiently early understanding of the client's equipment in present and potential attitudes to make the relationship we would wish to be therapeutic anything more than a blind clash of his forces against the worker's. More than this is essential if casework is to have any confidence in itself as treatment for human ills. This much at least is necessary: first, that the worker be able to analyze the forces active in the individual at the time when she enters into relationship with him; second, that she be conscious and intelligent concerning the way these forces interact with her attitudes and with each other in the progress of the relationship; and third, that she have some definition of the therapeutic limitations and possibilities of the relationship.

Two illustrations will clarify the distinction between history and knowledge of the present situation and the part they play in casework. In the first, a boy of twelve, under care of a child-placing agency, while in a temporary home awaiting permanent placement, exposes himself to a girl in the school yard. Half a dozen people testify to the occurrence. The boy is sent home and the irate principal refuses to take him back. The foster mother, devoted to the boy, cannot believe him guilty when he denies it. The caseworker, a student in training, identified with the boy, accepts it as fact with difficulty. She is able to forgive the boy in her own feeling about the occurrence by the study of his background in a disreputable section of the city, his lack of training and his poor associates. History serves in her thinking as an excuse for behavior which she cannot accept as such. But as long as the student places the explanation of the boy's behavior in past experiences which excuse the behavior she cannot help him through his present problem. Her attitude carries with it, as an almost inevitable consequence, the feeling "this must not happen again." We see here three typical levels of reaction to undesirable behavior: first, rejection of the individual; second, rejection of the behavior and denial of the individual's guilt; and third, forgiveness for the individual through finding an excuse or alibi for the behavior.

To understand the boy at this point in his development it is essential to accept his behavior as an expression of the boy's own self; to know his impulses and attitudes; his satisfactions and dissatisfactions as they operate in the present. What inferiorities pursue him in his relations to other children? What problem in his relation to the woman is this behavior attempting to solve? His attitudes towards the girl in the school yard, towards the foster mother, towards his own mother and father (both dead), would help build up an understanding of his problem. Every factor that is active in his attitude is an essential part of the present situation and invaluable for an understanding of his needs in determining placement. Probably with this inarticulate boy it will be impossible to get sufficiently fine enough detail of attitude to define the problem. History might add other illustrations of the way his problem expresses itself and the reactions of other individuals to it. History could not define its inner meaning nor locate its origins in causative circumstance. The skilled worker must eventually base her decision for his placement on the material that gives the best picture of his present orientation to his environment in terms of his positive and negative attitudes, not on background material about parents and grandparents and the child's early experiences.

In the following illustration the value of an initial study of the dynamic attitudes in a situation in preference to history as such is clearly indicated. Mrs. A., a widow with three children, comes to a child guidance clinic for help on the personality problem of her youngest child. In the first interview, she offers, of her own initiative, a statement of the child's problem, her backwardness and timidity in school, her inability to make friends of other children. Her whole picture of the child creates at the same time an equally vivid picture of the mother's disappointment, her pride stung by the child's failure. She then describes two older children, brilliant, efficient, successful, and their scornful treatment which amounts to positive cruelty to the youngster. Her satisfaction in them and in their rejection of the youngest child is obvious. The caseworker will ask any question here necessary to bring out the attitudes in the present problem. It is clear that the mother adores the oldest child, accepts the second as like the first and a tool for the advancement of the first, and rejects the last and different child as an interference with her own ambitious drive of which the first two children are a part. Also the mother is convinced that the situation cannot be altered, that the blame lies in the makeup of the youngest. To accept the possibility of change would mean an admission of her own responsibility against which she is very successfully defended. Nevertheless there is a faint stirring of guilt fanned no doubt by the teacher and others in the school interested in the welfare of the youngest. This underlying guilt leads her to the clinic that she may have an outside source on which to place the responsibility for the situation. She repeatedly assures the caseworker that nothing can be done and raises insurmountable obstacles to every obvious suggestion such as "had she ever considered sending one child away to school to relieve the rivalry among them." The caseworker's aim in this interview is to analyze the forces in this home situation as has been briefly indicated here and to decide why the mother is bringing the problem to her and what use she intends to make of her and of the clinic. If she is using the clinic to fortify and justify herself in her attitude towards the child, to prove them wrong and herself right in every suggested change, then the caseworker's further question must be to determine whether the mother will perhaps get enough release from being able to project her guilt on the worker to modify her vindictiveness towards the child. In this case it may be worthwhile letting the mother work out her problem on the clinic to this purpose. Or if the clinic decides that the mother is not likely to change her attitude, it may nevertheless decide to go into the situation further to see what other factor might be capable of some change to relieve some of the pressure on the youngest child. It may be that one of the other children might be able to enter into a relationship with the caseworker which would enable her to accept the youngest child (with all due regard of the effect on the mother and the third child if any change in the balance of power in the situation as a whole is produced.) Again, the caseworker might decide to try a relationship with the youngest child directly for what it might do for her to find herself the object of interest, attention, and concern from someone outside the family in a hope that if her behavior improved sufficiently of itself the mother might find her a child to be proud of.

In all this the worker has had no concern with history as such. The mother will advance it from time to time in self justification and explanation. She may offer her own experience with a good-for-nothing husband as one more proof that the youngest who resembles him is hopeless, but it will not aid any in the solution of the worker's problem to know this fact as fact or to seek to build up more of a picture of the domestic relations of the two by interviews with their respective parents. This fact has meaning only as it is active in the attitude of the mother. If her introduction of this material about her husband indicates any admission of failure on her own part and consequently a point of contact at which change may be acceptable then the worker will seize this as a treatment opportunity, i.e., as an indication that Mrs. A. has been able to come far enough in her acceptance of the worker to lay aside her defense and admit into consciousness an awareness of her failure in marriage. A later step in this growth process might be the acceptance of her own failure and a toleration for the child who is a personification of it.

In such an approach to a situation the analysis is made in terms of the dynamic factors within it and the possibilities of their interaction in the new dynamic situation set up by the caseworker's presence. This kind of analysis is in use in child guidance clinics, in children's agencies and in family societies to some extent. It is too tentative as yet to have voiced itself clearly in the records even where the worker may be thinking about and discussing her case in these terms.

Summary

The preceding chapters have traced the development of the treatment process in social casework from impulsive action in the client's behalf through the period of increasing respect for the client's essential individuality to the present decade when, some critics argue justly, treatment has almost disappeared from case records. We see in this development a necessary identification with the client's experiences until casework shall have built up enough understanding of personality variations and a sufficiently organized genetic psychology to be able to separate from this identification and accept the full responsibility for the client's problem as it expresses itself in the present within the limits of the casework experience. The acceptance of this responsibility involves the caseworker in a treatment relationship whose essential characteristic is dynamic interaction between client and worker and by this distinguished from the early "doing for" or "doing something to" the client or the later "understanding the client through his past." In one, the worker projects herself upon the client, in the second, she escapes herself in identification with the client, while in the third, "the treatment relationship," she accepts responsibility for herself and for the relationship as well.

A distinction has been offered between history of the client's experiences and knowledge of his present reaction tendencies in the hopes of clearing up some of the existing confusion about the place of history-taking in a treatment process. With the exception of this distinction and the subordinate place it assigns to history except as material in the treatment relationship, this chapter does not go beyond the analysis of the trends which seem to the writer to be very present in some of the casework that is being done at the present time. It is recognized that the formulation of such trends in this didactic form may call forth much controversy as to their existence and interpretation.

14. ATTITUDES AND TECHNIQUES

We have seen that there is one common quality underlying the attitudes of clients seeking casework help—the active search for a relationship in which to solve a problem. Similarly, the caseworker universally holds out this answering quality in her attitude when she accepts the problem:—"I am here to help you solve it." No other factor in the relationship is apparent to the client. The client knows nothing of the conditions, the possibilities, the limitations of this casework help he is seeking. Sometimes he intends to present what to him is a very slight and temporary problem—he would like a load of coal to tide over a hard month, or help in getting work during a season of unemployment. Rapidly he becomes involved, through the caseworker's interest and concern for his whole economic situation, his health, his family relationships, in asking and taking help on his fundamental problems, and consequently in a relationship with the caseworker which was unsought on this level and therefore not accepted and understood in advance. Even where the individual seeks help on so fundamental a problem as his relations with his wife or children, he rarely has any idea in advance of what he will go through in the process of reaching a solution. In this respect, the knowledge and control of the conditions must seem to the client to lie entirely within the caseworker's control. The giving or withholding of relief, the time she spends in listening to his story or the time she denies him in listening to some other member of his family, her special attentions, such as affording opportunities for recreation or health care:—all these seem to locate in her some arbitrary and variable authority and power over his situation beyond his control, often beyond his understanding. The sense of this power in the hands of the caseworker precipitates at once the client's fundamental problem in relation to the "other" and his typical reaction of dependency and subservience to that control or negative assertion against it, both so familiar to the caseworker in their concrete manifestations. In respect to this factor of control it is interesting to note the striking contrast between the casework and the analytic relationship. While control of the situation in the former is arbitrary and variable and neither understood nor accepted in its conditions by the client when he comes into this relationship, in the analytic experience the patient knows and accepts the conditions when he applies for an analysis. He accepts the unchanging condition of a limited time period daily and furthermore he realizes that he is entering upon a relationship which will gather deep significance for him and will inevitably eventuate in a separation experience.

This arbitrary control with which the caseworker is endowed and the fact that the client does not understand or accept the conditions or the relationship before he may be caught in it raises grave problems for the caseworker which are scarcely even as yet realized as problems. One may wonder whether it is possible to reduce the arbitrary control which the worker exercises, or at least to define it in advance so that the client may understand and accept it. In the light of our increasing sensitivity to the client's state of readiness or unreadiness to enter upon a casework relationship, we must ask the question whether it might not be better to give the load of coal and let it go at that as a simple relief procedure, rather than to intrude upon his fundamental problems when he has indicated no readiness to have us there. The answer should lie not in the discovery that the situation contains problems or needs casework treatment, for in respect to this all situations are much alike, but rather in this question: "Do the individuals in this situation seek casework help at this point or are they making an adjustment fairly satisfactory to themselves without it, and what kind of use will they make of casework aid if offered?"

The second quality which the casework relationship holds for the client is understanding, of a depth and penetration which almost without exception gives to this experience at once a unique character. Here the rehearsal of history in its treatment value is apparent when the client offers himself to the worker, through his story of his past experiences, and is accepted without criticism or disapproval. The records show a steady increase in the intimacy and completeness of these histories as caseworkers have grown in their understanding and capacity to identify with more varieties of experience. An illustration in point is the growth in detail and intimacy in the record of the individual's sex history in recent years as a result of the worker's growth in understanding sex problems and her capacity to accept the client's experiences without judgmental reaction.

The greatest limitation in the caseworker's equipment in understanding at the present point seems to lie in her failure to understand ambivalence in reaction. Her training in history has accustomed her to look at the events of experience in the large as a causal chain, to seek in behavior explanatory unit patterns. The concentration upon the finer detail of reaction which the acceptance of a treatment relationship forces upon her will bring about eventually a keener awareness of the complex ambivalence back of every reaction. On the other hand, this awareness is delayed by the necessity which the caseworker is under to accomplish something, to effect a change in an attitude or situation in conformity with her conception of a norm of personality growth or a social norm. As an illustration, a client about to give birth to an illegitimate baby discusses with the worker the possibility of an abortion. In this discussion it is easy to read all her conflicting attitudes. The worker, under the pressure of her own fear of abortion and the moral values attaching to it, reacts immediately to the client's slightest expression of desire for the baby without giving the client a chance to express freely her desire to be rid of the child. A plan is quickly made on the basis of the desire to have the child and the birth takes place. The mother gives it the worker's name and shortly after she comes out of the hospital asks the worker to place it for adoption apparently with a free conscience and the feeling that it was the worker's responsibility. The opportunity which this situation offered for the client to accept her own responsibility for the child was lost by the caseworker's assumption of that relation so that the client could easily project her guilt upon the caseworker's shoulders. The illustration could be multiplied by numbers like it in which the worker's necessity for constructive action inhibits her from seeing clearly the forces at work often to defeat her plan later.

The problems which the quality and depth of her understanding plus its limitation raises in the treatment relationship seem insoluble at the present time. The client responds to the understanding with a sense of release and of being accepted by another and in turn accepting the other, never before experienced. Here is a relationship in which he knows union and freedom to express himself. Inevitably in this deepening experience of release and freedom, conflicting attitudes come into consciousness and inevitably these attitudes must be checked by the caseworker's necessity of favoring the socially right, the constructive attitude. Jealousy of the caseworker's interest in his wife and children is a natural by-product of the reaction to her understanding of his problems on the client's part, but this attitude the worker would find it hard to admit into her necessity of having the whole situation move forward constructively. Very rarely do we read of the worker's permitting an expression of negative reactions towards herself and the agency, though they are undoubtedly present in every situation at some points. So the client is again caught and held in the network of his own patterns by the limitation in the caseworker's understanding, as he is by the arbitrary and irrational control which she exercises over his destiny.

Aside from the necessity of working towards a norm which we shall discuss presently, there seems to be no reason why the caseworker's understanding of ambivalence should remain static. Records indicate that it is growing steadily in spite of every obstacle and there seem to be no real limits to her increasing consciousness of the client's complex attitudes.

A very interesting secondary problem in connection with an understanding of ambivalence is the question of how to handle it with the client. "Interpretation" or "interpreting the client to himself" is a valued technique of casework at the present time. In many instances it seems rather the worker's interest than the client's and one wonders how much value it may have to the client. Records today abound in illustrations of the caseworker's efforts to give the client insight into his own mechanisms. She offers him elaborate explanations of behavior which have been but recently acquired and passed on in the full flush of their interest to the worker, often poorly assimilated by her and usually incapable of being assimilated by the client. It would be salutary for our procedure in this respect if we could more often get the direct come-back to our efforts to offer insight that a student recently received; the come-back of the door slammed in her face in response to her carefully prepared history and interpretation of the client's habit of exaggeration and prevarication. "So I'm a liar, am I?"—this dramatic summing up by the client of the meaning of the interpretation indicates the distance between the worker's insight and the client's readiness to receive it. This factor of readiness, a time factor, in developing insight, is one we have only begun to sense dimly in our dealings with people. Until we are more aware of its import we should be very wary of attemptting interpretation which, without consideration of this factor, is so apt to operate as gross intrusion into another's life.

The third quality with which the caseworker is endowed for the client is an identification with the morally right or the socially right as he conceives it. He approaches this in the abstract in first contacts either with admiration and respect or with resentment and protest. The unexpected tolerance with which the caseworker greets behavior which violates his moral code, invades his abstract picture of her as arbiter of right and wrong and permits him to accept her as identified with his own morally condemned strivings and desires. Here again she is apt to fail him midway in that her conflicting identification with the socially right, or what is right for this family, or for this individual, inhibits his condemned and negative impulses. This forces him either to a premature identification with her in this effort to achieve a norm against which the conflicting impulses continue to protest, or in a flight from the too great pressure which this effort entails. An interesting illustration of both these reactions is seen in Mr. B. who, in his first contacts with the caseworker, revealed his whole story of struggle and failure and seemed eager to put forth an effort to become self-supporting and a help to his family again. When the caseworker began to act upon this identification with her constructive desires for him and to offer him jobs of various kinds, he disappeared without word to her and involved himself again triumphantly in protective contacts with his old gang in a flight from the pressure of social responsibility which seemed to have fastened down upon him before he was ready. To him there must have seemed an inexplicable conflict in the caseworker in that she accepted his worst self in his past and yet so quickly and firmly desired him to be different in ways that condemned his past. On the other hand, many constructive therapeutic adjustments have been made by individuals on just this basis of identification with the caseworker in her ideals. It requires fine analysis on the caseworker's part to determine when this identification is one which can really organize the client's own impulses at that time and operate effectively in his reality contacts and when, on the other hand, it is a premature taking over of her ideal in denial of his own will and desires. In the latter case this identification will serve to further increase his conflict and will operate to disorganize the situation as a whole. Again we see how the case-worker's own stake in the situation, expressed as the necessity of doing a good casework job, of considering the family as a whole, or the attitude of the agency or of society towards this situation, must operate to prevent her making this discrimination in terms of what the identification with "the right" means at this time to the client in his total organization.

We arrive here at a fourth characteristic of the caseworker's attitude, her objectivity, her detachment from a personal stake in the client's problem. This perhaps more than any factor in the entire situation creates for the client a unique opportunity to change. In every other experience his need has been met by an opposing or an answering need, his will by conflicting or conquered will. In her function of understanding and accepting the client, the caseworker asserts no will of her own, but becomes at his service. This attitude depends upon her integrity and freedom from designs of her own in the situation and varies with the caseworker's development, a problem which will be discussed further in a chapter on the worker and her training. The client's response to this quality of impersonality is always ambivalent in that he, on the one hand, wishes to arouse some personal response as a token of his power to do so, and, on the other hand, he finds a new satisfaction in this impact with a force which permits his self-expression without having to retort in its own behalf.

Objectivity is an aim for which the worker must strive consciously in every situation through deepening her understanding of the client's problem and separating her own personal interest from it. It is never a goal which can be attained once and finally. It must be sharply differentiated from a detachment which is lacking in understanding and identification. It rests upon the finest possible feeling, identification with the client and intelligent analysis of the factors in his problem, and eventuates in a perspective which leaves both the client and the worker free. The worker does not have to take over the problem but can let the other solve it in his own way and time. Caseworkers have been so involved in their own necessity to give that it requires a new appreciation of the client's reactions to accept the fact that a gift is not necessarily therapeutic in itself as given. Only the development of a true objectivity makes it possible for a caseworker to reject and close cases, to extricate herself from situations when she realizes that the client is only using her in order to project an old pattern and is not able to change this pattern through anything the relationship can offer.

The supervisor's handling of a worker in the following situation indicates a rare capacity for objectivity. This worker presented repeatedly her discouragement with her own performance, projecting it on first one failure or situation and then another, but in moments of insight laying it squarely on herself. The worker, in the discussion of her cases, seemed always to seek the encouragement but could never accept it as convincing. Any discussion of the difficulty seemed to drive it back to the worker's conviction of her total inadequacy. The supervisor might have continued to treat this problem on the basis of its symptom and pointed out success and given continued encouragement. Actually, she decided that encouragement, while it accepted a projection and satisfied a temporary need, was really a constant source of dissatisfaction to the worker in that it failed to admit the problem for the all-devouring, completely inhibiting thing it was. When she became thoroughly convinced of the depths of the problem she granted to the worker the reality of her complete sense of failure and suggested that she seek help in solving this fundamental problem of her destructive attitude towards herself. The worker left the organization with a minimum sense of rejection and sought psychoanalytic help. In a similar situation another supervisor found it so important to have the worker succeed that she could not extricate her own need for success from the situation and continued to bring praise and encouragement to bear on the worker to make her see that she could do a good job. Under this pressure the worker grew more and more depressed and finally failed actually.

As objectivity develops in casework, perhaps we will see a decrease in relationships carried on an intensive level, and greater skill, in terms of deeper knowledge and understanding, to limit the goal of treatment. Only the most unflagging efforts to achieve this kind of objectivity will enable casework to think through the reactions which casework in its offer of help precipitates in those in need, and to rigorously limit the treatment goal in each situation, not in terms of the extent of need and what might be ideally desirable, but in terms of the individual's capacity for change within the limits of the relationship.

Some of the most well-established techniques of casework must be considered here in the light of the problems just stated. Approval, praise, and encouragement; stimulation, motivation, leadership;—by whatever terms we call them, such methods are generally accepted tools by which caseworkers attempt to organize an individual's attitudes along constructive, socially acceptable lines. The negative attitudes of disapproval and blame have gone so generally out of use that we need not discuss them here except to comment that the expression of the positive attitude implies always to the client the possibility of its opposite, as to the schoolchild the teacher's praise carries with it the fear of a reversal of this attitude on another occasion.[1] Praise and approval are symbols of power which, actually as we have seen, the caseworker wields over the client in a fashion which to him must seem arbitrary and variable. His response to praise and approval then would seem to be based on the same fear and dependence-resistance attitude which underlies his reaction to her power expressed in other ways.

The skillful teacher learns to use praise and encouragement so sincerely and so wisely that they build up the child's relation to the material which he is trying to understand. For instance when he is trying to make a chair with new and unfamiliar tools she will know at what moment to tide him over his discouragement by mentioning the good points in his efforts or indicating how it will look when one more step is taken. That is, when he becomes thrown back on himself in a sense of failure and inadequacy she relates him back to his material by her belief that it can be accomplished. She permits a momentary dependence upon her to relate him again to his own organization and purpose. By the shadow that this encouragement goes too far in emphasizing the teacher's interest in the project or her responsibility for it, it ceases to be the child's plan and his relation to it and becomes the teacher's. Her praise also is rare and always related to the task or project accomplished and therefore external to the child rather than applicable to the child himself. It is even possible for the teacher to give criticism of a performance when it is sufficiently external to the child and when he is more interested and active in finding how it can be improved than she is. It would seem as if the essential quality of the teacher's attitude here is her respect for the child's purpose and effort and relation to the material and her own detachment from it. So long as praise, criticism, and encouragement do not assume a control and responsibility on the teacher's part and deny it to the child they seem to be productive of independent growth. This illustration may be suggestive for casework though it offers no guide as to the application of this attitude to the more difficult problem of the use of praise and encouragement with the adult.

The techniques of "stimulation," "motivation," "leadership"

imply an even greater control over the client's will and development. Here we see the caseworker clearly identified with the norm or plan which she has in her own purposes for the individual and the situation, attempting to project this plan in the interview. In the discussions of interviewing which have been appearing particularly in the reports of the work of the Chicago Chapter of the American Association[2] and of the Kansas City Chapter[3] and the Twin City Chapter,[4] this point of view is apparent.

Pearl Salsberry's paper presented to the National Conference at Des Moines[5] gives the most complete formulation of the techniques which the worker uses to influence the client to some end. She quotes from H. A. Overstreet for psychological authority for the relationship of control by the worker of the client which she is advocating: "the salvaging of human life consists not simply in having high ideals. It consists as much in having the knowledge how: We need, in short, to know how to interest our fellows; how to arouse their expectations; how to build up habits of favorable response; how to lead and adjust and control. All this is the groundwork of our human ethics."[6]

She describes the work of a committee which studied over a two-year period the "how" succeeding in isolating and naming eighty-six different techniques in ten interviews analyzed. These are grouped into seven general classifications the subheadings of which listed below indicate clearly some of the attitudes involved. Under the classification, "Techniques used for breaking down defense mechanism," the subheadings are as follows: (1) "Anticipating ultimate outcome." (2) "Abusing for defense." (3) "Puncture." (4) "Rushing." (5) "Swaying by oratory." (6) "Taking client off his guard." (7) "Using acquired information." (8) "Putting cards on the table." (9) "Chasing into a corner." (10) "Instilling fear." (11) "Negation."[7]

Here clearly the assumption is that the worker knows what is good for the client and her task is to see that he does it. The worker's authority is kindly but complete and patronizing and denies the will and individuality of the client. He is a child to be "led, adjusted, controlled." This authority to control behavior seems to rest upon a conception of an absolute right and wrong and a final norm for social and individual adjustment. The technical processes described seek to establish a control over the client's inner life and behavior as definite as, in the earlier days of active treatment, the arrangement of his social situation.

This approach to casework which attempts so frankly to manipulate the client to its own ends brings out clearly the two contrasting and conflicting pulls which operate confusingly in all casework.[8] One is the active, aggressive desire to help, to change, to reform, to control, which projects itself upon the other individual and his social situation. This projection operates, no matter how delicately it may be expressed, as force or pressure of one will upon another. The other drive is the need to understand the client's very different reality which absorbs the worker through identification into the client's problem. Here and there in rare analytic moments, caseworkers are withdrawing both these projections and becoming self-conscious of the relationships to their clients in terms of the client's reactions as determined by his own growth process released in the relationship. The "control" in such a relationship lies only in the integrity and self-consciousness of the worker which enables her to keep her will free from that of the client.

A helpful test of the casework relationship and of all descriptions of the attitudes and techniques involved can be applied by considering it as reversible, the worker becoming the client and vice versa. As long as caseworkers feel, as some do, that they would never want to enter into a casework relationship as a client, "to have casework done on me," there is something fundamentally unethical in that relationship. The most elementary concept of an ethical relationship rests upon a mutual respect for the integrity and individuality of the other. Without this as a foundation the casework relationship is a travesty. But if this fundamental is accepted the casework relationship by virtue of its depth and meaning to both client and worker must open up constantly a clearer consciousness and a finer appreciation of the more and more that is implied in integrity, individuality, and growth in relationship.

By way of summary it may be said that this discussion of attitudes which the client finds in the casework situation has forced us to recognize certain essential, perhaps inevitable, conflicts. We see the caseworker holding out to the client promise of help, understanding, objectivity, and respect for the client's individuality and right to work out his own problem on the one hand, but at the same time she exhibits marked limitations in understanding and wields an arbitrary power over the client's destiny, manifested in the variable factor in the bestowal of time, attention and relief and her insistence on a constructive plan, the socially right. Her understanding and acceptance operate to stimulate and encourage a growth process, while her failure to understand ambivalent attitudes, her inability to receive negative destructive impulses which conflict with her picture of what is right and desirable for the client or the family as a whole, may immediately check, perhaps inhibit completely that growth process.

In the second place, we have recognized two extremes of attitude taken by caseworkers towards the client's part in this relationship which define themselves more and more clearly in discussions of technique. In the one, the caseworker's part is very active in knowing what is right for the client and "motivating" or "manipulating" him to this end. We may see in this development a continuation of the older interest in active environmental treatment transferred to control of the inner life of the individual. In the other tendency, we see an increasing respect for the other individual accompanied by a corresponding reservation in taking active part in his affairs. In the former, technique consists in a repertoire of tricks by which the worker controls the client's movements in an almost point-by-point scheme. In the latter, technique lies rather in creating a relationship environment in which the individual growth process of the client can be released. This internal process itself then becomes the center, the growing point of change, rather than any external manipulation of the client from point to point. There is little known and everything to be learned about the elements in relationship which favor such a growth process. Experience points to understanding and acceptance as the most essential factors in attitude of one individual towards another to create sufficient security in the other to permit the expression and release of his own impulses. We have seen the obstacles to the maintenance of these attitudes which seem inherent in the casework situation. The only hope of solution for these conflicts may be seen to lie in the worker herself and her capacity for objectivity, not only in relation to the client but in relation to the pressure of community and social standards.

15. THE WORKER AND HER PREPARATION

From friendly visitors to paid professional workers, and from professional workers with no equipment, except human sympathy, to the standardizations of equipment today in terms of college degrees, training in a professional school and experience in a good caseworking agency— these stages describe a long upward trend in increasing educational standards for this task of social casework. But the qualities we have been defining in the preceding discussion are factors of attitude, not of knowledge. The capacity to accept another individual may grow through knowledge of individual difference obtained by a study of psychology, literature, history, sociology and other social studies but depends primarily also upon an attitude towards the "other" which knowledge cannot guarantee. Even in a professional school of social work, where the classes in social casework and problems of personality attempt to organize knowledge around this focus of individual difference and to develop an attitude of acceptance of it, there is no uniform response to this teaching. With the same background of knowledge, students vary widely in their capacities to understand and to accept the different individual. We find some students who cannot acquire this attitude at all and must be directed into another field of work.

As we explore this acceptance of difference in its relations to other attitudes which the student exhibits, we find we are dealing with a fundamental factor characteristic of his ways of relating himself to people and things and of his way of regarding himself in these relationships. Perhaps we have not as yet the knowledge to analyze our understanding of the student from this point of view but at least we begin to see its significance in case after case. We have always recognized a factor independent of knowledge upon which the worker's success might depend under the vague name of personality. Pictures of a desirable personality equipment for social casework have been painted, including every admirable quality in human make-up. Sometimes this equipment has been thought to be native, "born —not made," but recently there is an increasing tendency to believe that certain personality factors are developed in the process of casework training itself and can never be "given" per se.

It is recognized also that a student may have a delightful, pleasing, outgoing personality in ordinary social contacts with her own group and never penetrate deep enough into the different personalities she must work with in casework to have anything of value to contribute in her contacts here. A shy, inhibited student, on the other hand, to whom social contacts with her equals have always been effortful, may surprise us by the ease with which she goes out to a client in need and she may develop more sensitive understanding and greater strength in meeting human problems than the student who seemed to offer better equipment in her natural social responses.

The terms, "good," "attractive," "pleasing," "outgoing," "friendly," "sociable"—in their usual connotations do not describe a personality equipment which will necessarily succeed in social casework.

The exent to which this matter of the worker's attitude involves the integration of all her attitudes of her entire adjustment, and is not a superficial acquirement of a technical training to be put on for purposes of her job only is well brought out by Lucy Wright in a delightfully human and philosophical discussion of "The Worker's Attitude as an Element in Social Case Work" in 1924.[1] She says, "I believe that social case work is a search for the truth for creative purposes in the personality of the client and in all his relationships. It will share in the creative purposes of social discovery and social education in proportion as it rises out of a creative attitude on the part of the worker. I am assuming that one's attitude depends upon one's religion, one's philosophy of social work and of life, and upon the plan of action resulting therefrom and checked up by experience."

While accepting this statement of Miss Wright's as profoundly true and appreciating that the worker in action in her casework contacts is a whole person where all of her experiences and her unique individual reactions function in an organic integration which defies analysis, nevertheless for purposes of interpretation and training I am attempting to isolate and define a single essential attitude which the worker must acquire for fruitful casework. The problem as it has been formulating itself in my mind is to choose an attitude sufficiently general and fundamental to include and interpret specific attitudes towards individual objects and classes of objects. At the same time, it must be an attitude which we can see exhibited in reactions towards specific objects and consequently study in its movement and development through casework experience. In discussing this problem with different people, I get different ways of conceiving this fundamental attitude, different terms and different contents. One says that the caseworker must have "emotional balance," "security in herself," or have "solved her own problems." Others state it from the opposite point of view, that she must be able to identify with the problems of other people rather than to project her own self upon them. Each of these statements emphasizes one side of the problem. the worker's attitude towards herself, or her attitude towards the other. Both are regarded as essential attitudes in the casework relationship. It would seem then that an inclusive definition of the essential attitude would have to state both emphases, the attitude towards the self and the attitude towards the client. In other words, we seem groping to define a balance in relationship, in which the worker has sufficient security in herself ("has solved her own conflicts," "is well adjusted," "has handled her own needs") to leave that security and enter into the reality of another individual's feelings. This participation, described as "identification," must be not merely intellectual or verbal but a genuine feeling experience, a living through of the other's attitudes and experiences in their essential meaning to the other.[2] The third phase of this balance would be again the phase with which we started, the worker's own poise in herself which would secure a proportion for this identification with the client in his own experience, that is, the worker would not be personally lost in that experience, be overwhelmed, depressed, or elated by it. The phrase that seems best fitted to carry the fundamental meanings in this balanced attitude is *acceptance of self and acceptance of difference.* Or I would like to borrow a word which Piaget uses to describe logical thinking and say that the casework relationship is a reciprocal relationship in which the caseworker must accept herself and the other equally, in which all of her attitudes towards the client would be such that she would be content to be at the other end of such a relationship herself. Such a description of a fundamental attitude must necessarily be abstract and contentless, because it must be recognizable to us in any content through which it is expressed. One worker will have problems in contact with colored people, another with superior clients, another with men, another with women, one always bungles a contact with a school principal, another is unable to get any information or cooperation from a doctor, one can't get anywhere with a particular Mrs. X or Mr. Y. "I just can't talk with that sort of person." Or it may be the worker cannot accept a particular type of behavior —"I can't go any further if the client lies to me." Sometimes the rejection goes into a general content such as a different racial group, sometimes into the individual personal content of a particular individual or particular behavior. The wise supervisor will see in all these varying contents the fundamental problem of the individual's acceptance of himself as well as of the other in each situation and will watch the development of this capacity to accept difference as the surest index to the student's growth and progress.

From this point of view, those of us who are interested in professional training must ask ourselves, what can classes and well-supervised casework experience expect to accomplish in furthering the growth of this attitude of acceptance of self and of the other, upon which a fruitful casework relationship seems to depend. The first responsibility of the training schools upon whom the burden of this task falls is the selection of students who are capable of the development we seek. This is to measure potentiality, not actual present ability or performance, in applicants, for no student fresh from college has sufficient experience in relationships or enough understanding of differences in people, their backgrounds and behavior, to be able to meet the clients that come to the application desk of a social agency intelligently and helpfully. A test of the worker's emotional adjustment has been suggested,[3] but I have no conviction that this is possible or even desirable to attempt. In my own experience I have found the personal interview the only situation in which we can sound out the applicant's attitudinal equipment. Such an interview can be very profitable to the applicant and the interviewer if it is entered into by both with the common purpose of attempting to find out whether social work is really the field for which the applicant is best fitted and for which she wishes to train. Background and history are unimportant and out of place in such an interview unless introduced voluntarily by the applicant himself but everything in the applicant's present situation, interests, ambitions, relationships, are pertinent and revealing. In such interviews certain students are being discouraged and eliminated constantly for reason of attitudes which do not show promise of development or change in casework experience. But there is as yet no body of experience in the hands of the schools on which we can base any conclusions as to where to draw the line in doubtful cases. We must still give a chance to the individual who shows any promise of growth and any desire for it and trust to the field work to provide the real test of capacity later.

A second responsibility of the training school is to provide an atmosphere in which the student is free to learn, to think, to experiment, to grow, to change. The attitudes we are interested in having the student acquire which will give her responsibility in relationship are not to be learned by accepting the authority of greater wisdom or experience or even by identification with a caseworker who may provide an ideal. The student can only hope to become responsible for others by first becoming responsible for herself, her opinions, her ways of acting, her decisions. The school can never teach this type of responsibility but it can provide the opportunity for a student to work into it for herself if she can. This opportunity can be created

by the school specifically through giving the student complete responsibility for her own attendance, and preparation, by doing away
with grades and examination requirements, by emphasizing professional accomplishment rather than academic attainment.

The greatest opportunity for change, however,will come to the
student through the field experience and in the classes which interpret this experience. This field experience has two important aspects,
the student's actual work on case problems and the supervisor-stu-
dent relationship in which this work takes place. If the teachers of
casework and "personality" classes in the school and the supervisors
in the field have in mind this attitude of acceptance of difference as
a criterion of progress, problems will be selected for discussion and
cases assigned in the field which will give the student opportunity
in proportion to her readiness to identify with experiences and attitudes different from her own. The more usual path of the student
as I have watched it, is through over-identification with an individual, first on the basis of certain like and understood, or perhaps
different and desired, characteristics, the identification being in
terms of the way the student would feel about it. In other words,
the student's first reactions to clients are naïve and limited identifications, perhaps more accurately termed projections. Further experience with the client, however, invariably reveals difference which
refuses to conform to this limited identification. As an illustration, a
student getting experience as field worker in a reformatory for girls,
identifies completely with a girl of unusual intelligence and culture,
arrested for shoplifting, a charge which the girl denies. The student
accepts the girl's story as absolute fact and sets out to defend to
the world the character which she has projected upon the girl. When
investigation proves the girl's story a fabrication, the student reacts
to the shock of this discovery to identify with the girl not as she
behaves, but as the student believes she really is underneath, which
is what the student wishes her to be. In this phase, the student is
very active in projecting her plans, her ideals, her interests on the girl.
Her efforts might be successful if the girl had enough satisfaction out
of the relationship and enough likeness to the student in ego-inter-
ests to be able to maintain an identification on this level. But actually, the girl feels strange and uncomfortable in this atmosphere of
high expectations and attempts to escape the student's pursuit with
one series of lies after another. At this point, if the student can accept
defeat of her plan, realize the subjectivity of her projection, and di-

rect her energy into an effort to understand the girl as she is, to learn the meaning of the lying and stealing, there is tremendous educational value in the whole experience. In this event, the student puts no need upon the girl beyond the need to understand the meaning of her reality, the identification is no longer naïve and limited, but disciplined, comprehensive and objective, and the relationship possesses a true relativity of reciprocity in that the student reacts to difference in the other with true appreciation of that difference in itself and in relation to its own background instead of with a fixed personal response of her own as with "I can't bear to have her lie to me."

I have said that the supervisor's and the teacher's first responsibility lies in the selection of material with which the student can identify naïvely, which in turn disciplines the student by its refusal to fit into her mold completely. An equal responsibility of greater importance, perhaps, to the student is the supervisor's responsibility for the relationship in which the student must work. This relationship has two aspects; first it is essentially a teacher-student relationship in which the supervisor brings greater experience and knowledge to the common project of the casework job on which both are working together. But the student brings also to every case problem for which she is responsible the superior knowledge of her first-hand contacts. When the focus is on the common problem with this more or less equal contribution from supervisor and student, the relationship is sincerely an equality relationship. The student just out of college, working perhaps for the first time, has great need for a relationship on this level and for recognition of herself as an ego, a professional person. She longs to do things her own way, to make her own decisions, to be responsible, just as strongly as underneath she may doubt her adequacy. The supervisory relationship which in the early stages gives her the greatest amount of ease and confidence in her own way, is perhaps the one in which her development as a caseworker is most soundly rooted. From this security she is most free to experiment, to make mistakes, to build up her own confidence in her contacts. As supervisors and teachers we have much to learn about how to create the situation in which the student is free to learn.

The supervisory relationship, however, cannot always remain simply a teacher-student relationship on an ego basis. Almost inevitably the fact of the supervisor's greater knowledge, her understanding of human experience, and her interest centered in the student, precipitates in the student the same type of reaction it precipitates in the client, a libido movement to work out her own relationship problems in this understanding atmosphere. Some students resist this movement successfully, showing more or less ego stress and sensitivity during the conflict. Others accept the relationship on this level, some very simply, often unconsciously, keeping an ego-identification with the supervisor throughout and growing and learning steadily through the whole experience. Other students react on a deeper level and precipitate the relationship into analytic depths, frequently with painful and embarrassing consequences for the supervisor who is not equipped to see it through on this level. As to the supervisor's control over this aspect of the relationship, one point seems clear: the supervisor herself should not push the student into this relationship by her own need to know the student's history and personality, rather should protect her from it as far as possible by the keenest sensitivity to and respect for the student's desire for independence.

One essential function which the supervisor must fulfill in her teaching capacity combines with the fact of her understanding of human experience to drive the relationship into one which has personal, libido value for the student. At the point where the student finds her naïve identification rejected by the client as in the illustration quoted when the student finds the client is guilty of stealing and later of lying to her, that is, when the student finds her case is not going right —at this point, what is the function of the supervisor? Of course, to let the client and the situation discipline the student first as far as she is able to see it and change her attitudes. But where the student is blind to her own part in it and blames some element in the situation, the supervisor may have to give the student some interpretation of her part in the situation. Sometimes, largely depending on how it is given, this may operate as ego criticism, very painful, often destructive to the student. Frequently, however, the ego hurt is less important than the sense of union which comes from being given such intimate consideration, from being understood even in one's mistake. Here again the relationship is driven deeper and can only be handled by the supervisor's unfailing respect for the integrity and independence of the student and of her right to solve her own problems.

As the training experience progresses, the student must become increasingly aware of herself in every contact, must become conscious and analytic of her naïve identifications and forego her old security in spontaneous contact for a security painfully achieved in professional contact where the client's reality, not her own, is of paramount importance. Frequently there is a period here of very depressing experience when the supervisor's security and taken-for-granted and accepted confidence in the job, and people, and in the student may be an important factor in making it possible for the student to persevere in training. Again, in this period the supervisor's function in guiding the choice of cases and controlling the case load is valuable in that it enables her to see that the student has sufficient spontaneous and successful contacts not to lose her security too completely on her old basis before a new security based on true understanding and acceptance develops.

The length of time which a student should spend with this first supervisor should be an individual matter, dependent on the student's growth and readiness to take over her own responsibility. Actually it must be arbitrarily determined by school terms and agency emergencies. Leaving the supervisor to whom one has been a student and transferring to a relationship with a supervisor in which one is regarded as a worker constitutes a separation experience through which, if the supervisor has left the student really free, the student should develop the attitude which will permit her clients to leave her in true independence.

The training school must emphasize experience and relationship, as well as subject matter and knowledge, as elements in the curriculum if the student's growth in acceptance of difference is important rather than merely her acquirement of knowledge content. The business of certification becomes more difficult on this basis, for it is comparatively easy to measure knowledge acquirement but impossible to measure or define a standard for a growth process. The student's experience in her training period at the school releases something, stimulates a new development of self-consciousness, a new awareness of others. Where this growth process will carry her, no one can say; at what point we could stop to measure that process and say "this is a trained caseworker," can be only arbitrarily determined. Of just one thing we can be certain: that only as this process is profound and deep-rooted and continuous will the worker be able, with safety to herself and others, to take over the tremendous responsibility which the social casework job puts upon her.

The multifold delicate problems involved in the supervisor's task of making the supervisory relationship educational for the student have been merely hinted at. It is only very recently that the supervisor has become self-conscious about her part in the student's development and willing to attempt to articulate her problems. Some of the problems of relationship I have indicated in this chapter were formulated by a small group of supervisors in Philadelphia who had students from the Pennsylvania School of Social and Health Work meeting over a period of a year for discussion of common problems. Other groups of supervisors are meeting on students' problems in connection with other schools. The major problem which such discussions reveal was brought to the surface sharply in the reaction of young workers and students to Miss Marcus' paper given at the Des Moines National Conference on "How Case Work Training May be Adapted to Meet the Worker's Personal Problems."[4] They evidenced a real fear of the relationship on this basis, and unwillingness to have supervision extend to the personal problems of the worker, to be "case-worked."

Two factors seem to lie back of this reaction, first, the natural fear of the naïve person who has not yet analyzed his own reactions, of change, of becoming different. Students just out of college entering a school of social work expect to *learn* but not to *change* in any degree. The second factor, which operates with the worker more than the student, is her disbelief in the supervisor's capacity to maintain the relationship on a truly reciprocal basis. As long as her own relationships with her clients involve any manipulation of his situation or control of his will, she dreads the same interference with her integrity on the part of her supervisor. Through her relationships in ordinary life, with parents, relatives, friends, she very rarely gets the kind of experience in understanding and being understood which produces an attitude free of personal need which can see and respect the reality of the other person. Perhaps the worker's only chance to learn this attitude is through the experience in relationship with the supervisor who has this attitude and can give to her worker the acceptance and consideration which she in turn can hold out to her clients.

In conclusion, we have found the worker's security in her self and her acceptance of the unique difference of the other to be the fundamental equipment for therapeutic relationship in casework. We recognized this attitude to be a growth process starting in the student's reactions to likeness and difference in her contacts with clients and in her relationship to her supervisor. The supervisor plays the most strategic role in the student's development in that she has control over the choice of material to be worked on and since, through the experience in relation to her, the student learns the attitudes which she will take in her treatment of her clients. We believe that this relationship is most acceptable and constructive for the student if it is entered into on a teacher-student basis of working on a common problem, giving to the student as much responsibility and freedom as she will take to solve her own problems. But we recognize also that the very nature of the relationship problems in casework forces a concentration upon the student's part in the situation with the client, which may involve the supervisor in a greater responsibility for the student's relationship problems. This demands of the supervisor a truly "analyzed" self-consciousness as to her own attitudes and the keenest sensitivity to the attitudes of others. The evolution of such self-consciousness takes place only in experience in analyzed relationships.[5]

16. CONCLUSION

In conclusion we may look at this whole development in casework which these chapters have attempted to survey as a relationship problem, the relationship of the agency and the worker to other human beings and their maladjustments under social conditions. The first approach was corrective and disciplinary as human problems first forced themselves into consciousness under such guise as "poverty," "dependency," "disease." A second stage growing out of actual human contacts followed in which "poor families," "widows," "drunkards," and "neglected children" emerged, more or less as types for whom definite, authoritative social treatment could be prescribed. A third stage, described in *Social Diagnosis,* carried this line of development to its logical conclusion, leaving the problem carefully analyzed but still located in the "other," in the environment. The concept of the social self on which *Social Diagnosis* rests, though a very much more evolved conception of the individual than that inherent in earlier social treatment, nevertheless lacks intrinsic unity and true individuality. The process of diagnosis scientifically conceived by Miss Richmond, is therefore, an effort to put together a patchwork of external impressions gathered by the process of investigation, while treatment becomes a rearrangement of these pieces in the environment in accordance with some social plan of well-being which the worker has in mind for the situation.

Along with this trend, which culminates in thorough study of

environmental factors and in a sound social treatment plan, goes
another trend, a drive to know the client himself more intimately.
If we think of the first trend as the worker's projection of her own
problem and her own need to solve it on her material, in the second
trend we see the worker becoming lost in identification with the
problem of other human beings. In the first, the problem is external·
ilzed and causes are located in the environment; in the latter, the
problem becomes more subjective and causes are sought for in the
meaning of the individual's own experience and in the individual
himself. So casework moves from a sociological into a psychological
phase of development.

In the brief span of its history in the psychological phase, the
decade 1920-1930, we have recognized two phases in the relationship problem of the caseworker to her clients. In the first stages of
this movement, she is absorbed in her identification with the client's
past and history is emphasized sometimes at the expense of understanding and usually at the expense of treatment. Or rather, to put
it differently, history is used to escape from the responsibility of
treatment as increasingly the deepening knowledge of the client and
his complex individuality makes it impossible for the worker to continue to project a "sound social plan."

The second stage—in which we are working in 1930—reveals a
new development in the worker's growing acceptance of responsibility for the treatment relationship between herself and the client as
the dynamic new experience in which therapeutic change may take
place. There is still great vagueness, uncertainty, and insecurity about
the nature of this relationship, and the treatment of the client is very
differently conceived in different places, an outstanding difference
being between the school that maintains a point-for-point relationship in which the worker manipulates the client's inner life as before
she manipulated the environment, and between the school which is
interested in the relationship as a new environment which gives the
client opportunity to work out his own problems.

In this latter point of view, with which I have allied myself in
this presentation, problems of technique and method fall into insig-
nificance before the all-important problem of the worker's own attitude towards herself and the client. It becomes increasingly clear
that an acceptance of herself and of the other, a development of
self-consciousness in relationships, a constant process of analysis of
herself and the other in interaction, beyond what is required for the

contacts of successful everyday living, is demanded of the worker if this emphasis on relationship is to be safe and therapeutic.

We have analyzed but a few of the many conflicts which lie in relationship of the one seeking help to the helper. Other conflicts will force themselves upon our attention for analysis and solution as we concentrate more intensively upon the relationship aspect of treatment.

One of these conflicts prominent in this discussion will probably have emerged in the mind of the reader as the focal point of criticism for this whole point of view. What of the essential conflict between the emphasis on the relationship with the individual and the relationship with the community to which the agency is to some extent responsible? Is there an insolvable conflict of loyalties here? From time immemorial, social betterment, family welfare, child welfare have been the large terms through which social casework has been interpreted to the public to justify expenditure of time and money. Among caseworkers themselves there is great confusion as to whether the ultimate aim of their efforts is to increase the sum total of human happiness, to further social welfare, or to give to the individual client a sincere and objective understanding of his problems. As the latter aim seems insufficient to some workers, the next decade will see a resurgence of active treatment methods and of advocacy of social reform such as old age pensions and health insurance, the latter a wholesome corrective for the intensive concern with the individual's inner life in which, I believe, one group of caseworkers will remain increasingly absorbed. Perhaps this division of interest may develop as, in medicine, the distinction between public health and individual medicine.

If the history of social casework teaches anything it teaches this one thing outstandingly, that only in this field of the individual's reaction patterns and in the possibilities of therapeutic change in these patterns through responsible self-conscious relationships can there be any possibility of a legitimate professional casework field. If casework accepts squarely this responsibility for relationship it has a field for research, for experiment, demanding the most untiring scientific accuracy and the most sincere unceasing self-discipline. It must always remain closely related to scientific research and therapeutic efforts in psychology, psychiatry, medicine, psychoanalysis, and education, as these are also working in the large field of human relations, but it need never be dependent upon any of these disciplines.

I believe that already we see increasing acceptance of casework as individual therapy rather than social welfare, in such agencies as Child Guidance Clinics, but even here the pressure of parent, school, and community to make the child "good," "conforming," throws a constantly interfering factor into the relationship with the child through which the clinic is trying to release the child to find the courage of his own way of meeting his problems.

In every enterprise which deals with human beings, the attitudes of human beings towards each other constitute the conditioning, limiting and at the same time the potentially creative factors of the enterprise. Perhaps the individual caseworker's responsibility to the community lies not in justification of the community's expectation of a casework job as for relief of poverty, cure of disease, and reformation of character, but in attempting to permeate the community more thoroughly, through her own attitude, with an attitude of tolerance for the individual in his failures and faith in his possibilities for constructive self-development.

There are fascinating professional problems which this group of individual caseworkers must tackle in the next decade. First among them, I see the problem of how to distinguish between an individual's behavior picture and his fundamental reaction pattern, secondly how to diagnose that reaction pattern in early contacts and to foresee its possibilities for growth and constructive change in a therapeutic relationship, and third, how to determine the conditions of therapeutic relationship and control the level of its development for different individuals. On the solution of the first and second problems, that is, on early diagnosis, I believe, will lie the possibility of controlled therapy. If relationship must be entered upon because of the worker's need to learn the individual's pattern for diagnostic purposes, control of treatment is out of the worker's hands before she begins. All three problems will relate the caseworker to psychiatric and psychoanalytic technique and force an understanding of therapeutic relationship in these fields in comparison with the caseworking relationship necessitating analysis of what problems can best be handled in one type of relationship and what in another.

This concept of social casework as individual therapy through a treatment relationship may seem to imply that the only legitimate and worthwhile casework efforts are in intensive relationships. On the contrary, however, this approach lends an increased interest and significance to the most limited contacts, to single interviews and

referral work. If the worker brings sufficient background of knowledge of relationship problems and is able to identify with the client
and at the same time maintain her own difference, the task of receiving and analyzing applications for help becomes a fascinating one
and may also have its own therapeutic value. To be able to reject
cases on the basis of the client's inability to use help, to refuse to
lift the burden from the client's shoulders when it would be to his advantage to solve his own problem, to withdraw when the only need
the client has of her is to receive his blame, demands the greatest skill
and knowledge a caseworker can develop. In addition, it demands
the most developed and genuine objectivity to be able to conduct
these interviews in such a way that the application is rejected and
not the applicant. Only if the worker has a really profound understanding of the factors at work in the client's situation, has really
accepted herself as well as the client so that she has no separation
problem of her own involved in these rejections, will she be able to
refuse to give to the client, simply, without accusation, apology, or
protest.

Problems of training new workers and students must be in the
foreground in the next decade and of the interpretations of a casework point of view to other professional and lay groups, again through
contacts and relationships rather than verbal interpretation.

When we consider the worker upon whose education all therapy
depends, we shall be wise if we maintain a profound skepticism as to
the possibilities of human nature to measure up to so tremendous a
task—a skepticism which will modify our expectations of results in
a one, two, or even three years' course of training.

Today the worker is having to resign her reliance upon social
norms, moral standards, and sound treatment plans, in favor of limited treatment ends and the stimulation of growth processes within
the individual which may carry him she knows not where. She has
no security in the casework job except as she is able to find it in herself, and in the other, in a faith in the growth process and capacity
for change which she knows in the client because she has experienced them in herself through relationship. The assurance with
which casework will move ahead experimentally and courageously
to professional status in spite of skepticism is founded on steady
development in the understanding of personality stabilized in substantial knowledge content, on the gradual accumulation of a body
of experience in discriminating and defining reaction patterns, and

above all, in the growth of an attitude characteristic of progressive movements today, of acceptance of the individual's unique difference and of the dynamic, creative possibilities in relationship.

III

Psychoanalytic Contributions
to Social Casework Treatment

On June 15, 1931, approximately six months after her book A
Changing Psychology *had been published, Miss Robinson read a pa-*
per in Minneapolis before the fifty-eighth annual meeting of the Na-
tional Conference of Social Work. It can be safely inferred that the
"changing psychology" following the publication of her book, was
still in a phase of heightened movement in her thought and feeling.

While the emphasis in the title of the paper is upon "psychoan-
alytic contributions," Miss Robinson after a few general observations
about psychiatry, psychoanalysis, and psychology, soon departs
upon an expanded elucidation of her own theory of casework prac-
tice. In point of fact she concludes the paper with an effort to differ-
entiate casework from these other disciplines—a question that was
to continue over many years and which is even now, one might say,
a recurrent question—in what way does casework differ from ther-
apy, or does it indeed differ at all?

In the paper which follows, Miss Robinon sets in motion a num-
ber of vital points at issue which the reader will encounter again and
again throughout this book. She deals with: relationship between
caseworker and client; the tantalizing contrast between so-called
"passivity" and activity; the difference in role between helper and
the one being helped. She uses words such as "treatment" and "trans-
ference," which do not appear in her later writing; instead she speaks
of "the helping process" and relationship in the immediate present
situation.

In concluding her paper, after once more giving passing notice
to the "contributions" from the other disciplines, she writes: "On
the other hand, I believe that social casework has the opportunity to
make a fairly workable distinction . . ."—But the distinction which
she makes in this early writing is one that changes as her writing and

153

teaching, over the years, expands and deepens. Here she places the difference upon the depth of change expected—the focus upon external factors in which problems are centered, avoiding the intention to touch the inner life of the person seeking help. In her later writing she clearly states that help given on the most tangible problem can touch the client to the bottom of his own individual self.

    Social casework has acknowledged its indebtedness to psychology, psychiatry, and psychoanalysis for their contributions toward an understanding of the human material with which all three disciplines are concerned. From these sources has come a substantial genetic psychology which describes the individual's growth and conditioning in the family environment and seeks the explanation of his behavior in terms of his dynamic attitudes as developed in this process of continual growth and interaction.[1] This paper will assume a general understanding and acceptance of the principles of this psychology. It will assume, further, an emphasis, attributable largely to psychoanalysis, on the internal motivation and determination of behavior, of personality as dynamic and creative, rather than acted upon as a passive agent by external environmental forces. This conception, when really assimilated into casework thinking, will clarify many of the problems raised in this paper.[2]

    My discussion will limit itself to an analysis of the contributions of psychoanalysis to social casework treatment. If a psychoanalyst were presenting this topic, he would probably give at this point a detailed description of the psychoanalytic process and of the ways in which it is differentiated in the different schools of psychoanalysis, of which no less than four may claim an influence in casework development. Perhaps the reason for the choice of a caseworker rather than an analyst to present this topic was that a caseworker would feel neither equipped nor called upon to present this detail. So, if the analyst will pardon it and caseworkers will bear with it, I am going to present merely a summary of the factors that seem to me to characterize psychoanalytic therapy of any school, in order that we may have a common starting-point for a discussion of the effect of this therapy on the treatment process in social casework. In order to get agreement on these factors, it is necessary to make so general a summary as perhaps to be disappointing to any particular school of psychoanalysis.

Psychoanalytic therapy contains these elements: it offers to a person seeking help on his own problem a relationship experience, of limited duration, under fixed conditions, which are explained by the analyst and accepted by the patient before treatment is initiated. These conditions include a regular time and place of treatment, a fee, and some notion of the duration of treatment. The treatment process, so far as the analyst is concerned, does not extend beyond these office periods—that is, he takes no responsibility for any arrangements in the patient's practical life, as a doctor might do for a specialist's examination, if indicated. Within the interviews, the activity of the analyst varies in the practice of different schools and even from individual to individual. But on the whole, in comparison with the practice of the doctor or the psychiatrist or the social caseworker, it might be agreed that the analytic process is a passive rather than an active one on the part of the analyst.

I should like to begin the comparison of casework treatment with this last factor, since it is at this point, I believe, that casework has been most influenced by analytic therapy. The word "passive" is quite generally used to describe a modern variety of casework and to differentiate it from older varieties. But in spite of its general usage, it seems to me most vague and misleading in its connotation and operation in treatment processes. The word "acceptance" has also been used— and for this, perhaps, I must admit some responsibility—to define the caseworker's attitude to people, an attitude that has been growing for many years in the caseworker's increasing sensitivity to the client with whom she is associated so closely. Long before the caseworker had heard of psychoanalysis, "sympathy," "understanding," "tolerance," "non-judgmental" attitudes were thought of as essential to her relationship with a client. Whatever word may be preferred today to describe the caseworker's attitude to her client, I think we would agree that it includes a finer and more penetrating understanding of the client's needs and conflicts and a more disciplined willingness to let him be his own self. The words "understanding" and "acceptance" perhaps best bring out these two sides of the attitude that the caseworker offers the client. Both have been carried to the limits of the caseworker's capacity to understand and accept herself, her own impulses and emotions. This capacity has been most influenced by the direct contact with psychoanalysis that many caseworkers are obtaining.

The word "acceptance" may continue to have value for some time to come in that it emphasizes the uniqueness and integrity of the other individual, and the necessity for the withdrawal of the caseworker's will from the effort to solve the client's problem. But it carries an essential confusion in its implication of passivity in the caseworker's treatment.

The confusion in casework thinking around this question of passivity and activity in the treatment relationship is indicated by the caseworker's use of the word "contact." A first essential of treatment is to make a good contact with a client. Responsibility for the contact seems to lie in the worker's hands, and there are certain definite skills she can use that further the contact. Or, through other forms of activity, she can "spoil" or "break" her contact. Analytic terminology, on the other hand, lays the emphasis on the patient's share in the relationship. The patient makes a positive transfer to the analyst, or at times a negative transfer. The analyst has no power and no will to create or force this relationship. When the patient seeks analysis, his need has already gone out in some way to the analyst; he is ready to deposit the burden of his problem upon this other person; he is fearful of the power of that person to destroy him. He puts over upon this person his ideal qualities and at the same time may endow him with the qualities he most dreads. In the essential and inevitable pull of his own conflicting emotions projected on to the other person of whom he seeks help lies the real meaning and significance of the transfer. We do not, I think, necessarily need to undergo an analytic experience ourselves to understand the meaning of this symbolic use of one person by another. All of our own relationships —in friendship, in love, in casework—illustrate it abundantly. Examination of any of these relationships will reveal that the person who is creative and active is the one who has need in the relationship, who is using the other to solve his problem. In friendship and in love both individuals are engaged; both, therefore, are active and creative. In self-conscious, professional relationships, on the other hand, the caseworker and the analyst are not solving their own problems; therefore, they are not creating the emotional bonds in the relationship. For this reason, the client, like the patient in analysis, should more correctly be said to make a good contact or a poor contact— or, better, to be using the caseworker positively for this purpose, or negatively for that.

Insofar as the establishment of the relationship is concerned in early contacts, it is clarifying, I believe, to give full weight and significance to the client's activity which brings him for help and enables him to use the caseworker as an instrument through which to solve his problem. With this emphasis on the worker's passivity in the first phase of treatment, the caseworker's dilemma is transferred to a further point in the therapeutic process. Is the trend of casework treatment, under the influence of psychoanalytic technique, toward greater passivity on the caseworker's part? Is there any change or treatment goal which the caseworker strives for in the relationship? In the older objective environmental casework treatment, while the ultimate goal might be a vague, indefinite change such as "rehabilitation of the family," the immediate goals were clear-cut and defined. The caseworker had a plan outlined in practical steps. Through the performance of these, she maintained a kind of control of the process and effected the changes she determined upon in the environment, if not in the individuals concerned. But as casework has retreated from the field of environmental adjustments to that of the inner life of the individual, the goal of a treatment process becomes far more intangible and elusive. The caseworker recognizes that she has no control over the individual's capacity to use her, or of the inner process of change, reorganization, and growth with which he may react to her help-giving function. The quality and extent of the change that she attempts to bring about or does bring about may seem so irrelevant to her efforts that the procedure can never be reduced to an exact technique. The word "passivity" has covered our blindness as to our share in this process. Under this classification the most various kinds of activity are carried on—praise, encouragement, approval, interpretation, suggestion, and so forth. Even interest of a certain kind in the client's story and problem may constitute a very active response, operating as definitely as approval and having that quality, both as given and as received. Probably real "passivity" is most nearly approximated in a listening process, when the client may tell a past history clearly for the sake of the relief of telling, while the caseworker accepts it without comment, except such as may indicate the value of its meaning to the client. Passivity of this sort can seldom be sustained for any length of time in a treatment process, for in most cases the client, dissatisfied with the lack of response, will attempt to draw the caseworker into active participation in his problem. He will make her take sides for or against him, if his problem is being fought out in the environment, or he will use her to strengthen or support one or another aspect of himself, if the conflict is internal. A wife's long story of marital difficulties which has been received with such patience by the caseworker may, in direct proportion to that very patience, be followed by the client with an effort to ally the worker further with her need and her defensive efforts to thwart her husband's attempt to escape from her. "Will you talk to my husband?" may mean, "You will help me against him." Or her story may end in the question, "Shall I leave my husband?" with the effort to involve the caseworker in the responsibility for the decision and for action. If the conflict is centered internally, the involvement may seem very slight in the question, "Do you think I can ever solve this problem?" but actually it is no less a seeking for response.

In no type of human relationship is one individual satisfied to use another continuously without knowing the response of the other. It might also be questioned whether any human being is willing to let himself be so used for any length of time. The very nature of the process set up between two individuals, when one seeks help or tells his story, is progressive in character. It demands something more or something different from what has been first received or expressed. Therefore, I would question the use of "passivity" as a casework attitude or technique, on the grounds that it is impossible to achieve or maintain in any but the rarest instances and then only for a brief contact. The use of it in a first interview at once precipitates us into the serious question of "What next?" if the client does not put this question to us first and involve us in the answer.

Here the analytic technique has much light to throw on a treatment process. This same point is reached in an early analytic hour, and the analyst becomes active here by removing the problem from the environment and the analyst and putting it back on the patient. To the questions, "Can I ever solve this problem?" the analyst might say, with full recognition of the seriousness of the question, "I cannot tell. You will find out." Perhaps, "Why do you feel yourself unequal to it? Why do you ask me?" To the query, "Shall I leave my husband who has so mistreated me?" the analytic answer at some time or other would be, "Why do you want to leave him?" Now this process of putting the problem back on the patient, pointing out the significance of the effort to lay it elsewhere and to seek response from the analyst, is a highly active process on the analyst's part. It is felt as such by the patient, since it constitutes a barrier to his natural

pattern at every step. It throws him back into another effort at solution, which operates as a fresh projection on to the analyst. This in
turn is analyzed, understood, and accepted as his own by the patient.
The analyst has been described as a mirror on which the patient projects his experience, his feelings, his attitudes. But there may be no
more than baffling repetition, unless the mirror permits the patient
to see and feel what is projected. Change and therapy take place for
the patient when he is able not *only* to see and feel these projections,
but also to accept them as a part of himself. The essence of the analyst's skill consists in the sensitivity with which he responds to these
rapidly changing projections. To be at every moment aware of what
the patient is feeling and willing, without controlling it, necessitates
the most active type of response that the human organism can learn
to make. We have been misled into calling it passive from the fact
that it does not put its own will into the process to direct or interfere with the patient's movement.

I have called attention to this characteristic of analytic technique, this process of analyzing projections, in order to criticize our
undiscriminating use of "passivity" and its attribution to analytic
influence. But I am far from convinced that the way out of the dilemma of passivity for the caseworker is in taking on more of this
active aspect of the analytic technique. To use this safely requires a
continuous, long-time contact, in which the client can become secure
enough to bear the burden of the problem consciously. It may have
occasional use in the hands of the sensitive, skillful caseworker whose
relation to her client is sufficiently clear for her to know whether
he is ready to accept the problem as his own. It must be the client's
readiness that determines its use, not the caseworker's eagerness to
display her knowledge, nor her determination to give the client insight. Another problem involved in its use, which caseworkers have
not as yet faced, is the inevitablility with which, if accepted at all,
it moves the relationship to a deeper level, where the caseworker may
be unable to follow; or, if rejected, it may involve the client in a new
problem, the struggle to refute the worker, to prove her wrong and
himself right, which is subversive of any goal of casework treatment.

One treatment function commonly practiced in the development
of a casework relationship which is frequently ascribed to the influence of psychoanalysis, but which actually has little in common with
it, is seen when the caseworker takes on and continues to play actively a role that the client puts on her. The client seeks an approv-

ing, protecting mother and finds it in the caseworker, not only through his own projection, but in her response. She responds generously, bountifully, on this level of his need, in the hope that he will get enough satisfaction to give it up of his own accord and move on to another level. Or, if he cannot get enough satisfaction to change in terms of it, he sometimes gets enough release on one level to ease the burden of his pressure on the family group.

This treatment, through the active assumption of the role of parent or friend, is at the opposite pole from psychoanalytic therapy, where the analyst accepts changing roles as the patient projects them, only in order to let the patient experience these attitudes as his own, but never actually to give response on any level. If the worker gives a real response as parent or friend, she runs the risk of creating insatiable demands on the part of the client to make the relationship more and more real on the level on which it is played. The children become worse that the good mother may advise; complaints of the husband's drinking grow louder. Invitations that would draw the worker into the family as an intimate member become more pressing and difficult to refuse without rejection. The worker who is trying to play the good-mother role may find herself forced into an equivocal and untenable position.

We are driven back to question what treatment activity is legitimate for the caseworker. If complete passivity is impossible, if the analytic technique of analyzing material in terms of its meaning to the patient precipitates movement that cannot be handled, if the good-mother role tends to be paternalistic and equivocal, what ground is there for treatment by the caseworker? I have been able to get a clearer approach to this problem in my own mind, first, by making as sharp a distinction as possible between the goals of treatment in a psychoanalytic process and a casework process, and, second, by applying the aspects of psychoanalytic therapy that set conditions and permit the patient to take responsibility for his share of the process. I will take up these two steps in order.

First, I would make a sharp distinction between the goals of psychoanalytic and of casework therapy in the extent of the change they hope to effect. A psychoanalytic process disturbs the patient's whole adjustment. In it his most fundamental relationship patterns are utilized and to some extent modified. A new balance grows out of the readjustment experience. In a casework process, on the other hand, the caseworker may change any aspect of the environment to relieve pressure on the client or to permit him greater opportunity, or she may attempt to change the client's use of a particular aspect of his environment. In doing this, she enters into a relationship with the client which he will use in a characteristic way and in which he will display his fundamental relationship patterns. It seems essential that the caseworker should understand these patterns, but I would suggest that it is not the function of the caseworker to change these patterns in any radical way. In analysis, a patient is learning to handle his own fundamental problems and the conflicts in himself; in casework a client is learning to handle a particular problem usually outside himself, in its projection on to the environment.

Two vocational-guidance cases may be used to illustrate this difference. A boy of eighteen comes to a school counselor for advice and help on the question of his college education. The father could afford to send him, but the boy's relationship to the father does not permit him to ask it. The caseworker's function in this situation would be to determine the strength of the various factors in the boy's conflict, to see whether she could in any way assist in the release of the conflict at that point. Could the boy use the caseworker to release his negative feelings for the father so that his underlying positive feelings might be left free to take the money? Could the father, given a better understanding of college education, offer the money less grudgingly? Or is the lack of money only a cover for an underlying fear of leaving home? If so, can the caseworker let the boy see this and accept it in himself through discussing it with her, through hearing her tell of other boys with similar problems? In any instance, she would be dealing with a particular problem in its reference to a concrete environmental difficulty. Her treatment aim would be satisfied if she enabled the boy to solve his immediate conflict at that point.

Another boy presents a similar educational-guidance problem, but this boy's statement takes the form: "I wouldn't ask my father for it unless he wanted to give it. I couldn't take it from anybody. I don't want a scholarship. I wouldn't be able to do good enough work to deserve it." The negative, destructive attitude toward himself that underlies these statements reveals a deep problem in which the boy is caught—the problem of not being able to take anything from another because he cannot give, of not being able to take because of the very need, which inhibits him from giving—a vicious circle that permits no immediate solution, necessitating a long relationship experience before any change can be hoped for. The caseworker's skill would lie here in her decision not to engage in this problem, perhaps in suggesting other forms of help if the boy wished it.

If this distinction between psychoanalytic and casework therapy can be accepted, it is possible to find in the former a new and, I believe, a most clarifying contribution toward relieving the confusion that confounds casework treatment. Up to this time the influence of psychoanalysis has been on the side of developing finer identification, deeper understanding, and greater acceptance of the patient. This understanding must be constantly refined, but our problem as caseworkers is to keep our need to give understanding to the client from working to the detriment of treatment in casework situations. We must learn how to give acceptance without approving and reinforcing the client's pattern; how to express understanding without setting up a process in the client that may break up his present adjustment only to involve him in a relationship with the worker that has no end, no solution, and no satisfaction. We have seen the psychoanalytic process in its earlier phases, characterized by passivity on the part of the analyst, projection and use on the part of the patient. If the patient can find security and can create a union in this experience, he has accomplished an important step in a process the goal of which must be the finding and acceptance of his own self as different and independent, not lost in this union. His ultimate security must lie in himself and not in the relationship. We need next to learn to understand the separation aspects, the end phases, of the analytic experience through which the independent self emerges. This, it seems to me, demands much more personal development and more self-conscious discipline than the understanding of acceptance. The therapist needs to have become conscious of his own separation reaction pattern and to have had some experience in which he could see it change before he can be intelligent and active in separation experiences in the patient's behalf. I am using the word "separation" to cover all experiences, no matter how slight, in which one feels a barrier between one's self and a strange, alien, or opposing environment. One may feel separation whenever one's own will senses a difference from another will. So, in a casework relationship, any withdrawal of interest, any criticism, disapproval, or refusal may operate as a separation experience. The negative will of the client aroused in opposition to this interference constitutes one of the most active factors in a dynamic relationship process.

This concept of a separation experience as one that contains difference or conflict of wills between two people makes it possible to isolate the briefest contacts for purposes of studying the dynamics of interaction between individuals. Application interviews offer abundant illustrations of a situation in which definition of the function of the agency, its requirements or limitations, brings out the opposing will of the client in his effort to control conditions in his own way. He will, for example, make the appointment at a slightly different hour from that suggested. From this point on, one can watch his constant effort to control conditions, to get his own way, to use the worker to accomplish an end, rather than to take responsibility for it himself. Whenever there is real recognition by the client of the worker's different purpose, even on so slight a point as his acceptance of her inability to change an appointment for his convenience, there is a slight growth process in the client's development. He absorbs another's difference into his own ego and in doing this accepts a new responsibility for himself. In this acceptance of difference, the separation experience becomes constructive and growth-producing. To think of a therapeutic experience as an effort on the patient's part to achieve, with the help of the therapist, a clearer definition and acceptance of himself and of the therapeutic situation as a will problem at every step seems to me to offer a new tool of approach to treatment control in the hands of the caseworker. The client comes seeking help and bringing a problem usually described in very practical terms: "My husband is sick and out of work," "I cannot manage my own child," "I want to place the baby and go to work." In each case the problem needs most careful definition and exploration on the part of client and caseworker before all the interacting forces and involved factors are clear. One of the most important factors in this situation for the caseworker to determine is the use that the client seems likely to make of her (the caseworker) in solving the problem. A few problems are largely environmental—such as unemployment in 1931, a child's problem in a home where he is mistreated—and can be handled as such by changes in the environment put through by the caseworker in the individual's behalf. But by far the greater number of problems lie in the individual's attitude to his situation, and here the question of the degree of responsibility that the client can accept for his own situation, for changing it himself or for changing his attitude toward it, is of paramount importance in treatment. There is no way of knowing how far the client can go in accepting change and taking responsibility for himself in a treatment process, but two things that can be determined to some extent in the first interview decide whether he can do anything at all in this direction and, therefore, whether it is profitable to enter upon a treatment process. One clue is whether he can accept any responsibility for a share in the process in the first stage of working on the problem; another, whether he can make any use of the worker other than to project his total need upon her, which does not permit the caseworker to contribute any element of difference.

From one point of view, the patient's whole problem can be seen to oscillate around the question of acceptance of responsibility for himself and acceptance of the other's difference. And this oscillation can be observed at work in every practical problem that he presents and in every stage of work on that problem. If there is any capacity in the client to accept separation and face his own will in terms of taking responsibility, it will appear in the earliest contacts in his discussion of the problem. The function of casework treatment in relation to his problem can be defined and his own capacity to take over responsibility can be furthered in the first interview, if the caseworker's approach includes an understanding of separation phenomena.

In respect to the handling of these separation aspects in treatment, analytic technique differs most radically from present-day casework practice. The patient applying for analysis learns in the first interview the conditions that he not only must accept, but for which he must assume some responsibility, as the fee, the definite time period, and so forth. In deciding to come, he takes a tremendous responsibility for his own treatment. He has considered and is willing to pay the price. On the other hand, the client applying for help at a social agency may know of no conditions but his own need and pays no price. The worker comes to him and brings gifts, material and immaterial, often overwhelming and destructive to his capacity to find and free himself in his problem. While casework is certainly in no position to consider charging a fee, there are other ways in which I believe the client could be enabled to take a more definite responsibility for his own treatment than is now permitted. It seems to me it would be very possible and wholly profitable to define the relationship clearly enough to the client to permit him to decide whether he wants to see the caseworker or not, and when, and to make some effort for this purpose.

The whole question of home visits versus office appointments would need to be reconsidered from this point of view. Do we go to the home to investigate the general conditions there and the family interrelationships? If so, one visit would surely suffice for our information. Or do we go to save the mother trouble, to find her most at ease in her own surroundings, to get her to talk unawares? If there is a problem to be discussed, it must be of as much importance to her as to the worker, or discussion will be futile; if she needs to talk to find release from her problems, she will be glad to seek the worker at the office. In a few cases visits must be made to the mother, as she cannot leave home on account of young children. But in most cases, I am convinced, frequent home visiting either deteriorates into a social chat in which the worker feels her role to be completely trivial, or into a maternal responsibility for the client's practical problem, the worker observing progress in housekeeping or care of children and administering approval, suggestion, and sometimes kindly, welcome reproof. Or sometimes, when the relationship is meaningful and the worker is less active, the client finds encouragement in a use of the worker that, because of the slight opportunity for payment, may block up his guilt to a point where no further treatment is possible.

It is possible to apply much of the technique of the first psychoanalytic interview to the first casework interview, to make this interview more sharply diagnostic for client as well as worker. The worker's skill and activity in this first interview should be directed very clearly and consciously to clarifying the problem on which the client seeks help. The problem is the center of discussion and activity, not the whole person. To attempt to give the client so much interest and understanding in that first interview that he will have enough security to want to come back is to involve him beyond his readiness to accept responsibility. If the problem is the center of the contact, the worker is freed for direct activity in understanding the factors that contribute to it and that her entrance into the situation will effect. She has need also of the most conscious self-discipline in inhibiting her own interest when it threatens to run away with the client's interest.

It seems to be profitable to have the worker think of every new contact in such terms as the following: "What problem did the client present?" "What factors did he try to put on my shoulders?" "How did I leave him in relation to this problem?" "Is it still his, so that he has an active, responsible drive to its solution, or have I taken it from him by assuming too much responsibility or showing too much interest?" The nice balance with which a client leaves a first interview when the problem is still his—perhaps even more consciously than before, but more bearable because shared—augurs best for therapeutic results in treatment. It should be the next step, practical or psychological, which the client wants to take about his problem that sets the date for the next contact, not the caseworker's initiative or the vague pull to see again the kind, understanding person. Sometimes the first step must be the caseworker's, as when, in a child-guidance clinic, the mother has brought the child for a psychological examination and interpretation of the results would be the next step in treatment. The mother's initiative here could be to come to get the interpretation rather than have the worker drop in to bring it. Everything that makes for greater directness in the relationship frees both worker and client for a more constructive experience. Our fear of the direct question, which might seem to savor of investigation or formal history-taking, has carried us sometimes to the ludicrous extreme of actual indirection.

The question of the distinction between passivity and activity in treatment, and of a legitimate field for the exercise of activity on the part of the caseworker, becomes clearer if we consider as fundamental this emphasis that I have attempted to place on the specific problem. In a psychoanalytic relationship, as in a casework-treatment process, the patient and the analyst also have a common problem on which they are working from hour to hour. Here it is the problem of the patient's whole self. He accepts this intellectually, it may be, at the beginning; he may evade it again and again with concrete issues; but again and again he comes back to it. In the social casework application, the client presents some specific need, which may be an indication of a deeper problem on which he is really seeking help. It is the function of the caseworker to help the client get at the problem on which he wishes help and to determine whether this is a problem in which she can function. If so, this problem, which may of course develop and change and bring up other problems, is the center, the basis, of their relationship.

An illustration may bring out more clearly the points of difference, which words are so apt to obscure. A social worker asks the advice of a caseworker as to whether she shall leave the field in which she is placed for another. It would be the function of the first interview to bring out her attitude toward the present job, to determine, first, whether the problem lies in her relation to this particular job.

There is no criticism of the job or the conditions under which she works, but a feeling that she is not doing her best work, that she could do better if she had a change. Here is sufficient indication of a problem to make it worth while to help her see this if she wishes. In response to one question—as to how she feels about changing in other situations in her life—she brings out with a good deal of feeling a necessity for changing frequently. She herself states the real problem of her present dilemma: "I never think I can make anything different. I have to leave and begin over again." This, it seems to me, could be considered the real problem of the present situation, a legitimate problem for a social caseworker to whom it has been presented to try to help with: "Do you want to think this over and come back to talk with me further about it next year?" Any further interviews would be at the client's seeking and would relate to the significance of this attitude in her job adjustment and what she might do to change it. In reality, in the case in question, she decided to keep the job and work on certain definite factors in which she might hope to effect changes. The deeper roots of this problem—the fear that makes flight necessary, the manifestations of this fear in other attitudes—were not touched in this contact—except as there is the possibility that after this experience in becoming aware of her problem, she will not be content to leave it on the surface in a particular application, but will want help on the problem of her whole self. When she becomes conscious of this more fundamental need, it will be necessary to refer her to an analyst.

I would see the caseworker's function in this case, which I use as typical, as highly active in helping to define the problem and to bring it to a point where the client can do something about it if she wishes. This activity necessitates the skill to read interacting forces as in a magnetic field—the skill to touch one ever so lightly in order to permit the action of another to be revealed. Above all the worker's activity would be turned on herself to see that she did not set in motion a new field of force by her own interest in solving the problem one way rather than another.

Finally, I am led to the conclusion that social casework treatment, since it is a relationship of help, must display many of the same phenomena of dynamic interaction that characterize the psychoanalytic process. Many of these reactions cannot be handled within the limits of a casework relationship. On the other hand, I believe that social casework has the opportunity to make a fairly workable distinction which will operate to protect the client and to release the caseworker to greater sincerity if she concentrates on the problem as presented and does not permit herself to be involved in answering the total need. Up to the present time, the contribution of psychoanalysis has been to understanding and acceptance, to the positive, giving techniques of social casework. Equally valuable contributions will come through understanding and assimilation of the techniques in psychonanalysis that, from the initial interview, set the stage for the growth of the patient's separate, individual self. These tend toward greater directness of approach, toward clearer definitions of purpose of agency and caseworker, toward finer analysis of the problem, toward permitting greater initiative and responsibility on the client's part at every step.

As truly as in psychoanalysis, the casework relationship may constitute a unique experience. If therapy results, it will be because the worker has entered into the client's problem with an understanding that enables the client to reorient himself in relation to it, but leaves him free to find his own solution. The worker's technique grows out of her sensitive awareness of the development of the process, combined with a self-discipline that enables her to keep herself from involvement, except to the extent of realizing her purpose, her treatment aim, which is to help the client get to his problem and work on it in his own way.

IV

The Meaning of Skill

The following article was written in the early nineteen-forties when the nation was still at war. It is placed in this position in the present volume (even though written later than the first book on supervision, which follows) because it continues to explore the question: Does social work have a unique skill that differentiates it from other professions? Miss Robinson writes: "The grave question which the professional school of social work must answer today is not what should be the content of the courses in the curriculum but are there unique skills in the practice of social work and has the professional school isolated and defined the situation and the methods by which these skills can be taught?"

It is to be remembered that the decade of the nineteen-thirties, immediately preceding the writing of this article, was a decade of painful and frightening experience for everyone—the decade which began with a major depression and, in its concluding years, took the nation into World War II. In the mid-thirties, the need for relief of the unemployed reached an unheard-of volume, and all the resources of social work were called upon to weather the crisis. One might assume that this could have meant the end of individual helping because of the mass programs initiated under such pressure and organized with personnel limited in number and without experience in these critical times. In general, it might be said that interest in the psychological helping process would inevitably be overpowered for the time being by the necessity to meet the bare practical needs of daily life.

However, it is significant that this very period offered the Pennsylvania School of Social Work the opportunity to discover a new method of helping, from this point on known as the "functional helping process." Faculty, supervisors, caseworkers, and students discovered that it was possible to give significant and effective help through the stages of application, determination of eligibility, and continuation of the financial grant from public funds under new laws. Also, it was a decade when some of the most important social legislation in this century was enacted by the congress: Old Age Assistance, Social Security, Unemployment Relief, with its sub-programs of public work, civilian conservation corps and other particularized programs. Perhaps one of the most imaginative was the program of public assistance to artists and writers who also were in serious need. Today, the basic programs of public assistance continue, but show the change from an emergency basis to one of permanency, as for example the unemployment insurance program which succeeded unemployment relief.

The Pennsylvania School was during this time involved in public assistance in many ways, especially with the development of the training programs. It was during this same period that Miss Robinson was turning her attention from a primary interest in the casework process to the underlying problems of training and supervision. In the introduction to Training for Skill *she writes:*

"This insistence on the integrity of the agency and our determination to hold to and make the fullest use of the factor of difference in the field experience has led to the discovery of the value of function in the training process, a discovery which I believe to be at once the most realistically practical and the most profoundly psychological for the understanding and control of student training."

In the critical era in which we are living, when democracy and all its values are on trial, the profession of social work must examine its contribution carefully for proof of its validity and usefulness in the democracy of the United States. Social work, though preeminently a democratic institution, a defender of human values, of the rights of the individual to health, economic security, and happiness, no longer carries a major responsibility for sustaining these values. The social security program, the national health movement, child welfare services, aid to farmers, labor legislation, all indicate the trend of government in the past eight years in accepting responsibility for safeguarding the rights and well-being of its people. The value of these social welfare programs to the people they are intended to serve will depend on the personnel which administers them, and it is far from clear as yet what forces will determine the quality and training of this personnel. The federal social security program has recognized social work training in its requirements for workers, but state and local set-ups in many places make no training requirement for personnel. Social work must ask itself what contribution it has to make to these programs. Does it possess any special and unique skills to bring to the performance of the tasks of the agencies set up to carry them out? Can these skills be described and demonstrated? Is the professional school equipped to teach them?

The professional school has come to the task of defining skill and training for its development only recently and through a tradition in which ideals, purpose, and attitude, rather than skill, have been emphasized. In this tradition the words "philanthropy," or "social service," carry more accurately than "social work" the spiritual values, the ideals and attitudes, which have characterized this movement throughout its history. The change of name from "social service" to "social work" has not altered the fundamental purpose and characteristic effort of this field of human endeavor. It is rooted firmly in an ethical ideology, in an immediate sensitivity to the other person, in a recognition of individual difference. The democratic state, because it accepts this fundamental reality of individual difference, must persistently and forever strive to balance innate difference by equalizing opportunity. Of all the various efforts to equalize opportunity for all citizens in a democracy, none has stood closer to the very heart of this problem of difference than social service. It has drawn into its circle of activity men and women whose sensitivity to injustice and inequality determined the devotion of themselves, their time and their means, to righting wrongs and alleviating suffering. Their passionate conviction created the social agencies in which the impulse-to-give of those who have could be organized and directed for the service of those who have not. These agencies rest for their support, psychologically and practically, upon this sensitivity to difference, this capacity to respond with feeling and with actual giving, to the other person's need.

It might be said that the social agency let itself take over the role of the conscience of the community in the latter half of the past century. It kept itself close to the needs of the disadvantaged members of the community on the one hand, and on the other held itself responsibile for stirring the complacency of the advantaged to respond to need by giving. Often this response went no further than a feeling of guilt which could be paid off in money, but a recognition of this superficial relationship should not obscure an acknowledgment of the deeper, more responsible connection which the private agency has fostered between those who have something to give and those who need this help.

Private philanthropy was just moving into the somewhat greater objectivity of social service in its understanding and use of this giving and taking process at the turn of the century when the professional school came into existence to train workers to carry out the manifold activities developed by the social agencies in offering service to clients. While these tasks ran into great detail and differed widely from one social agency to another, they were held together by the tremendous sense of conviction of man's duty to man. It was this conviction, too, which expressed itself in the curricula of the first schools of social work. Around this core of conviction, courses were organized presenting the special knowledge gained by social workers in their contacts with clients and social problems, and actual practice was offered in the social agency in working with its clients. A student entering one of the early schools of social service, forty years ago, by his original choice of this field and by the devotion to service fostered in school and agency, took upon himself the total symbol and responsibility for service to his fellow men. The impulse which operated in this choice was similar to that which drew others into the ministry, and the dedication to the task and the field had some of the same meaning as a dedication to the service of the church. The student was identified in his own mind and the minds of others with the conscience of the community, its sensitivity to wrong, its passion to help. Perhaps this willingness to carry so much symbolically beyond what can be carried really is one explanation of the opprobrium which frequently attaches to social workers today.

Whatever differences existed in these first schools—and they were great—between content of curriculum, courses, and methods of teaching, they were united in attitude, spirit, and purpose as they represented the "field" of social work in which this one principle of unity, the ideal of service, operated. Other factors have come in since to influence the development of the professional curriculum, particularly in schools which originated in the university departments of sociology or economics where academic standards outweighed vocational influences. But the major influence has continued to be the field itself with its concept of service and of practice.

The twenty-five years of development of professional education for social work between the two world wars have seen two major emphases in curricula as curriculum-making has followed the trend in social work itself. The first emphasis showed itself in a predominance of psychiatric content accompanying the popularization of psychiatry and the introduction of the mental hygiene movement after the first World War. As unemployment increased in the late twenties, the inadequacy of the resources of the private agencies to handle the need it created, forced upon the field and the schools the recognition of another area of content and a requirement for definitions of new tasks and for the development of new skills. Public programs began to take the place of private philanthropy, and the social security program written into law in 1935 clearly defined government's responsibility for taking over from the private conscience the burden it had been struggling to carry. In the curricula of the schools of social work, content from the field of economics, from the history of the labor movement, from political science, tended to decrease the emphasis on psychiatric knowledge.

Examination of the curricula of schools of social work today, in 1941, cannot fail to bring the realization that there is no special content of knowledge peculiar to this field. Everything that can be known about social, economic, and political problems is told on the radio, spread in print in papers and magazines, acted out on the stage or the movie screen. These presentations bring human need before the eyes and ears of the public more vividly, more immediately, and more movingly than can be done by lecturers in a school of social work.

Furthermore, it seems obvious that, in a world engaged in total war, social work can no longer carry the burden of social reform. If the world is to be reconstructed after the war into a place where human beings may live and grow and develop their capacities in peace, it will take the experience and the knowledge, the judgment and the skill, of all those who care for human values. A new dedication will be required for this task and the name "social work" will not be sufficient to carry the depth and scope of its purpose and meaning.

In this new era which social work and the professional school are facing in this country, no one can say whether there will be more or less recognized need for social workers. This depends on many factors over which social workers have no control, most important of all on the capacity of the public social programs to hold their own with the defense program. It depends, too, on whether there is recognition of the equipment of social workers as bringing a necessary contribution to the administration of social programs.

I believe that this recognition of the contribution of social work can only be established if the profession of social work can separate itself from its identification with the social conscience and social reform and find a role for itself in a more limited and more effective relation to social problems. Can social work, itself, define and stay within its own area of competency, an area in which its knowledge and judgment supply something different from the contribution of other professions and where its practitioners can do something by virtue of their training which cannot be done without it? The grave question which the professional school of social work must answer today is not what should be the content of the courses in the curriculum, but are there unique skills in the practice of social work and has the professional school isolated and defined the situation and the methods by which these skills can be taught? Has the professional school comprehended a sufficiently generic and fundamental base so that these skills may be considered professional rather than merely technical in character? An equally pertinent question for the future of professional social work is: Are these skills recognizable by others than those who practise them?

Ernest Bevin has been quoted as placing skill at the head of a nation's resources—a nation's wealth is not land, not machinery, but human skill. What, then, is skill?

Skill implies first of all an activity, an ability to perform, and while it rests on knowledge it is clearly distinguishable from knowledge. We speak in common language of knowledge about a "subject," of skill in handling an "object." One has a knowledge of the subject of mechanics, skill in handling a particular machine. This difference in the language is suggestive. For knowledge may remain in the possessor of knowledge, the knower, while the development of skill necessarily leads out into contact and engagement with an object. Achievement of skill demands that the object become known in its reality, its make-up, its ways of behaving, its capacity to respond to efforts to change its behavior. Most skills grow out of this engagement between a workman—a craftsman, a mechanic, or an artist—and his object around some point of change initiated by the workman. The nature of the object, its pliability and its resistance, sets the limits of the problem.

All crafts, all trades, all mechanical work, all professions, and all creative activity, have their special, distinctive, and recognized skills. The sculptor carving in wood or stone, the scientist handling the elements in his experiment, the cook preparing a meal in his kitchen, the gardener tending his growing plants, learn, through training and experience, a skill in controlling the process in which they are engaged. It may be possible to accomplish the process and achieve a finished product without skill in the performance, this lack of skill expressing itself in awkwardness, bungling, poor timing, perhaps in mistakes which ruin material or turn out a defective product. The skillful workman, on the other hand, seems to move easily and with direction. We admire his efficiency, his timing, the perfect gearing of himself and his energies in the process.

This skillful way of working obviously develops out of some relationship between the workman and the material in which he works. The force which will emanate from him to produce change in the material—his intention, his idea, his plan—starts the process in motion. His understanding of his material and his capacity to work *with* it, instead of *against* it, to utilize and not do violence to its essential nature, determine his ability to develop skill in his handling of the process. Skill might be defined, then, as the capacity to set in motion and control a process of change in specific material in such a way that the change that takes place in the material is effected with the greatest degree of consideration for and utilization of the quality and capacity of the material. It develops out of these two elements— the strength of the goal, purpose, aim, or idea in the workman, and his willingness both to struggle with and yield to the characteristics of the material with which he works. With increasing experience, as the workman learns how to handle his material, his skill becomes focused in himself. Hand, eye, self, and object, become one. The workman's skill is his way of working, natural and spontaneous. I recall a plasterer I have seen at work whose hands and body seemed molded by the process in which he was engaged. He worked in bricks and mortar with the loving care of an artist, building chimneys which could be depended on to draw and to endure, molding his own muscles into tools adapted to the task.

When an individual makes a choice of a vocation, the areas within which he will relate himself to reality and the contacts in which his skill will develop are laid down. In a world as mechanized as the world of the twentieth century, processes are so finely specialized that a vocational choice may limit a man's use of himself to one field of activity, one kind of material, even to one part of a machine. Industrial processes are standardized and patterned by the machine, and the workman's skill becomes a matter of adjustment to the speed and operation of machinery. No creative impulse and purpose of his own can be expressed in these mechanized performances. The choice of a professional vocation, on the other hand, that of medicine, for illustration, may engage the whole of the individual in a life-long struggle to master the knowledge and develop the skill with which to treat illness.

The extent to which the self becomes involved in the development of skill depends first on the strength and depth of the original purpose or creative drive, and secondly on the nature of the reality problem with which it engages. If the problem is slight, easy of solution, or partial, cut off from relation to other problems as in machine operation, the self is engaged only superficially and partially. Where the problem is complex, difficult, and related to other problems as in medicine or engineering, the self must be engaged more actively and more completely, and may be drawn into a field which constantly sets new and more challenging problems. It would seem that the fields which engage the individual most deeply are those in which the problems have the scope and nature of life itself, where the material is most human, most like in character to the self. Art, science, and some of the professions, especially medicine, nursing, and social work, involve those who engage in them in problems of life and death, of growth and change in the human being. Consequently, the skills that must be developed to work in these fields involve the commitment of the whole self, and necessitate the development and deepening of the self to the extent of its human capacity.

In the development of skill the influence of the organized craft or profession made up of those who have acquired the skill on those who enter the field is an important factor. Here apprentice training or the professional school operates powerfully, setting standards and controls, creating conditions and situations within which skill can be learned. In no field of human activity except perhaps the arts can the individual develop purely individual skill without going through a learning discipline set up by others. Only the greatest individual genius can afford to learn in his own way wholly through his own experience because he contains in himself that which goes beyond the ordinary human experience. Even the creative genius, in spite of his capacity to develop an original contact with his material and to wrest his own skills uniquely out of his own experience, must recognize and make use of his connection with the world of art itself and with others who have created in the same medium.

With these points in mind relating to the definition of skill and its development and training, we can ask ourselves the questions: What is the specific skill which social work has to offer? What change does it seek to effect? Through what processes does it work, and can these processes be described and taught?

One must keep in mind the handicap the field of social work has been under in moving from its original identifications with goals beyond human capacity to achieve individually or in the span of a lifetime to an orientation to social problems sufficiently limited to permit of the development of skill. The traditional concern of social work, the human being in need and the ills of society, have proved too complicated for any influence social work could bring to bear, while realistic points at which effort can be exerted upon these problems are not easy to find.

In one field of social work, the field of social casework, social workers have been forced to confine themselves within boundaries that define a point of operation and a relation to the material which are necessary for the development of skill. To the doors of the casework agency comes every variety of human problem. They are brought by individuals, by individuals representing families, and this fact of individual presentation constitutes the basic point of approach on which casework has always relied. But one must wonder what assumption could carry the caseworker into trustworthy activity in relation to the problems and circumstances of an individual in need of help. The impulse to help in response to need cannot always be relied upon to result helpfully to the other person. How different this problem of developing a skill is seen to be from the use of skill in industrial and mechanical operations! The mechanic or craftsman acts directly upon his material, but the caseworker is faced with another person, a human being like himself, seeking help in an effort to change something in himself or his circumstances. Has the worker anything to contribute that is valid and useful? Can any control of his activity deserving the name of skill be developed?

In the history of the casework movement, one sees that the approach to this problem of how to help, in relation to a person's need to bring about change, has moved through two phases. The earlier effort was a direct attack on the client with the intent of making him over in the image of the caseworker and for the good of society. In reaction against this will-to-control of his first efforts, we see the caseworker in the next phase of the movement resigning his own activity in a passionate identification with the client, a need to understand him in his difference. Neither of these approaches could lead to an effective relation to the client's request for help. In the first the worker was caught in his own pressure to change the client; the second left the whole burden on the client's shoulders. Through neither approach could the caseworker feel any confidence that the casework contribution was effective in producing change. Results might be good in one case, bad in another, but to what extent these results could be attributed to casework was uncertain.

No more difficult skill could be demanded—skill in setting up and controlling a process in which change may take place in a human being. If even the beginnings of such a skill exist, why is it not more widely recognized? Certainly no skill could be more desirable; none would be more deeply feared. For man's fear of and resistance to change within is in proportion to his desire to produce it outside himself. The power to effect change in human beings directly is permitted only to parents and religious workers.

Perhaps, then, the most fundamental and necessary basis for the development of any skill in effecting change in a human being is an understanding of human resistance to change and an appreciation of an individual's right to refuse any efforts directed at changing him. As long as social casework approached its clients with the intention of producing direct change, there could be no development since the other person could be involved in nothing but resistance. Social casework has long been in possession of this knowledge. Its literature abounds in assertion of its belief that the client must bring about his own change, make his own plan, participate in any effort to help him. But these are still words to a great extent. Young people continue to bring to training in social casework just this purpose, the will-to-change the other person, to make him better or happier, or to give to him what he ought to have or what the worker wants to give. How can the variable, temperamental nature of this impulse-to-give be disciplined into a steady reliable help which the other person can depend on, and how can the will-to-change the client directly be transformed into a willingness to play a part, to fit into what he is doing in his own behalf? These questions must be answered before the word "skill" is appropriate.

Now social casework has always operated in a reality situation which possesses to a singular degree the power to restrain the impulse and will of the worker from direct action on the client and redirect it in a way that permits the development of conscious skill in controlling a process in which the client can participate to effect his own change. But it has not recognized and made use of this situation consciously for the control of skill until recently. This reality situation is the social agency and the defined, limited service it offers to clients. If this reality is accepted and used it stands between the person-to-person relationship of client and worker in a way that makes possible the seemingly impossible task of effective change.

An obsolete definition of the word "skill" used as a verb is "to differentiate," "to separate." Certainly no skill in controlling a process of change can develop unless there is a separation between self and object, between the will-to-effect-change of the workman and the material with which he works. Where the material is another person, this first problem—to establish sufficient separateness so that the other person is not confused with the own self—seemed for a long time insuperable. The social agency with its purpose, its function, its services, its policies, structure, and procedures, effects this separation between worker and client. Since it offers a specific service it enables an individual to come seeking that service intending therefore in the natural, characteristic way of human beings to effect a change not in himself but in outside circumstance. "I want a job, or money to pay the rent, or help through an illness. I want to place my child, I want to leave my husband." These are some of the requests indicating the client's move to change his situation as he comes to a social casework agency. The client is not asked to change himself or to accept change at the hands of a social worker. He is told what the agency has to offer for his need as he states it. He is told the conditions he must meet. In a public relief agency, for example, he is asked to establish his eligibility, and it is made clear to him that his continuing relation with the agency will be a continuing process of eligibility. Thus he does something about his own situation and something with the agency. He involves himself in working with the representative of the agency, takes a new kind of responsibility for the facts he presents, feels and expresses a new concern in looking for a job and in discussing his progress with another person. Actually he does change in relation to a limited area of his problem and through contact with a specific, objective, external factor, a social agency.

Experience demonstrates that it is exactly these limitations which permit the client to venture into this dangerous area from which change may emanate, risk the fearful involvement with another person, and come through with some use for himself of what has been given him. What he brings away is new because the agency and the worker have given something, but it is his own since he has come to terms with it in the taking.

The effect on the worker of the reality of the social agency is even more electric than on the client. A student, beginning field work in a social agency, makes his first contact with a client not in his capacity as a person, but in a new role as representative of agency. The implications of this are immediate and far-reaching. The natural impulse-to-give and the total will-to-change directed at the client are suddenly invaded by the agency's requirements. There can be no coming to terms with this simply. Any attempt to describe what happens here oversimplifies a complicated psychological process. It is as if an ongoing force is broken in two parts, one part being diverted from its outward expression to be directed upon the self as object. Where the artist works upon his canvas, the mechanic upon his machine, both external objects, the student in training for social work must direct some of the creative energy, ordinarily directed outside, upon himself. An artist may recognize at some point that his own immaturity limits his conception, but he has no way of working on his growth process. In social casework, however, it is precisely with his own capacity to change and grow that the student must be concerned. Around the point where direct expression of impulse or will is checked by a supervisor in a training process, if this expression is internalized, change actually does take place in feeling and attitude. The student is brought up short before his own will, which perhaps he has never felt as such, detached from an object. He may feel himself convicted of error, of aggression, of meanness, of hostility, or of a generosity which proceeded only from his own need without consideration for the other person. With the help of the supervisor he can feel this force as something in himself with power to work harm to the supervisor, to the client, or the agency, unless he becomes responsible for it. Through this internalization, the conviction is established that the self is the tool with which he works in this process of helping another person, and that the tool must be formed anew in harmony with its chosen task.

The process through which these new feelings and attitudes

are assimilated into the self eventually follows the form and movement of a growth process, but it proceeds on a deeper level with more awareness of itself and with more capacity to see the other person as separate and different from the self than is the case in ordinary growth process with its slow organic rhythm, moving unconsciously and always in some connection with natural human relationships.

This new self, immediately the student feels it and takes any responsibility for it, calls itself "I" in the record. In sudden sense of its own separateness and strength, it often becomes aggressive and overbearing in its definition of difference, rigid in its adherence to the new-found support in agency function and structure. In this early phase of training, the student may be over-assertive of his professional role in his insistence that the client must carry responsibility for asking for help. He finds it easier, in the first flush of his own sense of separateness, to say "no" for his agency than to say "yes." Only teachers and supervisors who understand these attitudes as phases in a training process can bear with them and the harm they may do the agency and the client. Family and friends, particularly, react against these manifestations in training which seem to set the student apart from his natural human connections.

This new professional self varies from student to student in relative strength and power to express itself outwardly and to develop inwardly. The structure of the self has been disturbed by this change. Reorganization will depend on the individual pattern, on time, and on the capacity to continue to take help from supervisor and teacher in a training process. The role of the supervisor is seen to be essential, first in understanding the value of agency in setting up this representative-of-agency role and making effective this point of differentiation between student and client. Even more important is her role in helping the student carry responsibility for the professional self through its first use of itself with clients until reorganization eventuates in a self that can carry its own strength with less and less dependence on the supervisor. Through this relation to the supervisor, in which the supervisor consistently maintains a difference from the student that supports his development while it checks his undisciplined expressions, the student learns how to use himself helpfully with his client.

The student, once he has had this experience with a supervisor which differentiates him from his client and enables him to take in

the function of the agency, understands the beginning of a professional training process. He learns, too, in the midst of his own uncertainties, to trust the experience of the School in accepting the fact
that there will be development and eventuation in this two-year training process. Can the student also have the experience of seeing the
development of skill in shorter units of process than the two years of
his own training? Can he engage in a process with a client and see it
through to a point of ending?

The word "skill" cannot be applied to anything less than this—
the control of a process in which there is effective change. A student
cannot have any real understanding or use of skill until he can feel
himself present and active from the beginning to the end of a process
of change and know that what he as caseworker put into the situation has been an effective agent in the client's response. This problem has presented such difficulties when caseworkers let themselves
be confronted with the total life problem and total needs of the client that not even a step could be taken in the direction of teaching
skill to a beginner. Only an experienced worker who already understands the client's life problem and depth of need would be competent to try to help a client in these terms. But once the helping agency
has accepted responsibility for offering to the needful client some
specific service instead of total help, it is possible to see where a beginner can fit in, find a role, and define himself and his service to the
client so that the client's response is specifically related to this offer.
Here, then, is a unit of experience marked off in time by the conscious, deliberate act of agency and worker. Every contact with the
client can become such a unit for training purposes. Responsibility
for what the student puts in can be clearly defined, and the client's
activity can be examined thoughtfully to see how it is connected
with the student's activity. The student can bring an interview into
casework class and gain greater conviction of what went on between
himself and the client as he discusses it with his fellow students and
the casework teacher.

The clear definition of function, policy, and procedure in a public agency gives the beginner the kind of support he needs in taking
responsibility for his activity with a client, and affords too the most
satisfactory opportunity to see the effect upon the client of the
worker's activity. In the space of a single interview, a student may be
able to see his ability to clarify a policy with a confused client lead
to a real change of attitude on the client's part. He may see that what

he contributes in the interview in understanding a client's confusions and resistance and interpreting the agency's conditons has had the effect of enabling a client to establish his eligibility. Or, in other situations, the student may have to recognize that his own failure to bring out the client's real attitude or to be clear about agency requirements was an actual obstacle between the client and the relief check he needs so badly and for which he is eligible. Out of many such experiences where responsibility is fixed and the client's reactions to it recognized, the student learns the meaning of skill in the single interview.

But the single interview is by no means all there is to a social casework process, and while the beginning student is learning to analyze worker-client activity in these isolated units of experience, he must also be learning what makes for continuity and movement between interviews, in a series of contacts. Strange things happen. The client fails to appear when the student had set the date for the next appointment so carefully; he turns up with a job when the student was sure he was ready to accept a relief check. After expressing gratitude for an allowance worked out with him in one interview, he returns in the next to complain that it is inadequate for his needs. Just at the point where the student-worker has made all the preparations and gained the consent of the family to the much-needed tonsil operation for a child, the child runs a temperature or the mother goes back on her decision.

What do these changes in attitude on the part of the client indicate? "Is it due to what I have done or failed to do, or is there something else in the client's own movement which I must learn to expect?" the student asks. Again the student works on these questions with the supervisor and in the casework class. He learns that it is possible for the person who is giving help, if he holds to his responsibility for constantly defining and redefining what he puts in, to gain conviction about the relation of the other person's movement to what he has contributed. From a wealth of illustration provided by his own clients and those of his fellow students, and from his own experience with his supervisor and teachers, he learns to know that there are certain general characteristics of movement in a process where one individual takes help of another. It becomes obvious to him very soon that this movement rarely goes in a straight line. Rather it goes backwards and forwards, or with marked swings from side to side. Only a great deal of experience brings the sure knowledge that there is a general direction in this movement which seems at first so erratic. The supervisor and the teacher carry this conviction as to direction and outcome while the student struggles in the middle of the process. The phases of movement in time—the beginning, the middle, the ending—become familiar concepts to the student. The school year is patterned so that classes naturally bring an awareness of this patterning of movement and of the importance of recognizing and dealing with these differences in time phases. In all the field-work agencies of the School, the same concepts of movement in relation to a focus and the patterning of movement in time are in use.

In addition to the understanding the student must achieve of the general characteristics of human movement in relation to a helping function—its ambivalence, its positive and negative phases, its direction and its rhythm in time—the student must also learn to appreciate that each person individualizes these general characteristics in a way that is unique to himself. The client whose way is most different from his own, who baffles him completely, will probably afford the experience in which the student learns most deeply. The casework class in the school, and even more the class in the area of personality which accompanies his field work, will constantly supply additional illustration of different individual ways of reacting to and using help and will seek to build up and deepen the student's understanding of processes of change and movement in human beings.

A second-year student must go further and deeper than the first-year student in his capacity to take in and carry the function of the agency and use it fully in helping the client. One second-year student, a man with a year of experience in a public agency before he entered the professional school and his first year of field work in a private child-placing agency, began his second year of school in the same child-placing agency with a case load of older boys in foster homes. In the first month of school he brought to the practice class the case of a sixteen-year-old boy whom he had recently placed in a new foster home. The boy was behaving badly and the foster parents were asking for his removal. The student was approaching the problem *de novo*, seeing only a boy whose behavior problems he must understand and help. He felt himself to be understanding and helpful in his approach to the boy, and was baffled by the rejection of his offers. As the student worked on this case in class and with his casework teacher and supervisor, he struggled through to a realization that his approach was subjective and superficial in that he was ignoring the reality of the boy's long connection with the agency. (He had been placed by them as a baby with a family which gave him its name and treated him as an adopted child; recently, after the death of the foster father, he was returned to the agency without explanation.) To comprehend the meaning of this boy's experience with the agency and accept responsibility for what had been done to him by the agency demanded of the student a deeper internalization of function than is achieved in a first year of training. To stand up to the hostility and bitterness which the boy harbored asked more strength than the student knew he possessed. This student was eventually able not only to help this boy express his bitterness and place it on him as worker-for-agency but to face some of his questions about his own mother and the cruel inescapable fact that she had deserted him when he was a baby. To see a boy through these realizations of feeling while placing and replacing him in homes which his behavior threatens to make unusable requires a firmness and sureness of role and direction to be expected only in an experienced worker. The support of agency, supervisor, and teacher was necessary here to enable the student to carry this process through the difficult struggle involved until the boy accepted placement and his relation to the agency. The student used his thesis to abstract the movement in this case, and reached his own understanding of the problem, the process, and his own part in it through separating himself from the living experience.

It can only be regarded as amazing that any training could enable a student in his early twenties to help a boy of sixteen face and live with so painful and difficult a problem. There will be many who believe that such a problem could only be assimilated with the help of deep psychoanalytic treatment. That this boy would ever seek such treatment is highly unlikely. Failing the help which the student worker gave, his behavior would probably have taken him into a reform school. This help indeed is limited, limited to helping him live in a foster home and with the realities of foster parents, agency, school, and community. One could wish, of course, that a boy with so great a problem might have met the skill of the most experienced worker in the agency. Some bungling in the first contacts would have been avoided and the case might have moved more quickly and more directly. I do not believe, however, that this contact could have had any deeper reality or more satisfactory eventuation for the boy. For the essence of help is here, in this meeting of the boy's problem where it was, in feeling about himself and the agency, and in moving with it through its struggle to express the bad and find something he could depend on in the agency and in himself.

In seeking to understand the skill required to help a boy relive and assimilate sixteen years of experience, one needs another concept more comprehensive than the concept of movement in relation to a function. Only the concept of psychological growth can afford an adequate explanation of what is happening in this experience for the student, as well as for the boy, his client. Only a profound trust in this growth process enables the supervisor to stand aside at times and wait until a deeper development comes to pass rather than to exert her own pressure to force a result quickly. In the last analysis, it is on the understanding of growth and its slow time rhythms, different for each individual, that skill in supervising a training process, such as the one I have just described, depends. A young supervisor has not reached this understanding and must depend on the teacher in the school for the support which enables her to move ahead with this training process even when it goes beyond her own experience.

Not only in the child-placing field, but in any social casework agency, the worker who stands as representative of the agency's service to the client must learn that he never operates *de novo* and as himself in beginning a casework process. The client never comes *de novo* but brings inevitably, if not a continuing contact, as in the case of the boy just described, some relation to a previous contact or some attitudes from contacts with others who have used the agency. The worker must have a deep conviction of continuity to say to a client at the Intake Desk, after studying the agency's record, "You were here three years ago and you left without getting what you wanted from us. Why are you coming back now?" Skill here rests on an unequivocal identification with the agency, and a firm holding to its reality and meaning for the client through three years when he has not contacted it, in order to particularize and define with the client the different significance of his present turning to the agency.

These three years may have been a period of disorganization, of disintegration, instead of constructive, directed movement and growth in the client's life. Perhaps his failure to get help from the agency when he came before was a factor in his inability to move ahead. The skilled worker must take some responsibility for that failure and utilize his understanding of it in order to strengthen any positive movement toward reorganization that this present approach to the agency may indicate. The worker cannot know all that has happened to this client in three years, but he must be aware, if he is to be of any use to him, of exactly what has happened to him as a result of contact with the agency. He may see it more clearly than the client, must hold to it and affirm it even against the client's denial, in order to utilize it for the client's movement.

Skill that has reached this degree of firmness and sureness in its use of itself in the role of a particular helping function has the capacity to affect a client very immediately and very deeply. Not only does it individualize him in his difference from other clients, but it may actually create him as an individual in that it brings him together in his strivings and his confusions at last and enables him to feel himself whole in being met at this point by a responsible and responsive person. As he is met, too, with recognition of continuity that connects a past expression of himself with his present, he may be able to feel himself more really and responsibly present and persistent through changing circumstance.

I should like to say here, parenthetically, that the recent emphasis of casework on starting with the present problem, while it has been necessary in order to extricate caseworkers from the involvement with the client's past which made action in the present impossible, has gone at times to the extreme of denying the validity of the client's past as it affects the present. For purposes of training this emphasis may be exaggerated in order to give the student his role in a present point of contact, and to help him get a sense of focus in agency function and the client's immediate relation to it. But the further the student goes in experience in helping processes, the more he realizes that a contact really focused in the present must handle all the forces that come together there. A focus introduces more struggle, more meaning, more sense of reality, more conviction of self in the present moment. This feeling of self in the present inevitably stirs up a sense of past selves, deepening instead of limiting the contact. In every helping process that goes below the surface of the immediate single use of a function, the need for recognition of the whole self must express itself at some time. This is most obvious in the supervisory process where the skilled supervisor knows that every student, in order to achieve a development of the disciplined professional self, must touch at some point in his learning process a bad, impulsive self that he may be giving up, a weak, fearful self that may be moving toward greater strength, or perhaps certain rich, creative aspects of the spontaneous self that are holding themselves aloof from the process. These aspects of the self may express themselves in any content from the student's experience, and the supervisor's skill lies in her capacity to include them through her understanding of their meaning in the process. By maintaining her focus in the process, in what the student is learning and she is teaching, she sustains the structure, the environment, as it were, in which his movement to professional development can find its own form and shape without denying his human and personal self. The criticism which some caseworkers have directed against a use of function as limiting, rigid, and negative grows out of a failure to understand the universal problem of creativity in its search for form. Fundamental in the problem of creativity is the need for limits, orientation, and focus. Without these, form cannot evolve.

These considerations take us into problems of skill that go beyond what two years of training could be expected to compass. On the other hand, it is not possible to limit the client's use of help to the student's capacity to give help. The school has no power to limit what the student will be expected to do except by the selection of the field-work agency. In the public-assistance agency the student's responsibility for function can be definitely limited. But even there, the use some clients make of that function will strain greatly the student's capacity to understand and handle himself in the process. In the private casework agencies there are few field-work assignments which do not call at times for more than the student has learned how to give. Only skilled supervision and the integration of supervision with the practice class and the personality class in the school make it possible to handle these problems.

While I am limiting this discussion of skill to the field of social casework where we have built up structure and method through which skill can be trained, I believe this skill which is developed so specifically is generic in its basis and applicable to any field of social work, to administrative processes as well as to the processes of casework and supervision. The familiar concepts of lines of responsibility and flow of work in administration imply that the same basic understanding of movement can operate here. In our experience in the Pennsylvania School we understand skill in classroom teaching to rest on the same basis as does skill in supervising and in helping the client. In generic terms this basis consists in definition of a professional role in a situation with full understanding and utilization of the other person's relation to it. The student's professional role in relation to his client, the supervisor's role in relation to the student, and the teacher's role in relation to the class are all different, all interrelated. The training movement develops soundly only if these definitions of the professional role are kept clear.

The answer to the question whether this skill can operate and sustain itself in the public agencies lies in whether the public agency with its large case loads can permit enough sensitivity to the other person, and enough dedication to professional development, to ask for discipline of skill and professional training. If not, the relation to the client will be carried in routine procedures, while job security guaranteed by the union and by civil service will take the place of professional discipline.

In my opinion, any service which calls for individualization of the clients to whom it is offered must make use of this skill if it is to render service effectively. If social work understands skill in these terms of setting up and controlling processes of movement in professional relationships it might indeed look forward to a broader field of usefulness than it has ever envisioned for itself. There should be a place for this skill in extending the use of any service, educational and health services as well as social, from any agency or institution. Wherever people come to get something they need, to which they may be entitled but to which their relation is not yet established, they require help in making use of it. If the service is to realize its greatest effectiveness, this understanding of the individual's problem in making use of it should be inherent in set-up and administration. Particularly it should be expressed at the point where the individual applies and at the point where he is ready to end his use of the service.

This psychology of movement in relation to a function lies at the basis of the new skill which I believe is being created uniquely in the field of social casework today. It is difficult to teach because it cannot be learned from books or by the intellect alone, but must be comprehended through an experience in which the student risks himself really. Only courageous and able students will make the sacrifice which this professional development requires, will accept the discipline of the personal self which it entails. The school that undertakes to develop this skill must select its students carefully and must guarantee them a learning experience in which field work under skilled supervision and class work are set up and integrated through this understanding of the meaning of skill in social casework and the learning movement the student must undergo in acquiring it.

Summary

    In examining the question of the nature and meaning of skill in social work, I have used as a definition of skill the following statement: "Skill is the capacity to set in motion and control a process of change in specific material in such a way that the change that takes place in the material is effected with the greatest degree of consideration for and utilization of the quality and capacity of the material." The definition emphasizes the nature of the relationship which must exist between the workman and his material if skill is achieved, whether the workman be a laborer, a craftsman, a mechanic, a member of a profession, or a creative artist. The psychological task in the development of any skill was seen to lie in the discipline of the natural will-to-change the object into the will-to-create the object.

    For social work, whose traditional tasks have been to right social wrongs and to help the individual in need, there could be no definition and training of skill until these tasks were limited. I have pointed out that in the casework field alone social work found a limitation of its task which makes possible a point of control of effective change. Examinations of the problem of change revealed it to be fundamental in living. It revealed the necessity to change opposed by an equal resistance to it. In struggling with the problem of how to produce effective change in clients and their situations, social casework has clung to one conviction that the client must produce this change himself through his own effort and by his own growth. This left the worker still without an effective role. The discovery of the use of the social agency as the reality which introduces a separating factor and an objective focus into the personal client-worker relationship has revolutionized our concept of casework and made possible the development and training of skill in control of a professional relationship. When the service agency carries the helping function and states the conditions under which it will give help, professional roles can be defined and professional relationships sustained.

    The skillful handling of professional relationships, whether it be a direct contact with the client or his connections, with a worker or student as supervisor, with members of the staff or board members as executive of an agency, necessitates an acceptance of professional difference, an understanding of the dynamics which this difference introduces, and the capacity to sustain the movement initiated in the other person until he reaches an end in his use of it. This understanding of dynamics and of processes of change and growth constitutes a special psychological knowledge. This knowledge cannot be taught academically but grows out of the student's experience in a process of change in the development in his own professional self and in his capacity to feel his client's movement and growth as like and different from his own. In this training process the will-to-change the object is transformed into a will-to-create the professional self and the process of relationship in which it works.

In discussing the training of skill I have described three levels. First is the simple skill which the beginner can initiate and carry through in a single interview around a point of definition of function or explanation of a policy to a client. Second is the skill in controlling a process of movement in time where the student becomes responsible for his continuing part and for carrying the continuity of the experience with the client through to an ending. A third level of skill involves an understanding of growth as well as movement in relation to a function. The second level can be isolated only arbitrarily for purposes of training. Actually, as we have seen, any casework process requires the use of skill on all three levels, and only with the help of the supervisor and teacher can the student sustain his role until he has attained a development which enables him to use himself skillfully.

The Development of a
Professional Self: Differentiation
between Academic Theory
and its Practice in Relationship

V

Supervision in Social Casework — A Problem in Professional Education

We now turn our attention from the casework process – theory and practice that underlie the help given by the caseworker to the client – to theory and practice in supervision. Miss Robinson's first book on supervision was published in 1936. Again, it is extraordinary that in the midst of this decade so full of social and economic problems, when burdened with the necessity to contribute to the massive task of public assistance, Miss Robinson was yet able to produce this book. She states it thus:

"I have set myself the problem here of lifting supervision out of its confusing entanglement with the casework process in order to see it as a unique teaching process which has grown up inside of casework, indigenous to it, but different in important ways. My concern in this discussion is to define supervision as a distinct and unique educational process, to describe its form and its limits and the essential constant elements in structure and movement which underlie the differences that appear in different situations with different contents."

During this decade she was teaching classes in supervision heightened and enlivened by necessity, namely, the supervision of caseworkers without prior training who were already administering public assistance. She dedicates her book "To the Supervisors of the Pennsylvania School of Social Work."

From this first book on supervision we have included here only Part One, entitled, "The Dynamics of the Self in Learning." Part Two, of which only one chapter is included in this new edition, is entitled, "The Learning Process in Supervision." This same subject is dealt with in the second book on supervision, published in 1949 – twelve years after the first – and reflects there the increasing clarity and depth that characterize this process.

The quotation above and those which follow are from the preface and introduction (not included in the present volume). From the preface we quote once more the clear statement by the author of her purpose:

"In many years of experience in professional education for social work, I have found no set of problems more challenging and more baffling than those connected with the student's practice of field work and teaching through supervision. Two years ago I offered a class on problems and methods of supervision in the advanced curriculum of the Pennsylvania School of Social Work and through that class and others which followed it, have attempted to define the problems and build up some illustrative material for teaching in the field."
She goes on to say, in a key statement that may be applied to the whole of her work on supervision: "The field of social casework, and supervision with it, is moving so fast that one cannot write anything about it that has value beyond a very brief present. On the other hand, if I have succeeded at all in bringing out of this changing social casework content the underlying problems of learning and teaching in the supervisory relationship, I believe that there is here a fundamental basis with more than temporary meaning in professional education for social work."

PART ONE. THE DYNAMICS OF THE SELF IN LEARNING

1. A DEFINITION OF LEARNING

Education for any profession aims not only to teach the specific knowledge and skills necessary in its practice, but it undertakes also to make over the personal self of the "lay" student into a professional self. This is particularly true in education for social casework whose helping function demands the most conscious and responsible use of a professional self. This educational process, necessitating reorganization in the structure and functioning of the self, can only be understood from a point of view that considers all learning as organic, as movement and change, which emanates from and in turn modifies the self as a whole.

For the human organism, learning begins in the uterus and continues to be a major activity until the organism has exhausted its potentialities for growth and modification and closed finally its dynamic relations with the environment. Learning is the most characteristically human of all experience, at the same time it is individually patterned by every learner. All individuals in our culture, except those who through extreme intellectual handicap or isolation escape its influence, learn the minimum equipment required for self-maintenance and association with their fellows—to eat, to walk, to talk, to read, to write. They acquire some factual knowledge and certain skills and attitudes. But each person individualizes his performance in his method and speed of learning and the final quality of his learning achievement. Beyond a point each is selective, rejecting much more than he learns. Learning, once acquired, becomes in varying degrees a part of the organism's equipment, at times laid down almost as firmly as structure. Other learning may be very superficially related to the organism as a whole, like a fact learned for an occasion and forgotten tomorrow.

All learning situations present a common characteristic to be reckoned with by all individuals who come under their influence. They represent unknown experience, a threat to the equipment and structure previously acquired. Whenever the individual enters the range of influence of the new situation which presents skills and techniques or facts and interpretations unfamiliar to him, he may, if he will, become conscious of the threat and the pressure which the new exerts. At certain points, every individual resists this pressure and refuses to be engaged. Finally, however, he must yield and relate himself vitally to it if he is to make the new skills or the new knowledge his own. He can never be drawn into learning against all of his will.

The question that concerns us is what happens to an individual from the time when he begins to feel the influence of the unknown situation and the pull of his own internal movement through disorganization and reorganization to the new balance when he is master of himself again in possession of the values of the situation. This problem has been broken up into relatively simple terms and studied in laboratory situations where tasks can be set up and learning speeds and performances measured. The real situations of education, however, strike other levels of the problem which do not enter in to the laboratory conditions. The important factor of actual learning situations which can never be lured into the laboratory for measurement is the extent to which the self is involved. A laboratory task can never matter enough to become a test of the self. At the other extreme, professional education is always a test of the self. The process it sets up must ultimately engage the self as a whole and must penetrate deeply into the existing structure of the self until a new organization has been achieved.

Three stages of this fundamental learning process can be marked out, each presenting a special set of problems. In the first stage appear the reactions of the individual to the learning situation in any cross section of time. I believe this can be most helpfully comprehended as one aspect of the part-whole problem which underlies all the movements of the organism in use of and in reaction to its environment. The types of problems which can be studied on this level are those which have to do with the way the individual enters into a learning situation, whether he feels the teacher to be using pressure or giving help, how much he can learn from what is given and how much he must do himself, to what extent he can learn positively and to what extent negatively, the effect of resistance, and how the activity of the teacher can be related to the learner's movement.

A second stage of the process can be defined when the process is internalized and the will has accepted its own essential activity in giving direction and form to the part-whole movements in the total organization of the self. These movements do not appear clearly in the immediate situation but require extent of time to be convincing. This problem can be seen as an aspect of the problem of growth and individual creativity about which little is understood.

A final stage can be described when the process eventuates into form and organization which can operate as firmly as structure or be projected in attitudes and behavior as tools of the self. Problems of importance here have to do with the establishment and utilization of limits in learning situations.

These three stages will be illustrated and discussed in the material of supervision which is the content of this book. I have further attempted to present the basis for understanding the part-whole reactions in learning in a more abstract statement of this problem as a problem of change and movement apart from content in Chapter 1. I realize that such a description is open to every possible criticism from those who are interested in scientific accuracy and that it becomes purely hypothetical in the early physiological experience where I have purposely placed it to separate this picture of movement as widely as possible from the concrete learning experience in supervision. If the chapter conveys some feeling for the part-whole movement of the self determined by fundamental and individual patterns in its way of using the outside object in early parental relationships and in the learning processes from kindergarten to professional school, it will serve its purpose.

2. THE DYNAMICS OF THE SELF IN EARLY EXPERIENCE

The Organism as a Whole: Its Constant Movement

To understand learning as an organic process it is valuable to begin with the concept of the organism as a whole in terms of which the self must be thought of as a dynamic system, never static and never completely closed while life lasts. In constant flux throughout its own growth changes, it seeks balance and equilibrium which is achieved momentarily, only to be broken up again into new movement by energy or impulse contributed by change within or by the impact of force impinging from without. We may describe an organism's movement from three points of view:—first, as it is a system of highly active forces which are in constant motion to control each other and the environment, a system which changes radically in its total organization by a growth process which operates steadily as a disintegrating as well as an integrating force; second, as it reacts in contact with an environment which it must make use of at every point to sustain its own life and equilibrium, taking in sustenance here, unburdening itself here and there. Thirdly, we have to consider the movements set up within the organism by the action upon it of other organisms in constant traffic with it in pursuit of their own ends.

This movement can be comprehended in its most abstract terms by the fundamental law of motion—"a system tends to change so as to minimize an external disturbance"—a law which holds throughout the universe in every realm of phenomena, on the physical, physiological, psychological, and social levels. The application of this law to psychological phenomena would lead us to expect, around every point of change, movement that is made up of ambivalent forces pulling in opposite directions, forces of aggression and resistance.[1] Since change is inevitable, the individual is in constant movement and conflict, forever striving for a balance which can never be maintained for living forces.

This balance is portrayed in emotional terms as fulfillment and peace for the individual, equality and harmony in the group, and projected beyond this world of struggle and conflict to an ideal world beyond. On the other hand, this goal of fulfillment and perfection threatens as much as it allures. Achieved momentarily, it becomes a trap which ensnares and must be broken through at any cost. There is real fear of happiness which does not end, of satisfaction which contains no flaw, of unchanging love. Reality is instinctively and rightly felt to inhere in change rather than in the perfect whole. So the process of living may be felt as a movement in search of wholes which break themselves up into parts each of which has power to seek insistently a new whole which again splits up into dynamic parts unendingly.[2]

The Organism as a Whole: Its Principle of Self-Determination

Through this stream of change in each individual life, there remains a deep principle of self-determination, an identity convincing to other people and to the person himself. This principle for which every name is misleading, call it will, ego or self, is fundamentally resistive to change from without and is even slow to recognize as its own and accept responsibility for any process of change from within. Its fear of loss of its own identity and control may inhibit even its normal growth process. It seeks its own likeness in the world outside, selecting elements here and there that can adhere to it without changing the unique organization which sustains it as a separate self unlike every other self in the universe. It fights to maintain a whole at any cost, to defend itself against being made a part of any whole alien to its own. This principle of self-determination operates to produce some degree of cohesion, organization and stability within a total self which is in constant contact with the forces about it. Its own needs entangle it with other selves. Their needs in turn create new needs and active traffic goes on between them. Control may go to the self with the stronger organization. This relationship may enrich the individual who yields his own organization to it and may not threaten him with loss of self unless the other individual asserts a difference or puts out a demand which forces the first back into a sense of himself as different. Against this difference the individual will react defensively to protect himself from an alien element.

Even the immature self of the child, highly unstable in its organization, exhibits amazing strength and tenacity in pursuit of its own ends. It moves in and about its environment, feeling itself into some situations, putting itself over forcibly on others, in each case spanning the gap between itself and the strange outside with a bridge over which it can travel. The child goes out to other selves who welcome his advances and who never become too threatening in theirs—people who will pay attention to his feats, who will listen while he talks, who play with him or tell him stories in a way that makes him feel comfortable. No line can be drawn between himself and these other selves at times when he is most united with them.

The Self Defined as the Central Point of Particular Experiences

To understand the movement of the self it will be more illuminating and perhaps even more accurate to think of the self of the child as a movable point lodged at the center of each experience in which he participates. He is nursing at the breast and his experience initiated and organized by his need contains himself and the mother in a whole which obliterates his sense of need and separateness. He is playing with a younger child, bossing the younger in every movement, and we can believe that he feels himself, his own plan and purpose, the center of this activity and the other child merely an instrument in his hands, an annex to himself. When this same child participates in the play of older children, if he can actually lend himself to their plans and become a part of them, the total experience may again become the whole in which his own self finds meaning. As an adult, he will move into a relationship along the path that has become most natural to him, making use of the other person to sustain the role he has chosen for himself. It will be the rare occasion on which he will stop to define himself separately as a part of, or distinct from, an experience.[3]

The Movement of the Self in Projection and Identification

I am borrowing two terms "projection" and "identification" which have been widely used in psychoanalytic literature, to describe the movements of the self in relating itself to objects and forces in its environment. In using these terms, I hope this point of view will not be identified with psychoanalytic interpretations of the child's early relationships which it is far from representing. I am concerned here to develop a picture of the movements of the self in relationship as a whole-part problem. From this point of view the experience of the child at any moment constitutes a whole within which the self is being defined. Through the movements of projection the self organizes external elements around its own center; through identification it merges itself into some other organization. I should like to illustrate these movements, first, on the simplest level of physiological need in the infant, and second, on more complex levels in later development where behavior has acquired psychological and emotional value for the complex organization of the developed psyche.

Projection on the Physiological Level

On the physiological level, in the uterus, the experience of the foetus is one of almost perfect wholeness maintained in a physiological relation with another organism. This experience must change and enlarge as physical growth proceeds until birth which breaks into the whole so cataclysmically that all feeling of wholeness may be shattered forever. After birth, each separate organ may strive for its own existence, for some union of itself with some element which will relieve tension. The lungs must find air, the mouth must achieve a relation to milk that the stomach may be filled, bladder and bowels will empty themselves automatically. Each experience is, in a sense, a partialization, a reaction of a single organ of the body, but in a truer sense it is a use of an organ in the service of the entire organism for the sake of establishing a whole again. In sucking milk from breast or bottle, the infant incorporates into himself an outside object thereby affecting a relationship with that object which becomes the center of his existence. He projects his need upon the object and the whole or the relationship immediately becomes the total experience. Where the object is the mother's breast, the relationship develops in an alternation of projection and identification as the child first projects his need and then submits to the mother's necessities in making use of the breast. If he cannot achieve the breast he may project his total discomfort in crying and shrieking in an effort to get the discomfort outside himself. If satisfied, he may project this feeling in gurgling and cooing. Once outside, his feeling is no longer himself alone, but a new thing to be played with, worked on, experimented with. Any of these expressions of feeling may call out response which sets up a new center in which the baby may operate, as when his cooing brings a laugh and baby talk. Then the relationship itself, the play of response, has become his interest. But this is a secondary effect. The original and primary aim of expression of feeling is to put it outside, to break it up. Kept inside as a whole it is too much and moves to its own change, its destruction or its elaboration. If crying brings the mother to the crib to minister to his wants, crying soon becomes a projection of need or of will to control the mother to get what he wants in order to reestablish a whole of his own making.

Urination and defecation may be seen as projections in which a product or a part of the organism itself is put outside, regardless of environment. On a purely physiological and segmental level these products are excreted automatically without problem. But as the organization of organic segments of the body is effected in the service of the whole organism, each segment and each product may assume a meaning beyond its physiological function in the whole-part problem of the organism.[4] It becomes of tremendous moment to the organism to control its own output in these segments, as to time, place and conditions. The inevitable entrance of the mother's effort to control the movements of the segments sets up new centers in which the child struggles for control against the mother's effort to dominate.

These illustrations may suffice to give content to the word "projection" on this level of physiological needs and tensions. It has been seen as the organism's effort to throw off some element. This element may be a part of the organism which is causing tension, as the products of the bladder or intestine; it may be feeling expressed in crying or cooing, or a need which annexes another object and incorporates it into the organism as in sucking. While this removal of parts of itself is a natural biological process essential to life, from a psychological point of view, it spells loss and separation which is the fundamental source of fear.[5] Consequently the determined efforts to control the projection, as in the use of bladder where the child's behavior so often seems to have back of it the attitude, "I will have this relief when I want it, freely and fully" (enuresis); or in the use of the intestines where the attitude often expresses a more complicated control, as "I will hold on to this product until I am ready to give it up" (constipation).

Withdrawal of the breast and weaning precipitate new tensions, feelings of incompleteness and fear of loss of control. Driven by need and fear, the organism reacts with determined strivings for restoral of these lost parts outside or inside the organism. As the breast or bottle moves away and is no longer at the beck and call of the infant's feeling of need of them, he is forced to accept new organizations of the whole and new limitations in his control over it. How he finally balances the parts in the whole-part problem of weaning, whether he feels the center to be in the mother who comes when called, in the bottle or food she brings, or in his own cry of persuasion or demand is very important for his late use of himself in relationships.

The movements of projection as observed in these early activities of the baby bring about constantly changing wholes of activity or feeling in each of which the self of the child is involved in some way. This movement has its own rhythm, different in each individual. The natural pattern may be so characteristic or it may become so set through early experience that succeeding experience cannot perceptibly modify its way of using the environment in this part-whole movement. Certain factors in this pattern are organic and spontaneous, others seem to appear in reaction to environmental factors. The problem has successfully defied scientific analysis. Obviously an individual can never become aware of his own pattern except comparatively if experience forces him to recognize a pattern different from his own. If this experience and the resulting sense of difference is sufficiently important to him, it may stimulate him into further self-consciousness. Consciousness of movement itself, and of self and object as phases of movement, is rarely achieved in psychological development and then only by years of self-discipline and self-conscious responsibility for one's activity in relation to others.

Identification on the Physiological Level

Definitions of objects proceed at points at which the world outside affords satisfaction for a want and later refuses satisfaction where it had been given previously. Even pure expressions of feeling which seek and receive no response, and the activities of elimination alone, as projections regardless of the environment, may define the environment to a certain degree in that wherever a part of the self is projected that point may become a center of interest in relation to which surrounding objects are organized. In nursing from a bottle the child can project his want and satisfy it without comeback from the object. But in nursing the mother her response creates a new center in which definition proceeds. He is forced to deal with certain differences, with parts which must be recognized and taken in to modify his whole or which force him to abandon his center and become a part of another whole. "Identification" may serve as a convenient term to describe this opposite swing from projection. It implies a taking in of something which can be accepted because it feels like the self but whose differences modify the whole in some ways. It may occur as a secondary result of a projection on to an object to which the self yields its own whole and becomes a part. The intake of milk is the simplest illustration of this process. Here need is first projected, the breast is seized upon as a part of the self, and in the satisfaction which results from the achievement of object and milk, the child yields to the whole which the mother's behavior and attitude set up and becomes "identified" with her. Around points of projected need and satisfying-depriving response the child's focus must move outside himself and the balance may be thrown completely in the other direction so that the other person becomes the center of the circle into which the child is drawn. His feeling is one of wholeness but the process through which it is attained is a breaking down of the wholeness originating within the self, a yielding of himself to a larger and more compelling whole.

Identification can take place only with an object which satisfies need or accepts projection. It may be a projection on to some fragment of the object only which has use for the projector. The one who projects may continue to use only the part of the second object which symbolized what he wanted and so is yielding to a whole which feels like more than himself but actually is only an extension of himself. In this case the individual may have an experience of self-expression and release, but he takes in nothing of the reality of the object he makes use of. Definition of the environment through identification takes place as the individual who projects can accept an identification with the other object as a whole and can bear to feel differences in the whole with which he is identified as parts of the other are projected back on him. Two people in love project on each other, perhaps united by the feeling of need, of readiness for love, which each indicates. On this projection of a self each puts out his feeling which radiates over the other object like a halo. Inevitably with the passing of time different needs, attitudes and feelings arise in each and may be projected on to the other. The original unity may be shattered around a pinpoint of difference and whether unity can be restored and maintained depends on many things, chiefly on the extent of real psychological likeness which exists.

Enlargement and enrichment of the self can be seen as the result of the process of identification as the individual takes into his own psychological structure aspects of the different wholes of which he has become a part. As the self becomes organized through separation and deprivation experiences, it gains greater awareness of its own wants as inside and the objects which satisfy, oppose, deny or punish as outside. As this takes place, the physiological level of impulse, organic tensions, and feelings is passing into the psychological level of will and emotion. With the recognition of the capacity of the object to frustrate come the conscious emotions of fear and anger, acute realizations of the separation between the self and the world outside, of the pain of partial experiences. There is no fear as long as there is perfect wholeness within the self or between the self and the environment. The processes of projection and identification still carry the movement in which the self seeks to maintain itself as a separate entity, while it is building itself up by adding what it needs, sloughing off what threatens its structure if kept inside. These movements determine all the activities of life from physiological activity to the most complicated processes of thinking, from early learning reactions to creative expression.

Projection and Identification on the Psychological Level Developing into Patterns of Relationship and of Learning

In the school situation, we can observe the child's activity as constant movement in these two phases, giving out, taking in, projecting, identifying, putting his own plan over on a group, becoming a part of another's plan. Work and play, lessons and sport, friendship and enmity have taken on the pattern of these fundamental movements, permitting children to relate themselves to the group in terms of leadership or following, of dominance or submission. The child wanders about the school environment always selective in relation to what surrounds him. What will have meaning for him so that he stops and works in it for a while, what will he pass by unseeing? He lingers near a group of children in a game and, feeling his body move in participation with theirs, is drawn in more and more by the pull of his identification with their activity. He will turn over the pages of a book and find some picture which for reasons unfathomable to the teacher compels his attention. He is very selective among people: some have less value for him than inanimate objects; others he avoids with obvious distrust and dislike; with some he seems simply and quietly at home; others he pursues aggressively and possessively.

Some children will reach out into experience eagerly along one avenue, hesitating, perhaps blocking completely in others. Some will use hands and body actively and freely; others will use speech, words, books and be too awkward to succeed in large muscle movement. To some, figures have meaning; others are lost here, but become at home with words. Individual differences in intellectual, sensory and physical equipment operate to some extent in determining selection, but to a greater degree the selection and development of interest is determined by the fact that attention is focused at the point where the object comes alive to the child as it permits him to project his need and work on it in relationship, or as it interferes with his purpose in some way which stimulates him to further effort to conquer it.

Even in the early years while the self is relatively undifferentiated and unstable, characteristic ways of learning make themselves apparent to those who know the child well. One is quick, one is slow; one takes help readily, another must do everything alone; one works positively in pursuit of his own interests, the other only negatively in opposition to others. These differences do not depend on intellectual equipment alone, but also on the way the child uses his equipment and his relation to the learning situation. They seem to be fundamental differences growing out of each individual's different ways of solving his whole-part problem as these ways become patterned in experience. Children bring these learning patterns to school with them and the wise teacher adjusts her teaching to them, as far as a school system built to promote a uniform way of learning and standardized results will permit. Children learn to adjust to these requirements and standards with a minimum of change in their essential selves. They learn to say the words, to go with the group in action. The school constitutes the whole and the average child rests upon this wholeness, finding his place in it as part with only enough protest to sustain his difference. There is real security for him in his relation to a whole which is greater than his individual difference and striving, a whole by which he is sustained as well as limited. The exceptional child, the creative as well as the neurotic, does not so easily accept this limitation put upon him by the school situation. He may not be able to work in it or to learn of it except as he may do it negatively.

Reactions of the Self to Education Interpreted as Pressure

The total effect of a public school system in its elementary grades as it works for a standardized product is to exert pressure. As pressure it is interpreted and used by its pupils. As pressure it can be kept outside and conformed to more or less cheerfully. But because it does not really carry the child's own choice and positive will, there is a split in the self which permits him to be educated against his will while the will engages positively in other pursuits. Athletics, for instance, may carry the real will to learn in devotion to which the child will submit to a self-chosen discipline more severe than that imposed by any school system. On the other hand, there may be no will organization or expression except what is manifested in a negative resistance to pressure. The child's life may move in impulsive expression or in secret fantasy which comes to no organization which the child can project and pursue as an educational goal. The real self may be withdrawn from educational influence and does not educate itself. The child may protect this self from change and from invasion, while at the same time he distrusts it. It is the "bad" self which he can neither give up nor incorporate into the whole self.

With a change from elementary school to high school, or from high school to college if the child goes from his own choice, particularly if it involves sacrifice or a decision to go against another's resistance, a change in the child's relation to learning may appear. His will may be engaged positively to back his own choice and may carry him into a freer and more positive use of himself in which real change and learning may take place. Remnants of the impulsive self, however, still regarded as "bad" may be carried on into adult life, refusing education and modification until the end.

Summary

This chapter has attempted to place the problem of learning within the larger problem of the development of the self in its part-whole movement in reaction to, and in use of, the environment. It was recognized that from the beginning, on the physiological level of experience, each individual manifests a characteristic pattern of movement in projection and identification phases which is in some aspects organic and unchangeable. Other aspects of pattern become set in early experience. Change, or learning, seems to take place within this spontaneous flow of projection-identification activity at two main points:—first, at the point where a projection fails or is broken up by the environment and when the individual can take back his projection as his own, accept it as a part and work through it into a new whole which takes account of the factor of difference in the environment. A second point at which change or learning takes place is where identification with a larger whole brings into the self new factors not too different to be accepted as part of the own self and which can then function inside the self to enrich and stimulate change. These learning experiences soon become crystallized into patterns of learning which characterize school behavior from the beginning.

We have stated that "school" functions as outside the self to force the child into the mould which society has set for him. As it sets out to teach him and to change him he feels it as pressure, accepting it irresponsibly, conforming where he must with change in the superficial layers of himself, retaining other selves apart from educational influence. High school and college, if voluntarily chosen, may bring more of the self into an active responsible relation to education.

3. THE DEVELOPMENT OF A PROFESSIONAL SELF IN SOCIAL CASEWORK TRAINING

Professional Education Calls for a Professional Self

By the end of high school for many children, of college for others, formal education has accomplished its purpose. The child has subjected himself to the maximum of pressure laid down and controlled by the environment. Work and family relationships will put new demands upon him but in more informal and personal ways. From now on he is accepted as he is. He may be directed, criticized, nagged and scolded by those closely related to him, but no organized effort is made to train him or change him unless he puts himself voluntarily under a new educational influence. If the individual chooses to follow a trade or a profession, however, a new educational process is set in operation. The extent of this education will depend on how much of the self is engaged in this process and the pattern of learning which the individual has developed in previous experience. If he chooses a trade such as carpentry or plumbing, for example, he will be required to learn many new things and to develop skill in doing them, but this knowledge and skill may be taken on as additions to his equipment and he may still remain essentially the same person in his relationships and his expression of himself. Obviously something very different happens if he chooses a profession such as law or medicine, teaching or nursing. A longer, more rigorous training discipline is required, greater responsibilities are undertaken. A new level of development is foreseen in making the professional choice and if the training is persisted in, this development is accomplished and a professional self emerges with new ways of relating itself to other people, with responsibilities, attitudes and behaviors that are outside himself. So there is carried over into professional education something of the resistance to educational pressure which is so characteristic of learning reactions in elementary and secondary education.

The Demands of Social Casework Training on the Self

Social casework has not achieved the full professional status of older professions but it has established a recognized, required training discipline on a postgraduate basis. Only two years of this training have been clearly laid down in the curricula of professional schools but this training period is being extended in a few schools to a program for full doctorate work. In casework agencies of good standards, the training process is carried on for years beyond the school period through the process of supervision.

Professional training in social casework includes three kinds of equipment: (1) knowledge which the professional school supplies in its classes; (2) skills which are taught in the field work experience;[1] and (3) the controlled use of the capacity to relate oneself and one's service to people in need. A student may bring to the school an interest in helping other people and a will to learn how to relate himself to their problems, but his capacity to help is a very limited and bungling tool until he has undergone severe discipline, accepted change and achieved reorganization in himself to the end that his thinking and action may become truly responsible. The beginnings of this change must take place in the two years of professional school experience, but it is by no means finished in this brief time.

Young people who choose to enter upon a profession which carries the helping function, to identify with this profession, and to develop the capacity to help, initiate in themselves a process of development which goes beyond what is required for the average person. The demands of social casework as a field of work cannot be satisfied by a use of the self as it has already developed, well-adjusted and adequate as it may be to the demands of the life situations in which it has been formed. The patterns of learning which this self may have found satisfactory in school and college are upset by the impact with obstacles that do not yield to their attack. New patterns must be built up slowly and with the struggle which any new important adjustment requires. This process of change, adjustment and reorganization must become conscious with the student and realized as his own process of change and reorganization if he is to make the best possible utilization of it for his understanding of other people's struggles and his capacity to help them. We are accustomed to speak of this process of change and reorganization of the self as a growth process, but in using this phrase it is important to bear in mind that it is not a natural growth process such as is required for biological maturity with its accompanying psychological and emotional maturity. On the contrary, it is a stimulated growth process brought about by the setting up of the function of helping. The fact that an individual chooses to prepare himself for this function indicates that some part of his already developed self is expressed in this choice, but the extent to which this self must be remade in working through to the real acceptance and use of this function is something he cannot know in advance. Nor could anyone who has gone through this experience tell him to his satisfaction. There is a genuine unknown here which must be accepted both by the applicant and by the school. The school, even with the finest, most careful application procedures of reference and interview, can only succeed in eliminating certain extreme types of applicants which experience with many students has proved unadapted to this educational process. The majority, however, will have to try it out and bear the uncertainty of the lack of guarantee of success. By the end of a first semester, both the school and the student should know whether he is able to sustain himself in this process.

An emphasis on this lack of guarantee of success, the uncertainty which must be accepted as characteristic of the initial stages of this

experience, may serve to bring out in clear relief one sharp difference between this learning experience and the more ordinary learning experiences of life. The accepted and approved attitude towards
learning is that it is within the learner's control. "If at first you don't
succeed, try, try again," emphasizes this positive side, the under-own-
control aspect of learning. We have been afraid of the negative aspects so that they are consistently minimized in any picture of the
learning process. In order to get them in their proper perspective as
of equal importance with the positive aspects, it may be necessary to
over-emphasize them in this picture. The determination expressed in,
"I *will* learn," sets out to conquer the situation, to embrace it and
make it one's own. It may win its way through to some kind of possession of the situation or it may destroy some part of the situation
or some part of itself in this attack. True learning may require all the
strength one has and all one's will concentrated on the other object
to be learned, to be made one's own or a part of one's self, but equally it necessitates a willingness to yield to the strength and difference
of the other. If the new learning situation is very foreign and strange
and one has no reason to feel confidence in one's relation to it, the
will to take hold and make the situation one's own may be lost,
temporarily at least, in the overwhelming sense of the power of the
situation. It may become a matter of being overpowered by, rather
than an acceptance of one's own will to yield to, the differences in
the situation. This is strikingly the case in the first stages in a school
of social work and results in a predominance of negative reactions,
of fear and resistance, present in all first reactions in new learning
situations but more insistent and apparent under these circumstances.

Three Aspects of Social Casework in Relation
to Which Learning Must Take Place

In order to analyze a student's reactions in learning in the field of
social casework, it is useful to distinguish three aspects of the work
and analyze the effect of each upon a learner. First, we may put together the routine elements of the job, such as learning to be on time,
to hand in reports and expense accounts, to work in a systematic,
orderly fashion. The kind of responsibility to be developed here is
not essentially different from that required in any job except as it is
related to the responsibility required for the second aspect of the job,
the carrying out of the essential helping function of the agency in

services to clients. The third aspect of the casework job is supervision, the way provided by which new workers are to learn. I should like to illustrate different levels of change and learning in reaction to these three aspects.

1. Learning Reactions in Relation to the Case Records and Routine Procedures

The record is for the use of other workers who depend upon having its facts available and up to date. The student has to learn how to use the record and how to incorporate his work on the case into the record. To do this he needs to understand and use office files and stenographers and must fit into the office time schedule. Very frequently a student will fail to get his dictation ready in time for use. The supervisor will treat this as a single piece of behavior. The student may not have understood; there may be a real excuse. If this is the case, he will take responsibility for this behavior when it is pointed out to him and do it differently. Suppose, on the other hand, the behavior is repeated. The supervisor may well assume that this is a point where a newcomer in social work might easily fail to be aware of the importance of the record and his part in it. The student's attitude towards the record or towards his own work in the case will need to change before he can appreciate the need of dictating. This could be discussed with the student; the use of the record illustrated. The student might admit that his own findings did not seem worth while, or that they seemed too intimate and too personal to be included in a typed record. The whole attitude towards recording what the client gives to the worker comes up for discussion and the student may even in one conference find this attitude changing to the point where he is able to dictate. More experience is necessary before this changed attitude is really stable and his own so that he operates on a basis of true appreciation of the value of the record.

In the case of a third student, this discussion of the record may seem to be intellectually understood but the behavior persists unchanged. His knowledge and his action are in conflict and do not support each other. The supervisor is forced to assume that some resistance to learning is operating against the new knowledge. It may be no more than a confusion growing out of the student's fear and uncertainty in the whole strange situation and if so, it will change with time and more experience that gives the student a foothold in this job and with the supervisor's ability to wait and her skill in clarifying without putting pressure. If she puts too much pressure on this resistance by her desire to change it, no matter whether she expresses this in encouragement and suggestions or nagging and insistence, she will become aware of the negative force expressed in this behavior. It has the feeling of a refusal, or will-not-to-learn. She may try withdrawing her pressure and may find some students released from their resistance and able to take over their own responsibility at this point. Or she may point out the resistance to the student and he may be able to feel the embarrassment his behavior causes other people in the situation and change it.

There will be a fourth student, on the other hand, whose behavior will not be affected by time or the supervisor's efforts, whether positive or negative. The attitude involved here seems to be a total attitude towards time for which the student has never become responsible, not caused by this situation but appearing in it. The student may explain his delay with, "I never have been able to get any work done on time. I am always late."

I should like to parallel this illustration with one from the child's early learning experiences to bring out the same problem. A child entering nursery school or kindergarten is required to learn to put back on the shelves materials and toys he has been using when the bell for closing time rings. The teacher shows how this should be done. A new child may pick up this behavior very quickly by listening to the teacher or watching her and the other children. He may forget on the next day, but a word or a reminder from the teacher may be enough to send him back eagerly to do what is expected. This behavior may be very superficially oriented and may drop off in the next classroom where different rules of order prevail. Another child may be slower to pick up what is suggested and repeatedly leave his things lying about until a serious talk with the teacher or a catastrophe to some of his treasured playthings may bring him to a different realization of his responsibility for this bit of order. This behavior would seem to be taking root in a deeper level than is the behavior of the first child. When the child cares about finding his things in shape to be used and realizes the relation between this and putting them away properly, a real attitude towards order is being developed. A third child, on the other hand, will not learn in spite of explanation and suggestion, rewards or punishments. This may be a problem of his reaction to a new situation and the strange demands it puts upon him, his resistance to the new teacher, or his necessity to be different from the other children. These factors may all change with time and wise handling on the part of the teacher. The child may work through his resistance in this situation and become as responsible for his behavior as the other children. A fourth child, however, and there is always at least one such child in every group, will never succeed in getting the things put away on time. He may seem to try as hard as the others, but it is as if he struggled against a greater force than his own conscious desire to finish with the others. He will be sent back to do it over and watched to see that it is done, he will often be helped by the others in the friendliest spirit, or sometimes derided because he holds up the whole class from recess. Such a child, the experienced teacher knows, will go through school and through life, defeating his own ends and getting in the way of other people in pursuit of theirs. "Johnny is like that" will be said of him with kindly tolerance or with irritation and annoyance, depending on whether his other characteristics are sufficiently lovable to excuse him or not.

In these two illustrations we see four levels of learning behavior: —first, we see behavior taken on in response to the custom or the requirement of a situation, motivated superficially, easily put on and as easily dropped off, learned and unlearned without much effort. It is an easy adaptation to circumstances and makes no demands for change in the learner. Second, we see behavior growing out of a change in attitude towards a particular situation. This change in attitude engages more of the self and will continue to determine behavior that is reliable and stable. It may continue to grow and involve more and more of the self, influencing more attitudes and determining new ranges of behavior in many different sorts of situations. Attitudes that determine neatness and order and promptness and care for one's own and other people's possessions may all be involved here. In the third place, we see an individual blocked by fear and resistance to the new and strange, refusing to take steps which will relate him to the new situation. The whole organism seems to be blocked negatively against the situation or the person who as teacher or supervisor may symbolize the power he feels to be over him. Obviously this is not a matter of his conscious purpose or intention because as soon as he becomes free enough to use his intelligence he will change this futile and obstructive behavior.

It is difficult to find a word which expresses the whole self which is involved here as clearly and intelligibly as behavior and attitude describe the parts of the self which are involved in the first two learning reactions I have illustrated. The word "will" as used by Otto Rank[2] is the only word I have been able to find that is truly psychological and that carries the full meaning. This usage is different from the commonly understood concept of the will or the meaning which it has been given in the criticisms which have stricken it from modern psychologies. It is not the moralistic, virtuous will of religion or the partial, structural will of the older faculty psychology nor is it the "illusion of volition" which Harvey Fergusson so ably criticizes in *Modern Man*.[3] Under the term "will" Rank describes the most fundamental reality of psychological experience, the very essence of the self which underlies all expressions of that self, a dynamic concept of energy and motion. Thought of apart from its content, its forms, its objects of projection, it is pure force and movement, too total, too alive, too abstract to become conscious. It can come to consciousness only as it is in operation, positively or negatively, in relation to another will or an object, or as it operates as an organizing or integrating force on parts of the self treated as separate forces. It is impossible to handle as idea or formulate as concept since it is essentially the life principle itself. Awareness of one's willing self comes ordinarily only when the will is expressed positively and in partial ways and in specific situations. The will to succeed, to get what one wants, the will that decides one way rather than another and having decided carries out a series of acts which accomplish its end—these are well understood. The will in these situations is positively engaged, specifically and partially expressed. In most cases the will so engaged is socially approved and so can be accepted. If, however, the end the will seeks involves harm to another person, it is not so easy to be conscious of and responsible for this will. It is even more difficult to admit the use of the will which is intentionally negative and destructive.

These words "positive" and "negative" are not used moralistically but simply to describe opposite poles of life forces. One is a binding, uniting force, the other tends to break up into parts, to separate, to destroy. Both are essential phases of life and growth. Neither has any ethical or moral value except as these values become felt through appreciating the effect on the other person or the object on which the force is expressed. When the other person or object is taken into consideration, either use of the will may turn out to be harmful to the other person, as either may put something on him which is not his own and which he may not want. Pressure, for instance, to go another's way, to join an enterprise, to go on a party may be well intended, positively motivated but offensive to the other person's mood or purpose. I shall use positive in this sense to describe the will which is outgoing and uniting, creative or constructive, without regard to what the effect on the other person may be. The negative will, the "evil" will, feels pain and separation and its expression intends separation to whatever is related to it. If it can act and become aware of its action in a partial specific situation which does not involve too much consequence in damage to the situation or pain to another person, it may be possibe for it to move, through a feeling reaction of guilt and regret, to taking responsibility for the consequences of its action and on to a positive will phase which includes more sensitivity to the other and more responsibility for the self. This is what happens in the case of the third student or the third child whose resistance to the new situation has blocked it off in a separating and negative phase which permitted no positive outgoing impulses to come through. The child cannot take help or make the effort to do what he should. The student persists in his refusal to get the record material in on time. If this behavior can be recognized as an expression of negative will put out against the teacher or supervisor in so far as he is holding up the class procedure or the agency's use of the record, the student may be able to get the feeling of his own will through his sense of what he is doing to the other person. In this lies the value of criticism or punishment for the individual if it can be related specifically to the "bad" act and not to the whole will or the whole person. Through the feeling of being surprised or shocked at his own behavior and sorry for the annoyance it has caused, a new phase of positive feeling and will is reached which may take hold of the problem and make up for lost time in doing correctly all that is required by the situation.

When a student reaches the place in his professional development where the record is completely accepted as an essential procedure, where he dictates into it to carry the continuity of his own responsible work on the case, the word "will" must be used again to express the positive organization and use of the self at this point. From the standpoint of this relation to the record, the first reactions in all the illustrations now appear to be impulsive and undisciplined. Even where the behavior was correct in the first place, it was facile and adapted on too superficial a basis to be reliable until it became incorporated into the self. When this change begins to work in the self, fundamental learning is taking place. The original impulsive behavior, characteristic attitude, and blind will in its negative and positive expressions have been checked by other forces. The will has become conscious of itself and of the other factors in the situation which its behavior was affecting. It has become responsible for itself and has organized the impulsive reactions into a stable reliable tool.

Feeling may be defined here as the moment of awareness of movement initiating in one's self or in reaction to environmental pressure. These moments of feeling indicate the break-up in habitual pattern and organization in which change is beginning to take place. They must be utilized by the teacher and the pupil constructively for the ends of the learning process.[4]

In the case of the fourth child or student, however, a problem is presented which is insoluble. The student says, "I am never able to get my work or my papers in on time." In other words he is saying, "I will not get them in on time." What is indicated here is a negative use of the will in a way that blocks it off from movement or change at this point. The implied attitude in its bearing on the teacher or supervisor is, "I am as I am and you cannot change me." There often is no negative intent to the other person in this, though the effect of the behavior may be most upsetting to the whole situation. It seems clearer to see it as related to the protection of the own self, a reaction pattern that has grown up to defend the self from change or movement at some point. It seems lacking in awareness of any outside person or object who may be affected. Obviously no learning can take place at the point where the learner cuts himself off so totally and so unconsciously from any relation to the teaching situation. It can only be affected if some particular piece of behavior can be recognized as related and the student can feel and see the relationship and want to become responsible for changing it. He cannot accept responsibility for his total will at any point, certainly not until he can become aware of it as partial expressions of his force exerted at spots where he can see the consequences and work on the results.

I have used these illustrations perhaps too exhaustively in order to bring out the meaning of the terms behavior, attitude, feeling, and will in its positive and negative phases, and to show different levels of change in learning reactions. I hope there emerges from this some picture of how responsibility for behavior, attitude and will can develop in this learning experience. I have purposely selected the simplest level of experience in the casework field, the relation to the record as objective procedure. In a sense it is the most routine aspect of the job one can find; in another sense, as any caseworker knows, the record holds more than routine importance. Routine or not, the record possesses the power to pick out a spot where the will of the worker may gather itself together to fight external pressure or to protect itself from internal change.

2. *Levels of Learning in Relation to Functioning as a Caseworker*

The next type of illustration leads into the major acitivity of the casework job, the activity of giving help to people at some point of need. Students are assigned for their field work experiences to different casework agencies offering different services for different needs—relief-giving agencies, public pension funds, family societies, child-placing agencies, school counselling agencies, child guidance clinics and medical social work departments in hospitals. This field work experience throws the student into immediate contact with the individuals and families who are obtaining help or who, as applicants, are seeking it. Since his relation to these cases is in some degree a responsible one, this contact precipitates him into an expression of himself, engages his will as he responds to demands and needs as they are put upon him and as he projects in return his own will upon them. On the surface, it would seem that the will he puts forth should be no more than the carrying out of the function of the agency. The actual giving of relief, the arrangement for convalescent care, taking the child who is to be placed to the foster home, would be simple objective instances of points where the student might be acting in this way. But it is the decisions that lead up to the activities and the way in which they are carried out which constitute the essential quality of the casework job and a student must be related to these decisions and to the way they are expressed from the beginning of his training. An office boy can be trained to carry around the relief checks safely. A boy in training to be a "visitor" in a relief agency must wonder and question on his first visits why this family gets relief, why another gets less; must meet the family's requests with more interest than the office boy will feel. The child-placing agency may use a chauffeur to take children to new homes and bring them to clinics. Of such a worker no more is expected than responsibility for getting children to and fro safely and happily. The student who is in training for social work, however, must become interested in the child, curious about the home. Why is this home selected for this child, what will happen to this child in the home?—these questions arise in his first contact and take him at once into deeper relation to the situation than the office boy's or the chauffeur's who are carrying out a function of the agency on a superficial level.

We will follow this relationship to the case with the student in the child-placing agency for illustration to see what must be learned before responsible action can be expected. As the student becomes more and more interested in the child whose placement he is to carry out, he will naturally bring into play for his deeper understanding of the child's personality and experience, his own background of childhood experience. If he is in his early twenties, these experiences are very accessible and many are still actually present. A bond through feeling like the child, or in identification with him, is very easily established on some basis real or unreal. With this feeling of likeness between them, it is easy for the student to project upon the child many more of his own characteristics, to make the child into a replica of himself. As he takes the child with whom he is identified in this way to clinics and does the various things necessary while he is in a temporary home to prepare him for a permanent home, the relationship becomes stronger and may grow to have a real basis in the experiences they go through together. Contacts with the foster parents in the temporary home may be determined entirely through the student's identification with the child and may even antagonize the foster parent if the student, over-active on the child's behalf, fails to consider her. To be adequate in this situation, it is necessary for the student to separate himself from his identification with the child sufficiently to see the foster parents also.

In this situation, the student tends to use his own experience, his own attitudes towards parents as these have developed in his own childhood, as an approach or a bridge as it were, to understanding the new situation. He may get the new situation so tangled up and involved with his own family relationships that his action expresses no more than his own feelings and his own will as called out by his family. I believe this kind of involvement is inevitable in learning how to work with people and relationships. But I am sure that we can help to clarify the issues more quickly for the student, if, as teachers or supervisors, we insist upon emphasizing the new characteristics of the casework situation in which the student is involved instead of encouraging him to work through his own attitudes as they have developed in the past. The learning process that must take place here is the separation of attitudes that relate to the new situation, in this case the child and the foster parents, from the attitudes that belong to the student's own parents. The supervisor facilitates this development, as she by her own attitude and interest remains related to the present casework situation, pointing out what the student is doing here, and so cutting off the escape into the attitudes that belong to an older situation. An occasional student may not be able to reach the level of development required to deal with antagonized foster parents. He may be so much of a child still in his whole way of feeling, thinking and acting that every adult calls out in him a necessity to fight the authority they represent. If this fight persists in spite of every effort to help him to see what he is doing, the student is obviously not ready for the responsibilities involved in social work.

As the student has contacts with more individuals and family relationships, separates them from his own experiences and learns to see them more nearly as they are, independently of his old projections and his own will to do things to them, it becomes clear that the learning process involves a great part of the self, of his attitudes as they have been projected upon objects and figures in his life. New attitudes, as they are being developed here towards new relationships, may reorganize older attitudes towards other objects and individuals. But these changes in personal relationships are by-products of casework training and not its ends. The end is the development of a professional self which can relate itself to people and situations not in terms of its own past experiences, but in terms of the factors in the professional situation. This is not a goal which can be achieved in any training once and for all, but once the goal is recognized and the movement by which one approaches it is felt, it is possible for a student to make progress in every new case in becoming aware of the attitudes which are irrelevant to that situation and which block him from seeing it as it is, and to become responsible for his own feelings and will as he projects them. This means constant change and reorganization of attitudes into responsible and efficient tools of work.

These illustrations of the learning problem have been taken from two aspects of problems in the casework field, one involving the routines of the work in case records, the other the very stuff of the casework job, the human problems with which it deals. The adjustments required of a new student in learning the routine procedures of the agency are not essentially different from that which would be required in any job where he must learn to work as one among many on a staff or in an office. The one respect in which it does differ, the keeping of a record of his own contacts with clients, brings it into the other area of relationships with people in which social casework differs fundamentally from practically every other vocational field in the kind of learning it requires.

3. Learning Reactions to Supervision

I wish to introduce at this point a third aspect of the casework job which will bring into clearer light the quality of this difference. This third aspect is supervision, an essential area of the job to which the student must learn to relate himself in a new way, as he must learn to relate himself to routine procedures and to his clients. Not only has supervision come into being in this field as a convenient way of getting work done and of introducing new workers to their tasks, but supervision of the responsible sort which is offered in connection with a school of social work and in truly professional casework agencies, is the only way in which the student or new worker can get the experience in which the reeducation of his own attitudes and the discipline of his own will can be achieved. The supervisor stands between the worker and his clients, mediating the effect upon the client of the worker's natural spontaneous impulses, providing the student in the conference discussion with the opportunity to express in words his attitudes, his feelings and his plans of action. Through her own responses she starts a process that may lead immediately or later to change of attitudes, to a shift of feeling, or a reconsideration of plan. If everything had to be worked through on the client, no agency could afford to train students.

The student has been in relationship with people all his life and has been expressing himself more or less spontaneously. He has built up patterns of relating himself, ways of using other people. Perhaps he has been self-critical, analytic and self-conscious to a certain degree and feels that he knows himself well enough. This may be true for ordinary purposes, but if he is going to relate himself to people in the professional service of helping, he must become conscious of what he does to them, how he uses them and how they react to him, and how he reacts to their reactions with finer discriminations than he has been able to make hitherto. There is a new level of sensitivity and self-consciousness opened up here which goes beyond his previous experience. It is impossible for the student to proceed far in this direction without the help of another person who has developed awareness and responsibility for his own part in a situation and so can help the student to see and accept his part. The relationship with the supervisor has value in this respect, in that it is actually a new experience in relationship in which the student is required by all the demands of the situation to put out more of his real self than perhaps he has ever done before. The supervisor has superior experience, knowledge and understanding of which he wants to make use and she also represents authority and the power to pass upon his professional progress which he dreads and fights. He fears her knowledge of his reactions before he has control and possession of them himself. These attitudes may not be conscious. They may be covered by the conventional eagerness to learn and the assertion that learning is under one's own voluntary control; but underneath they operate in every person who attempts to work under supervision in this field. They set up a movement in the self, a process of reaction, disorganization and change, which eventually must come through to a reorganization of the self under its own direction and its own control. The detail of this process is the material of the following chapters.

The full gamut of professional training in relation to supervision should include three levels:—first, learning to work under a supervisor; second, learning as an experienced senior worker to work with a supervisor on an equality basis; and third, responsibility for supervising new students and workers. These are three essentialy different experiences, requiring that one relate oneself in different ways, and take different roles in this process. I believe that they represent three levels in development of the professional self, of internal change and experience as well as the acquisition of knowledge, and that each one depends upon the other so that they cannot be learned in reverse order. There would always be exceptions to such a generalization as this, since other experiences might of course substitute for certain aspects of this training experience. Each student brings different capacities and different problems in working under another person's direction, in working on an equal basis with others, and in taking the teaching role in relation to others. But each one has something new to learn, since casework is a new field and the learning situation here has the peculiar and unique form given it by supervision in which learning takes place in a relationship with one person.

No learning process contains more dangers than this one for the reason that since it is a relationship with one person, it may precipitate the student into greater fear and more violent struggle, fear of becoming too dependent on the other person and struggle to maintain independence itself. To some extent this risk is run in every relationship of importance. In friendship and in love, in partnership and in working relationships of any sort, the question is present whether consciously faced and articulated or not:—how much of myself will be risked in this relationship? Will I keep myself intact or will I be changed, will the other person gain control of the situation or can I keep it? The more the self is involved, the more fearful the individual will be of the invasion of the other and the greater will be the necessity to maintain his own control and his own integrity. In ordinary relationships two people take equal chances and each works out his own solutions sometimes in true consideration of the other and sometimes with regard for nothing but the expression of his own will. The supervisory relationship, set up, as it is, for the benefit of the learner with definite forms and known limits, permits the student to risk himself with more concentration of himself than many relationships since it offers the guarantee that he will not be used by it or lost in it. It has its end defined in advance and if he can make use of the process and come through to the end, he will have the experience of finding himself in possession of more of himself than before. Instead of a continuing dependence upon the supervisor which he dreaded there will be built up a new confidence in his own thinking because it has been tried out and modified where it is limited and in error by the greatest test of one's own thinking, the different thinking of another person in the same field of work. The blind struggle for independence born of fear of its precariousness will be reduced by the discovery that one does not lose it but finds an independence which is more reliable as it is rooted now in experience. Occasionally for some people the fear is too great to permit them to try at all, and, unless some other experience outside of training reduces this fear, such a person should not attempt to enter the casework field to help other people. Such a statement makes the capacity to relate oneself to supervision, to take the risks to the organization of oneself involved there, to accept this kind of help from another person, one important criterion of readiness to do social casework. I mean it as

such, but it can never be used as a test situation for applicants for it
will only work as test as it is entered upon really and for a long
enough time, at least several weeks, to work through the initial fear
reaction which every student will feel.

Summary

I have attempted in these two chapters to build up a picture of
an organic kind of learning which is more than intellectual, in which
every level of the self must participate undergoing change and reorganization. Knowledge and wisdom which goes beyond knowledge
must eventually be achieved and must retain its capacity of changing with new experience. In the most meaningful sense of the word,
knowledge in any field only becomes real to an individual as he re-
lives it for himself, puts himself into it as new experience and is
changed and made over by it. This is peculiarly true in the field of
knowledge of human problems and social relationships, where there
is so much knowledge that is as old as human experience, and so
much that is new and little tried, much that is right and more that is
wrong. An individual's relation to this knowledge only becomes sure
at the cost of living it through in action or in feeling. Only where he
has really had experience can he say, "I know." By experience I do
not mean overt behavior, but the internal experience which comes
only in feeling awareness when spontaneous action is checked, and
feeling and consciousness can develop. This is the essential training
in the field of social casework facilitated peculiarly by the supervisory experience which I have tried to sketch here and will analyze in
detail in subsequent chapters.

PART TWO. THE LEARNING PROCESS IN SUPERVISION

7. THE STUDENT'S UTILIZATION OF THE LEARNING EXPERIENCE

The Will-To-Learn

An interesting learning experience was reported by a blind student who was trying to teach a client, an elderly blind man, to read Moon type. He was practicing on a deck of Moon type playing cards. The student recorded: "We had gone through the deck a number of times and he found it very difficult to decipher the denominations. He seemed very discouraged and finally ceased to mention the cards when I visited. I decided to let the matter drop until he brought it up. About five months elapsed. (There were regular visits to the family on other problems.) Now, Monday, when I called he immediately said to me, 'You know I've thought I might like to go through the deck of cards.' Just as if we had been recently talking it over and he had been asked to decide the matter for himself. We went over each card and it was a very successful venture, judged by the number of cards he could recognize in comparison with the number he could make out previously. It interests me to wonder how and why he made the decision and what went on in his mind during these five months when he never mentioned the subject. It seems as if there had been some continuous relation to it, however, which came out finally in his decision to risk it."

The student writing this episode recognizes a continuous learning process here of six month's duration, though nothing seemed to happen for five months. The initiative was hers, but after a few lessons in which she puts her effort into trying to arouse his interest and effort, she is wise enough to recognize that he is not taking hold and drops it. After five months he comes back to it, asks for help, and takes over the problem into his own control.

The story illustrates in its simplest form the essential nature of learning. Whatever may be put into the teaching, in the last analysis, the learning results are limited and determined by the learner. Teaching provides the subject matter, the stimulus, the materials, sets the tasks and defines the conditions, but learning is the process of utilizing opportunity and limits in one's own way for one's own ends. The learner determines the speed of the process and its quality, the level on which it proceeds, whether superficial or fundamental, and the final results achieved.

With all that has been said in the preceding chapters about the supervisor's activities and the form and structure of this process of casework training as it is set up in the school, in the casework job, and conditions of work, it is important to remind ourselves that the final form which the process as a whole achieves and the results which are accomplished in any individual student depend on the student himself, the learner not the teacher. A supervisor of many years' experience who has followed many students through this training process states it in these words:

> In going over the material that I have recorded in these students' conferences, I am impressed by the fact that it is the individual student who determines to a large extent what the supervision will be. I think probably any experienced supervisor is aware of this, but I did not know it so clearly in words until I read these records as a whole. I know that the supervisor does not become a different person for each student, but the student is able to feel what part of the supervisor's personality and intellectual equipment she wants to use. I would see the supervisor as exercising a certain control in the procedure, but on the whole a rather limited one. She maintains limits at definite places, but in the process as a whole, it is the student who establishes control through his own limitations. It seems then that the teaching process from the supervisor's point of view consists in the ability to adapt herself and what she has to teach, to the learning needs of each individual student.

Individual Differences in Learning

The student's learning needs extend into three areas; first, the obvious need for an extent of factual knowledge including agency function and procedures, resources of the community, social conditions, social planning, and other such questions. Second, is the need to develop a greater understanding of people, of their needs and and reactions. Third, is his need to learn to use himself more responsibly in relation to the problems of his clients within the function of his agency. The first need may be satisfied externally and intellectually; the other two involve deeper uses of the self and changes in its structure.

The most important differences in students which affect the way they use supervision and determine the forms and results of this learning process are not in intellectual equipment, for at least a superior degree of intellectual equipment is guaranteed by the fact that all students have successfully completed four years of college. The student's ability to see the manifold facts involved in a social situation, to discriminate between the essential and the unessential, to come to a decision and act upon it, are capacities that rest upon intellectual ability it is true, but even more upon the willingness and the freedom to use the intellect sensitively, penetratingly, and decisively. Feeling, intelligence and will must cooperate in balanced decision and action. In the freedom to use these faculties and in the responsibility taken for them, students present the greatest degree of difference. They differ also in the extent to which they will engage themselves in a learning process and take over responsibility for change and for a new integration of impulses, feelings, attitudes and thinking. All students expect and intend a little change, but this ranges from the most external change expressed by learning how to do certain things by rules and getting new ideas from a book, to internal reconstruction of the self in a growth process which carries it to deeper levels of freer feelings and appreciation, and to more responsible disciplined expression. The student, typically here as in any new learning process, presents his most disciplined correct self ready to be taught, determined to learn. Determined as he may be to keep out of the situation his impulsive self, or his "personal self," it is sure to appear sooner or later owing to the meaningful nature of the content and the quality of the supervisory relationship. As this impulsive or spontaneous self appears in supervision conferences, in behavior or in expression of feeling, the growing student comes to accept responsibility for it as his own, to be aware of its relation to and its effect on other people, on the supervisor, or the client, or the agency, and to take responsibility for disciplining this impulsive expression in relation to the needs and demands of the outside situation. The most able and successful students are those who become most deeply engaged in this process and go the greatest distance in accepting responsibility for self-discipline.

Different Uses of Supervision

In the process of becoming conscious and accepting responsibility for their own actions and feelings, students will use the supervisor very differently. Some will react to the slightest suggestion of a problem from her, work alone on the problem and bring back a changed attitude, a new understanding which seems all their own and which carries them far ahead in development. Others must almost force the supervisor to do it for them. They seem to ward off insight and defend themselves against any effort to penetrate this blindness. Some students seem to progress only by a series of bad experiences, of making mistakes and having to take the unpleasant consequences. Some learn chiefly negatively, differing with the supervisor and trying out their difference as far as possible. Each student has his own way and within a certain range these ways are acceptable so long as the self of the student is really engaged in the process and struggling to learn and as long as he is moving towards more understanding and more responsibility.

Some things about the student's individual way of learning, the part of himself that he is bringing into the situation, the way he will relate himself to the process and the use he will make of the supervisor, will be apparent in what he presents in the first conference and the use he makes of it. Two contrasting uses of supervision appearing in the first conference and continuing characteristically throughout, are described below by the supervisor of the two students concerned:

> In the introductory interviews one sees these differences in the students so clearly—the contrast in their approach to the agency work, the relation to the supervisor, and the feeling about the self. These interviews foretell pretty clearly not only the trend of the supervisory contact, but the whole future mode of operation of the student in relation to clients and something of his ability to modify this.
>
> A.'s acceptance of herself, of her security and her apprehension, enabled her to lightly touch on both feelings. Her enthusiasm and interest are freely related to the content of this new experience. She has little to unlearn and she has a positive attitude toward learning. She welcomes the use of others' material expecting to get help from it. She assumes responsibility for bringing her own interests and questionings to the interview and apparently enjoys discussing the supervisor's response to

them. One is aware of her consideration of the other and her ability to modify her own impulsive behavior.

B. brings only the problem of herself to this first meeting. Quite defensively she assumes control of the interview presenting this self as an able, interesting person. There is a decided effort to relate to the supervisor as at least a contemporary, if not an equal. Except for the simple questions as to routine office hours there is no concern about the content of the field work and no curiosity as to agency function. There is, however, a great deal of insecurity expressed in a veiled manner culminating in her whole doubt of the school because it is the one she has chosen. Her negative approach to this situation is self-obscured by her will to put herself across. Absorbed in building up an idea of herself into reality, she is unaware of the other person except as she tries to dominate and control his activity to meet her needs.

In the first real supervisory conferences, the pattern of each student's behavior in relation to it is more clearly shown. A. is so articulate and frank about her fear of and insecurity with this new responsibility. Her willingness to learn not only through her own experiencing but also through others is quite pronounced. B.'s insecurity is expressed in her need to be authoritative in relation to clients and destructively critical in relation to the agency. It is the "other" or outside that is wrong. She cannot bear to be in a learning situation, becoming increasingly argumentative after introducing any question. Some of this bitterness is relieved in our joint appreciation of the hardship of "change," although I do not articulate the feeling I have that B. resents the inequality of our positions and is finding the role of student very unacceptable.

Although there is a steady sort of progression in both of these series of conferences, A. seems to develop more smoothly and naturally in both a personal and professional capacity. Her attitudes are pliant and easily affected through the intensity of her field work contacts. Her impulsive enthusiasms respond to an increasingly conscious control. At the end of this first term one begins to feel the emergence of a professional self with a growing sense of its power and a greater use of personal equipment being put to a constructive service of the other.

It is much harder to follow any kind of professional development through the conferences with B. who has so much to learn about herself that there is nothing left for her to use in learning about others. Briefly one traces an increasing awareness of her own impulses, the negative destructive use of her will, the feelings motivating her behavior. It is as if in this first term B. finally discovers a bit of solid foundation within herself. To me this seemed like real achievement for only from this basis can one actually begin to develop, to get to any creative use of one's own abilities. Strictly speaking, her operation in the field was not acceptable, but her personal development gave much hope for future activity of a different quality.

Three Phases of This Learning Process

The first six weeks, roughly, mark the time period for the first phase of supervision. In general, it feels like a struggle between the supervisor and the student, to define on the one hand and to accept on the other, the conditons of supervision and of field work, to reach a basis of working together. This phase may be prolonged beyond six weeks, and for some students the struggle against supervision is never completely given up. But in every case the first phase of blind struggle must yield to a phase in which the student recognizes that his own will is engaged *with* the process, not *against* it. In this second phase the student learns more easily and is conscious of change and growth and new capacities. The amount of progress which takes place in this phase, and the responsibility which the student is able to accept for it, varies greatly. In the third or end phase of the learning process, every student should take over what he has learned and recognize it as really his own. His independence of the supervisor and his ability to leave his studentship is established for him by the end of the school year. He may return and go on in a job experience or a second year of training, but his relation to supervision will be on another level. The whole school situation brings this end-phase forward into consciousness, and prepares for the actual leaving by everything that goes on in the last six weeks of the school program. Final papers are being written. There is discussion of next year's program and students are asked to make their plans for next year. Some will apply for fellowships or jobs. In working on these plans each student takes over more clearly and decisively than before his relation to professional training. In the field work, he begins to plan with his supervisor for leaving his cases, summarizing his records and turning over his case load to another worker. Even if he is to stay on in the agency for a summer or a second year, there should be a sharp, clearly marked change in his work and responsibility at the end of the first year. For the experience of giving up cases, of winding up records, and getting one's work in shape to pass it on to another person is a very important learning experience in the opportunity it offers for coming through to clear-cut thinking, for decisive action, for self-criticism and evaluation of what has been done during the year within the limit which the end of the year sets. The supervisor's knowledge and experience may be used more actively at this point while the student works more independently since because he is leaving he can feel freer to take and not become dependent on it. In leaving also, all the student's individual and unique ways of handling separation come into play. There may be a period of greater fear for the student who dreads taking over his independence and an insistence on his inadequacy, or there may be the contrary premature assertion of readiness to leave and do everything all on his own. There may be a deepened realization as the student separates himself from the learning situation and realizes its positive meaning for him, or there may be for some students no way of leaving except by finding something to criticize in what they will be giving up.

Illustrations of Different Ways of Reacting in this Learning Experience

To illustrate the range of difference in the ways students use supervision, take what they can assimilate, and create that process for their own needs to learn, I will use [three] illustrations of student experience. The first illustration will show the extreme at one end of the range—the student who, on college grades and recommendations and satisfactory references from a previous office job, is able to satisfy the requirements for entrance to the school, but who demonstrates undeniably to the school and to herself that she cannot adjust and make use of the casework training. In the second illustration, the student makes a very negative use of supervision until the end of the first semester but at that point becomes aware of what she was doing to her training experiences through the supervisor and brings herself to another attitude. The third illustration portrays a very able student who works on every aspect of her job very independently and responsibly from the beginning. She takes over her own training positively and makes use of the supervisor to help her work out her casework problems. I will quote briefly from her field work reports to show the way casework goals have become her own and are used by her for her own thinking.

1. Student whose limitations make it impossible for her to learn in this process.

Student is a college graduate with one year of office work after college. In the small town in which they live, her mother, a very able, powerful person, is a leader in church and civic work. She apparently leaves her daughter complete freedom to make her own choice of work, but it is clear that the girl is deeply attached to her mother, both positively and negatively, and that her choice of social work as a vocational field is involved with her whole relationship to her mother.

She was intelligent in class responses, has learned how to "say the words," but in the field her attitudes were predominantly punishing. The relationship to the supervisor was maintained on a polite superficial level while doing everything contrary to the supervisor's point of view and suggestion. She could not see or admit her negative, punishing behavior when it was pointed out to her in specific situations. Finally it was decided to try to interpret to her the problem her attitudes constituted in the field of social work and give her our judgment that unless there was a real change in these attitudes she should leave the school.

This process of interpretation took place in eight interviews with four people. The supervisor initiated the process with an evaluation interview based on the actual casework and the relationship to supervision. The student claimed not to understand this at all and sought interviews with three different teachers in the school who knew her work best. The final interview with her adviser in the school follows:

Interview, January—

Student made this appointment a week ago and has evidently had it in mind as a final interview. I left it to her to begin and conduct. She did this very soberly with complete poise and control. Said she had not been able to get enough assurance of success to feel it would be worth while to continue classes in the second semester. In what has been told her about herself, she finds nothing she can work on. It seems that people see her problem as a personality one. One side of this seems to be, as she tried to interpret what has been given her by her supervisor and teachers, an uneasiness in herself which doesn't leave the client at ease. If this were the whole problem she could work on it. But she has come to believe also that what we are all talking about is a certain quality which she calls "outgoingness." She sees this as "God-given" and if you don't have it there is nothing to do about it. I asked if her supervisor had it, and with a slight hesitation she said, yes, she thought so. I then asked if she admired this in her, if she wanted to be like the supervisor and with her characteristic laugh she said, no, she didn't think she did. I said this seemed to be a very satisfactory solution on her part. She had really put her finger on the quality that is essential for casework and doesn't want it for herself. She really wants to be a different kind of person. She didn't answer this, but brought out that her mother has this quality to a rare degree and in her it is certainly God-given. I said that perhaps it was important for her to be a different kind of person from her mother and this was a difficult task when her mother was so strong and so powerful—perhaps it would be easier for her to be herself in a different field. She showed real surprise at this, saying she had never thought of it that way. Seemed not to want to pursue it further, covering it up with a little picture of how happily she and her mother were related. Of course they differed on some points, but each accepted this and they never disagreed fundamentally.

Somewhere in her discussion of the quality of "outgoingness" I attempted to add a little to it by saying that the caseworker did have to have a feeling of wanting to go out to the other person and take some responsibility for it. She corrected me very firmly for this statement saying that the caseworker shouldn't take responsibility for another, she should only act as a channel through which the other person could work on his problem.

On the whole, my attitude was to accept her solution as wise and right for her. I told her I thought she had handled it very maturely and with logical thinking. I tried to permit some recognition of the rejection aspects of this situation for her by saying I wished she could express a little resentment for these people who seemed to pass judgment on her. But she rebuked me with, "Why should I feel resentment? Anyone going into any field of work accepts this possibility. You have to weed out undesirable people." I told her this sounded like a 40-year-old philosophy. She wasn't entitled to it at 22. She said she had gone through a great deal in the past two weeks in reaction to our criticism and I agreed that she had gone through as much as one can in keeping criticism *outside*. She questioned my meaning, but when I explained that I meant not letting it in to the point where one really accepts it and *changes* in terms of it, she agreed.

At the end I disagreed with her determination to have the quality of "outgoingness" God-given. I said I had known people to change in respect to their feeling for other people. She dismissed this as impossible. This quality cannot be worked on. It must be spontaneous. She sees no possibility of change in herself in respect to it and does not desire it.

In this illustration it is clear that it is the girl herself who, by her behavior, by her rejection of the quality of the social worker, and by her insistence that change is impossible, determines that she will not go on further into this training process. She is not able to take the full responsibility for deciding this and acting upon it. She forces that responsibility upon the school, on the supervisor and the adviser. She will probably tell her friends that she was rejected by the school but she will not be able to offer any reason even as clearly as she does in this interview. The difference between the kind of person she is and the "outgoing" social worker whom she comes near to seeing in this interview is not one she can affirm in her own favor. It is the essential nature of her problem that she is doomed to prefer the opposite nature from her own but fight it and refuse to try to be like it. The strength back of this organization of herself as she is, as "born that way," her determination not to change seems too great, at this point, to yield to any learning process. The powerful dynamics of this casework learning drive her very hard and against it she pits herself with greater strength and more punishing behavior. It is this negative strength of hers, this tightly organized will which forces the issue and determines the end of a process rejected by her from the beginning.

2. Student who makes of the supervision situation a constant struggle but eventually puts her whole will into the process and learns positively.

This second student had not been as conspicuously poor in her work as the first, but she had done nothing outstandingly good in field or class. She seemed to withhold her contribution rather than to fight aggressively. But her lack of class contribution and one particular paper in casework class, in which for the first time she expressed strong feeling about the possibility that a client might resist the caseworker and the futility of casework in this instance, led her casework teacher to seek an interview with her. In this interview, the teacher pointed out the feeling back of the paper, the lack of interest shown in the casework class and raised the question as to whether she was at all identified with casework or whether she really resisted being a caseworker.

The student was deeply disturbed and initiated a discussion around this question with her supervisor. In several interviews she worked on her problem, which she had been unconscious of up to this point, of taking supervision and relating herself to clients. When she had worked this through so that she understood it and could express it, she took the following interpretation back to her casework teacher.

> I see now that in the first semester I have made all my supervisory conferences simply a contest between the supervisor and myself, a battle to see whether I could refuse to take up anything she suggested in regard to my cases. I resented her knowledge and her experience. I always tried to make myself believe that her opinion was wrong and mine right about the client. Suddenly when I was able to express this to her and talk it out and see that she understood my feeling, I realized that the client never had anything to do with it. It was myself. If I gave in to the supervisor about a client I would have to give in about myself and I could not bear to do this. Now that I have given in and expressed this feeling, I can be interested in the client as I never have really been before. I have tried to be interested and be nice to them but I have always interpreted their feeling solely in terms of how I would feel in their situation. Because I have not wanted to talk or express any feeling of my own freely, I have not wanted to let clients talk. I feel now as if I could have real interviews.

From this point on this student puts more of herself into her casework contacts and learns more freely. It is never easy for her but she now puts herself into the learning process and works with it instead of against it. There remain very real and distinct limits in what she can get from people and give to them, but unlike the first student she has accepted change and takes responsibility for it.

3. Student who takes responsibility for her own learning from the beginning.

The third student comes into the professional school directly from college with no previous experience in working. She has a fine mind which she has always used in college in thorough scholarly work. She has learned how to think independently but her thinking has been related to facts and ideas as laid down in books. Her social contacts and experiences have been limited to a small family and town and determined by strict religious and moral standards. Many situations confront her in a big city and in the children's agency where she does her field work which conflict with her own philosophy of life and her standards of behavior. She reacts to each new experience deeply, permitting herself no escape but seeking always to understand the reason of the strange behavior of the child or the child's parent in terms of the factors of their own lives. She takes with the utmost seriousness her responsibility for what she does with the problems of her clients when they are put upon her. She uses supervision actively to talk about what she is trying to understand in other people. She is infinitely careful and painstaking in accumulating all her facts and can never act until she has surveyed her problems from every angle and thought herself through to a relation to it as a whole which seems right to her. She can get entangled sometimes in the too-intricate web of her own thinking and on such occasions the supervisor had to go ahead of her for the sake of getting action which the client needed. The student found this hard to take from the supervisor in the first year, since it went athwart her own responsible way of working out everything for herself, but she learned to see her need for this kind of help at certain points and in her second year we see her seeking this help from the supervisor very consciously. At the same time, in the second year her own speed in getting through to effective intelligent action has increased as she has become more secure in her understanding of the meaning of the behavior she is dealing with and is more sure of her own capacity to react to it and handle it helpfully.

The following quotations from her own field work reports at two points in her first year show the responsible attitude to the field work which characterizes her from the very beginning, and its steady progress towards independent professional judgment and action. I have added the supervisor's report of her work in the second year to show the supervisor's opinion of her quality and performance as it matures in the second year.

Comments on field work experiences at the end of second month:

> In general, these last two weeks have been the least exciting and stimulating period of my field work so far. None of the six children whom I am supervising in temporary homes has developed any startling problems and the mother of the little boy who was to be taken into care has disappeared with him, so that so far all I have done in that case is to hunt for her and speculate as to her reasons for evidently changing her plans. My last visit to the home in which this woman, Mrs. H., had been living with her mother and an indeterminate number of relatives, indicated that her mother had decided that Bobby ought to be placed and probably brought some pressure to bear on Mrs. H. in the matter. The sister mentioned that Mrs. H. wanted to place both of her children if she had to place either, though she had always told me she only wanted to place Bobby as she could care for the older boy or trust him to be alone. There is in my mind a question how much of the desire to place Bobby and not his half-brother arises from the fact that the former is half Jewish and that the father of the latter has been paying the mother for his support. However, it is perfectly obvious that Bobby's hyperactivity and tendency to fight and snatch does make a problem for her in her attempt either to leave the children alone or to find a friend or relative to care for them gratis. It is also interesting to me to realize that a home composed of a mother who has evidently been extremely promiscuous, an illegitimate gentile child, a Jewish man (not her husband) and their child could be even as stable as this one seems to have been. A letter from the Warden of the Penitentiary in which Mr. H. is imprisoned indicates that Bobby's father feels deeply the separation from Mrs. H. and the children. I am repeatedly being surprised at the combinations of emotions and behavior of those people whose standards are not those to which I have been accustomed—the similarities and differences in people's reactions. I am afraid, also, that where there are similarities I attempted to show that, therefore, their complete reaction must be the same as mine.
>
> The problem of family ties was again emphasized when I received a frantic telephone call one morning from the Aunt of Oliver who lived with her for the last three years, since he was eight years old. She was eager to have me bring Oliver to see the

dying grandfather who lives with her. Whether or not to take the child was a difficult problem for me to solve myself as my own reaction in such a case is to stay away from a very ill person. Also, I am very doubtful of the advisability to taking children into the very emotional, tense situations which accompany death so often, as they so seldom understand the significance of the thing. It happened that I was too tied up with previous engagements to have time to take the child anyway. Nevertheless, the problem is still there. In asking my friends whether or not the visit should have been made, I found a wide range of opinions and attitudes. Certainly the Aunt would have enjoyed having Oliver come even though it developed later that the grandfather was not as ill as she thought.

It might have been interesting to see how Oliver would react to a very emotional situation, as so far we have never seen in him any sign of emotion or great interest in his family.

As a whole, these experiences tend toward a broader experience and an increasing realization of the complexity and interrelation of human problems as influenced by varying personalities.

Comments on field work experience in second month of second semester (after 6 months):

This period in my field work has meant the realization of several very fundamental problems but has not solved them. In fact, the first and most disastrous problem is this inability to satisfactorily solve my problems which results in a failure to accomplish results. When the Court asked that we place Doris C., although her mother wanted her at home, I hesitated to see the mother, feeling that if she objected so violently to placing the child, she would create an impossible situation for the foster mother to deal with the child. After seeing her several times, however, I have come to feel that her need is more to be accepted as a person capable of doing what she desires and defeating the opposition—the Court—than any real desire to care for the child whom she left pretty generally to friends before. I am hoping, now, therefore, that with our continued acceptance of her and interest in her as a person she may be willing to take us on in the capacity of the friend who used to give Doris physical care. However, I still fear that inevitably her opposition to the Court will be transferred to us when Doris is transferred if the Judge refuses her request to have Doris.

At the point of indecision, there, I have waited for someone else to indicate the course and have, therefore, placed on them the responsibility for results. When I do so I am thoroughly ashamed of myself for being so dependent but I've been independent in general for such a short time that my fear of the stranger is stronger than my self reliance. Because of my own lack of self assurance, I was uncomfortable when visiting Bobby and his grandmother as Bobby seems most independent and self-assured. Finally, a realization that the grandmother really enjoyed having someone come in to visit and talk with her about her problems—which so far have not been very serious—made me feel at ease in the situation. On the other hand, there were the parents of Mary, who couldn't seem to get to Court to file an application, though they seemed anxious to place her. They wanted to put the entire responsibility on visitor or someone else and were greatly afraid to take any steps alone. For them I wanted to help get things done—ask the Court to hurry through the case, etc.—instead of waiting until they took the responsibility of doing so themselves. Possibly they may have felt, as I do when another takes the responsibility I put on him or her, that I took from their self respect if I had obviously taken the responsibility.

The inability to come to a conclusion results in a lack of standards on all issues. Doris's mother seems perfectly accepting of her life which includes working in a beer garden, fist fights with other women, probably immorality of various kinds, and certainly when she had Doris giving her any kind of care with the responsibility left with any friend who would take it. If she is adjusted to this life and wants Doris to share it and Doris wants to do so, might she not be as happy in it also as she would be having a tie to a mother with whose life her own in a foster home would be incompatible? Of course, I doubt if this is the case here as I do not believe Doris's mother really wants Doris that much. Nevertheless, the question of standards is presented. If in a case like this, one were to work with a mother primarily on the basis say of health or relief for which she desired assistance, would our attitude be one of complete acceptance of such a plan of life or an acceptance of the possibilities which she possesses to become a "moral" and self supporting member of society? In other words, is it possible to accept anyone without accepting the behavior which is satisfactory to him?

Closely associated with and underlying standards there are the values of life to each individual. How much will it mean to Johnny if his Uncle, whom an out-of-the-city Children's Aid

Society asked us to meet, desires to take him because of a feel-ling of family responsibility and will give him excellent physi-cal care, while having little interest in him as a person rather than as a family responsibility. He does recognize his right to make his own decisions as he grows older and may have more affection for him than appears, but if not would a foster mother who wanted a child as a child be able to give him more than a very fine physical setting and a feeling of being in his own family?

I've come to see human life as a more varied and really in-teresting pattern, but have not entirely accepted the necessity of finding my own thread in the weave. Yet, I am unhappy when I do not do so, so that I go neither one way nor the oth-er. So long as a parent or child has a plan, I'm glad to help it but have no standard by which to call it wise or right. Perhaps for him this is better, but for the accomplishment of some-thing else it does not serve and how secure can he feel in deal-ing with an individual so lost in uncertainties?

Supervisor's report of first semester of work in second year:

Student has been carrying a city load which at present num-bers eleven homes and fifteen children, three of whom are clas-sified as inactive. She took over this group of children and homes in the permanent foster home department as soon as the first year of school was completed.

Although her load is small, it has been very active, partly because she is alert to problems and quick to think a situation through to its ultimate conclusion. She has had quite a range of experiences within a six months' period, covering every phase of child-placing except the long time placement and the responsibility of planning for sixteen year olds for whom no board can be given by this agency.

One of her first difficult experiences was the removal of two foreign children, whose father speaks no English and is deeply suspicious of any change, from an old but undesirable foster home where the children had been dumped. The reason for this change was really student's conviction of the bad effect of the foster mother's protective but repressive attitude to-ward "dumb foreign" children. The medical clinic's recommen-dation that the children be given preventive care for tubercu-losis furnished the leverage for removal, since country place-ment seemed to offer a better health opportunity, but this was not a sufficient cause in the opinion of the foster mother, and student had the experience of facing a most unpleasant situa-

tion in which the foster mother fought in every way to prevent
the carrying out of the plan. She got the children and their father on her side, so that the removal was painful in the extreme. She also tried to go over the student's head by appeal-
ing to the supervisor. Student herself was almost shaken in her
conviction because of her uncertainty about the home to which
the children were to be taken. She had only the assurance of
the supervisor that it would probably work out. In fact, at this
point she had to accept the supervisor's taking it out of her
hands because the selection of the country home rested with
supervisor and country visitor.

After this experience in which supervisor acted quite decisively in the interest of getting the children placed, the character of the conference hour changed. What had been free and
comfortable, seemed to become rather formal and uninterest-
ing. Realizing that I had probably seemed high-handed in the
placing of these children, I asked her if she did not feel somewhat resentful. At first she denied it, but soon came through
quite freely with an admission of feeling and from that time to
the present there has been only the greatest frankness between
us.

I consider her courage and decisiveness in breaking up this
old situation most unusual, even for an experienced worker.
She certainly grew under it. A second equally difficult removal
was carried out later, with no external excuse, on the basis of
the future of the child and the absence of any good prospect
in the foster home. This was done at considerable cost as the
foster mother was abusive and the student not so sure herself
in this instance, but on the whole she felt it was worth doing
and has gained confidence in her own judgment. In this case
she had a decisive part in the choice of the new home and her
judgment was sound.

Student has studied five new homes, one of which was
closed before investigation, two were rejected and two accepted
for use. Into these two new homes she has placed two little
girls, with a thoughtfulness and careful follow-up which I have
never seen bettered in any young worker. She has a remarkable
faculty for seeing and weighing all the significant details of a
situation. She does this in such a sensitive feeling way that the
result is a living picture, not a mechanical assembling of facts.
Her problem is how to cut her way through the many-sided
identification to the action indicated. She seldom fails to see
what should be done but she finds it hard to act on her decision.

However, she is not seriously blocked but is finally carried by her own conviction despite the effort it costs her.

In addition to these valuable experiences of removal and placement, student has gone through the unusual experience of the death of a foster mother and the return of a foster child who was like an own child, to her real mother. This painful adjustment of an adolescent girl has been a fruitful source of discipline in community contacts and in the functional limitations of our job.

Student comes to conference hour, which occurs once a week, bringing her most immediate and difficult problems for discussion. She had never asked me to read a record until a short time ago when I myself was about to suggest that we might survey her case load. Then she took it over and told me what to read and from what viewpoint. I think she would find it hard to handle a supervisory relationship in which the supervisor took much initiative or responsibility for her. Student gives the impression of a worker who has taken full responsibility for her work. She comes for help only when she has formulated the problem and thought it out as far as possible. She never has any trouble using the conference hour. Is apparently fearless in stating her difficulties and what she has done in a situation. Takes disagreement on my part with great courage. Is not negative but has to be convinced within her own self before she can take over anything from me. I have always talked with her as an equal, but with a frank admission of the advantage which age and experience give me. I never feel any need to soften my reaction on her account. We are remarkably comfortable together as far as I can tell and she seems to grow steadily in her sureness and understanding. She needs to acquire more decisiveness and ease of execution, as well as a broader personal experience.

In order that the picture of the process of professional training may not be left with so perfect and onesided an emphasis as this summary of the last student's experience, I want to call attention to the "down" phases which are so characteristic and as important in a learning process as the "up" phases. Even where the will is involved as clearly as in the case just quoted and takes possession of its training process so that the professional self seems to develop gradually and with more and more control and organization there may be moments when the self seems unequal to the task and the confusion overwhelming. I will quote one comment from an able student who came through to distinguished accomplishments.

> To try to write what I have 'gotten out of this term in field work' is dreadfully hard at this point with my mind in a hopelessly confused state. One thing is quite certain and definite—the old props and illusions I had six months ago won't do at all—they've simply disappeared, most of them, and this process of groping for something to take their place is a baffling (and stimulating) experience. At times it can be also depressing. At others it seems simply ridiculous, and if it weren't so often amusing it might be quite unbearable. The result is an acute self consciousness that is, to put it mildly, disconcerting. I never have the slightest idea what I am going to do or say or think next. One viewpoint and its exact opposite are apt to take possession of one's thinking within five minutes of each other and I find myself saying one thing one minute and quite another the next. Realizing the inconsistency doesn't seem to be enough to remedy it. It is exasperating enough to feel this bewilderment, but not to be able to express it when a paper is due and one has torn two attempts to shreds, is a dilemma.
>
> It would be awfully 'interesting' to me to know what in the world has happened to me and why I don't know myself nor seem able to trust myself any longer. If it is only another growing pain, inevitable in a learning situation, one may allow one's self to hope a little. It seems quite hopeless at this moment.

Desperate as this state may seem to the student, the experienced supervisor knows how to evaluate such moments as natural phases in the whole process.

Summary

In a consideration of the learning process as a whole, we have come face to face with the fact that, in the last analysis, the control and the utilization of the learning process rest with the learner. The situation provides opportunity within limits which set standards and determine goals. The student who puts himself into this situation establishes his own relation to it, must find his own direction and form himself anew in terms of what he takes from the situation. The student's way of making use of the supervisor as helper in his learning experience, his speed, and what he finally makes his own, are different for every individual. We have said that individual differences in students here seem to be due, first, to differences in their freedom to use their capacities and the balance with which the total organization of the self functions in respect to feeling, impulse, consciousness and will; and second, to differences in the extent to which individuals engage the self in this learning process.

Underlying all differences, I have indicated a fundamental likeness, when one looks at this learning process as movement, in the organization of the self determined within the limits of an educational situation. I have described three characteristic phases of this movement:—a beginning phase in which the student feels the situation as pressure and influence and struggles to make it his own, to control it by his own pattern; a middle phase when he has accepted his own will in the process and learns freely and rapidly; and an end phase in which he prepares to leave the situation and take over what he has learned as his own. Many points of knowledge and of skill are clarified in this end phase which were confused before as the student puts his own strength and pressure into acquiring what he needs. It has been pointed out also that into the end phase as into the beginning will enter all the confusing ambivalent reactions which appear in the struggle with which individuals move in and out of any relationship which has engaged the self.

The problem of this chapter belongs under the second set of problems indicated in Chapter 1. As was said there, the individual's utilization of a fundamental learning experience and the change and reorganization of the self in time through this experience is an aspect of the deeper problem of growth and creativity about which little can be known. We can only describe results while we remain in as great ignorance of the internal adjustments back of them as the blind teacher of the blind student of Moon type.

VI

The Dynamics of Supervision under Functional Controls

A PROFESSIONAL PROCESS IN SOCIAL CASEWORK

The preface to the original edition of this second book on supervision opens as follows:

> *Twelve years have elapsed since the publication of my first effort to define supervision in social casework practice. . . . In these twelve years I have clarified the preliminary statement of the meaning and nature of supervision which I formulated in my book in 1936. . . . My experience in working with the professional function of supervision in these twelve years, in teaching its use in class and in individual conference, in supervising staff members for whose work I was responsible, in advising supervisors of students in training, has enabled me to lift my description of the process of supervision out of its connection with its early biological and personal roots to a description of a process in itself, with its own characteristic function and dynamics.*

The Dynamics of Supervision *is organized in four parts. About Part One—"The Nature of Social Casework"—Miss Robinson writes in the introduction:*

> *It has seemed to me necessary to begin with an examination of the nature of social casework itself, to describe the basic process which characterizes it, the process which supervision undertakes to teach. In Part I of the book, therefore, I have attempted to show how the helping process of social casework has evolved in use and through what experience it has achieved understanding and control.*

Thus the two opening chapters focus upon "the development of social casework from a personal to a professional service"—in essence the theme of this present book. In addition, the second chapter offers a brief but comprehensive statement of the principles underlying functional helping. Miss Robinson recognizes in her opening paragraph a "divergence in point of view in the theory and practice of social casework [which] began to make itself apparent in the late twenties and early thirties." She will not "attempt to deal in any way" with the differing theory and practice, but notes:

> *The discussion of casework and supervision in this volume will limit itself to the practice that has developed under the Rankian influence now known as functional social casework, a term truly descriptive of a characteristic psychology and method growing out of the experience of the profession itself.*
>
> *This change of name from "Rankian" to "functional" could only come about in the passage of time through a process of assimilation of all that had been learned from Rank's point of view.* *

Parts Two and Three discuss at length the nature of the supervisory relationship and its role in the structure of the professional school. Most significant here is the definition of the supervisory position as that one which extends recognition and respect to the self as a living whole—in the form of the person seeking help or the student in training as well as in her own self—and which accords that self "the right to its difference while holding it to the change which must take place in the learning process."

Omitted from the present volume are the preface, the introduction, and Part Four, "The Graduate in the Social Agency."

---

*For further discussion of the principles of functional helping, see "A Conception of the Growth Process Underlying Social Casework Practice," by Jessie Taft, included in *Jessie Taft, Therapist and Social Work Educator, A Professional Biography*, edited by Virginia P. Robinson, University of Pennsylvania Press, 1962. Also, "Preparation for the Annual Meeting — The Relation of Function to Process" by Anita J. Faatz, *Journal of the Otto Rank Association*, Vol. 9, No. 1 (Summer 1974).

PART ONE. THE NATURE OF SOCIAL CASEWORK

1. THE DEVELOPMENT OF SOCIAL CASEWORK FROM A PERSONAL TO A PROFESSIONAL SERVICE

What is social casework? Have the community fund drives of the last few years with their red feathers and modern advertising methods made the meaning of this service as clear to the public as is medical or psychiatric service? On the contrary, the public may contribute to help the poor, the sick, the friendless, without understanding any more of the nature of that help than that it is offered by reputable established agencies responsible for collecting and disbursing funds to those in need. Few members of the contributing public would conceive of the service of these agencies as anything they would seek or use themselves. How much does the tax-paying public understand of the nature of the service extended to their clients through the public agencies that operate under the Social Security Act, Aid to Dependent Children, Old Age Assistance, Aid to the Blind, or of General Public Assistance? What is known of the casework service to veterans set up since the last war as an essential part of Veterans Administration?

Those who administer these services to people in need, the social caseworkers themselves, who constitute the staffs of the social agencies, are a small group of highly responsible, professional workers. Professional training is fast becoming a requirement in all agencies except in many of the agencies administering public assistance. Back of the practice of social casework lies a tradition, a history, of less than one hundred years in which the idea of social casework has been gathering meaning in use. The date of the first training course for social workers, 1898, out of which developed the New York School of Philanthropy, may be used to mark the beginning of professional definition and development of this field. Actually, its beginning is more accurately marked by the publication of Mary Richmond's *Social Diagnosis* in 1917 and it is in the period following the First World War, in response to the profound changes in human values and relationships, to the deeper understanding of the individual and his needs opened up in these years, that social casework has found its challenge and its opportunity. Today fifty schools of social work are offering two years of training in social casework. There is a national professional association of social workers, there is professional literature to the extent of perhaps a dozen books in the social casework field, and extensive pamphlet material. *The Journal of Social Casework,* a technical publication, is issued monthly.

If one studies this literature one cannot fail, I believe, to get the conviction that there is something vital, alive, and meaningful in this field, something which has genuine help to offer to individuals in need, despite the confusions, the waste of words and efforts, that are at the same time so apparent in many of its writings. One can only bear with its confusions, the lack of clear professional purpose and direction in the field as a whole, if one is willing to understand it in process, to remember its youth as a profession, to realize that thirty years is a short time indeed to make a beginning in defining a service which, resting on the oldest, most personal bases in human relationships, at the same time aims at something so new, so unique and different in the utilization of relationship.

It is significant that with all that has been said and written about social casework there is no brief and ready-to-use definition one can lay hands on. Nor am I ready to offer a definition that would attempt prematurely to simplify the problems and unify the differences in this field. I shall, on the other hand, attempt to state the nature of its task, to examine problems it must solve if it is to accomplish this task, and to look at how far it has come, and by what road, in understanding and defining its own unique process. This much is necessary if we are to gain any understanding of supervision, the unique teaching process which has been developed in this field.

One has only to listen for a few minutes to the radio broadcasts in a community fund drive to realize the deep personal sources from which this thing called social casework springs. Every appeal reaches out to touch the wound of human difference, to arouse guilt for what one has of equipment, possession, or opportunity that another lacks, and to mobilize for action the ever-ready desire to wipe out or equalize difference. Underneath the superficiality and sentimentality of the words of the appeal lie the fundamental psychological and ethical problems growing out of the inescapable fact that each human being feels himself to be different from his fellows in circumstance and opportunity and in something essentially characteristic of himself as a person. The guilt for this difference no individual ever resolves finally for himself; no government, democratic, fascistic, or communistic, has succeeded in eliminating it for its citizens.

It may well be that the sensitivity to the other person, the response to need, out of which the institution of social work has developed, is more active in a democratic society where the fact of human difference is admitted and acted on in all the structures and processes of governmental organization. It is true at any rate that in the democracy in which we live, the United States, the problems of the person in need have always been consciously felt. Out of this sensitivity and responsibility of each man to his fellow, a persistent effort to respond to his need, to discharge some obligation to him, can be traced through the years, taking organized shape and solidity in many institutional efforts directed toward various problems of society. Within these institutions and agencies financed by individuals, sensitive to need and obligating themselves to meet it, the development of a service to individuals in need, known as social casework, has moved ahead to a professional status beyond that which has been attained in any other country in the world.

However, it was not until the passage of the Social Security Act in 1935, when through the depression years the burden of need had mounted to a weight far beyond the capacity of privately supported agencies to meet, that the obligation was really shifted to the tax-supported sources of government. Today these public agencies recognize, as do the agencies supported by voluntary individual contribution, the essentially individualized professional nature of the help they have to offer to individuals in need. In all these agencies, no matter what the source of support, the practice of social casework is defining itself, is developing skill and competence.

This fact of the institutional support for social casework service is of fundamental significance and importance in shaping the unique character of its professional practice. It was just this step, taken when a group of people decided to come together into a Charity Organization Society to administer relief responsibly as an agency, rather than in individual response to individual need, that marked the beginning of the possibility of creating a professional service out of such purely personal sources. This difference continues today to distinguish the social caseworker, who operates always as a representative of an agency bound by its function and policies, from the doctor, the psychiatrist, or the psychoanalyst who, whatever his institutional connection, operates in his own private office, on his own professional responsibility. The implications of this difference for the training and development of the social caseworker are fundamental.

A third factor which has marked the service of social casework as different from other types of service is that, until recently and only in a few fee-charging situations, there has been no money payment from the client to the agency. In all the ordinary transactions of living through which a man satisfies his needs in the environment around him, there are two well-understood ways of relating. One's personal needs for love and affection, for comfort and support, for differing and fighting, for uniting and separating, are projected on people with needs like one's own. One gives and takes and controls in the coin of personal payment so well accepted, if so poorly handled, in the personal relationships of friendship, of enmity, of love, of marriage and family life. Certain needs can be projected onto objects or tangible, defined professional services. Characteristic of these need relationships is the fact of money payment set by the one who has the object to sell or the service to offer and accepted by the one who comes to buy. True, that into the process of buying an object or a tangible service goes something more than the mere payment of the money value set upon the object or the service. The individual choice, the felt impulse or need in the self, which extends itself out to an object, chooses among several objects, and takes possession of it thereafter for his own use, can be a highly exhilarating and life-giving experience. But the aspect of the process that is emphasized is the money payment which carries the relationship between buyer and seller, stabilizes it, and keeps it within bounds.

Contrast these need relationships, the one kind carried in personal payment, the other stabilized in money payment, with the relationship set up by a social agency where the client comes seeking an answer to need and has not the wherewithal to pay or the accustomed controls of the personal relationships. Often he is asking for money, for food, for shelter, for the basic necessities of life for which all men in our culture expect to pay, or for help in a personal situation which has become intolerable. If self-respect is to be maintained and hopefully to be increased in this experience, in what new coin can payment be made? With this problem social casework has struggled, at first more or less blindly but with increasing consciousness, understanding, and responsibility.

What are the problems of a relationship created by one human being's need of something which he cannot obtain in his accustomed way by his own efforts projected onto another human being. From the moment of birth, when the organism is precipitated into an external and alien environment, it must satisfy organic needs through establishing connections with the environment, with the object which contains the answer to need and always in relation to a person who has some control of the source of need satisfaction. As the organism succeeds in establishing its necessitous connections, the ways in which these are established, the very connections themselves, become specific and necessitous so that any interference with these ways may become as threatening or even more so than the loss of the object satisfaction itself. The baby nursing from breast or bottle, or being taught by mother or nurse to control the processes of elimination, gives evidence of the deeply rooted, intricate nature of the connections between need, its sources of satisfaction, and the inevitable role of the other person in the process of need satisfaction. In this process, the child is patterning, not only his own ways of satisfying and controlling his own needs, but just as exactly and specifically his ways of reacting to need in the other person.

Many individuals who succeed in establishing patterns that serve their organic needs satisfactorily and with a use of the other person which is not too destructive or unacceptable to the other person may go through life without having the consciousness of need break through too painfully and without any necessity for change in the patterns of connection or of control in relation to the physical environment and to the other person. Even the sex need when it arises may find its object so quickly and so characteristically that no fundamental change in the individual's patterns of connection takes place. Other individuals find no such easy and simple connection but seem alway conflicted in relation to the object choice, rendered confused, obstinate, or negative by the presence of the other person. Some remain confused and conflicted, never able to find direction or satisfaction. Others may seek satisfaction determinedly with the exercise of a powerful will, accepting as little as possible from the other person, sometimes able to get their own ends only by a negative, destructive relation to the other person, or by controlling others through dependency and assertion of weakness. The way the other person, parent, nurse or relative, handles the child in early relationships is deeply determinative of the way this pattern of control and relationship develops.

Whatever the pattern may be that develops in this early childhood experience, it does not easily bear change and interference in any of its established parts any more than with the ends it seeks or with its time rhythms. Certainly some change takes place in these patterns with natural growth and new experience in relationship but always within the limits and along the lines set up by the original experience.

It may profit the reader who is trying to make a decision as to whether he will enter this field of social casework—if there be such a one who has wandered into the pages of this book—to look into himself to see how he reacts in a need situation, to face himself in imagination with the need for some object or person to which he does not have access, or with the loss of some object or relationship that has become necessary to him. Let him add to this the painful realization that, try as he will, he cannot satisfy this necessitous need in himself, or by any reliance on his own exhausted resources, or by his own unaided efforts. It is precisely this grim and desperate realization of impotence that brings a person to the doors of a social agency which has help to offer in this need situation. If the reader can hold himself further to this identification with the one in need, he will know that one does not go to an agency joyfully, with the hope of solution paramount, but apprehensively, suspiciously, with a mobilization of strength to get what he must have in his own way. Perhaps the reader who has consciously lived through an experience in which he has tried to recover a lost object of need can feel the blind rush of defenses to control the object, the other, through whom satisfaction can come. Perhaps he can then guess the overwhelming feeling of this pressure to ward off and gain control as it attacks that other person.

The day-by-day experience of the social caseworker appointed by an agency to carry out its social purpose consists of impact with just such individual need in its most critical shapes, with hunger and suffering; impact with human weakness and strength projected in confusing forms, one masking under the guise of the other. The very life stream of social casework flows through this sensitivity to need, sustained in the feeling response of human beings who act as caseworkers. The individual who decides to enter this field of service to persons in need will be faced immediately and inevitably with two problems: his own tendency, if he is open and sensitive to the other person, to become involved in the other's need as if it were his own; at the same time his reaction, whether it be resistance or yielding, to the kind of will control or pressure which the other person inevitably exerts on him.

What is asked of the worker who elects to enter this field of social casework is not a sacrifice of sensitivity but rather a deepening of sensitivity to the other person and an extension of the areas of his sensitivity to needs different from his own. But more than this, he must learn to find some detachment in himself, some separation between himself and the other person that can enable him to know and accept himself as different in relation to the need and will of that other. In this acceptance and use of difference lies the essential discipline of social casework as a profession. True, some use of professional difference is a part of the training and discipline of every professional person, but in no other profession does it constitute to the same degree the very essence of the discipline without which there is no service. Other professions have more tangible services to offer: medicine, its diagnostic skill, effective drugs, hospital care, operations; law has knowledge and technical advice not in the possession of the layman. But social casework has had to learn that even when it has tangible satisfactions of need to offer—money, an assistance check, a home for a child—the object is never the right answer, is never the solution of the problem, or enough in itself as an answer to need. Only if something can happen in the casework process which enables an individual in need to shift his relation to the need object, to modify his ways of seeking and controlling it, to find a new relation to external resources and to his own strength and weakness in himself, is there any real service rendered.

The choice of this professional field cannot be made by the young person just out of college, no matter how carefully he has studied the catalogues of the professional schools, or how widely he has inquired. The real moment of choice can only come later when he has had experience in using his good ability, his fine mind, his sensitivity, his intense desire to be of help, in actual practice under supervision. When he discovers himself inadequate, perhaps even destructive, in the way he naturally uses himself with a client, then only is he ready to make a choice. If the realization of problem in himself, in his own equipment and patterns of relationship, penetrates deeply enough into his consciousness, then he may really choose to undergo the change in the self, the discipline involved in learning how to use himself helpfully.

Here, in this moment of realization of his own problem and his own need, the student worker can experience most truly his likeness to the client in their common humanity but he experiences this now in a way that moves, not in the personal way of identification and the creation of greater likeness, but to the acceptance of difference between himself and the other. In the first steps he must take here, only the function, policies, and limits of the social agency can provide him with any stable, legitimate basis for acceptance of his right to set himself in any way apart, in difference from, or opposition to, the client's need and control. This conviction of difference can never be sustained as personal difference without guilt and involvement, nor can it be long sustained as professional difference in even the most experienced, skillful worker, without the support and limitation of agency-defined structure and conditions.

When the client comes asking, "Will you help me with the problem of my husband, my child, my job, or myself?" the worker can meet this projection of need with a statement of what the agency he represents has to offer, the conditions and requirements the seeker for help has to meet if he uses the agency, so that the relationship is lifted at once in the very beginning, for both worker and client, out of the depths of personal involvement into which any projection of need is naturally precipitated. It makes possible the initiation of a new kind of relationship, one whose limits and boundaries can be touched, which will involve client and worker in a use of themselves very unlike the way that is natural to them in personal relationships. The movement through such a relationship to its eventuation is without precedent in the previous experience of student-in-training or client. Each will strive unconsciously to make it into something more familiar and natural to him and will inevitably become lost in his old patterns unless there is firm, sure help for the student from someone who has been through this before, who knows its course and its possible outcome—the competent supervisor.

With this brief sketch of the development of social casework from its impulsive sources in the need-to-give to the one in need, to a skilled service extended by a professional caseworker who has undergone change in his use of himself in need situations, the profession of social casework today would be in agreement. There is, however, a marked divergence of point of view and practice within the profession as to the nature of the social casework process and consequently a difference of understanding as to the change which the training process effects and the method and practice of supervision. The school of thought which I have helped to develop and with which I am identified, now known as functional social casework, is the practice I will describe in subsequent chapters.

2. FUNCTIONAL SOCIAL CASEWORK

A divergence in point of view in the theory and practice of social casework began to make itself apparent in the late twenties and
early thirties. It was not easy for this young profession, so conscious
of its good intention, its positive will to help others, to admit that
difference could exist in its own ranks. For social caseworkers to differ was in itself bad and wrong, not to be tolerated. Only when difference could be frankly recognized and discussed was a more vigorous phase of professional growth initiated.

This difference was at first identified, strangely enough, not with
the names of teachers or schools of social work but with the names
of two psychoanalysts, Sigmund Freud and Otto Rank, a fact which
in itself indicates the reliance which social casework found it necessary to place on something outside its own professional experience.
In psychiatry, social casework had discovered a new understanding
of human nature. Now, in the early thirties, its practitioners were
turning to psychoanalysis, not so much for help in their personal
problems, as in behalf of learning greater skill in helping others.
Whatever the admixture of reasons for which they sought this psychoanalytic help, it gave them a new experience of themselves, of
their own needs and motivations, and a new understanding of the
meaning of seeking and taking help which had a profound influence
on their own relationships with their clients. In these contacts with
psychoanalysis they found also an illuminating philosophy of relationship, a psychology of growth, and conscious, articulated therapeutic method. This is not the place to attempt a description of the
fundamental differences in psychology and therapeutic method expressed in the contributions of Freud and Rank.[1] The fact remains
that these differences found response in already existing differences
in social casework point of view and in turn sharpened and deepened
them. As a result the profession of social casework now recognizes
a division in its theory and practice into two schools. With the one,
which still goes under the name of Freudian, or psychoanalytically
oriented social casework, I shall not attempt to deal in any way. The
discussion of casework and supervision in this volume will limit itself
to the practice that has developed under the Rankian influence now
known as functional social casework, a term truly descriptive of a

characteristic psychology and method growing out of the experience
of the profession itself.

This change of name from "Rankian" to "functional" could only
come about in the passage of time through a process of assimilation
of all that had been learned from Rank's point of view and a shift in
focus from the experience of learning and taking help for the self to
a new relation to teaching and giving help to clients. It is interesting
and characteristic of Rank's own understanding of differentiation in
growth processes that, when the powerful influence which emanated
from his therapy, direct personal teaching, and writings began to be
assimilated by the faculty and supervisors in the Pennsylvania School
of Social Work, where his relation to social casework was most fully
expressed, there was no tendency to introduce into casework or supervision any imitation or adaptation of the therapeutic form or
method of treatment.[2]

On the other hand, there began to appear a sharper sense of
focus and responsibility developing around specific services or functions of agencies and deeper sensitivity to the feelings and movement
of the clients in using those services. Irene Liggett's article entitled
"Agency and Child in the Placement Process"[3] was outstanding in
these early efforts to describe the conflicted process of seeking help
on the part of the client of the child-placing agency, and the vital use
of agency structure in making foster-home placement a helpful service to parent and child. Almena Dawley's article "Diagnosis: The
Dynamic of Effective Treatment"[4] described this process for the
parent seeking help in a child-guidance clinic. My book *Supervision
in Social Casework* analyzed the learning process of students as a
process of taking help in relation to the function of supervision.

By 1937, this process of taking and giving help had become sufficiently clear, through the use of various specific functions in its
fieldwork agencies, to enable the Pennsylvania School to see this
process as a universal helping process. Jessie Taft in her introduction
to the first number of the *Journal of Social Work Process,* published
by the School in November 1937, states this universal base in these
words:

> In science the hypothesis, the problem, the experiment, the con-
> trolled situation, are only various forms of putting up a man-
> made limitation to nature, to see what will happen and what
> characterizes the process. In social work, the limitation with
> which we operate is necessarily the function with its expression

in agency policy, structure, and procedures. Certainly function is never completely static or inflexible, certainly it alters over a period of time in terms of changing social conditions or should alter, but relatively it is the known factor, the comparatively stable, fixed point about which client and worker may move without becoming lost in the movement. Every helping situation is an experiment for the worker and for the client. The worker sets up conditions as found in his agency function and procedure; the client, representing the unknown natural forces, reacts to the limitation as well as to the possible fulfillment inherent in the function, over a period of testing it out. He tries to accept, to reject, to attempt to control, or to modify that function until he finally comes to terms with it enough to define or discover what he wants, if anything, from this situation.[5]

In the ten years that have followed this statement, graduates of the Pennsylvania School of Social Work have dmonstrated the applicability of this concept of function and its use in all branches of social casework. Herbert Aptekar's book *Basic Concepts in Social Case Work*[6] has been of great value in setting forth the concepts of functional casework in a form usable by students. Most recently, its application in that difficult, unpromising field of work with promiscuous girls has been described and illustrated by Mazie Rappaport,[7] and its value for the oldest traditional field in this profession, family casework, has been definitely established by M. Robert Gomberg.[8] In the two publications just mentioned and in other earlier ones, there are ample definitions of functional casework and analyses and illustrations of its use in various fields. For a brief, comprehensive, and definitive statement of its point of view and method in contrast to the school of casework which is psychoanalytically oriented, nothing better has been said than is contained in the paper of the late Kenneth L. M. Pray, "A Restatement of the Generic Principles of Social Casework in Practice in 1946," presented at the National Conference of Social Work in San Francisco, in April 1947.[9]

Dr. Taft in her introduction to *Family Casework and Counseling: A Functional Approach,* and in her discussion of Dr. Gomberg's article, and Dr. Gomberg in his article on counseling[10] with the two case records give an authoritative, detailed exposition of functional casework in operation, an analysis of the psychological point of view on which a functional helping process is based and of the laws of its movement within a time structure in an agency situation. These articles also differentiate this point of view and method from psychotherapy and from the social casework theory and method that emanate from a Freudian point of view.

In preparing this book for publication during the summer of 1946, Dr. Taft realized that, while the meaning and nature of help and helping had been taken for granted throughout this book and illustrated specifically, these concepts had nowhere been defined in universal terms. In recognition of the need for a statement of a concept of professional helping, as a generic psychological process underlying all specific forms of casework as well as psychotherapy, she supplied the following:

> I would draw a distinction between what might be called "real" help, by which I mean a realistic meeting of need without hindrance and on its own terms, and *psychological* help whose meaning and value are registered in the very experience of taking help through the medium of a helping person whose difference from the applicant is maintained and becomes effective in the process. To take help in this sense is, we believe, the deepest, most fundamental form of personality change and of learning because it penetrates to the roots of human relationships as they are developed from the beginning in the manifold forms of giving and taking, of relying upon, yet struggling to control, those who supply the answer to urgent need from the mother on. Because the original human need is of necessity placed, not on things but on a person, it sets the pattern of all our later efforts to develop within the self enough integration and self-possession to grant to the "other" his equal right to a self of his own, a self which is not there just to meet our need in our own terms. Perhaps no human being ever gives up completely that first image of the all-giving one who has no self-interest to consider, no desire beyond that which is attuned to our own changing necessity. But if maturity, as a result of psychological growth, has any meaning surely it must relate to the degree of success which has been attained in that unending struggle to develop a strength and integrity that can accept and bear internal need without assuming the obligation of the other to meet it and without exerting pressure upon him to fulfill our requirements regardless of his own desire or willingness.
>
> When a man is brought to the necessity of asking assistance from an outside source because of his own inadequacy, inability, or failure to manage his own affairs, whatever has been faulty in his way of relating to the other will be brought into focus as he tries to find his role as client of a social agency.

While he is free to concentrate on his own need and to try to get it satisfied in exactly the way he has planned, he is met in the person of the caseworker by something that is quite unknown to him out of his experience in purely personal relations. He has no personal claim or hold on this worker or this agency, although he may try to establish one, yet she meets his request with a consideration for him, an understanding of what it costs him to ask, that answers to an unmet hunger of which he has probably been unaware. He finds also that this worker is not there just to meet his need but that she represents an agency which has a character of its own, a defined purpose, a service with limitations as well as resources. This applicant, whose request has been received with such respectful and thoughtful consideration, is now faced with the fact that the agency presents a difference which must be taken into account and that to use its service, he must go beyond the pressure for immediate fulfillment to a reevaluation of his own situation in relation to the service which the agency can give. He may decide that this agency does not have what he requires and go elsewhere but, if he stays, he will have to modify his idea of his need and his determination to have things his way in terms of a new plan or purpose which includes the agency in its difference. This does not take place easily or at once but, if the need is acute, the pressure for fulfillment intense, and the worker skillful in meeting it, the struggle to find a way to use the agency that is right for both can precipitate an experience that goes to the very roots of the client's faulty relationships.

No difference in the other is so painful, so unbearable, as that difference which threatens the satisfaction of a need that seems vital. How then can a client who is forced to ask help, not of a friend but of an impersonal agency, ever find the difference which the agency represents to be anything but intolerable although he may be forced to submit by the urgency of his need? That this experience can be a source of fundamental learning, of actual reorganization of the self with which he comes is due to the fact that the agency is known, is differentiated, through the medium of his relation to the worker whose human understanding, professional skill, and genuine readiness to help, give to the client increasing awareness and possession of himself as an individual whose right to differ is thoroughly respected. It is this combination of regard for him and his need, together with the worker's affirmation of agency as something which goes beyond her power to alter in his favor, that can break up the client's impulsive or willful presentation of himself and finally permit a true yielding to the reality of the situation, the agency's and his own. Not blind submission to superior force or inner need, but a new willingness to let the other have a part in the giving because that other has recognized the true nature of the asker, has not tried to control, although he has refused to be controlled.

This, then, is what I understand to be the essence of the helping process, which can take place as a professionally determined process only when the helper has developed in his own person a professional self to which the personal need is subordinated and by which it is controlled when responsibly engaged with a client as the human representative of an agency whose purpose and raison d'être is to give a service so that it will be truly helpful to the individual who can use it.

With this understanding of the meaning of a helping process basically accepted, functional social casework must now struggle with the problem of finding limits for the time structure within which this process can most effectively operate. These limits can be realistically determined where tangible services are offered as in child-placing, day care, protective service, medical social service, relief-giving, and public assistance. In such services as child guidance and counseling, no such realistic basis exists. Therefore, determination of the time limit must grow either out of a responsibility for the psychological movement of the client in the process itself such as the psychotherapist accepts or out of a relatively arbitrary limitation of time based to some extent on agency necessities.

Dr. Taft summarizes this problem in its present stage in *Family Casework and Counseling: A Functional Approach.* There she suggests the use of an arbitrary time span offered in advance as an agency-limited and agency-defined service, and likens the resistance both agencies and practitioners exhibit to the use of an arbitrary time structure to the "older fear once experienced by many workers in relation to any firm definitive utilization of agency function." She goes on to say:

> It is apparently very difficult for us to look at time in the same objective and realistic way (as the relief budget) when it becomes not the medium for therapy, individually determined by the therapist who is individually responsible, but the particular service which the agency offers to meet a family relationship problem. Neither agency nor worker needs to take on

therapeutic responsibility for the length of time it can offer. Instead, on the basis of its past experience, it can offer what it
has found to be a useful length of time for dealing with certain
kinds of family problems. There is a practical element in this
arbitrary limiting of time, just as there is in the limiting of a
budget. It should represent what the agency can afford to give
in terms of the available time of its workers and the needs of
other services. What we evidently fear to trust is the capacity
of a client to make his own best use of the time offered, if he
can accept its limitation in advance, indeed can choose it as
something impersonal and a general policy of agency and not
the decision of an individual worker for his case. Although we
have learned that clients are helped through the very process
of finding and asserting themselves, in the struggle with the
agency's conditions and limitations, even in the instance of
learning to use a far from ideal budget,or to accept the visiting
restrictions of a foster care agency, we still do not believe, apparently, that the client is equally capable of wrestling with,
and creating on, the very limitation that a definite time-span
imposes. In my opinion, the agency's authority for a time-limited service, even more than its setting of a fee, marks a reliable differentiation between therapy and casework, not only
for the client but for the worker.[11]

With this indication of the problems of the use of fee and time
limits with which functional social casework is engaged today in its
newest, most experimental venture in counseling services, we can
leave this brief survey of the development of functional casework.
We must ask next what equipment it requires of a worker to practice in this field in this way, to offer the service of a functional
agency, to carry a helping process through to an ending with a client,
to be a responsible, participating member of the staff of a social
agency.

These requirements can be summarized under four headings:
First, the worker must have an acceptance of agency as the creator
of the helping situation, the whole, greater than himself, of which
he must become a part, which limits as well as supports his professional activity. Second, the worker must come to an identification
with the function of the agency which from the beginning provides
the wedge of separation and differentiation between himself and the
client, out of which a professional rather than a personal relationship
can develop. Third, the worker must have the ability to enter into

this process with the client, to feel and utilize his own reactions as his own while he remains constantly sensitive to the reactions of the client. Dr. Gomberg gives fine accurate expression to the meaning of this participation in the helping process when he says:

> I believe that the true power of the relationship as a possible source of help for the client does not lie in the ability to piece together intellectually the meaning of earlier experiences, so that one thus understands the genesis of a problem, important and useful as this may be for the *worker*. *Help* for the *client* rests in the vitality of the immediate contact as an emotionl experience, in which the worker takes full responsibility for his own realness and that of the agency. He does not exist outside the sphere of the client's life and conflict, merely understanding, interpreting, and guiding, but rather for the time of the contact he takes responsibility for becoming a part of the client's emotional life experience.[12]

Finally, to practice functional casework skillfully, the worker must have an acceptance of the time-limited nature of the process and some experience with the movement of taking help as it develops in a limited time structure.

Obviously, no purely intellectual learning can give the worker the understanding of this relationship process and the ability to use himself in it. Only an experience of his own, similar to the experience of a client in taking professional help in a time-limited structure and the spontaneity and discipline in the use of himself which eventuate from that experience, can enable him to function as a responsible practitoner of social work. It will be the purpose of the rest of this book to show how this can take place in a training process and to analyze the role of supervision in this process.

PART TWO. SUPERVISION AS TEACHING METHOD
IN SOCIAL CASEWORK

3. THE DEVELOPMENT OF SUPERVISION IN
SOCIAL CASEWORK

Supervision, with its literal meaning "to oversee, to watch the work of another with responsibility for its quality," has in practice taken on itself the additional responsibility of teaching the learner the skill required. In every field of work—in the crafts, the arts, the professions—supervision has evolved its own peculiar method appropriate to the field and the nature of the skill it teaches and supervises. In industry today, supervision derives from administration and management as a method of inducting workers into the organization, of teaching them the skills and processes they must perform, of holding them to standard performance in time and quality. It is through supervision that the quality of the product is tested and assured. In the fields of education and nursing, supervision has evolved as a means of training nurses and teachers, of standardizing the service of hospitals, public-health nursing agency or school, by maintaining a continuing supervisory control over the quality of service offered.

In those professions where service is offered by the individual practitioner rather than under the control of the institution, as is the case in medicine and law, supervision has not developed to the extent that it has in institutionalized services. Even in hospital and clinic service, the chief of staff, teacher though he may be, does not carry true supervisory responsibility for the internes or young doctors who must learn from his demonstrations, as does the chief nurse on the ward for her nurses in training. The practice of law has developed through an apprentice method of training in which the young lawyer learns in the office and through association with the older, experienced lawyer who takes a paternal or teacher's interest in the young learner, but not the continuous supervisory responsibility as the practice of nursing, for instance, understands it.[1]

During the war, the public had the opportunity of becoming acquainted with several types of supervision developing along different lines appropriate to the particular organization within which it functioned. In the army, where a huge organization is trained and made effective as a fighting force by lines of authority reaching down into small units, supervision develops at every level of authority and responsibility as a method of training, overseeing, and directing the work of the men under supervision. In the air corps, with its smaller units set apart in plane or bomber necessitating a more immediate responsibility for the mission carried by all members of the crew, an entirely different type of relationship and of supervisory control was developed.[2]

In the field of social casework, as in other fields, supervision has evolved in response to the development of the practice in this field and to the agency situation which controls and directs that practice. Since supervision in social casework teaches a helping process, it must itself be a helping process so that the student experiences in his relation to his supervisor a process similar to the one he must learn to use with his client.

Historically, the development of supervision in social casework was slow and at first unconscious. As agencies grew beyond the original staff of one or two workers and new workers had to be inducted, training by apprenticeship evolved as a first step in professional education, bringing with it a certain kind of supervisory responsibility carried by the experienced worker for the beginner. A next step in the development of professional education followed when agencies pooled their resources and sent their new workers to lectures on social problems and methods in the practice of casework taught by the executives of the agencies. At first only a few hours a week were spent in these lectures and classes, the meager beginnings of the curriculum of the professional school of social work, while the real business of training the worker in practice remained with the supervisor, herself without training but with competence gained by experience in the performance of the job. The agency as a whole was actually the training situation in which new workers took on the attitudes of the executives and older workers, became identified with their goals and purposes, and adopted their methods of work as far as it was possible. The very nature of the day-by-day job and service of the agency, helping people in need, tended to bring its workers together in intimate personal association where likeness was at a premium and natural relationships of the character of family relationships were fostered. The small size of the agency, or of the district office of the family society with only three or four workers at the most, was an important factor in the development of this pattern. There was nothing in these situtions, in either the nature of the service or the relation of staff members to the agency as a whole, to encourage the use of the authority with which the function of supervision has been endowed in other fields. Responsibility for the cost of the service, for its financial support, for the relationships to its board and to the community which might have furnished the limits out of which acceptance of authority for supervision rightly develops, tended to be left on the shoulders of the executive. This split of the administrative function from the agency's real job of helping clients left the supervisor, who was originally a caseworker herself, identified with the client and the worker in the casework process and separated from the authority inherent in an effective supervisory function.

The stimulus of the professional school and the authority inherent in its teaching function were necessary in order to lift supervision out of its complete identification with casework and the worker and enable it to take over the authority and responsibility it must accept in order to fulfill its teaching function. It has not yet fully accepted the authority which belongs to its function deriving from its relation to administration and to agency as a whole.

A different development of the supervisory function and responsibility can be observed in the public social agencies where the large, hastily recruited staffs necessary to handle the overwhelming needs of the unemployed in 1929-30 called for a form of organization held together by supervisors who could assume heavy administrative responsibility while at the same time they supervised the workers in the processes of establishing eligibility and getting relief to thousands of clients. A typical supervisory load in the days of the depression might be from six to ten workers, each worker carrying from one hundred to several hundred cases. Final responsibility for the relief check, as well as for helping the worker to learn how to meet her client and assist him to establish his eligibility for relief, fell upon the supervisor.

The problem of developing any kind of professional helping service in these relief agencies at the height of the depression seemed almost insuperable. The workers were untrained and in many cases close to the client group; frequently they themselves had suffered from a depression which was no respecter of persons. The meager relief check aroused intense negative feeling in the worker in his identification with the client. In the supervisor alone was there any hope for the development of enough detachment and separation from the client to furnish a basis for offering a professional service. Since these supervisors were in most instances recruited from the private social agencies, they brought to this public job the determination to try to offer an individualized service even to the overwhelming mass of individuals in need. In the small district of the family agency which constituted a common background of experience for many of these supervisors, they had known the community and the families they served. There they could expect to know all the cases carried by their workers; frequently they had carried some of these families themselves. Transferred suddenly to the public agency, these supervisors found themselves responsible for from six to ten workers, each carrying several hundred cases. It was impossible to know those client families directly or even by record reading. Some way of discharging the responsibility vested in the function of supervision had to be found other than by the way of knowledge of the case load itself. Here for the first time in social casework was exerted the pressure of a responsibility out of which a new orientation to supervision and a more professional process could develop. The necessity of training workers and supervisors to meet the demands of this job brought the professional school into the field at this point to claim a professional service and to lift both casework and supervision out of the routine, mechanical job into which they can so easily deteriorate, to the high quality of professional service they have actually developed.

The first efforts to develop supervision as a technical process in its own right began very tentatively in professional schools by bringing together groups of supervisors from different fieldwork agencies to discuss the problems of student training with the teachers and advisers in the professional school. These discussions continued on the assumption that training was a joint enterprise in which agency, supervisors, and school were equally responsible—a natural enough assumption, since the student spent more than half of his time in the fieldwork agency. Only when the professional school moved clearly into its position of responsibility for the student's learning and his training movement was it able to clarify the role of the fieldwork supervisor in its partial place in the total process. Only then could the school take leadership in developing supervision as a technical process in classes taught by members of the school faculty rather than in group discussion with leadership developing where it might.

The first classes in supervision were offered at the Pennsylvania

School of Social Work in 1934-35, in the Smith School of Social Work shortly after. Others followed rapidly. A small body of literature has developed, including two books and several pamphlets and articles on supervision published in the technical journals. Very little recorded material of supervisory conferences is available for study. The Pennsylvania School of Social Work library contains some ten or twelve valuable theses on supervisory problems but these are not in print and cannot be made generally available.[3] From my experience in working with supervisors and teaching classes in supervision, it is my belief that skill and competence in the possession of supervisors goes far beyond what the meager published literature would indicate. It is to be hoped that the next decade will bring a development of this literature.

In *Supervision in Social Casework,* I defined supervision as "an educational process in which a person with a certain equipment of knowledge and skill takes responsibility for training a person with less equipment. . . . In the field of social casework, this teaching process is carried by a succession of conference discussions between the supervisor and the student."[4] To this definition of 1936, a decade of training experience in the use of functional supervision has contributed one revolutionary change. It has clarified the understanding of a time structure with a beginning, focus, and ending, and its utilization for the movement of a relationship process. This difference between a "succession of conference discussions" and a time-structured process is crucial.

Nothing has been more effective in bringing out an understanding of the learning movement in the student than the use of the arbitrary time form in the hands of the professional school—the two-year training program, structuralized into fifteen-week semesters. This movement begins with the student's choice of the field and the particular school in the application process, proceeds into his use of each part of the prescribed curriculum, until it comes to an eventuation in his thesis statement of his learning and conviction presented from his own practice. From the beginning to the end of this two-year training process, the Pennsylvania School maintains its focus in the practice of the student, the use the student makes of himself, and his understanding of this use, in other words, in a developing professional self and its expression in professional skill. This emphasis on a focus in the self and its use in a functionally defined helping relationship is wholly new to every student and cannot fail to arouse deep apprehension until there is reached a turning point in the process, a new balance in the self, when the student can feel the focus in his movement as his own rather than as external requirement and pressure from the School.[5]

This description of the professional curriculum in social work as a single training movement focused in the student differentiates this concept of professional training clearly from academic education and professional education in other fields where the focus is lodged in curriculum content. At the same time it must be recognized also that, in this emphasis on the use of an arbitrary time form which derives from the educational institution, the professional school introduces into the practice of supervision in the social agency a more clearly defined and sharply limited time structure calling for greater decisiveness in its use for evaluation of the student's progress than casework and supervision in general practice have as yet accepted.

The question will be raised as to why—if the Pennsylvania School so clearly accepts responsibility for the student's training process as a whole—it does not set up its own fieldwork situations with supervisors appointed and paid by the School, as is the practice in some schools of social work. I have discussed this question in *Training for Skill in Social Case Work* and quote from it here:

> Our original connection with the agencies offers the obvious historical explanation. But more important is the fact that in using this existing school-agency connection we have learned to value the actual agency experience as an essential element in student training. His field placement gives the student from the beginning a responsibility as a functioning part of an agency offering service to clients, more real than is possible when he is placed in a training district set up and controlled by the School.[6]

The very fact that students have their practice in a variety of agencies, each with its characteristic function and organization different from each other yet alike in their conception of a service agency and a helping process, provides the reality and the richness which students need for their development in this professional field. Students understand that in learning to offer the service of a social agency responsibly they are learning also the professional nature of this service as a typical helping process. Through this conviction, their identification is not limited to the particular social agency or agencies in which they have had their practice but is firmly and soundly established in the profession of social casework. As the Pennsylvania School grows it may become necessary to set up special training situations in the field. If this is done, great care must be taken to secure in these situations the essential characteristics of the social agency in its extension of a functional service to clients with all its realistic problems of organization and community connections.

Between the professional school and its fieldwork agencies there is a constant flow of students into the agency, of graduates in and out of the agency. This mutual dependence creates a special set of problems, which I will not attempt to examine except in respect to the one problem created by the introduction into the agency of the kind of supervision I am describing, focused in a training movement set up in a rhythmical and clearly limited time form sustained by the School. In the succeeding chapter, I will look at the personal and ethical problems inherent in the supervisory relationship for student and supervisor-in-training. In Part Three, I have undertaken to present a detailed description of the way in which this relationship so fraught with personal need can become a reliable professional process of learning, change, and growth when the professional school carries responsibility for the process as a whole and for the training of the supervisor as well as of the student.

4. THE SUPERVISORY RELATIONSHIP: ITS PERSONAL SOURCES AND FUNCTIONAL CONTROLS

No amount of clarity in the definition of supervision, no statement of its role, its function, or its controls, can eliminate the problems which the very nature of the relationship itself arouses for the student and the new supervisor. The School itself, in its tested experience in using this relationship for students, in introducing the concept of functional difference, in its conviction as to the value of functional limits in determining the ongoing, forward movement in this relationship, seems both to the new supervisor and the student to deny the very problems which the relationship creates. There is, I believe, some truth in their accusations, in that the setting-up of any function that brings out into the open or emphasizes a psychological difference between two human beings is a denial of the unity of connection, of the deepest sources of relationship. I believe that any relationship process, whether it be therapy, supervision, or casework, must inevitably stir those deepest sources of connection in the individual who is using it. Unless the professional person responsible for carrying the helping function, at the same time that he holds to the limits of the function, is also able to feel these sources in himself without denial and without personal involvement, the process will be blocked in its movement or limited in the extent to which it involves the whole self of the other person and permits the change he needs.

In every association between two people which has sufficient depth, continuity, and meaning to be called a relationship, there takes place some exchange between the two individual selves involved, an effort to achieve a new balance in the self. Each puts out something of himself upon the other, tries out his likes or dislikes, ventures an expression of his prejudices, his opinions, or the ideas by which he lives. Sometimes one risks behavior which reveals the bad self that can feel anger, jealousy, resistance, the feelings not permitted recognition in the well-trained "good" self that has been built up in family, school, and social relationships. Along with this inevitable tendency in the self to split up its organization, on the one hand, to free itself of what it needs to be rid of as no longer of a piece with the whole, or perhaps simply as too burdensome, too much, to be contained in the self, on the other hand, to give to the other what is precious and dearly valued, goes an opposite tendency. This tendency may be in exact proportion to the first tendency to project what the self can no longer carry alone. It seeks to take back from the other on whom it has deposited parts of itself something in exchange for what it has given. A subtle psychological process impossible to describe with sufficient fineness goes on in the necessity of each individual in relationship to equalize the exchange, to annihilate the difference between them, to make the other like the self through projection, or the self like the other through identification. Each must struggle to control this process in terms of his own pattern and to his own ends.

This fundamental need in relationship has its sources deep in the relationship in which the child is carried in the mother's body and later nursed at her breast. In the uterus, the growing fetus dominates the relationship for nine months and comes into the world a complete, fully formed organism always with some feeling of its own organic unity, no matter how that unity has been threatened with disruption in the throes of the birth struggle. At the same time there is an equally great sense of loss of unity in the birth struggle as all sources of connection with the mother are cut off and the child must establish connections with the sources of nourishment and other life processes in new ways unknown to him. The mother enters into this moment of isolation and disunity to offer the child a new source of connection whereby he can achieve wholeness again through the partial relationship with her which nursing at the breast provides. This nursing relationship between mother and child in which there is the highest degree of mutuality, of giving and taking, serves as the prototype of all mutuality in later relationship.

No matter how carefully and how considerately the child is weaned from this relationship, no child leaves it wholly of his own accord with what belongs to the mother truly resigned, and all that is his own completely possessed and affirmed. Some struggle of wills between them is necessary to produce the separation essential for the child's growth as an individual and out of this struggle some negative elements, anger and hate, fear and resistance, remain as deposits to reappear in later relationship situations. The positive counterparts remain also where love has been given and taken between mother and child, and the need to experience again this mutuality in living is the most powerful craving in relationship.

In the supervisory relationship in social casework, where two individuals enter into a process set up in a rhythmical time structure, this tendency to mutuality must be understood as the basic fundamental trend, it overrides all the obvious factors of difference which would seem at first glance to take precedence over likeness. True, there is an initial phase when student and supervisor alike must go through some struggle to accept each other in this relationship at all, but once accepted even though superficially, the tendency then to create likeness begins to operate between supervisor and student of different ages, of different sexes, of different races, of different temperaments. It is a common observation that a supervisor's first student seems strangely like herself and is so described. The student, I believe, begins with a more painful consciousness than does the supervisor of the difference between them which he struggles to annihilate in every way familiar to him. For him too, as well as for the supervisor, there must be some thread of likeness on which he can bridge the difference and move into the relationship. He may find this likeness in his own most personal terms. It may be as superficial a thing as the color of the supervisor's eyes or the clothes she wears; it may be almost wholly a projection out of the need of the student rather than the supervisor's quality. It may, on the other hand, arise truly out of a deep and sensitive recognition of some characteristic quality with which the student can identify. However real or unreal it may be, some sense of likeness in the beginning of this relationship is necessary in order that there be a beginning but it must be tested and retested, torn apart and built up again on a more substantial basis, until finally it develops into a reliable professional identification.

Given this natural tendency to identification as an early and necessary phase of the supervisory relationship, it is essential that the supervisor recognize it and the trend to mutuality in the process which grows out of it so inevitably and overwhelmingly, as something she must deal with and control in herself if the movement is to develop into a professional learning process for the student. For the new supervisor this ability to differentiate herself from the student, to check her own natural use of relationship, does not come easily or quickly. For her, too, a learning process, a reorganization of the self, is required which begins with her ability to accept a professional difference from the student.

The phrase "professional difference" is glibly said, taken for granted. How natural and easy to slip by it with evasion or denial of its implications! Present this concept of professional difference to any group of supervisors and watch the inevitable struggle against its implications. Typically the opposition gathers under the banner of democracy and contends for equality in professional relationships. One may answer that equality is indeed an end result, that one hopes that the student will in the course of training and practice attain the skill and the competence which is in the possession of his supervisor. But to start with an assumption of equality is to deny to the student his right to any learning process. Add to this, in answer to protest, all the concrete, real illustration of actual, undeniable difference. Remind these supervisors of their own training, of their years of experience, of their knowledge of the agency, of its policies and procedures, in contrast with the student's inexperience and ignorance. Bring out for them some realization of the responsibility they carry for the agency's work and service, which the student cannot possibly be asked to sustain as they do, and the authority that the school places in their hands for the evaluation of the student's progress.

But this answer and these illustrations of actual factual differences do not reach to the depths of the fundamental human problem which is stirred here by the requirement one is setting up in asking a supervisor to begin to take on herself the role of supervising another person entering the profession, to affirm her functional difference. As teacher of this practice of supervision, one must comprehend the depth of the characteristic human aversion to assuming the role of supervisor and know that there is no escape from the guilt that such an assumption of the right to assert and sustain a difference from another human being arouses in everyone. Even though a caseworker has learned to affirm and use her difference in the role of helper to the client, she cannot move into the role of supervisor and affirm her difference from the student or worker, so much more nearly her equal perhaps than her client, without experiencing new depths in this problem of separation and differentiation.

I know of no more touching and meaningful illustration of this guilt for difference and the problem it can create in a supervisory relationship than in a story told by St. Clair McKelway in his articles on "A Reporter With the B-29'," published by *The New Yorker.*[1] I quote from those articles:

> Everybody seemed to realize that everybody else was working his head off. Requests were made, commands were given, in quiet voices. Everybody seemed almost miraculously full of tolerance and understanding.
>
> There was a major who had worked all night in his Quonset office and was about to grab two hours' sleep on his office cot before going on with his work. Around 6 a.m., he telephoned a staff sergeant, a clerk who he knew was on duty in the main administration building of headquarters. The major had to have an envelope that contained certain secret matter. The sealed envelope, with his name on it, was in the headquarters safe. He had to have it, he told me later, in case the information in it was required of him at a conference he was to attend after the nap he was about to take, and he had decided it would be better if he had the envelope in his breast pocket when he took his nap. He wanted to get it into his pocket and off his mind. He called the staff sergeant whose duty it was to look after the safe, to put things in it and take things out for all the officers who used it. The major explained about the envelope and asked the sergeant to get it and bring it over to the Quonset office right away. The staff sergeant, who had been working all night too, asked if he could wait and have the clerk who was to

relieve him in about fifteen minutes deliver the envelope. The major said no, that he really wanted the envelope right away, that he hated to ask the sergeant to do it, but would the sergeant please bring the envelope over to him right away? The sergeant started to say something further and the major, a bit tense but still good-tempered, told the sergeant he didn't want to talk about it any more, told the sergeant just to do what he had asked him to do, and then hung up while the sergeant was still talking. Five minutes later the sergeant brought the envelope to the Quonset, saluted, and laid it on the major's desk. Then the sergeant stood back, saluted again, and asked, May I say something, sir?"

The major sleepily replied, "Sure, sergeant, what is it?" and leaned back in his chair and looked at the sergeant.

"Sir," said the sergeant, "I just want to say that I consider your having hung up on me just now a very rude and unpardonable thing for an officer to do. I work hard and I do my job and I have never been subjected to such treatment before by anybody and I have been in the Army for three and a half years."

"My God, sergeant," the major told me he managed to say, "I'm sorry as hell you're taking what I did that way. I know you're a damn good man, you know I do, and you've helped me out several times before—done work for me you didn't have to do. I apologize, sergeant, for hanging up on you, and I don't want you to think for a moment—even though what I did was wrong—that I meant any lack of respect for you when I did that."

"I consider your having hung up on me, sir, the same kind of mistaken thing General Patton did when he slapped that soldier."

The major says he sat there looking at the sergeant and that tears were suddenly in all four eyes in the Quonset office.

"There he stood," the major said, "a middle-aged fellow, a good guy and a good man all through and up and down, and I'm telling you he taught me a lesson and did something to me as he stood there that I'll never forget and that I hope I'll never get over. I didn't know what it was he represented at the time. All I know is that it made me want to shake hands with him and then maybe cut my throat. I've figured out since that he was the dignity of man personified, if you see what I mean. He stood there and I looked at him and I apologized again. And then *he* began to feel bad because he could see that he had somehow hit me below the belt, so there we were, with

> tears in our eyes, and he wanting now to apologize to me. I'm still a little hazy about how the hell we ever got the thing straightened out. I think he started to apologize to me while I was apologizing to him for the third time and we both laughed and he saluted again and I told him never to lose whatever it was that had made him tell me what he had and he said something about how he hoped I would just forget the whole matter and finally we saluted each other a couple more times and he left and I lay down on my office cot and cried for a second and laughed for sometime and then went right to sleep, feeling wonderful. It's the damnedest experience I ever had, and I thought I had had some in this war."

Here in this brief episode between a major and a sergeant is personal guilt as it inevitably manifests itself in relationship, deeply felt and sensitively described. Guilt such as this dissipates and confuses the strength of purpose and direction of movement in both individuals. Both are precipitated into personal and ethical questions of debt and responsibility to the other and must handle them personally as best they can. Only the obligation to the common task, the functional difference can restore clarity and direction to the relationship.

This guilt reaction must be expected to arise again and again in the supervisor who is learning to take on the role of supervisor for the first time and can only be handled as it is honestly faced in feeling. Only when the supervisor has come through a process with a student to an ending where she can clearly see the use the student has made of her functionally defined and sustained difference, will she have in herself the true differentiation and partialization of herself which enable her to supervise with conviction.

While both student and supervisor alike feel the pull toward mutuality which this relationship arouses, the student's struggle against it is very different from the supervisor's. The supervisor has chosen and accepted the role of supervisor, difficult as she may find it to hold to the role in actuality. The student, on the other hand, even though he has chosen training with all the consciousness and will he has to put into a choice, has not yet accepted the role of student, will struggle against it and try to control the relationship in every way. He must oppose the will to teach him which the training situation places on him no matter how much he wants it. He must test the supervisor's strength and his own choice until he is

sure it is his. Against the supervisor's assertion of her difference and
ability to teach him, he will oppose his effort to make the relationship equal, a social, casual, friendly contact. The use of first names
between them, the habit of staff lunch, and the discussion of common interests encourage this effort on the student's part to wipe out
the threatening difference. He needs protection from these casual
associations which invade the supervisory relationship and the supervisor should find ways to help him avoid them.

One may well wonder what stays this pull to mutuality from
drawing the student into a deep personal and therapeutic use of the
relationship. It is only the inescapable reality of the function he has
chosen in electing the profession of social casework. This function
is the helping function which he begins to carry with a client in
terms of the agency service from the day he begins his training and
enters into a supervisory relationship. There is no preliminary period in which he learns to take help from a supervisor in order that
he may later give it. But at one and the same time he must take help
in a learning process with his supervisor and give it in a helping process with a client. This training experience asks that the student be
both student and helper simultaneously. Seemingly contradictory as
this is, the fact that it works in practice is incontrovertible. It is not
achieved by the student's deserting his side of the desk and trying
to take on by any effort at imitation the supervisor's function and
methods. His process must be exactly the opposite. Nor, as might be
anticipated, can he derive his strength to act as helper to a client in
reliance upon the supervisor's undeviating support. Support there
must be for the process throughout, but to his work with the client
the supervisor must be able to react with her difference, with criticism. Although this may precipitate the student to the depths of inadequacy in one moment of feeling, he must be able to rally from
this guilt and helplessness to an assertion of his role as helper to
the client. What he pulls out of a conference in which he comes to
awareness of his error or his problem in relation to what he is doing
with the client, and what he takes back to the client in his next
interview, brings about some partialization and objectification of
himself that constitute a beginning of a professional use of the self
rather than a merely personal one.

This characteristic of the supervisory relationsip, that it is inextricably related to its content, the helping process with the client,
requiring of the student a constant partialization of his total im-

pulsive projection of himself, is the greatest protection against the
trend to personal and mutual use of the relationship. There is present always the controlling factor that the relationship requires from
the beginning the inclusion of a third person, the client.

This three-person relationship is characteristic, not only of supervision, but of the social agency itself in which this three-way process
has naturally developed. In addition to the client there may be another worker on the case who must be included in the student's
contact. There are agency policies to be considered and other members of the staff. There is also the school, the student-adviser, and
his teacher. Everything in the training process, in agency organization and structure, requires that the student who enters this professional field give up something of his own natural, individual relationship to what he is doing to include other realities that have a part in
the situation. This necessity to take in the third person, to become
a part of a new whole, requires of any individual a deep, new learning.

Those individuals who have never achieved a separation from
the first-person relationship with the mother may not be able to accept the partialization which this training asks. Some students take
hold of the personal help they feel extended in supervision but cannot rally their strength and difference to take on the function of
helper. When it is clear that the student cannot, or will not, move into
training but must use the relationship for his own therapy alone, the
school must discuss this with the student and refer him to a therapist
for the help he needs if he will take it. While he is finding that help,
in most cases it is necessary that he should leave professional training
in order that he may use therapy to the extent of his personal need.
When he has ended that therapeutic experience, if he chooses again
to prepare himself for professional casework and can stabilize the
will-to-be-a-helper sufficiently, he may attempt to re-enter training.
The ability of the school to evaluate these problems, to help the student who cannot use training to leave, depends upon its clarity and
decisiveness in the use of its own training function.

In concluding this examination of the basic human problems in
the supervisory relationship created by the need of both student and
supervisor to use this rhythmic time structure for their own personal
experience, I want to state again my conviction of the unique opportunity which this relationship can extend for professional learning
and development when the relationship is safeguarded for this purpose through the use of functional difference and the responsibility

to the common task, the service to the client. At the same time, as I have pointed out, the very assumption on the part of the school of the right to set up and utilize functional difference as the dynamic of movement in the supervisory relationship implies a denial of the trend to mutuality, of the personal sources which feed relationship, of the necessity to create likeness and make a personal utilization of difference in all relationship processes which involve the self deeply. Unless the school retains its sensitivity to these problems and can extend help to its supervisors as well as to its students, it will find itself constantly thwarted in its effort to carry out its training function.

The constant partialization and new organization of the total impulsive self which are in essence the requirement of the training process in social casework are asked for in every aspect of the training situation, in the supervisor-student-client relationship, in the adviser-student-supervisor relationship, in all the parts of the agency-school structure. All exemplify the essential three-way relationship characteristic of reality and necessary for living and for growth, which for all human beings who have accepted any partialization in early experience constitutes the guarantee of the essential naturalness and universality of the professional process as a true growth process.

PART THREE. THE SUPERVISORY PROCESS AS DETERMINED BY THE STRUCTURES OF THE PROFESSIONAL SCHOOL

5. THE DIFFERENTIATION OF ROLES BETWEEN SUPERVISOR AND STUDENT

The student entering professional training in the Pennsylvania School of Social Work is told in the catalogue statement and in conference with the application secretary and with his adviser that his fieldwork practice in the agency to which he is assigned will occupy three days a week of his time. He[1] is told and to some degree understands the importance of this practice in his training and the fact that his supervisor in the agency will be the person with whom he works on that practice in regular conferences, the person who will know and evaluate his practice with him and with his adviser in the School as the school year goes on. I say he understands to some degree, for this relationship created by his studentship under supervision is a new one, the actual character of which he cannot possibly comprehend until he has experienced it. He identifies it naturally with earlier relationships experienced in school and college, with the teaching and tutorial relationships which were sustained by content and subject matter, with all the typical student resistances to authority and with their individual and personal manifestations. No modifications in these reactions to authority were expected of him in these former teaching relationships, provided the subject matter was mastered. The good student felt himself at home and adequate in these learning relationships of college.

At the very beginning of his professional training, the supervisory situation is described to him by the adviser and set up by the supervisor with definiteness and clarity as to time and statement of purpose. There is content offered in the first hour, some picture of the agency, perhaps a case assigned to the student, a visit where he will have a role to perform in the situation definitely planned. He understands that he will make a record of that visit and that it will be read by the supervisor. He knows that he will return to the supervisor for an hour's conference on what he has recorded and with his questions about what he did, about the client's reactions, about next steps. He is told that he should expect her questions. But does he know that, even though she has told him? If he has really got into this new enterprise, he has likely projected his own way of working and controlling to a degree that has already excluded the other person, his supervisor. Or if he has not gone so far as to exclude her, at any rate he can have no idea what she will put into it. Young students fresh from college discipline frequently bring notes and take notes in these early conferences, are surprised and hurt by the suggestion of the supervisor that this formal note-taking may interfere with what they need to get to here. The formal, organized, controlled, businesslike use of conference time seems to them right and proper in contrast with the informal, loose, give-and-take, gossipy exchange of the personal relationship. Of a professional relationship, different from either of these, they have no conception but must learn that difference through experience.

If this learning is actually to take place in supervision, it can only come about by the supervisor's recognition and acceptance of professional difference between herself and the student—any student —as the basic factor on which the relationship begins.

A young caseworker supervising for the first time, and therefore as much a student in relation to this new practice as her student is in relation to casework, has much to do to establish her difference from the student in her own attitudes. She must separate herself from the case load where she is at home in order to help the student find his relation to it. She must sacrifice her own skillful relation to the client and let the student's awkward, bungling relation intervene. She will suffer for the loss to the client which this occasions temporarily, at any rate, and will wonder if the student's professional development is worth the cost. Sometimes she holds onto the case or intervenes to take it out of the student's hands or unwittingly separates him from it by her own interest and superior capacity to handle it. From these tendencies she must be helped to extricate herself by the student's adviser or the casework teacher, whose primary concern is always for the student.

This young supervisor will of necessity have to assert her difference arbitrarily at first and support it by every formality. The limits of the conference hour may have to be rigidly held to, the content of case discussion planned carefully in advance. Only experience can give her ease and flexibility in sustaining her role. The student will engage his will against hers at any point where hers is mobilized rigidly, and he will therefore have more than the usual training resistances to work through. Again the teacher in the School must help with this by her direct contact with the student as well as with the supervisor. Despite these hazards, experience has proved that a young supervisor can give a satisfactory experience to a beginning student if the whole training process is supported firmly and consistently by the School.

When the supervisor has had sufficient experience to be free to rest on and use her function easily and naturally with the student, there is opportunity to examine how the student begins to find his way into the fieldwork and the agency and how he uses her function in his efforts. First of all, it must be recognized that a careful application process in a school of social work brings to this point of fieldwork placement under a supervisor only students with good ability who are accustomed to success in academic work and in whatever jobs they have engaged in.[2] In coming into training for the field of social work, they have made a professional choice which involves them more completely than any previous educational or vocational decision. They have chosen specifically this particular school for various reasons and have had a chance to test the validity of this choice in an application interview. They may know of others, perhaps classmates, college friends, or fellow workers in the agency where they have been employed, who have been rejected. Many bring with them hearsay tales about students who have been rejected after the first semester or have failed to be recommended to continue after a first year. So the typical reaction of eagerness and assurance and the accompanying apprehension with which everyone enters upon a self-chosen new enterprise are deepened and reinforced here by the application process appropriate to the professional training ahead. The student goes to his fieldwork assignment with all the assurance he can muster, glad to have been chosen, ready to get to work. His previous training and education have taught him to deny or to make light of any indications of fear, if indeed he is conscious of any. The idea that he should actually have resistance to beginning anything he wants so much and has chosen so deliberately is foreign to his whole conception of himself and his way of working.

This positive constructive way of beginning may take many students through the application process which, no matter how hard it tries to present what will be involved in professional training, may be powerless through words alone to bring to the student's consciousness any awareness of other underlying attitudes. Classes, too, have

the familiarity of the college class for the young student and at first
therefore do not stand in the way of his getting to work to master
assignments.

The fieldwork agency and the supervisor, on the other hand, present him with a reality which opposes his constructive, outgoing energy. In the first place the fieldwork placement is the choice of the
School, not necessarily his own.[3] Even though it may be in the area
of his own choice, once the assignment is made, it becomes the
School's decision rather than his. He begins to question various things
about the agency, to compare his placement with that of other students. Occasionally he will protest it with the adviser; but more typically he will accept it, hiding his criticism and suspicions behind a
surface acceptance which asserts that the agency is wonderful and
everything is all right.

The supervisor, standing at the very center of this agency experience as he engages with it, becomes for him the focus of his unrecog-
nized suspicions and fears. Sensitive to the difference which she actually carries in her superior experience, knowledge, and skill to
which he cannot submit until he has accepted his own reactions to
being an ignorant student, he uses any personal difference he can find
to carry his criticism or his fear to level her to equality with himself.
She is too young; she never had a student before; she is too old;
there is a color difference between them, a racial difference, a sex
difference; she was trained in a different school. It would take more
courage and directness than he possesses to face this criticism with
her or with anyone in authority, but in some cases the adviser may
sense the attitude behind some tentative question and be able to
bring it out in the open for what it is.

For the young supervisor who also has difficulty in accepting
her youth and inexperience, it is hard to realize that these factors are
not really the cause of the problem the student is feeling and expressing. Yet she can help him get to an awareness of his negative attitudes if she can believe that they are inevitable reactions to this
new experience and that they will inevitably be projected onto her
person or her professional function. She will have to protect her personal difference and handle her feelings about it as best she can, perhaps needing to talk that over with her own supervisor or with the
adviser in the School, but with the student her attitude must be clear,
firm, and unequivocal. If she can hold to her professional function
and a conviction of the necessary difference it creates between them,

she will become increasingly more skillful in helping the student to recognize his attitudes and his projections as his own and to accept himself as a student, a role different from hers, which carries its own rights and obligations as well as its essential limitations.

A supervisor's use of this differentiation in role and her understanding of its meaning for the student in all of its implications in a training process and in the inherent similarity in the relationship between client and student is well illustrated in the conference quoted below. The supervisor has had many years of experience in a child-placing agency and is at home with her supervisory function; the student is young and inexperienced in the field.

> At our conference we spent a good deal of time on one interview. I commented on the fact that there was a great deal of movement shown in this interview on the part of both the foster mother and the worker and that I felt both had come a long way in understanding and acceptance of each other, as well as of the part the agency had in this situation. We reviewed the steps which had led up to this interview. I said that, of course, we could not expect the foster mother to maintain this level and there would be many ups and downs, but that a beginning had certainly been made. Student was quite aghast that this level could not be maintained and said, "You mean we are going to keep working at just this some more?" I said indeed I did, that learning and changing were slow processes and it was a long time before they became parts of one. I asked him if he thought the foster mother was as concerned with Stanley's relationship to the agency as she was with her own. Wasn't that really what she was trying to say to the worker? Student said, "Well, I certainly missed that." I said perhaps he had, but in discussing Stanley's problem, he had got a great deal over to the foster mother and in a way which she could accept.
>
> I said that maybe the student was having some problem himself in really knowing why the agency was going into foster homes and what his relation to the foster mother should be. He denied this at first and then said that it was hard for him to really understand all of it. I said I knew that, and that we only expected him to get it step by step, the same as we did the foster mother. He said, "Oh, you think I'm a client too." I said, "Well, aren't you? What is a client but someone asking for something from the agency. As a student, aren't you asking for something from a school which also might be an agency of its own kind?" He said, "Well, I'll have to think about that." I

said that I could understand that and it was only after thinking things through as well as experiencing them that we made them a part of ourselves.

The essential elements which a student needs for his training process are in this supervisor's attitude and brought out in words for his use if he is ready to use them; the unequivocal assertion that he is a student and like a client in that he is asking something from an agency, the School, and from the supervisor, combined with the knowledge that the process is slow, that he, like the client, is expected to get it only step by step in his own experience.

This illustration highlights the problem of the beginning phase of the training process for the student entering a professional school of social work as I have described it in this chapter. The definition of difference between supervisor and student must continue throughout the whole supervisory process and indeed may be said to be the fundamental underlying motif, the necessary condition in the training movement. In these early conferences that mark the beginnings of the relationship between supervisor and student, the definition of the difference in roles may seem crude and arbitrary. In every case, no matter how stated, for the student it amounts simply to the beginning of a realization that he is a student and in that role is, like the client, asking something of the supervisor and the school. When he has accepted this for himself to however slight a degree, his learning has begun.

6. THE SUPERVISOR'S RESPONSIBILITY FOR BRINGING OUT THE NEGATIVE ELEMENTS IN THE STUDENT'S EARLY REACTION TO SUPERVISION

Criticism is always leveled at the emphasis this School places on the necessity for maintaining the function of supervision in its professional difference from the role of the student and on the inevitable negative reaction of the student to this necessity. This criticism frequently says, "Why make it hard?" and "Isn't learning a positive experience, not a negative one?" The answer to "Why make it hard?" can be given from the experience of anyone learning in a new field if he is willing to be conscious of his own reactions. Learning on this level is always hard and painful in proportion to the extent to which it involves the self. It can be accomplished only if one is willing to admit the hardness and the fear and put oneself into the task of learning. If there is a teacher, somewhere, somehow, in the process there must be some admission that the teacher knows what the learner does not and a giving-in to this painful, fearful difference which permits an exchange between teacher and pupil. True, superficial learning of subject matter of skills may involve so little of the self that the essential nature of the learning process need never become conscious. But in all professional training the negative elements of the process, the fear, the resistance, and the struggle, can be recognized if one will but look at them.

In all professional education except social work, these reactions are taken for granted as elements to be overcome with as little dwelling upon them as possible. A student entering a medical school is committed to grueling study, to sacrifice, to discipline, if he is to arrive at his goal. He expects to resist it but stakes himself to accomplish it. But social casework, to a greater degree than any other profession, asks its students to become conscious of this conflict within themselves as the very basis for learning how to help others. In this sense alone there is some validity in the accusation that social casework makes training hard, since it requires the student who would deny the hardness and the fear, who tends to handle the new situation in which he finds himself with the superficial, one-sided assertion that he is having no problem, that everything is all right, to break up this assumption in order to gain true understanding of the forces involved in taking help, both for himself and for his client.

The supervisor who accepts responsibility for her function with a student should know from the very beginning of the process that she must help the student to get to some awareness and some expression of these negative aspects of his experience. She must look sharply into the situation, the fieldwork assignment and the supervisory setup, to see what aspects of it may bear harshly upon the student, new to its requirements, or which ones may be used to carry his whole diffused sense of discomfort and awkwardness. It would be wiser to assume that he does not altogether want to be there in that particular fieldwork agency under her supervision than to take for granted that it is exactly what he wanted. She can at least recognize the difficulties of getting to the agency, and for every student these usually loom large. Hopefully, many positive conditions of work will be offered him—his own desk and its equipment as well as clear and accurate information about how to find his way in the agency and the community. A conference hour, defined as to purpose, length, and frequency, for his use surely carries first of all its positive supportive meaning but the supervisor must be alert to recognize its limiting implications as well. It requires the student to organize himself and his material for discussion. He must send in a record of his interviews with the client in advance and present himself on time. Even the limitation of the conference period to one hour, or one hour and a half, has a negative aspect for him. Certainly it limits his freedom to come when he feels like it and to leave in the same way. It may feel too short or too long as it faces him with time that he does not know how to use.

True, these seem but little things, matters to which any student should be expected to adjust with more or less tolerance and a certain amount of healthy criticism of the powers that be. Any student is startled to find himself asked to go below his easy tolerance, to put his criticism out in the open upon a person who holds herself responsible for the conditions that irritate him. He withdraws from the first indication of the supervisor's effort to touch these unacceptable feelings that no one before has ever asked him to face as his own. And since he also feels this expectation in every contact with the School, with teachers as well as supervisor, it begins to constitute a sense of strangeness in the environment, to be felt and resisted as a definite pressure for some response that he has never given before. Students try to understand this in their own discussions with each other and, with the help of the teacher in the casework class, get the courage to articulate their fears of this unknown and dimly sensed demand. Their apprehension may be voiced as an accusation: "You are trying to change us." The answer, "Surely you must change if you are going to learn how to help people but no one can possibly change you against your will and yourself," does not satisfy until they have had more experience with the beginnings of change in themselves. But the experience of discussing their fear and of placing their criticisms directly upon the teacher, who stands for this whole training process and who accepts their reactions as natural, helps immeasurably toward a recognition of the validity of these reactions as a part of themselves. But it is with the supervisor in an individual conference hour that the student should have the opportunity to go further in expressing his negative reactions, to learn to place them courageously where they belong.

The supervisor, too, will have more opportunity than the teachers to see the student's negative reactions expressed in behavior as she is closer to his daily contacts with his clients and with other aspects of the agency. The best efforts of the most positive, constructive student to conform, to do right, to make good, must break down somewhere in relation to the multitudinous demands that a field-work placement in a strange agency puts on him for a new use of himself. Some of his errors are due to ignorance and inexperience and must be understood as such with patient explanation and with encouragement to try again. But other behavior which merits criticism may be due entirely to his resistance to something just because it is asked of him, or even more deeply to the limitations and controls that hem him in. The supervisor must be on the lookout for these manifestations of his unwilling or negative relation to the strange experience of being supervised and face him with it in some specific illustration if she can find it or in general terms when his problem of relating to agency seems more diffuse or more total. She may say: "Your recording has come to me too late for me to read it before conference several times now. I wonder why. Is there anything stenographic service can do about getting it typed or do you think there is something you can do? Perhaps you mind putting down what you have said in an interview in black and white or having me see it to discuss it with you. Could we talk about it?" Or perhaps the student is punctilious about getting his work done and his records typed, but the supervisor is disturbed by a vague sense of unreality in the student's conference discussion, a formality that seemingly accepts, but actually excludes, the supervisor's participation. She may have to take up just this aspect as something in feeling between them with no more to use as illustration than her own feeling that there is something wrong.

It is apparent that what is called for here is more than an external, superficial picking out of something to criticize in the student's work or of something wrong in the fieldwork situation on which the student can express his criticism. This would be easy enough to do and to teach if one had conviction that it was called for. But the more one tries to teach this to a succession of supervisors, the deeper grows one's realization of the forces in human nature that struggle against this responsibility. In spite of the fact that every supervisor has surely learned in a casework process that every client must project upon the worker the negative attitudes aroused by the limitations and conditions of the casework situation if a real and profitable relationship is to develop, she stands back, averse to taking any initiative in helping the student, her client in this training process, to uncover these attitudes in himself in relation to what the training process is demanding of him. Any caseworker finds it more natural to believe in the positive tendency of her own intentions as they bear upon the other person whom she wants to help and to move into a relationship by expressing these and by encouraging the positive attitudes of the other person. Even though she may have come to believe it necessary for the other person to find and face his negative feelings in relationship, she may well feel aversion for the effort it takes to withdraw herself from the flow of a positive movement into the kind of organization of herself and her own forces which is required to meet the other with a new focus that he must recognize and respond to.

More is implied here than the concept of ambivalence now generally accepted in psychiatry and so glibly used in social casework literature. What I am saying is not only that human behavior is characteristically ambivalent but that there is, in spite of every evidence to the contrary, a persistent and fundamental tendency in the natural helper to deny the negative aspect of feeling and to try again and again to build wholes which exclude those negative tendencies. This effort to exclude, to deny, the "bad" in the self, to control and punish its expressions in the self and in others, begins in the earliest relationship with the mother and continues on in the family into school and later relationships. Some individuals succeed in keeping the self all "good" in its intentions toward others and even in its behavior. Perhaps these individuals must make other people good too, are incapable of believing evil of anyone within their environment. Individuals who must have the world they live in wholly good are likely to need a devil to carry the burden of the evil they cannot assimilate. There are those who maintain goodness and rightness in the self only by distributing the evil onto others in the environment; they may tend to be apprehensive and suspicious of others, to blame them rather than to find anything wrong in the self.

True, there are individuals who build up the self aggressively on an affirmation of badness, who want to get the better of the other fellow, even to destroy him. But individuals with this pattern do not often come into training for social work. Those who choose social work as a profession have long since, probably in their earliest relationship, identified the self with goodness, and want to do good to the other. No theoretical teaching about ambivalence touches this fundamental organization of the self, but it must be touched if it is to deal with the reality of human "badness" as it needs to be expressed by the client in the relationship of taking help from an agency. Benevolence must somehow break up its own organization in order to find in the self, and be able to identify with, the evil inherent in all human nature.

This badness can be felt by any individual in a relationship that controls him in any way, as the supervisory relationship necessarily does. He will use his well-established ways of keeping knowledge of his own feelings from himself and, at any cost, from the other person. Any indication of the presence of feeling in himself which he does not want to recognize will be warded off with denial. If this denial is not recognized and accepted, it will tend to break through into consciousness in a sense of confusion and pain. Here is something coming at him from the outside, which must be given some credence by the student since it is accepted as valid in the training process he himself has elected. If he can really see and admit that he has done something wrong in spite of his good intentions, felt critical of the supervisor or the teacher in spite of his belief that everything was good and right in his situation, then actually something new and different has entered into the organization of the self that he brought to training. How deeply a student takes this depends on the nature of the expressed badness, the extent to which he has staked himself, and the amount of the self which is already involved in the training relationship. For young people in the first phase of training, this initial experience may be relatively slight and need not disturb the self very deeply.

While a supervisor may have the deepest conviction theoretically about the nature of the responses the student will feel to the supervisory function, of his fear and resistance to engaging in this new enterprise under the restraints of supervision, if she is inexperienced she often lacks the skill to help the student bring out the feelings he has been taught to hide. Perhaps she can offer only a verbal recognition of the negative feelings whose existence she suspects but cannot bring to a focus. Sometimes even this verbal expression constitutes enough release to enable the process to go on developing until the time when some circumstance precipitates it into a deeper level.

In the following excerpt from a supervisor's record of an early conference with a student, it is interesting to see how relievedly the student can place her fear and resistance on the record and on the supervisor's right to read and criticize it when she is given a little help from the supervisor in expressing her feelings.

Discussion of written material on student's first interview.

We had already discussed this visit briefly and spontaneously when student had come in right afterwards to tell me about it. I had said to her that if she were bursting with it when she came back after this first home visit, she could just call me and if I were free I would be so glad to hear about it. . . . Then last week she had brought me this written material to talk about using it for class purposes. At that time we had talked about how it felt to write and submit this first interview. We had not discussed the recording itself since I had not read it.

I had suggested it had probably been far from easy. She said thoughtfully that it was more difficult than she had foreseen and put it all on the problem of recalling what had happened, and its sequence. I asked lightly if this had been the whole difficulty, and as if searching herself she said, "Yes." I waited a little, and then I asked her if any of the difficulty had to do with me. She looked up at me startled, and then began to bring out how really hard it had been because she had to account for what she had done, and she had kept worrying over whether she had been aware of everything that had happened—whether she had understood it—and what was the proper way to handle it. And then almost whispering, she said, that as she wrote, it had almost become a question of whether to be honest or not. I said yes, it was that hard to reveal oneself. And after a pause I added that it was pretty frightening to see how deeply and even disturbingly involved you get in this learning relationship. We sat on a while thinking, and then I said something I can't recall, that expressed some very genuine confidence I had in her and called for some acknowledgment of at least a measure of confidence in herself that she could find her way in it, probably.

It is interesting to see how for the student this recognition of problem in her own performance begins to strike deep into the area of the bad and fearful in herself. "Almost whispering, she said, that as she wrote, it had almost become a question of whether to be honest or not." The supervisor's response to this is a warm recognition of the student's feeling as her own while at the same time it identifies that feeling as characteristic of this very experience of working with a supervisor and risking the involvement she was beginning to feel in it. One can feel here the beginning of something new in relationship for the student and the support which the supervisor's warm acknowledgment gives to that beginning.

In this period while the supervisor is engaged in trying to help the student express his negative feelings about supervision, classes in the School, particularly the so-called "Personality Course,"[1] either "Attitudes and Behavior," or "The Nature of the Self," challenge and encourage students to risk verbal expression of parts of the self that have been inhibited as impulsive or bad in previous experience. An article by Jessie Taft entitled "Living and Feeling," first printed in *Child Study* in 1933 and mimeographed for the use of students, has been found most valuable as it affords legitimate opportunity for students to focus their negative feeling on a point of view where they can differ and criticize freely. In working on this article in the classroom or in conference with the teacher who stands for the point of view it presents, students typically come to a new and revealing experience and acceptance of negative aspects of themselves.

To call this experience, as is so glibly done by the average caseworker, "releasing the negative" is to misunderstand completely its significance and value in the training movement. On the contrary, it indicates the first stirrings in the self of a spontaneity out of which may develop a freer, more creative use of the self in response to the client's ambivalence and leads to the discovery of hidden and denied forces concealed beneath the conventional and cherished patterns of behavior, potential strengths, without which the wholeness and flexibility essential for the professional use of the self in a helping process can never be achieved.

Students who put themselves into this training process most deeply often come through this phase of the revelation of their own negative selves with a positive realization of the value of feeling itself, both positive and negative, so well expressed in Dr. Taft's article in these words:

> The price one pays for success in denying negative feelings is a lessening of the ability to feel positively. Feeling is one. It goes with whatever the self admits as vitally important. To be able to feel, one must be willing to care. And to care is to expose one's self to loss or injury or defeat as well as to fulfillment and success. The goodness or badness of an emotion is determined, then, not by pleasantness or unpleasantness, not by its positive or negative, uniting or separating character, but

by the extent to which the individual accepts it as a part of himself, a necessary reflection of his own evaluation of living, instead of projecting it completely upon an external cause.[2]

7. HELPING THE STUDENT TO FIND A BEGINNING IN HIS CONTACT WITH THE CLIENT

Each time a supervisor launches a new student or a worker new to an agency into this enterprise of offering the service of the agency to those who seek its help, she must make vivid and alive for herself again the confusions and the difficulties that this new person encounters. No matter what her experience and skill, she herself must begin again in her own realization of and participation in this process. How can the student enter a client-centered situation already related to agency through countless complicated connections? How follow another worker? Does he study the record and attempt to follow through on what has already been initiated? Can that be done? The supervisor's own problem here is always in taking too much for granted, in not knowing how to get at the questions which every student needs to ask and does not dare to, at what he feels and cannot express.

The student in the interview cited in the previous chapter may be quoted again to give us the lively sense we need of the problems that confronted her, an inexperienced young person, in getting started with a foster mother and an eighteen-months-old boy recently placed in her home. The foster mother is a mature, steady person who has given years of reliable service to the placement agency. She welcomed the student cordially, talking freely about the child, how much the family likes him, etc. She introduced, however, some feeling about the members of the child's family who visit. The student responded on a warm, human level and came out of the interview with some exhilaration. She described her feeling to the supervisor as follows:

> Once she left the foster home she felt it had been all right. She had gone out to get acquainted and to give them the chance to get to know her too—they had made a friendly beginning, and that seemed good. Still she knew she had felt stopped, too, by the fear that she might have to do something that would not be entirely friendly.

How clearly this student states for us, what she herself does not as yet know, that the exhilaration she felt immediately after the interview was only the relief of having got through the dreaded visit at all. That it was friendly seems good, but she knows too well that this friendliness was of the foster mother's making and that her own stand has not yet been taken. She suspects and fears that "she might have to do something that would not be entirely friendly." Interestingly, she projects this fear into an unknown future and conceives of herself and the difference she may have to introduce into this good foster-home situation as "unfriendly." This projection of the inevitable fear that grows out of not feeling one's own part in a situation is characteristic. Characteristically, everyone skips the awareness of fear in the present and dodges the realization that hostility is felt in what is immediately going on between two people rather than in the vague "what I might have to do to them in the future."

The supervisor tries to bring the student into this present problem. How difficult it is for her to touch it, how impossible for the student to face it as yet, is evidenced in the recording.

> From this we explored whether it might have been helpful to her and Mrs. S. to talk about the change in visitors—to give Mrs. S. a chance to say whether she had been anxious over it— perhaps to say something about the previous worker—maybe to talk over together whether she would be visiting with about the same frequency—that Mrs. S. could feel free to call her at the office too. Student participated by listening thoughtfully, not filling in the gaps of time I left for her own suggestions, but saying she knew what I meant. There was a little questioning how, exactly, she could do it—a little feeling that the recording left out her beginning statement to Mrs. S. that she was the new worker—but she hadn't known how to carry it on, she still couldn't see. I thought perhaps she could use this kind of beginning around her own feelings: "I've been so anxious to meet you, Mrs. S."—and see where that took them.
>
> The student wondered if it were too late to use what she sees now. She really struggled with this and verbalized her thinking. She was sure the questions about her own family would recur. But could she begin with Mrs. S. when the beginning is past? She didn't think she could try saying, "We didn't get to talking much last time about," etc., etc. I agreed the time might be past for it. She wasn't even sure she could bring in some information about how they would be working together

as to spacing of visits for the time being, or the fact that she would expect to be the worker till summer.

She returned then to her question, vaguely stated, that she felt she didn't know exactly what things meant as they happened, or how to use herself. She did know her function in representing a child-placing agency. She knew quite certainly her focus was the child but the problem was in living this out piece by piece in her varying day-to-day experiences and relationships. I had to leave her with this. I thought she had the courage to work at it and share it with me. She wasn't sure—somehow she goes ahead in spite of a lack of great courage.

The supervisor ends her record of this conference with her own sense of bafflement for having worked on too much without ever succeeding in making a point clear to the student.

One feels that the supervisor is justified in her belief that this student will go ahead and work on this, but correct, too, in her own sense of failure to give the student help in getting hold of any real sense of herself in this situation. It could have come only if the student had been able to face what it would mean to feel her newness and its meaning to the foster mother. The supervisor, in talking round and about this, succeeds only in blurring all its edges. Evidently the supervisor herself construes the beginning with this foster mother as a purely positive experience when she suggests the student might introduce herself with "I've been so anxious to meet you, Mrs. S." Only if the supervisor herself can face this beginning in all its aspects can she help the student to state her own feelings of fear and inadequacy first and, relieved of them, to give some freedom to look at how it feels to a foster mother to have a new person enter her home. Out of this discussion they should come to a clearer conviction for the student of the immediate purpose of this visit and of the basic agency relationship to this home which can sustain the student and foster mother through the student's new contact.

An older student with several years of successful experience in a child-placing agency before she entered training reveals the same problem in beginning in a new fieldwork placement, the problem of trying to find a role for herself as counselor in a public school. In contrast to the younger student's feeling of vague, undefined fear, she is full of impatience and irritation, baffled by her ignorance and inability to act, in contrast with the sureness she had felt in her child-placing experience. Her vigor and determination to find a way forces the supervisor to struggle with her on the problem she brings to this conference at the beginning of the fieldwork placement. The interview she wants to discuss is her first interview with a boy referred as a health problem by a teacher. She feels only dissatisfaction with what she has done, confusion as to what she could do.

I quote the conference as the supervisor recorded it:

> I wondered then whether she felt that there was a problem in this case. "Oh, yes, she did," she said. There was no question in her mind that the boy's health was causing trouble, or would cause a problem in the future in his relation to the school. I asked whether she felt that as a counselor, she had a function here. She was sure that she did, implying that I wouldn't have assigned the case to her otherwise, but she added honestly that she didn't know what to do. She knew that there were problems in all the cases I gave her, and she thought she knew the treatment they needed, but she just didn't know how to go about handling them. "What do you say to a child, when you send for him, to make him respond?"
>
> I recognized warmly that it is awfully hard to know just how to begin with a child, and frightening, too, particularly when you have to initiate the contact and it is someone other than he who asks help for him. Perhaps we could begin to find some answer to these questions, if we examined the interview bit by bit.
>
> We began this carefully with my questioning her elaborate explanation to the teacher of her role as counselor. She followed for a few minutes, then suddenly interrupting me, she burst out that she was feeling so clumsy and awkward in handling interviews. She thought she knew something about casework before she came here; now she was feeling that she knew nothing, as if she had never talked to a child. She couldn't get hold of anything with him; she didn't know what she was doing, really. And then, not knowing resources in the school, or its regulations and standards, she could never be sure whether she was doing the right thing.
>
> I said that, of course, she couldn't know, and certainly she would be bound to make mistakes. Anyone coming into a large institution like this would feel confused and helpless until she could acquire a little more facility in using the mechanics. But, also, her relationship here was quite different than it had been in a placement agency, wasn't it? She said yes. Here one is concerned only with school adjustment; in child placing one is concerned with the total life of a child. Here she knows nothing about the background in the home or the family be-

fore talking with a child. I recognized that this could make her feel pretty insecure, and added that she felt less needed here, too, didn't she? Yes, that bothered her, although, she added quickly, she knew that a counselor must be needed here.

I said warmly that I thought I knew something of what she must be going through, and that this beginning as a student wasn't easy for her. It seemed to me, although perhaps it didn't to her just now, that her experience in working with children in another agency was not entirely useless, and that she was bringing something to this new experience. However, only as she acquired more experience in working on individual cases, and began using resources outside and within herself, could she begin to feel more comfortable. And through this, I'd be going right along with her, and trying to help her as much as I could.

Student sat back, still looking disturbed. I waited quietly for a moment or two, but she seemed to have nothing more to say, and so I went back to the case material.

I wondered whether she had any question about the way in which she had presented to Philip her understanding of his problem. She said she didn't think so. We talked then a little about the feeling of this boy, who, she recognized with me, was probably pretty frightened at being summoned to see this strange person in the school who seemed to know so much about him. Student could go along with me on this, but she looked puzzled when I stopped. I asked then if she thought she might have been able, at this point, to relate herself a little more to the school in the boy's mind, and at the same time give him a little more security by bringing in his teacher's part in the situation. She agreed but it was obvious that she herself was not feeling related to the question. I pressed her further by asking why she had thought it best *not* to tell Philip who had made the referral?

Her face cleared, and she smiled. "Of course," she said, "I should have told him that the teacher had told me about him." We discussed then the advantages of such an approach, in terms of her own relationship with the boy. It seemed to me that she had really found a point of entrance for herself into this situation at last.

The difference between this conference and the first lies, not only in the greater capacity of this experienced student to take hold of the concrete aspects of the boy's problem and her determination to seek for her own effective role in it, but also in the supervisor's keener awareness of the painful nature of the feelings aroused in the student by being caught in a situation where she does not know where to turn. She is more able to stay with this problem, to help the student verbalize it and bring out all the factors in it. Evidently, the most difficult factor in this situation for the student is the relationship of the boy's teacher who makes the referral. It asks her to find for herself a different and more partial responsibility for the boy to whom she will act as counselor than for the child whom she would place in a foster home. How firmly the supervisor holds her to facing this precise point when she asks, "Why had she thought it best *not* to tell Philip who had made the referral?" The student's relief at this is obvious. The barrier between herself and the teacher, between herself and the boy, is down as she can take in the supervisor's question. One sees that she is ready to make a realistic beginning with Philip as she is now identified with her function as school counselor.

Finally, I should like to look at this problem of beginning from the record of an experienced supervisor working with an experienced student. This student is in her thirties and brought to training some years of work as a visitor in a public agency and in Red Cross Home Service. She had taken extension courses in the School before entering training. In spite of the fact that she was coming to school on her own initiative and with a purpose which she had long had in mind, she approached the actual experience very negatively and had much to fight out, first in the admissions process and then with her teachers, before she could get herself into the situation at all. To the fieldwork placement, a coveted opportunity in the neuropsychiatric service of a large military hospital and her own first choice of placement, she brought her most positive efforts to learn what was there to be learned.

There is much to be mastered in the orientation to the external physical aspects of a large military hospital. Just to find one's way around constitutes a major problem. Beneath these spatial connections lie the much more complicated network of relationships of military, medical, and psychiatric authorities and the delicate thread of responsibility for the individual patient carried by the social worker, in this situation representing the Red Cross. The most skillful caseworker would be hesitant in finding her way into this situation. This student whose experience I quote is not skillful, but vigorous, powerful, quick to action, determined to learn. The following conference, which describes her effort to make a beginning with Private X, a plastic surgery patient, took place in the middle of November after six weeks of training.

The supervisor states her impression of the student's learning problem, her pressure on the supervisor to give her rule, policy, and procedure, in the following introduction to the conference.

> Student from the beginning spoke about *skill* repeatedly. It was what she wanted to learn. It was what she came to school and to X General Hospital "to get." At the same time she pressed me to tell her "what your policy is" or "what is the practice of the Military." I was much troubled by these questions, at a loss to know how to handle them. It seemed strange to me to speak in such grandiose terms of "the practice of the Military" in relation to such a simple thing as telephoning a medical officer to ask him whether it would be convenient to refer a patient to him for approval of a loan application.

The supervisor's record goes on to relate the discussion of the case of Private X. I quote it in full.

> I had picked up the case of Private X among several others student had given me for routine reading. He was a patient on a plastic surgery ward and during May had made a loan of $15 for the purpose of financing an unexpected furlough home. He had agreed at that time to repay the loan on June 20. This had not been done. Student had seen the patient on 10-26 in reference to a matter concerning a brother, also in the service, who had requested an extension of his furlough in order that he and the patient might have more time to spend together. I should not fail to mention that the previous worker on the case, who was the same worker who had made the loan in May to the patient, had seen the patient on 10-25, just one day before student had visited him. On neither visit was the matter of the delinquent loan mentioned. I was curious about student's failure to pick this up.
>
> During our conference on November 12 I discussed this case with her. I opened the discussion by asking her whether she had been aware that there was an unpaid loan in this case of Private X when she had visited him. She looked troubled and agreed that she had been aware of this but did not know what "one did in cases like this."
>
> I wondered what she thought should be done. She pondered on this in silence. Finally and cautiously she ventured that as a caseworker she thought the matter of the unpaid loan should be discussed with Private X but "as a Red Cross caseworker I don't know what should be done." She was puzzled by the fact that

the previous worker had not mentioned it and did not know what her own obligation was and also by the knowledge that her own earlier experience in a Red Cross setup had not given her a basis for procedure here.

I suggested that we might try to consider why it was important to pick up this matter of the unpaid loan, from the point of view of agency and from the point of view of the patient.

We discussed these two points fully, and at our conclusions student nodded solemnly. When I thought we were finished with the discussion of this case and looked down at the material on my desk to pick up the next case I wanted to give her, meanwhile handing the X case record to her, I was genuinely startled, when I heard her exclaim, "Oh, no, I'm not finished with it yet!"

I agreed to continue the discussion by asking her what more she would like to ask about the X case. There was a silence and then, "This takes skill. Where do you get it?"

This was said with such a spontaneous gesture of helplessness on her part, so different from her usual ability to raise logical questions that I laughed and said, "But you don't 'get' it, do you?" "Of course," was her immediate response, and then she went on to describe rather pedantically her concept of the acquirement of skill. I did not agree with this concept but did not express my disagreement at this time because it did not seem important.

What did seem important to me was to know whether student was afraid of getting into this situation of the loan. There was an emphatic denial, followed by a wordy dissertation on the cause of her hesitancy. I really could not follow what she was saying—it was so devious and complicated and I asked her if she would repeat it. She tried to but after a few words floundered helplessly.

I ventured that what she had really said, I thought, was that she was afraid, wasn't it? She nodded her head. We discussed further the reasons for this, her sense of discomfort about going to see a patient about a loan and her feeling of "dunning." We reviewed what seemed "right" for us to do here, "right" for the patient and "right" for the agency. When she seemed ready to leave the X case, I suggested that she might not be able to do this thing we had decided was "right." If she could not do it, I wanted her to know that we could discuss it again before she visited Private X on his ward. This appeared to finish the question satisfactorily for her that day and it was on this note that we left the case of Private X.

This conference contains the essential elements of what must be faced and struggled through between supervisor and student and student and client in making a real beginning in a process of learning to help through casework function. It is instructive to see the value which the actual negative element in the situation, the unpaid loan, contributes. Here was something between student and client which could not be skipped, something which her own sound feeling told her was troubling her and must trouble the patient. The fact that she herself was not responsible for making the loan seems an almost insuperable problem in finding her relation to him on it, but at the same time it introduces Red Cross into the situation as the consistent, responsible agent to which both she and the patient are obligated. Only when she can really admit her fear of facing the patient with his obligation, and of the personal feeling of dunning that overwhelms her, can she get beyond this to look at what is "right" for patient and for agency.

It is interesting to see that it is the student's sense of problem, her determination to see this through to something basic, that holds the supervisor in the beginning of this discussion. The supervisor had finished with the case and handed it back when the student refused to leave it. But how immediate is the supervisor's response to this indication of the student's need! From this point on she takes the lead to get beneath the student's verbalizations about skill to the simple admission that she is afraid to face the patient with a question about the loan. She realizes that this discussion may not settle it for the student and tells her she can discuss it again, if necessary, before she sees the patient.

One senses that the student leaves this conference with something basically focused between herself and the supervisor so clearly and definitely that it will inevitably move to some new resolution. The student brings this eagerly to the next conference.

> The following Monday, November 19, student gave me the case of Private X to read for our next conference. Her face fairly glowed with excitement as she gave me the case, saying smilingly, "I tried what you said and it worked!" I must admit to being startled. I could not recall that I had given her any formula and I wondered what it was she meant.
>
> I learned that she still had a great deal of feeling about seeing Private X, saying that it would have seemed more comfortable to her "if I had been in on the ground floor," meaning if

she had been the worker who had made the loan. This was followed by a wistful statement that she supposed that this "could never happen in Red Cross, though." I thought that was not really so and I asked her to examine this critically. She could not do this, it seemed, so I brought to her attention how even in a child-placing agency, which to her was an agency that seemed to represent the quintessence of all that was professional, a worker frequently had to go into the middle of a situation created or begun by another worker.

I continued by asking her to tell me what it was she did when she so directly focused on the purpose of her interview on 11-19 with Private X. She fairly glowed as she said excitedly that she "had cut through to get to the point." We discussed this further with my directing the discussion to the end of helping her see why this visit of hers for this purpose was acceptable to the patient, although it was not *she* who had made the loan.

She was very thoughtful as I pointed this up by saying that for the first time in her experience here she had projected herself as "Miss M., a Red Cross caseworker." It was she who crystallized this still further by commenting with excitement, "I see it now. That's why I had the *right* to go to see Private X about the loan."

We were able to go on from here to discuss what had been unreal in her previous, intense striving for skill as separated from function and—it was she who said it—that skill had to be related to function and that function was the purpose of your agency, of which the caseworker was representative. She could understand why Private X could accept her, because although she was new to him, the Red Cross was not new to him. It was the agency with which he had dealt in May when he had made the loan.

What has taken place in these two conferences on Private X? A complete shake-up in the student's identifications and attitudes toward casework which she brought to school in the first place and had been holding to tightly and determinedly. These attitudes maintained an effective barrier between herself, the untrained Red Cross Home Service worker, and the trained supervisor who knows how and should be able to give her the rule for proceeding in every contact. Her feelings of hostility against all those who know how when she does not, have been persistently pounding against this barrier. They had been released to some extent in a previous conference with her adviser. In consequence of this, she brings to this conference with her supervisor on Private X a kind of readiness to move out of this negative phase of relationship. With the supervisor's help, all her feelings become focused around the unpaid loan and she is able to admit fear of her own negative feelings as well as of the other person's negative. Actually, this amounts to realization of the fear of facing the other person with responsibility for her own feeling and action. To take the next step, then, is to move into the beginning of the professional helping relationship. In doing it, the student leaves behind the old Red Cross self and identifies with a new Red Cross self, exemplified in the supervisor. She is triumphant in her conviction about what she was able to do with Private X in the interview about the loan and can put into vivid words her understanding of what she had done: "she had cut through to get to the point." No words could describe better what the supervisor had done with her in the previous conference. As soon as this new identification is felt and used with the client, the student gets a completely different understanding of function. It comes with a sense of revelation that now she has a right to see the patient about the loan and that it is this conviction of hers that enables him to accept it.

These two experiences just quoted, that of the student in the school-counseling placement and the student in the military hospital, epitomize the beginning phase of the training experience. It is typical of the movement that must take place through the projection of negative attitudes and on to a new positive identification with the supervisor which enables a real identification with the function of the agency to be established. The one student can talk with the boy comfortably when she is free to identify herself with the counseling function of the supervisor and to recognize the teacher's role, not as one that threatens her, but as related to her own, yet different. She can use the teacher's referral now to make her contact with the boy, instead of feeling cut off from him by it. The other student as she identifies with her supervisor finds her right, as Red Cross worker in a military hospital, to talk to the patient about the loan.

This beginning phase of the training movement has come to the desired eventuation in six weeks in these two placements and should in every situation not be delayed longer than eight weeks. If the supervisor is not alert enough to recognize and focus the confusion for the student, there will be an increase of fear, a mounting of negative feeling, a pressure on the supervisor,which will ultimately explode in some way. Out of such an explosion, a realistic beginning can often be retrieved if the supervisor has integrity and willingness to see what she has done and the strength to make an honest admission of fault without giving up her function as supervisor.

Through all the various details of case situations and the differences in functions, in skill and experience of supervisors and students analyzed in this chapter, one fundamental and important point for an understanding of the activity of the supervisor in this training process stands out clearly. It can be generalized in these words: only when the supervisor finds a way to cut through the case detail and take hold of the student himself courageously, to focus on something immediately present in the student's feeling or attitude in the situation or toward herself, can the student get hold of a direct and responsible connection with his client. The new feeling which emerges for the student out of this experience first with his supervisor, then with his client, constitutes his earliest beginning experience of a focus in his use of himself and the responsible connection it creates between oneself and the other. Out of this experience can come a true conviction of the meaning and use of function.

8. THE TURNING POINT IN THE PROCESS

The learning movement which has come through the beginning phase in the training process now moves into an extended plateau on which the student is typically occupied with using this newly acquired sense of function throughout his case load. There seems to be a brief respite from struggle, a sense of effectiveness and achievement. There is consciousness of a new strength which comes from identification with the supervisor and the agency. The casework class, into which are brought illustrations of the beginning experiences of different students learning to represent their different functions, carries further the conviction of the meaning of this training experience and establishes the beginning of a new relationship in the group—a relationship based on professional experience, not personal liking or disliking.

The supervisor may find great reward and satisfaction in this period in the revelations the student brings back to her, in his positive sense of exploration and learning. However, there need be no fear that the student will rest content on this plateau if the super-

visor is free enough to trust the dynamics of the casework relationships themselves and the student's own movement in them and in his
relationship to the supervisor to call out new responses in the student. If she keeps her sensitivity to the student and watches for indications of his confusions and blockings, she should know when and
what to tackle with him in conference discussion and how to hold
him to working through his next area of conflict. On the other hand,
no supervisor, least of all one without experience and skill in this
process, finds it easy to break up a peaceful interval by holding the
student to a fresh realization of problem in order to engage him in a
new and deeper learning struggle. The beginning engagement may
seem to be enough, the positive gains as she sees them in the student's casework may appear sufficiently satisfactory to justify her in
continuing the easy way of going along at the student's pace.

One may well ask: "What is there, then, to set the pace other
than the speed of an intelligent and willing student?" No school of
social work, to my knowledge, has ever succeeded in setting up criteria for what should be learned in a first month or a second, in a
first or a second semester. Many have been intrigued by this possibility but have fallen down in the task with some realization, perhaps,
that the helping process we seek to teach is not of a nature to lend
itself to the one, two, three pattern of standardized, objectified learning goals. But the fact remains that there is a helping process to be
learned, a process whose rhythm and speed of movement take place
in a time form set up by the school. In the process I am describing
here, the pattern of the fifteen-week semester, the two-semseter year,
and the two-year graduate program has been in use for many years. I
believe that it does not matter what this time form is so long as it is
understood and used by the school as the unit within which movement takes place. The mere fact of the acceptance of a unit of time
within which something is to take place gives to both participants
in the process a certain relation to the time limits of that movement
within each hour and as a whole. Each moves with it or against it,
controls it or yields to it, fills the hour with content or leaves it
empty and barren, because of the deep underlying necessity of each
human being to move in relationship from a beginning to an end.
The pressure to finish, to accomplish within the time limit, at the
same time the fear of ending and of not being ready to end, operate
in every task and in every time-limited relationship. Inevitably these
fears and pressures operate for both student and supervisor in the

training process. To deny them only increases their potency. If they can be admitted and recognized they can be utilized for the student's learning, a learning that he recognizes first as his own experience but one that is immediately translatable into his relations with his client.

Only the structures and convictions of the professional school evolved out of long experience can offer sufficient support to enable the supervisor herself to be free to move and to help her student to move forward within the training structure of the time-limited term or semester. If she listens carefully to her student she will find in the very earliest conferences some question, some scarcely articulated fear, about "evaluation." "How will I know if I am doing well, or enough?" The plateau I have been describing, which follows the student's identification with agency function somewhere between the sixth and eighth week of training, will finally be invaded by some question which refers to evaluation and which is an indication that the student is looking ahead in time, if only apprehensively. The teacher regards this sixth to eighth week period as a mid-semester point when she herself, in her own thinking, is tentatively evaluating her students, returning papers to them with some significant comment or question. The students react to this with an increase of fear and questioning, with discussion among themselves and often class discussion that articulates and focuses the fear of movement on "Am I doing well and enough in class and in the field?" And on a second question, "How will I know how I am doing?"

To show how the supervisor can make use of this questioning on the student's part and help him to find his own role by focusing the problem specifically in the casework and supervisory process, I have selected two conferences occurring in the seventh and eighth weeks of training between a supervisor and a student placed in an agency offering a service to the families of boys committed to a reformatory. This student is past his middle twenties, an intelligent, able young man who moves into a new experience positively and eagerly. He is accustomed to doing well whatever he undertakes. He fulfills all assignments on time and with fine consideration for all the factors involved. He has made a good beginning in his fieldwork placement and is one of the first students in his section to offer case material from his own experience for class discussion. The supervisor is a man, a skilled caseworker, new to student supervision.

This material was selected and discussed fully in conference with his supervisor. When the class presentation had taken place, the supervisor told the student he would be making an appointment to talk with the class teacher, the student's adviser, about his work. Such a conference between adviser and supervisor is typical procedure at this time in the semester and it is typical procedure for the student to be told that it will take place.[1] Obviously this focuses fear on what takes place between adviser and supervisor which concerns the student so intimately. He must be helped to find his right relation to the actuality of such a conference through discussing it with supervisor, adviser, or both. Both will want to make some reference to it in order that it may be included in the relationship each has with the student.

The excerpt from the supervisor's record which follows shows the clarification and conviction the supervisor himself has gained from discussing the student's work with the school adviser as both were close to it and saw it projected in the case he had presented in class. This clarification has illuminated his whole point of view of the student's work. While he still feels warmly about the student's ability and good progress, he is able to cut through to a deeper focus of problem and face the student with it.

> November 16. We talked of my recent conference with his school adviser for the greater part of the hour. Student had been intensely interested in knowing how the adviser and I felt about him and I had told him that for my part, I felt he was making pretty good progress so far. I pointed out evidence of what I meant—his industry, his eagerness, his responsibility and conscientiousness, etc. I had felt that there had been a bit of anxiety on his part up to then and what I said was designed to reassure him. There was no mistaking the comfort and relief he felt. But he wondered how the adviser felt. This, I told him, was something he would have to get from her. I thought that in the main she agreed with me that he was moving along pretty well, but I certainly couldn't speak for her in the details of his progress at school. Student said he would see her next week. Previously he had rationalized his procrastination in making an appointment first by "waiting until a paper was returned" and then "until after I had seen her." I recognized the naturalness of putting off such a meeting when one feels so uncertain about oneself and one's work. He rationalized this again bv saying he had delayed until after I had talked with his adviser. "Maybe so," I said, "but I guess you are a bit afraid to go too." This he admitted, but he said he felt better about it in the light of our conference today.

We then directed our attention to some recorded material. This material, an interview with the mother of a boy in X Reformatory, reflected a trend similar to that in the case he had presented in class in the way student is handling cases and learning casework. I told him I sensed a note of urgency on his part to get things done, to put himself into the center of the interview, to get things settled without much regard for the client's need or pace in taking help. I pointed out specific spots in which he "said," "asked," "recommended," "acted," "directed." He dominated the interview almost to the exclusion of the client and her needs at that time. Student nodded and said he was in the picture a lot, wasn't he. I told him I thought it was important to be in the picture but equally important is how you get in and how much of the picture you have to be in so as to satisfy your own needs. Perhaps he would want to consider the pressure he puts on a client and the urgency he feels to get things done. I concluded the conference deliberately at this point saying he might want to think it over.

The supervisor's good judgment in leaving his question with the student at this point for him to think over is confirmed by what the student brings back to the next conference. The day after the conference described he submitted an "agenda" for the next conference listing for consideration at the end:

On my impatience and haste during interviews—my problem as I see it. If possible I would like this definitely on the agenda, even if it entails omitting or reducing the above points.

The record of the conference follows:

November 20. In accordance with student's agenda we started on his problem as he sees it. At the start he said he had thought a lot about what I had said and he guessed it was pretty important. He guessed it was the way he was with people before he ever came here. I thought it likely that impatience to get things done was not something newly acquired but asked him to explain. He went into considerable detail in describing personal relations: he argued a lot with friends and got impatient when they didn't go straight to the point. He cut them off and settled the matter his own way. He got annoyed with fuzzy arguments, disliked "lack of logic." I understood his reactions—they were the core of the academic and intellectual life which he loved and had not yet really left. I said as much. He nodded in agreement. I went on to say that such an approach could hurt a client. For example, he had "logically" and forth-rightly tackled with the mother of the boy in X Reformatory the problem raised by his getting a girl in the family way. Student had proceeded step by step in his way, not hers, to the conclusion—that the court would see to it that the boy paid support. "She seemed stunned" —and student left her that way. I pointed this out. Student said grimly that was bad. I agreed, and went on to say there was something good in this, too. His job is to point out what in reality she and her son would have to face; but it is also to recognize the difficulties this would involve for them and to help her with her feelings of fear. He said he guessed he hadn't helped. I didn't spare him; and then pointed out that just as in the case he presented in class, he had gone ahead at *his* speed, conducting the interview to-ward an end *he* selected, and doing these things without much regard for his client's feelings or need.

Student seemed to expect my reaction because in the agenda he had contrasted this interview with one in which he quite tenderly helped a weepy father of a reformatory boy under-stand the industrial school program. I recognized this differ-ence in his work. He explained it in terms of finding a weepy man easier to reach than a reticent woman. When I suggested they might both be afraid of him and reacting differently to this fear, he could see this. He could also see that *he* was dif-ferent in both interviews and that his problem aggravated the problem of the inaccessible mother because he couldn't adjust himself somewhat to her speed, her fears, her need for healing.

This experience in the middle of the semester constituted a turn-ing point in the student's training movement. This phase of his train-ing grows out of his own active, positive, well-organized self, his readi-ness to present his own work in class. But it requires his adviser's critical relation to that case and the coming-together of adviser and supervisor in discussion of the student's relation to the case, to enable the student to get beneath his own natural approach to a new use of himself. This evaluative activity also focuses the supervisor's attitude and gives him the conviction to go back to the student with a criticism which can penetrate the student's good adjustment in or-der to get at the problem his very clarity and logic create for the par-ent whose feelings they override. While doing this, the supervisor ex-presses his sincere and spontaneous appreciation of the student's good qualities, as well as sympathetic understanding of his fear of criticism, of evaluation—fear which the student rationalizes and denies to the same extent and in the same way that he overrides the client's fear.

This is not an easy conference for either supervisor or student. Both are involved in it, stirred by it. Left with his own feelings and the supervisor's questions, the student reacts vigorously, carries the questions further, applies them to other cases. There is defense of himself in this but at the same time a new openness to the feelings of the other person as he achieves a freer relation to his own feelings. Between the supervisor and student now there is a realization in more fundamental terms of the student's problem in learning to help a client. One can see that a deeper level of the student's personality has been touched. He refers to all his personal relations with people and is aware of his greater freedom in responding to a father in trouble than to a mother. Obviously this is but the beginning of a movement which will involve his feelings of himself as a man in personal relationships as well as in the helping relationship. But how wisely the supervisor, without cutting off the feeling, keeps it focused around the meaning of his functioning as a person who represents the agency to these troubled clients. Both the mother and the father might be afraid of him and both need something from him, he says. This is a new idea to the student. It pulls together the feelings that have been so personally stirred in himself into something tangible which he can use and move on in learning how to help. One can know that he will ultimately have to go deeper into an exploration and reorganization of these attitudes before he is in full possession of his strength and capacity to help women as well as men clients, but one can feel sure through the record of these two conferences that what he has done at this point is sound and sufficient for the ongoing of the training movement. The supervisor comments on the difference in the student's relation to conference after this experience. He brings his feelings more freely, asks more penetrating questions, and offers his own criticisms of his interviews.

I repeat in concluding this discussion of these two critical conferences that this supervisor was new to student supervision. He was a skilled caseworker, with limited experience in supervising workers. He is honest, frank, direct, and able to use the other parts of the student's school experience to precipitate and sustain the student's movement. His own relation to the school process and the adviser enables him to find the right timing for his action and to trust it to eventuate in the total movement, in spite of the fact that he himself has not experienced this movement through to an ending.

When the School carries full reponsibility for the total time structure of the training process and the relation of the parts of this process to the whole, it is justified in using inexperienced supervisors who are willing to lend themselves to this process in all of its newness and through this experience learn its direction and its controls. In doing this, the School can never afford to lose sight of the fact that these inexperienced supervisors are themselves in a process with the School and must be prepared to have them, like the student, resist whatever carries them beyond their own moorings in casework experience. No step, I believe, carries the supervisor further beyond her own known experience and involves greater risk of her professional competence than the necessity of finding a focus, a turning point, in the student's training movement. However stubbornly this step is resisted, it can be accepted, experience proves, through the use of the arbitrary time structures which the School maintains. When the supervisor has worked through this process once with the help of the School, through a turning point to an ending, she will have experienced in herself the feeling of the training movement in a time structure which will enable her to enter into the process with her next student with greater ability to appreciate the necessity for focus and to anticipate the timing of the turning point.

9. EVALUATION AT THE END OF FIRST SEMESTER

When a turning point has been felt and focused in any relationship process, every person involved begins to have some awareness of the impending end toward which the process inevitably moves. How personal and individual are the reactions to this movement taking place deeply in the organic self, rarely recognized as belonging to the self if indeed they are consciously felt at all, only those who work with this process can understand. What is happening is a shift in equilibrium, a change in direction, a return of the energy which has been so stirred and absorbed by the dynamics of the relationship into its sources in the self. The recipient in the relationship has overcome his initial fear in the beginning phase, has risked some part of himself, has taken in something different from the other person, and now must move away on this newly acquired strength out of the influence and control of the helping person.

This inevitable natural movement to a premature separation and independence is completely obscured by conflicting natural tendencies, by a deeper need for relationship, and by the fear of ending and of independence. In the professional helping relationship, while the tendency to separate must be recognized, the need to remain must be supported in order to enable the individual to stay in the relationship and trust to its deeper movement toward an ending less premature than his first impulsive reaction might dictate.

For the student, the recipient in the supervisory relationship, in order that he may have the experience which will discipline his own tendency so that he can help the client in a similar process, it is obviously necessary that he stay in the relationship. He himself has no question about this necessity, for he accepts intellectually the semester time structure of students in the casework class, at the time it is given to the supervisors in the supervisors' class or to other supervisors by mail. A date must be set by each supervisor for the evaluation conference well in advance to allow the student time for preparation. A later date is set by the School for the return of the completed evaluation to the adviser. The student, through this active relation to the content of the evaluation form, from class discussion which gives him ample opportunity to express his fears about it and at the same time to extend his own actual knowledge of what the evaluation is about, brings to the evaluative conference with his supervisor some ability to participate. He will have thought about the questions the form raises: his case load, his relations to his clients, how he takes help in supervision, his capacity to organize his work, to meet requirements of dictation and of agency schedules, etc. In this process there is an objectification of his work as such, a separation of the work from the self, which in itself constitutes the separation that prepares for and makes bearable the separating, evaluative attitude of the supervisor.

This description may have the effect of making the evaluation process and the evaluation conference between the supervisor and the student appear simple and easy in contrast to the strain of a written evaluation. It is never that for these two individuals who have been actually engaged in a vital learning process, since it necessitates a marked change in the relationship, a standing apart from each other to look at the semester's experience and its accomplishment as a whole. The beginning supervisor finds this detachment difficult to achieve and must be helped to reach it by the emphasis of the School and the adviser on the form and the date-setting for the evaluation conference and for the completed evaluation to be sent to the School. The supervisor-in-training will need to discuss it in class and with the student's adviser just as the student does. She will need to prepare for it by going over the student's work as a whole in her mind and by careful record reading.

If both supervisor and student have prepared for the conference in this way and bring to the actual evaluation conference the readiness to share their findings, there will be no lack of significant content for discussion. There is always some problem, however, when each participant is so well prepared through differentiation and separation and has organized himself and his material so well, in getting together again for participation in a process. The supervisor usually swings between two extremes: taking too much initiative and authority in her effort to establish the fact that this is evaluation, or, in her fear of doing that, leaving the student alone without sufficient support from her. The student, too, who in this experience of being evaluated is brought up sharply against all his fears of authority and criticism, struggles deeply with his fundamental need to control the relationship.

The test of a helpful, satisfactory evaluation conference lies in the feeling of each participant that both have had an effective part in it and that what has been said about the student's work and what will go to the school in the written form are acceptable to both. If the supervisor has expressed her difference and handled her criticisms of the student's work frankly throughout the semester as occasion arose, if she has focused her criticism in terms of a fundamental turning point as described in the preceding chapter, there will be no need to introduce new criticism in this final evaluation conference. Rather it should be the student who takes possession of the criticism now, sees his beginning work in terms of the change he has experienced with its indication of the need for new skill not yet achieved, but which he begins to perceive and reach out for. For the student who is able to do this, there is tremendous satisfaction in this evaluation experience.

Following this evaluation conference, it remains for the supervisor to write out the completed evaluation on the school form. There is much difference of opinion as to whether the final written evaluation should be read by the student. My own experience leads me to believe that if the student has really participated in the conference he will trust the supervisor to submit the evaluation. If asked he will say,

"I don't want to read it." Any lack of trust in the supervisor which leads him to fear that she will write something to the School that she has not already said to him implies a fundamental problem in the supervisory relationship which bodes ill for genuine learning. While students, many of them, bring distrust to the beginning of this experience, it should have been worked through by the end of the semester so that the student knows that his supervisor shares with him as well as with the adviser her opinion of his work. Difficult as this three-cornered relationship is for students to understand and accept, they come to do so to a great extent in the first semester, so that reliance and trust in it become stronger than fear and suspicion.

It is argued that there is no reason why the student should not read the evaluation since he knows what goes into it. Anyone who has had the experience of reading his own evaluation knows that a reaction to the finality of the written word produces a very different response from the fluid discussion of that same content. Process goes out of the written word and it becomes endowed with a definiteness and finality that one cannot bear to have placed on one's changing experience. Nor should a changing learning experience ever be asked to carry such definiteness and finality. The supervisor's written record of the student's development belongs in the School, where it plays its part in the total record of his training which constitutes the material out of which the School can draw its final evaluations, recommendations, and references.

The letdown or slump which follows the achievement of any goal in a learning or creative process is a common phenomenon well known to all teachers. Energy has been put out and used up in achieving that goal; the examination or evaluation marks a successful achievement, the finish. Certainly it does not mean the complete exhaustion of energy, but often the release of the new energy unused in the effort to achieve the goal. This fresh energy may dissipate itself in a variety of activities, or it may seek an impulsive expression denied by the obligation to hold itself to one end, or may quickly engage itself in pursuit of a new self-willed goal. All educational institutions understand this phenomenon and handle it in various ways. Usually a brief vacation period follows midyear examinations, a period in which the student can rest, have a good time, free himself from first-semester connections, and get ready to start again. He goes over his equipment, his clothes, his books, and his papers; he registers for the new semester, perhaps choosing new courses, setting up a different schedule. These activities all have their value as signs and symbols of another beginning which will carry him further into his total learning undertaking.

All the phenomena which characterize the output of energy and the renewal of its sources in any learning experience are present to a greater degree in learning to use oneself in a helping process. Constant consideration must be given by those who set up the structures for this training process to the necessity of providing time and opportunity for this shift in energy. That it has not received the consideration it deserves is due, I believe, to the fact that this training process in social work is being developed out of the helping process in social casework, and its timing is still involved with the timing of the casework process in the rendering of the agency's service. There is a fundamental problem here which requires special treatment. For purposes of this discussion, it is important only to see the extent to which students at the time of this midyear shift are already involved in responsibility for service to clients, for carrying a case load however small it may be. It is essential for the student to learn that while his own tendency to slump, to end, to move out of responsibility and relationship must be felt and recognized, he is in this agency and this profession to give to his clients the steady support of the service to which they are entitled.

The supervisor who, in her own training and agency experience, has accepted this discipline of her own impulsive movement will be able to help the student to achieve the same discipline. The necessity arises early, particularly with young students who have not been prepared by anything in college education for the kind of responsibility for clients which professional training asks them to take. Week-ends and Thanksgiving, Christmas, and midyear vacations have been their own time in a way which must be modified in the professional school. For every student, the supervisor's consideration with him of what will be going on in each of his cases during his vacation, or in absence for any cause from agency, is most important in developing in the student the professional responsibility he must learn to carry for his client. It is this deepening sense of responsibility which must function between semesters in order to carry both student and supervisor through the separating evaluation experience to a deeper, more solid level of relationship in this learning process which asks of both so much self-discipline.

With these two factors in mind, the student's tendency and need to experience change and ending, to feel the letdown and shift of energy before he makes a new beginning, and the necessity of learning to develop in himself the capacity to hold himself steady in offering the professional service, the School may be able to arrange a brief vacation, perhaps a long week-end between semesters, which recognizes the vacation need without interfering with the consistency of agency service. A period of a week or two weeks between semesters, when classes are omitted but work in agency continues, seems to be a helpful device in timing in order to emphasize ending and new beginning without interfering with service to clients. Such a period provides time and opportunity for advisers and teachers to confer with supervisors on evaluations, and for students who are having problems to confer with advisers. A few students may be dropped from the School at this time or may leave of their own accord. An ending process of this final nature requires much extra time from both adviser and supervisor in coming to a decision and in discussion with the student who is leaving. So from the point of view of all that the School faculty must handle at this time, a two-weeks period between semesters seems none too long.

Strange as it may seem, two weeks without classes does seem long to students who have become accustomed to the support of the group and the class discussion in carrying the training movement. The supervisor who is still seeing the student in weekly conference during this period should be aware of the feelings which this change must stir up in the student. First and most important, she must keep in mind the deep sense of change due to the experience of evaluation which they have been through together; in addition, she must be aware of the uncertainties the student is feeling in the immediate loss of the class contact and that, however unconsciously, he is beginning to face the requirements of the second semester ahead.

If the student is able and has made satisfactory progress in his first semester and if the evaluation has been positive in character, the supervisor will find it easy to use the assignment of new cases or the pointing up of new problems to be tackled in his old ones, to serve as a basis for a new hold on his work. If, however, the student's development has not been so satisfactory, if his evaluation leaves him unsure and not in possession of himself or of his skill sufficiently to make a new beginning in his cases, the supervisor has a more difficult task in helping him find his own base for a new and more real start.

But no matter what the ability and achievement of the student, the supervisor needs to keep before herself in this mid-semester peri-od the extent to which the focus of this training process must be maintained in the student himself as he can find and feel that focus in relation to her and to his clients. So, it seems to me, he should be helped to some expression of how he feels in this between-semester period, particularly in relation to the supervisor who after evaluation inevitably seems new and different. Resting on the development of their capacity to work together in the first semester and on the firm texture of their shared knowledge of the case load, they must learn to work together again on a new level of greater depth and spontane-ity. For supervisor as well as student, it is difficult to believe that this relationship can never be taken for granted but must be won again and again at every stage of the process.

10. THE SECOND SEMESTER

Students bring to the first meeting of the second-semester classes a gratifying sense of their greater responsibility for their own learn-ing, a deeper conviction of the purpose for which they are in school. In contrast to the personal beginnings of the first semester each stu-dent has a grip on something in agency function, in case load, in his own skill which unites students in classes on a professional basis. It often seems to teachers as if the two-weeks period between semesters had been much longer by the indication of what the student gained in understanding. At the same time the teacher understands the re-sistance that will be felt to the more difficult requirements set up for the second semester, the deep aversion to the pressure of form, of the movement itself, which classes emphasize and sustain. These resistances will inevitably find some expression, but this expression can be facilitated by the teacher and made conscious at times in ways that are helpful for the movement of the class as a whole, as well as for the release and additional insight of the individual student. The student's work with clients and his developing skill should rapidly furnish the content as well as the solid base of relationship in class discussion and supervisory conferences throughout the second semes-ter. There is the same rhythm in this semester as in the first: a begin-ning phase with resistance culminating in a turning point followed by a movement toward evaluation, ending, and plans for the second year. The content in casework in this semester is more extensive and complex than in the first, the student's relation to it more responsible, his understanding, finer, deeper, and more reliable.

The supervisor can take solid satisfaction in the substantial work of her student in this period and can feel indeed that her major contribution has been made, as the student finds so much in his case load to explore, learns from it, and recognizes his own problems in the casework process much more on his own initiative. This is not to imply that the supervisor becomes passive or withholds her own participation in conference discussions. On the other hand, her participation can become freer and more spontaneous as she feels the student's growing strength to be himself, to differ, to oppose, and to find his own function and attitude in the casework relationship. When the student's relation to his client becomes truly and surely his own, his fear of the supervisor's superior skill and knowledge vanishes and he can risk listening, taking in something of what she might have to say about the case, knowing that it is he who will go back into the contact, freed, enriched, and more clearly focused as a result of the conference discussion. If the supervisor loses sight of this increasingly reliable connection between the student and his client, forgets the student, and interposes between herself and the student her own interest in the case, the student will immediately feel this as a threat to his own control and will react against it. He may temporarily lose his hard-won relation to the case and may even drop it in confusion or in negative, impulsive action. The supervisor must be sensitive to his reaction as she finds it in the record of his next contact, or perhaps in his failure to record or to get the material to her. She can feel it, if she is free to, in his attitudes to her in the next conference.

As the supervisor acquires more experience in this process, she will know that in this delicate balance between herself and the student lies the essential skill of supervision. She will guard her own tendency to put in too much of interest, of knowledge, using the reaction of the person she supervises as test of her own activity. She must learn, too, that the student will project his own excessive fear of loss of control in this area where he is still a learner in various ways, and that he may in some moods allow her slightest word to disturb his own relation to his case. Here she must take hold of what is between them fearlessly and vigorously and help him to work through this maze of confusion, through the expression of his resentment against the supervisor, to a clarification of his function and his relationship to his client. This kind of blocking is to be expected again and again in any supervisory relationship and must be resolved as it arises. The supervisee will come through such an experience with deeper and more sensitive awareness of himself and of his place both in the supervisory situation and in the casework situation with his client. He will gain greater understanding and conviction about the meaning of help, the struggle against taking it, and the strength required to give it.

This new strength in the student wrested out of struggle and directed into his relations with his client is the basic force which moves toward a true ending of this supervisory relationship and of his first-year learning experience. He knows as a rule that he will leave this supervisor and this case load, and perhaps the agency where he has been a student. If he has gained the strength and skill required to continue in training, he will go on to a second year which will be different in many aspects from the one he has come through successfully.

The time structure of the School provides the dates for evaluation with the supervisor, for discussion of his work as a whole and of the point he has reached in training with teachers and adviser, and finally sets a time for planning for his second-year placement with the teacher in charge of such placements. These structures serve to objectify the student's reactions to ending and put within his reach the tangible, concrete steps which he can take in making his training process a continuing one in which his will can engage more actively and really.

But it must never be forgotten that this conclusion of the first year of professional training is for every individual student an ending experienced more deeply and more consciously than he has ever experienced this aspect of living in his life before, unless he has been exposed to analytic therapy. Supervisors and teachers carry this awareness more deeply than the students. Their experience and discipline enable them to detach themselves enough to permit the student's feelings and attitudes in ending to be fully realized and expressed. These run the gamut from fear, guilt, and a sense of loss, from regret and pain, to relief and satisfaction, even to the extreme of triumphant fullness, in the realization of the independent self. There will be negative feelings, too, perhaps some destructive attitudes or behavior in the student's struggle to free himself. Something in the old self and the situation now fast becoming old must be left behind to make way for the new organization. In this final stage the supervisor has to be prepared to receive some projection of what the student needs to abandon. It is not uncommon for the student filled with the guilt of separation to bring out in his final evalaution conference some criticism of her, to refer to help she failed to give. He does this impulsively and blindly as an expression of the negative feelings so sharply felt in this ending experience. For the supervisor, related to the whole value and meaning of the experience and aware of all she has given throughout, this criticism is hard to take, particularly so as it is often located on so slight a point, without rhyme or reason in the total relationship. But take it she must, for if she should attempt to argue it, to make it take its rightful place, she will only give the student occasion to falsify the relationship further. The only thing that enables her to take it is her conviction that she has made her contribution and that the student's essential and difficult task now is to end with her as best he can. He must save some difference for himself, some advantage that is his, on which to extricate himself from the relationship. The richer the person, the deeper the experience, the freer he will be to feel not only the reward of his own fuller use of himself but gratitude to the other person, the teacher or the supervisor, who has enabled him to have this experience.

11. THE SECOND YEAR OF TRAINING

The long intermission of three months between the end of the first year and the beginning of the second year of training in the professional school which operates on the semester time plan is an important and valuable part of the two-year educational experience. That the student regards it as such is indicated by the fact that not even the youngest student often has an inclination to return to the summer jobs in camp or other situations which had meaning and importance for him before he entered the professional school. Nor does the student feel that it is desirable or appropriate to take a three-month summer vacation. Even the youngest student has left behind the college student pattern and has become identified with a working, earning professional group. Of his own accord, as well as at the dictate of the school, he seeks a job in a social agency with salary attached.

The School, since it is not in formal classwork session, cannot undertake to control or direct these summer placements in any way beyond the part it has already taken in planning the student's second-year placement. By the end of the first year in early June most of these placements are arranged. Student, School, and fieldwork agency have each participated actively in this placement.[1] The student has made a choice among available agencies, the agency executive in conference with the student has chosen the student, has offered him a second-year placement. A summer plan for the student will offer itself naturally, either out of the first-year fieldwork placement or out of the second. Sometimes both agencies want the student for summer work, and he must choose between them, but in either case it is understood to be a limited job for so many weeks under conditions and supervision provided by the agency and without School controls. In every way, the difference between this working experience and the learning experience of the School year must be emphasized. The student will resist the difference to some extent but to a greater degree he welcomes this opportunity to feel himself a working member of a staff, to earn a salary, to do a real job in job terms.

It is no wonder that students returning to the second-year curriculum in October seem to have grown many inches in professional stature. They bring back a firmer identification with the profession, a surer sense of themselves as professional people. Each has much to tell of his summer work and welcomes the opportunity to share his experience with his fellow students. There is an immediate feeling of unity in a second-year practice class, a unity which had to be worked for through many long weeks of first-year class discussions. But this positive return to the training process by no means describes the whole picture. While each and every student has chosen to return, is truly identified with the School and the profession, and has engaged his will deeply in this learning process, at the same time he resists this return with greater strength than he did the original beginning, for now he knows, as he did not know before, how much is asked of him in this process. If the summer has given him an opportunity to use what he has already learned freely and effectively, he will surely feel that he has enough. No further change should be required of him. But he cannot completely blot out the stirrings of awareness that more is required or he would not be returning to the School. If he feels his first-year struggle to have been a very painful one, he may come to the second year determined that it shall not happen to him again.

For all students beginning again in the second year, the immi-
nence of ending, embodied in the thesis requirement of the second
semester, looms up more fearfully than ending in the first year,
both in its finality and in the skill and independent work it must evidence. They have studied the thesis case material of students who
have gone before them, and they have heard many rumors of the
difficulty of the thesis assignment from graduates. "Will I be ready
for it or equal to it?" is a haunting question. They handle it in different ways. Some students enter the second year with a thesis topic
already in mind; others shy away from the mention of the word. It
is the difficult task of teacher and supervisor to get through the seeming positive unity of the class group, the independence and ego asser-
tions unconsciously but forcefully set against learning, to a new
beginning, for the class as a whole and for each and every student.

The supervisor of the second-year student should be, and usually is, an experienced supervisor. If she has already had experience
with second-year students, she knows before she begins of the life
blood that must go into this struggle, her own as well as the student's. There is no way to remain aloof and untouched even if she
would save herself, for what the student has already experienced in
a first year means that in a second he will put a demand on supervision for all that he needs to see him through a deeper process of
change and reorganization to a surer use of himself in skillful service
to the client. This demand may express itself in resistance and may
fight every inch of the way any admission of what it needs and
wants. But we assume that fundamentally the will-to-change must be
operative or the student would not be in his second year. Sometimes,
of course, a mistake has been made; he is not able to see through his
choice. Then teachers and supervisors must help him to leave but
this should be a rare occurrence if the first-year evaluations, choices,
and decisions have been soundly made.

When the student begins his second-year fieldwork assignment
with his second-year supervisor, he may be starting in a new agency
or a new department of agency. If he is in the same agency working
from the function he learned to use to a degree in his first year,
there will be at any rate a change in case load. For every student the
feeling of newness in himself and in his relation to a new supervisor,
new teachers, new classes, is made real and actual in relation to the
clients where he must find his function all over again. The wise supervisor knows that she must struggle with the student in his efforts to

get hold of something familiar in the situation against his tendencies to control it all in his own terms. Since he feels all change so acutely, she can help him by pointing up the actual concrete differences in this second-year placement; he has a new supervisor, a new case load; perhaps both agency and function are new to him. Some aspects of this difference he will dislike and fight; the sooner and the more freely he can be helped to express his feeling, the more quickly the relationship can move into a more positive ability to work together on the cases.

Here in the case load the second-year student, no matter how much experience he brings, must be helped, as the first-year student must be helped, to get down to the actual beginning with the partic-ular, individual client. The supervisor knows well the vagueness and generality that pervade the early conference discussions before this real beginning has been achieved. Her rightful impatience with it, if nothing else, will speed her effort to cut through it, to bring out the student's expression of his genuine negative feelings. Only when these have been fully expressed and truly placed on something in supervision or in school is the student free to take them back into himself as the natural reactions to change that they really are. Then and then only he is able to get to the client.

I can find no better way to make vivid the sense of change and newness which a student feels at the beginning of second year than to quote from a student's statement in her thesis. This student in her early twenties came into the professional school direct from col-lege and made fine progress in her first year of training in the long-time care department of a child-placing agency. Her second-year placement was in the same agency in the reception department, where her case load was to consist of babies placed in temporary homes. She had learned well the function, philosophy, and practice of this agency as she had been the worker for some of its children al-ready placed in permanent foster homes. But what a different prob-lem faces her when she herself must actually receive the baby into care at the moment of separation from his mother and go into the foster home with him in a placement process which is temporary, leading to another separation, a permanent placement later! She says:

> I never sought for a way of helping more earnestly than when I entered the reception department of the X Child Plac-ing Agency as a second-year student and found that I was being asked to implement a movement toward separation between a

baby and a temporary foster mother. The framework with which I was presented was the placement of babies in temporary foster homes with a view to removing them when a more stable plan for their future was reached. Abstracted from the whole configuration of the baby's life situation, this practice seemed to me an almost impossible one for baby and foster mother. What I knew of the external factors that led my agency to use such a practice, though real, could not in itself bring me to a true acceptance of the practice. The conviction I lacked was that this procedure could provide a growth-producing experience for baby and foster mother. Without such a conviction I could hardly assume my role as a helping person within this framework. I needed a deeper understanding of the use of this structure before I could accept it as providing a growth experience for the baby needing foster care, and I needed to know how it is possible for anyone to separate from a deeply meaningful relationship.

She achieved this conviction in her second-year training experience and states its basis and identifies the experience out of which she reached it in another paragraph in the thesis.

Essential to being helpful is the conviction that an individual has the capacity to live through this precarious experience. We gain such a conviction only from living through a parallel experience ourselves, for in understanding our own movement through it, we become aware of our own strength and of the help we received. This knowledge of our own struggle is the only instruction we can trust, affirm, and use in helping another.

This depth and clarity of conviction can be reached only when an experence in a helping relationship has been lived through to an ending in the self. So this statement could only be written in the second and final semester of training in the form of a thesis that represents the eventuation of the training experience. To a greater or lesser degree, depending on individual depth and capacity, each student must come to this conviction and by means of a similar experience of his own internal struggle.

For this student, the struggle was focused in the painful problem of separation with which she was faced by her new function and in her relation to her supervisor. The foster-home placement offered her everything she could desire; the supervisor was ready and equipped to give everything she could ask for her second-year experience, of warmth, of understanding, of strength and supervisory skill. In direct proportion to the strength of her own need for the experience she might find in the second year, her very resistance to becoming involved in it necessarily organized her overt activity against it. She came back to school in October with a program of extracurricular activities planned for herself, calculated to protect her from too much involvement in class- and fieldwork. Not many conferences had taken place before her supervisor detected the barrier which the student had thrown up between them, and the frank discussion of the student's fears led to a complete revision of her extracurricular program. Once this initial resistance was overcome, the student threw herself into her cases and into the conference discussions with her characteristic sensitivity and intensity. Her learning was rapid; her understanding fine in quality. The cases provided a full variety of experience to give her all she needed of deepened and extended understanding of this problem of the child's capacity to use a temporary situation for his own growth, of what the agency and the worker must put in to help him.

But this student's own problem in relationship was carried to a deeper and more precarious level for her when she herself faced the midyear evaluation and the end of the practice class with all that it foreshadowed of the final ending of the school training and the separation from student supervision. Here she fought actively with a strength she had never known she possessed, and found herself capable of destructive behavior and bitter feeling inconsistent with her picture and ideal of herself. This sturggle was a matter of weeks, painful in its nature for the adviser, the supervisor, and the teachers involved in it with her. Her foster parents and babies suffered too during this period no doubt, but less than the other people concerned since, for her clients, she kept her professional relationship under the discipline she had already achieved. It delayed her thesis until the middle of the second semester when she came through the negative phase of her separation to an acceptance of herself in this process. The self that she achieves in this process, as she herself states in what I have already quoted, has a new maturity and in its use now with foster parents and babies she is in possession of the understanding of relationship, movement, and separation on which true ability to help must rest.

While this student may have a greater awareness of her own process than some others and more capacity to articulate it, she is not exceptional in her conviction about the nature of the process itself and in her possession of her own experience in it. Every student in his own individual terms must experience this process of change and growth in himself and must know it and affirm it as the basis of his understanding of his client's problem in using the service of the agency.

One more illustration of the second-year learning experience of a student will have value in illustrating further the nature of this process. In contrast to the student already quoted, this student brought maturity of age and experience to her training. She was in her late thirties, with some years in social work and with experience in an allied field in an executive capacity. It was obvious at once that she was an extemely intelligent, thoughtful person, thorough, logical and well-organized in her thinking, and dignified and reserved in relations with others. While her progress in the first year was substantial and solid, her teachers recognized in her aloofness and tendency toward rigidity, attitudes which she would need to change if she were to reach the full and free use of her able self in helpfulness to her clients. The fieldwork placement arranged for her second year offered the possibility for the experience she needed if she could use it, an agency well organized and administered, a function new and challenging, a supervisor sensitive, mature, and skillful.

The supervisor[2] has analyzed this training experience in her own record from which I quote.

> Student impressed me as a thoroughly responsible person with a great deal of strength and integrity. The school of social work described her as thoughtful and sensitive with a pleasing personality, which could not but make itself felt. She had completed a very productive first year of training and was considered as having excellent potentialities for casework. The school's very acceptance of her as of fellowship caliber was a recognition of her capacities. It was felt that she still had a great deal to learn, especially in the area of leaving to the client that which is his part in the helping process.
>
> From the beginning, she had been eager to work in a children's agency. She likes children and brought to this experience a strong identification with the child. She felt the pain in placement, that is, in separation, keenly, but had sufficient strength and identification with the service to carry through responsibly with the client to the end. At times her identification with the child and too-ready acceptance of placement as a

solution to the problems inherent in difficult parent-child relationships led her to overidentify with the child against the
parent.

Her very strength and determination, that is, the use she
made of it, created difficulty for her in her work with clients
as well as in supervision. She is by nature a very reserved person, one who does not find it easy to share her feelings. Beyond this, she seemed to exert an iron control and discipline
over herself, which gave her work at times an aspect of stilted-
ness, of flatness rather than one of dimension and depth. In
her interviews with clients she did not let her own feelings
come through and thus was not always able to help the client
with his feelings. This was particularly noticeable in her lack of
awareness of ambivalence as an ever present factor in the process of taking help and especially so in the taking of help around
placement of one's child. The decision to place one's child is
rarely arrived at wholeheartedly by the client, but is fraught
with guilt, indecision, feelings of inadequacy, and a painful
recognition of the individual's difference from his fellow men.
There was a quality of literalness about her which made her
take whatever the client might say at the moment as something that was whole or right for him. She became confused
and frustrated when the next moment the client seemingly re-
versed himself. Her conception of feeling had an aspect of totality and singleness. She found it difficult to experience it in
parts for herself and for her clients and she could not bear the
fluidity that there is in all casework helping. With this, she
took over too much for the client and carried too great a feeling of responsibility and stake for the outcome of her work
with him. Her use of structure, too, had this element of finality in it. If the client balked at a particular piece of structure
such as a necessary contact with the Department of Welfare or
working out financial arrangements, she would view this with
finality as proof of his not wanting to go ahead with placement, rather than to see what the struggle over this point sig-
nified for him and to help him move beyond it toward a more
integrated decision for himself.

While some of this is typical of all beginning learning in casework, there ran through it, nevertheless, a thread that was student's own unique relationship to helping and to taking help.
Since feeling held such totality for her, she was afraid of it.
She could not bring her feelings out in supervision any more
than she did in her relationships with her clients. When I dis-

cussed her work, she looked downcast. I tried to bring out her
feelings about taking help. I felt it was not easy for her, who
had been an executive, used to giving orders, to have to take
instead. At her stage of development, too, she must have arrived at some acceptable way of life for herself. Was she afraid
that this would mean too much change for her? She could
not accept understanding from me at this point. She could
only affirm the part in her that wanted help. Her reaction to
criticism and taking help, she felt, was a universal one. Naturally anybody would rather have praise. She felt, however, that
her very going to school was an acceptance of her role as a
learner. She valued my help and wanted to learn. I did not
doubt it. I knew she was putting a great deal into this training
experience and I respected her for it. Yet I knew that learning
could not always take place positively. It had a negative and
painful side. Could she let that part of her feeling come through
here with me? She was suspicious, she said, of what she calls
"trusting to feeling." The school and I emphasized this so
much. She thought a social worker would be disciplined in her
feelings. So did I, but said this could only take place professionally, if one let oneself know and experience one's feelings.
She, I felt, was withholding hers. She argued with me on this
point, instancing illustrations of destruction being wrought in
the world under the name of free expression of feeling. I said
her illustrations seemed extreme and very far removed from
what we were experiencing together here and now. Wasn't she
struggling with me right now and could she feel that? I knew
she had had many experiences that made her fearful of feeling
and I recognized her right to personal reserve, but I thought
she did not know what the school and I were talking about,
namely, about a freer, more creative use of herself in her casework and a letting go of that tightness and control. I knew
that she was capable of deep feeling. She has such very nice
feeling for people. Could she dare let some of it come through?
Of course, she knew what I was talking about, we had gone
over it when discussing instances in her work where her problem showed itself. She could see a little, too, how she was fighting me.

While she was fighting, there was at the same time a kind of
determination about her wanting to learn. She kept her conference periods with me scrupulously and always brought her
case material in time to discuss it in conference. Part of her
undoubtedly wanted help, and she was eager to get ahead and

to develop professionaly. Even while she struggled against change, some change did take place. So much of her work was sensitive, especially where she could identify more readily, for instance in situations where the need for placement was caused by external reasons, such as illness. She was utterly responsible as to every detail of the job and carried this professional attitude beyond her immediate case load. This, together with great concern and interest in general social welfare, reflected her deep identification with the field and her acceptance of her own role in it.

As time went on she began to have less of a stake in placement as such, recognizing that while it might help with the immediate situation, it did put into motion an entirely new set of problems. With this, she could leave the client freer to make his own decision. She began to be aware of how great a part ambivalence plays in the application process. She also used structure more imaginatively and altogether began to get a better hold of the intake job. We were both naturally pleased with her development. Yet in the one essential area of using herself more spontaneously, in just being able to "be with" the client in his feeling, change came slowly and hard. She was still struggling with that aspect of her development and part of her was holding itself back from yielding to learning.

In school, too, she was fighting. This expressed itself in struggling with the philosophy for which the school stands, accepting some of it, yet holding herself aloof from its very essence. She brought some of this struggle into her supervisory conferences and at first I was quite willing to talk with her about it, thinking that she was trying to find herself in relation to the casework philosophy taught at the school. However, it soon became clear that she was arguing with me and that I could not let it continue. Her struggle with learning was projected onto me and while that was all right as far as it went, it did not go far enough. It remained too external. I let her alone for a while, that is, I did not initiate a discussion of anything problematic in her work with me, so as to give her a chance to work on it by herself. But this did not bring much change. She could see what was wrong in her work, was dissatisfied, but seemed to have reached a blocking in her learning beyond which she could not go. Something decisive had to happen now, something that would shake her out of that rut she was in.

I arranged for a special evaluation conference and told her that I thought she was struggling against all learning at this point. While her work on the whole was not bad, in many instances, was even quite good, she had not made essential progress with what I considered her problem as a caseworker. Unless there were some decisive change, before the end of the semester, I could not give her fieldwork credit for the semester. (This was done in consultation with the adviser at the school.) This would be on the basis of her not approximating her own capacity. She became a little defiant and said with an edge in her voice, "Perhaps you overestimate my capacities." I said, "Perhaps I do." With this, she had to fight me a little bit more, and said that she for one believed in discipline and in being in control of oneself at all times. I thought that that was all right if that was what she wanted, except that it stood in the way of her becoming a caseworker. She was really quite mad now and said, "Well, there are other things besides casework." I said, "Yes, and these other things may not require as much of the self in the way of change as does casework." At this point I didn't know whether she could change or whether she wanted to. With a shrug of the shoulders, she said that neither did she.

She was visibly upset during this discussion, but would not give in to her feelings. She went on to discuss some cases with me as if nothing had happened. I felt I had to help her see what it was she was doing just here with me in the way of exerting control, and how this tended to cut herself off and shut out the other person. I told her that I was amazed at her being able to go on to a discussion of her cases and to act as if she was as unconcerned with what we had talked about. I told her frankly, that I, in her place, would not have been able to do this. After all we had talked about some pretty serious matters. I knew how much of herself she had invested in this training experience and at what cost and sacrifice. I knew she could not but feel concerned. Her first reaction to this was, "Well, you told me, and now I know." But then she yielded, broke down, and cried, half letting it be that way, and half fighting it. "What's there in it for me," she demanded, "in thus losing control?" I could not tell her what meaning it would have for her, except perhaps that she had dared to let it be. After crying for a time she walked out of the room, slamming the door behind her. I knew how painful this conference must have been for her and I thought she was certainly entitled to feel hurt and indignant at me at a time like this.

At our next conference I asked her how she felt and how things were going with her. In response, she handed me a paper she had written for school, saying that I might just as well read it, since I was in it too. This was a paper on feeling, the pain in it for her, and how she had tried to protect herself from pain by building a wall around herself. Now she was fighting anything which threatened to tear down the wall. The paper described the feeling of separation and utter isolation caused by this withdrawal of herself, the fear for her in it, either way, that is, in change as well as in remaining within her shell. The paper was beautifully written reflecting the depth of her feeling and the degree to which she was stirred and shaken.

I commented on this and said that it would be hard to forgive me for having aroused her so. This she acknowledged readily. On the other hand, she could now see the relationship of what she was experiencing with me to what had been blocking her in her casework. She felt that she also could understand her clients better. I said I thought that was important and I was willing to wait and see where all this took her.

At one point during this period, student worked with an adolescent girl who was in a rebellious phase of development. In describing the girl to me she talked with great glee of how negatively the girl, Bella, was related to all authority at this point. She said very wholeheartedly, "I like Bella." I said that I thought that there was a little "Bella" in her right now in relation to me. We both laughed and understood each other.

During the next few conferences she was much more sharing and was willing to let me in on what she was feeling. She told me that she had dealt with the painful experiences in her life by blotting them out of her memory and by not letting herself feel. Her feelings, she said, could reach such violent pitch that she was afraid of them, and so she tried to control them through sheer effort of will. I asked whether this was really bringing her the inner peace she wanted. She could see that it did not. I thought that one could not get rid of the past by merely denying it. Perhaps she could gain a new inner balance not through denial but through taking possession of her feeling, the good and the bad of it, through letting the past live, and herself outlive it, as it were.

All of this marked a very difficult period for this student. It seemed to her as if she were drifting and at loose ends. To her, who had always been so in control of herself, this was upsetting and disturbing. Yet this was just what she needed—to yield and give in to herself. I am sure she knew I was in it together with her. The school was in it too, and she found her contacts with her adviser extremely helpful to her during this difficult phase of her development.

Throughout this period, even while she felt so unmoored, there was a new direction in her casework. I am quoting from my evaluation of her, written at the end of the school semester:

"The change in her casework has been remarkable. She now uses herself creatively with the client and is able to let the fine feeling she has for people come through dynamically in her contacts with them. Feeling no longer holds so much totality and finality for her. She is able to be more tentative with her clients and able to bear the tentativeness in them and in the case situation. Above all, she now has a deep conviction of the client's part and she not only is willing for it to be that way, but is also developing skill in freeing the client to participate fully. She is able to sustain a process with the client, and the ending phase of her contacts is as meaningful as the beginning. She is generally freer and more relaxed and it is good to see the pleasure and confidence she derives from her own movement.

". . . I feel that the student has unusual potentialities as a caseworker and that the movement she has made during the latter part of the semester, certainly warrants my recommending her for full casework credit for the term."

Recently she had a client, a young girl who had a baby born out of wedlock. The client found it extremely difficult to share her feelings with student and did not want to talk about her experience, trying to deny to herself the reality of it. Student was most sympathetic with the girl. In one of her interviews when they were discussing the situation, she tried to help her see that one could not get rid of the past by denying it. These were the very words I had used with her. When she told me about it, I searched her face for a sign of recognition, but there was none, so much had she made this her own.

Now that the school year is drawing to a close, she is reviewing for herself what this entire shcool experience has meant to her. She is amazed at how much she has been able to change. She had not thought it possible at her age. I felt that it was what she had brought to the experience and what she had been willing to put into it that had enabled her to change as much as she had. She said it was wonderful to feel that she had "come through." This was giving her courage and confidence in her work with clients. They, too, can "come through." The school experience has been very meaningful for her and at present she is feeling the pain in ending keenly. She now lets herself experience feeling, and she can live with it.

This record of a second-year training experience needs no comment beyond the fine, sensitive analysis inherent in the supervisor's thinking throughout her description of the process. The supervisor's point of view, her activity, and her thinking are as clearly set forth as is the student's problem and part in the process. But I should like to draw from the record of the training of this one student several points which I believe fundamental to all training for social casework on the second-year level.

A record of an experience which penetrates so deeply into the very center of the self will inevitably raise the familiar question: Where do supervision and training leave off and where does therapy begin? I put the question in this form purposely because it is the form in which it usually takes shape and which implies in itself the fallacy, as I see it, of the basic conception of personality and personality change which underlies it. It implies a static and structural picture of personality organization and development and also the possibility of control both by the helper and the one who seeks help through an assumed ability to determine process, to decide what levels of personality will be touched and what will be kept safe and intact. This is exactly the point of view which this able, intelligent student brings to training, opposing it with all her strength to the point of view of School and supervisor. She is willing, more than that, determined, to use her logical, analytical mind to learn what she must in this professional field, but her feelings are her own. They are deep and powerful. She has learned to control them in ways that make living possible for her, in ways that make her an admirable character. She values her life adjustment and it would violate her conception of herself, her ideal for her development, to seek therapy. Nor would the supervisor or the School conceive of suggesting it to her. They, too, admire the fine personal adjustment this student has achieved and would have no reason and no justification for touching it except in a training relationship.

It is essential to an understanding of this training process to see that the question of whether this is therapy or supervision never presents itself to School, supervisor, or student for the reason that the distinction is so clear from the beginning in the function which determines all that happens in the process. If a school accepts the function of training students to help clients who come in search of this help from agency services, it is obligated to ask each student to meet the requirement of that training. This necessitates for each a new

experiencing of his responses, his feelings, his attitudes, and his behavior, in new situations; inevitably it requires change in his personality structure. How deep this change will go can never be pre-
dicted. It can only be pointed out step by step in the process as
teacher or supervisor becomes aware of the problem that the student's attitude is creating in relation to his client.

The student's attitude can often be handled partially in his
relation to the particular client or in his immediate feelings about
supervision, as we have seen in the illustrations of the beginning experiences of first-year students. But on the second-year level of training for many, perhaps for a majority of students, there comes a point
when the need for more fundamental change is indicated. Perhaps
it arises inevitably to a certain degree for all students from the very
nature of the process itself. Their experience is on a deeper level in
the second year, more difference has been taken in, and a final ending is approaching. Teacher and supervisor on the one side, student
on the other, feel deeply the sense of focus which this final ending
creates between them. One can only describe this as a training movement, with its own function, timing, structure, focus, and goal, clearly differentiated from therapy. It resembles therapy in results only
to the extent that the laws of personality change and growth are
basic in both processes.

The personality problem which the student quoted presents to
training is no different from the problem she would have presented
to therapy if it had been within her range of possible action to seek
therapeutic help. The reason for challenging her adjustment in training is to acquire a skill, not to correct a personality adjustment. The
possibility of change in this problem lies in the question of whether
she can give up any of her own already-established ego ideal, her will
and previous direction, her current organization of herself, sufficiently to accept something new, foreign, and different. At first
this comes at her as invasion by the School's point of view. It requires her to admit the reality of the feeling which she has both
fought and denied and to accept the validity of expressing it if she
wants to attain the training goal which she herself has chosen.

The supervisor's ability to accept and sustain the painful responsibility of requiring the student to effect some change in this fundamental organization of herself is clearly seen to be rooted in her twofold responsibility for clients and for student, focused as a single responsibility for the student's training movement. She sees the stu-

dent's problem in her records, in her inability to feel the ambivalent negative forces in the parent's movement toward placement. She knows that the student cannot become an effective caseworker unless she learns to recognize these forces and to respond to them. She knows also that the student's blind spots in relation to her clients are directly connected with her refusal to recognize these feelings in herself as they are deeply stirred by her positive movement into the training experience. The supervisor attempts first to give specific recognition to the student's problem in her cases, and makes every effort to penetrate the student's resistance, to help her see that she is fighting her and the School. Some students less tightly organized might have come through this period with sufficient change and recognition of problem to meet the constantly held-to requirement that they move forward in ability to use themselves more freely and with greater discipline in behalf of the client. But while this student does seem to make some progress in her casework, in the careful, considered judgment of adviser and supervisor it is not sufficient. One might argue that she will get it later in working experience. But to leave it to that, for the supervisor who is in this experience with her, would be an evasion of what is between them, a refusal to give her the completely honest judgment that, if this is the best she can do, she is handicapped in her chosen profession. In proportion to her own ability and integrity, this student is entitled to an equal degree of honesty of judgment from those responsible for her training; the supervisor from her own integrity and professional maturity can give her no less.

Only the keenest sense of professional difference and the deepest conviction of responsibility to use it to the utmost in behalf of the student can bring a supervisor to the difficult point of action described in the record as follows: "I arranged for a special evaluation conference and told her ... she had not made essential progress with what I considered her problem as a caseworker. Unless there were some decisive change, before the end of the semester, I could not give her fieldwork credit for the semester."

The authority inherent in this supervisory action is inescapable. It feels harsh and arbitrary to the reader as it does to the student while she is still fighting it. But it is no more than the gathering-together into one point of focus of the authority implicit in all training which asks the student to meet and take into himself an essential difference that requires change in himself. Even the most external educational standard and requirement contain the "you must learn this or else." At any point it may be opposed by the student so that this edge of difference as requirement is felt as sharply as it is felt here between this supervisor and this second-year student.

One has only to look at the negative attitudes that typically oppose themselves to the teacher in school or college in order to realize the extent to which this edge of authoritative difference is feared and evaded. Only the most responsible teachers learn to use it consciously in behalf of the student; only the rarest student in relationship with the rare teacher goes all the way in experiencing what is there to be experienced if this crisis is used, not evaded. This authority asks that one yield to the other's difference, to his superior professional development, to his greater knowledge and skill. The very word "yield" carries the meaning which must be resisted in some degree by everyone, particularly by the strong-willed, independent, well-organized person. One must experience yielding truly and deeply as at bottom a potentiality for growth in the own self in order to be free of the fear of dependence, of weakness, of loss of self, which haunts every individual in his movement into relationship.

The clear, fine line between personal and professional is obliterated at this point where difference meets difference so sharply. For at this point of impact, the self is driven back to its organic and impulsive sources and becomes total in its reactions. This experience which, for the supervisor, can only be undertaken out of professional function and responsibility must feel to the student purely personal. If he can give up his willful resistance and yield to the other, it is actually a yielding of the whole self, totally unlike the limited giving-in on a specific point, which leaves the self intact, wholly different from adjusting to a particular external requirement.

Because this yielding is a total emotional experience, felt as personal, that is, as individual and unlimited, the student's reaction will necessarily extend it to the supervisor. In its very quality and essence it is a uniting experience enhanced by the sense of the difference it has overcome. The student must resent the fact that his personal experience is not for the supervisor what it is for himself and he may set himself to make it so. At the same time, his strongest guarantee that this experience will eventuate for him in gain, rather than loss of self, lies in the supervisor's ability to hold to her professional difference throughout this experience. It is her capacity to do this that sets the professional limits for the movement of his powerful feelings, which he now truly knows as ambivalent. As a result they move back into the relationship with the client with new freedom, strength, and sensitivity to the client's ambivalence. The School, too, has an important part in keeping this relationship always three-cornered. It is interesting to see in the record of this second-year student that she found it possible to express the depth of her feeling only indirectly in a paper for her teacher which, however, she manages to share with the supervisor.

If the supervisor has not achieved the maturity and skill to maintain her difference in this process naturally, in behalf of the student, if she must assert this edge of authority arbitrarily and withhold her recognition of the student's reaction to it, the student will not be able to get the full experience of yielding wholeheartedly to all his feelings as was the privilege of the student whose experience we have quoted. One senses in every word of the record this supervisor's warmth of feeling for what the student was going through, her fine identification with every shade of feeling. As she says: "The student was not alone in this. I am sure she knew that I was in it. The School was in it too."

From an impact with the sustained and necessary difference of the professional person who carries the training requirement responsibly and skillfully, the student who comes through it learns the fundamental dynamics of a helping process from having experienced them. He becomes aware of his own natural ambivalence in taking help, the fear of loss of control, of involvement in relationship which inhibits his own movement, the strength of negative resistance which fights his own positive will-to-learn and to yield. He has felt the firmness of the other person's authority, holding him to the necessity of movement throughout his struggle with sensitivity and consideration for all his feelings. He discovers that he can "come through" this struggle with gain rather than loss of self.

For any student to know these dynamics in his own struggle to use help is to know also the client's struggle. Parallel with his own movement in taking help goes the release of his capacity to accept not only his own feelings, but those of the client. At the same time, he is achieving the discipline of his feelings which permits the client to have and to come through this experience of choice and change with the student as helper. As the student in the quoted record says: "It was wonderful to feel that she had 'come through.' This was giving her courage and confidence in her work with clients. They, too, can 'come through.'"

12. THE THESIS AS THE ENDING PHASE OF THE TWO-YEAR TRAINING PROCESS

The thesis project taken over from academic education when the Pennsylvania School became affiliated with the University of Pennsylvania in 1935 has become, in the course of its use in this two-year professional curriculum, the most effective structure that could have been devised for a true realization and eventuation of the whole training movement. The catalogue description gives a simple factual statement of the nature of the requirement. To quote:

> Thesis
>
> Candidates for the degree of Master of Social Work or for the Vocational Certificate complete a substantial discussion of a professional problem arising within their own practice. The problem is chosen and developed in consultation with a thesis adviser, usually the staff instructor most closely related to the field of specialization. In all cases the agency in which the student is doing field work must approve the choice of material.[1]

This statement differentiates the thesis project of the Pennsylvania School of Social Work from the typical research thesis by the requirement that the thesis must develop out of the student's own practice instead of in the use of materials gathered from records or from experience other than his own.

In order to qualify for the thesis work, the student must have demonstrated in the first semester of his second year of practice some basic understanding of the meaning of a functional helping process and the beginnings of a professional use of himself in such a process with his clients. The supervisor's record, quoted in the preceding chapter, shows the extent of the challenge that the responsible supervisor felt it necessary to present to that able student to help her to break through her inhibitions to use herself fully in the helping process. It shows, also, the careful, serious, and continuous process between supervisor and adviser by which the student's change and learning and her skill in practice were evaluated. It is on this progress that the student's readiness to undertake the thesis work rests. While the School recognizes the supervisor's essential role in bringing the student's learning to this level, it is clear that the supervisor should not be asked to go beyond the point of giving credit for the fieldwork of the semester in her evaluation and that the full responsibility of decision as to the student's readiness to undertake the thesis work must rest with the School.

In this final semester of training, therefore, of which the thesis work is the center, while the three-way relationship of School, supervisor, and student continues, the role of each in this relationship alters radically. The student must effect a certain separation from his supervisor and does naturally do this in the evaluation process which takes place between them at the end of the first semester. He must separate to some extent from the day-by-day ongoing connection with his case load in order to analyze part of that experience as thesis material. He enters, then, into a semester of work with a thesis adviser in the School, usually the same adviser who has been his casework teacher and adviser in the first semester. Whether she is familiar or strange to him, the student makes her and this thesis assignment into a new and strange undertaking in which he recapitulates his whole training experience and through it finds and organizes his new professional self in its basic convictions and its skill in practice.

When the student registers for his thesis project at the beginning of the second semester of his second year, he is given in writing a detailed description of the time structure and procedures under which he will work. There is a date for submitting his title and for discusion of it with his adviser, a date for working on his outline, a date for handing in the case material, a date for a final rough draft, and one for the completed bound thesis copy. In all, about six appointments with his thesis adviser are indicated and set up roughly in time.

The thesis adviser who accepts responsibility for carrying the student through the thesis work faces, first of all, the obligation to involve the student in using her help on the thesis against his temptation to escape this process by returning to his supervisor who knows his cases as well as he does. A major problem at the same time is to help him assert the validity of his own experience with his clients against his tendency to deny that he has anything to write about. It must be there in his records or he would not be certified to begin the work on the thesis but it is the rare student who can move easily into a choice of thesis problem, a statement of title, a selection of case material. Some students bring too much, others too little. Characteristically, students start with generalizations and must learn to break this down in order to get to the concrete and real in their own experience. They feel hampered by all that has been better said by other students before them or they tend to rely completely on what has been written by the faculty and must be challenged to bring out in their own words the essential bases for their thinking. Much of this is no different from the process that anyone goes through in attempting to state in organized written form for the first time the conclusions of his own experience and thinking. The significant difference in the writing process of the students in this school of social work is that it is undertaken and carried through in a helping process with a professional person, the adviser, in a definite and limited time structure. It is therefore essentially of the same nature as the other learning processes of the preceding semesters. It does not stand alone but is an integral part and a true ending phase of the total training movement. In the limited time unit of this one semester of work with its half-dozen appointments with an adviser, the student in taking such specific and defined help comes to a clearer understanding of his own pattern of using help and of the typical struggle and ambivalence of any human being in this process. In his writing he sees himself more objectively in his relation to his clients and gains greater capacity to evaluate his own skill. The final completion of a thesis, typed and bound and presented to the library and to the agency for the use of other students and workers, gives him a new and satisfying sense of his achievement as a professional person.

This description of the training movement in the thesis project as primarily a process between the adviser and the student with the focus on the student in his final organization and affirmation of his professional self may seem to leave the supervisor with a negligible role. This is by no means the case. One must state her role first in negative terms to realize fully the sacrifice and the discipline it asks her to maintain. Her stake in the first semester has been deep. She has contributed fully of her concern, of her supervisory activity and skill, in bringing the student through to a point where his casework practice can support a thesis undertaking only now to be obliged to resign him to a new process which will involve him more deeply. The kind and degree of separation this asks of her tends to be overlooked in the responsibility she must continue to carry for his work with his cases and his relation to the agency. She must be prepared to be the bearer of his negative projections and to see the final reward of his ending experience given to another person. Only the experienced supervisor who has weathered the sacrifice and the disappointments not once but many times has found a way to carry the very responsible and often odious part that is hers, not only without interference, but with an identification with his thesis process that can be sustaining and helpful to the student as well as satisfying to herself.

School as well as agency expects responsible practice work of the student in this final semester and little extra time or allowance is made for the thesis writing. Each year as students struggle with this difficult assignment, thesis advisers question again whether the School really asks the impossible! Each year they find the positive answer in the accomplishment of another class of students and must affirm again their conviction of the essential rightness of this process as a whole, which like all living must always seem too hard at the point where one engages with it fully and deeply.

13. THE ESSENTIAL BASIS FOR SUPERVISORY SKILL

In locating this description of the supervisory process in the particular structure of the Pennsylvania School of Social Work, I may seem to imply that I believe this to be the only structure within which this process of learning to help in a professional relationship can take place, and perhaps also that this structure is fixed and static. If this were so, the Pennsylvania School would not be willing to use as supervisors any except its own graduates trained in its own structures. On the contrary, the School welcomes as supervisors of students, graduates of other schools, asking of them only one requirement, that they be willing to engage themselves in working with the Pennsylvania School in its structures in training a student. The School does not minimize the learning that will be involved for a supervisor unfamiliar with this school and has set up a class for beginning supervisors which follows the movement of the first-year student in the time structure of the School year, sustained by supervisor in agency and adviser in the School in a focused relationship. A supervisor in choosing to undertake the training of a student in the Pennsylvania School of Social Work is facing for herself a new learning process.

While the graduate of a different school of social work cannot know in advance all that will be involved for her, she will not attempt it at all unless she knows enough about the Pennsylvania

School to make this initial choice for herself of a new learning experience. It goes without saying and is a matter of fact that graduates of other schools trained in the Freudian diagnostic approach to the helping process and who are satisfied with this approach and method of helping will hardly risk involving themselves with the Rankian-functional approach and method, exactly opposite as it is in its basic understanding of the self and its use in professional helping relationships.

As supervisors trained in other schools engage in this class and in this learning process they will undoubtedly ask: but what of the psychological point of view which underlies this functional practice? Can we supervise for the School if we are not taught this point of view *as such?*

There can be no question that the method and practice in use in a helping process rest upon a psychology, an understanding of the nature and organization of the self and of its processes of change and growth in helping relationships. This fundamental psychology determines the way in which help is given and the nature of the structures set up to facilitate and direct the professional helping process. The psychological point of view of this school, as I have said in Part II, derives from Rank's Will Psychology and his understanding of helping processes. Rank's articulation of this psychology in *Will Therapy* and *Truth and Reality* growing out of his long and intensive therapeutic practice is difficult reading. Its meaning eludes the typical intellectual approach and analysis. Only the student who brings to Rank's writings something more than intellectual effort, some ability to connect with his own inner experience and a sufficiently strong desire and purpose to hold himself to the exploration of and deeper understanding of that experience, can relate to Rank's content in a way which enables him to find in it its valid meanings. The School asks of its students and of its supervisors this effort to find meaning for themselves in some part of Rank's work. Beyond this limited use of his psychology it does not expect its students to go, for the additional study required for a comprehensive and objective evaluation of his contribution to psychological theory and therapeutic method goes far beyond what could be expected in a two-year curriculum in social work.

What, then, is the absolute minimum and essential basis of psychological understanding, the necessary unit of experience, knowledge of which is required of students and supervisors of students to enable them to use the practice of this school in helping processes?

I would say that the essential experience on which rests all ability and skill in helping in a professional process is an experience of change within the self which takes place in relation to a projection of this experience on another person who carries the stability which supports this risk of change. There is no experience so fearful, so threatening as the risk of change in the self, for the natural process of living takes place in relation to external reality and the slightest stoppage in this process which forces the movement of energy back from its outgoing expression on its object into the self disturbs the individual profoundly. The extent to which any living organism can tolerate this moment of interference with its movement is probably very limited. It finds its way to go around, to avoid, to overcome the obstacle. The human being alone, for better or for worse, has developed the capacity to take in this moment of interference with its own movement, to know it and deal with it. He alone can become aware of his own inner experience, can tolerate to different degrees his feeling and emotions of fear and of anger, of love and hatred for the other to whom he is related. But in the experience of natural human relationships in everyday living, the individual controls his inner experience, his love and his hate, even when he seems most at the mercy of the other person. It is he, obviously, who determines by all that is in him what he will feel and how he will feel it. No outside force, personal or impersonal, can wrest this control away from him against his will. The uncertainty, then, that an individual faces when he lets himself in for an experience of change in himself of which he does not hold the control constitutes a risk beyond comprehension or description.

It is precisely this risk of the self that the student who would use himself in helping others must face. On the other hand, it must be admitted that it is possible for a student to go through a two-year training process in a school of social work without actually risking himself in this way, just as it is possible for a patient to go to a therapist and prove that his neurosis is incurable or perhaps bring about some change in his neurosis himself against, or in spite of, the therapist. The rigidly organized, deeply negative, as well as the very creative, personality may succeed in sustaining its organization against the other or independently of the other and may indeed be eminently successful in certain undertakings but is surely disqualified for the development of skill in a helping process where sensitivity and responsiveness to the other person are basic requirements.

It is possible, of course, for an individual to experience change in himself in relation to another in life-giving ways without knowing the process by which change was effected. But if one seeks to make professional use of this experience, it is necessary that it be identified as a time-limited, structuralized unit with a describable beginning, a known focus, and a definite ending in time. Some of the detail of content and process must be open for examination and available for use in subsequent experience.

Here, I believe, one runs up against a fundamental human problem, the problem of holding inner experience, immediate, delicate, and fluid as it is, long enough to examine it, to bestow upon it any conceptual words which will not stultify the living quality of the process. Each individual has a unique relation to his own inner experience and describes it for himself, if indeed he attempts to describe it at all, in terms and images peculiar to himself alone. The passion to share this experience, which surely every individual knows at some moment in his life, may never be realized except in very fragmentary and unsatisfying ways subject to misunderstanding. In a therapeutic process, the individual learns to risk these fragmentary expressions of inner experience, trusting them to be understood for what they are, knowing that what is temporary and misleading today can be added to and corrected tomorrow. If this experience in sharing the inner self and its changing feelings and attitudes is to be more than personally therapeutic, ready for use in professional helping processes, some points of process, of movement and change, must be identifiable in language that has common professional meaning.

In the description of the two-year training process which I have given in this book, I have attempted to give meaning to a few concepts, to identify several points of process to serve as guideposts in this movement in a time-structured relationship. I restate these concepts now in conclusion. First, I have emphasized the concept of function, believing that this concept introduces the precise degree of objectification which makes consciousness of inner process possible and describable. Accepted and understood as the necessary basis of a relationship process, it begins to define responsibilities and roles, to indicate direction, to afford opportunities for partialization and deepening of psychological experience.

When function is accepted by a helping person in a professional relationship, there follows at once an understanding of the second concept to which I have assigned importance—the concept of functional difference. One does not need to go far into his inner experience to be aware of the psychological importance of his feeling of difference from others or look around him to any extent without realizing the problem this difference constitutes in the world today. It is only in a functionally controlled relationship, I believe, that the factor of difference can be truly accepted and affirmed by the helping individual because it has been justified by function. This acceptance of his own difference and the responsibility for the use it engenders at the same time develops an increasing sensitivity to the other's difference and greater freedom to relate to him in this process, always directed to helping the other rather than to an expression of his own impulsive feeling or willing.

I have used the word "yield" to identify the moment in process when an individual gives up his own inner organization in response to what the other person has injected of his difference. This word merely describes, but in no way explains, the complexity of this little-understood experience, in which the very essence of the possibility of change in psychological organization in relationship resides. The degree of yielding will differ from individual to individual, from a fairly superficial giving in of some point in the outer layer of the resistive, fighting self to a deep inner yielding of the whole self in fundamental trust of the other and of this relationship process. This experience in yielding one's own direction and organization is crucial for one's awareness of the strength and nature of his own will and its projection on the other. It marks a shift in balance in the beginning of a new organization of the process in the self, a different possibility of balance in relation to the other. The words I have used to mark out the time structure in this process are the everyday words in common usage: beginning, middle or turning point, and ending.

Granted the basic experience in the self, acknowledged as change in a professionally controlled relationship in learning a helping process, the individual has within his grasp not only a characteristic unit of experience upon which he can draw for the enlargement and deepening of his own understanding of relationship process but even more than this. What has been revealed of himself in this heightened moment of living in relationship, of hitherto unacknowledged parts of himself, its possibilities for good and evil, for pain and satisfaction, for destructiveness and creativity, is not limited to an understanding of the professional experience alone, but constitutes a deeper source of connection with the complex, living self and of its expression and projection in all its relationships. The process of change, professionally initiated and limited, becomes an organic growth process of the whole self formed and directed by the unique nature of each individual self. Within the controls and structures of service, supervision, and administration in the social agency, the discovery and expression of the creative self can find almost unlimited opportunity if the individual can accept the responsibility for himself, for the other, and for the process which helping demands.

This concept of the self as a living whole whose complex and manifold expressions can never be analyzed and interpreted but can only be understood as a whole underlies all understanding and skill in helping processes. It is this quality and respect in the understanding extended to the person seeking help or to the student in training that enables him to yield his defenses to the other. The supervisors's essential skill, I believe, stems from this respect for her self and for the other and extends only so far as she can truly take in and comprehend the unique self of the other and accord to that self the right to its difference while holding it to the change which must take place in the learning process.

The Dynamics of Psychological Change in the Impulse-Will Balance in the Organization of the Self

This article was written in 1950, just before her retirement, when Miss Robinson was Associate Dean and still teaching at the University of Pennsylvania School of Social Work. She wrote this manuscript as a member of an advisory committee of the U.S. Public Health Service.

Although she utilizes as content this specific educational experience, she is really working with the dynamics of inner growth—the movement which characterizes all psychological growth whether it be in individual therapy, group therapy, or educationally centered as it is in this manuscript.

Any person who has undertaken to teach or to train for a skill, no matter what the skill, who is at the same time sensitive to and aware of the relationship which develops between himself and the one who is ostensibly there to learn, will recognize at once the universality of the experience described: the early enthusiasm, the point of resistance, the two sides of feeling, the moment of change when, accepting discipline and conditions on a new level, the student takes into himself the will to learn. Miss Robinson herself states it thus:

> *There would be no justification for taking the reader through this movement if I did not believe this process to be a typical learning movement which reveals the characteristic phases of learning in any field.*

The reader will find in the pages which follow aspects of the teaching/learning experience which are the opposite of many popular educational and therapeutic theories; here there must be structure, form, limits, clear roles. The teacher is clearly a teacher, the stu-

dent a student. Requirements are held to firmly, so-called "flexibility"
is at a minimum. Within a clear gestalt of place, time, conditions,
and function, the student will find the chance to grow, to develop a
skill, to become more of a self, not in a boundless, amorphous way,
but with a specific purpose, a focus: to become a professional self.

There is no more inescapable reality in the world today than the
reality of change—social and psychological change beyond the power
of the single individual to stem or control. The utmost any individual can do is to reach out for some foothold in his own attitudes towards the rush of events only to find himself swept along in this
changing stream, so that it seems one cannot say today where one
will stand tomorrow. Our national character, our way of living, our
values, our goals are in jeopardy.

This ever-present fear in the present danger influences in ways
impossible to disentangle the fundamental psychological problem of
change and resistance to change. We have learned in this country to
be patient, even to value these differences and the struggle between
them as essential to democratic process, believing that out of this
open expression of opinion and the struggle itself a new solution of
the problem will emerge.

All those who work with individuals in the conscious effort to
influence their attitudes, to teach them, to help them, to counsel
them, to heal them, by whatever word in our own field of endeavor
we describe our professional or social purpose, know the gap that exists between the available information that we have to give and the
ability of others to use it; between the individual's need and seeming
desire for help and his readiness to take what is extended to him. In
some painful realization of this gap we face the conflict between our
desire and will to overcome this difference, to give to the other what
he ought to have and what he so desperately needs and his own resistance to taking it. We have been compelled at times to give up before
the force of the refusal to learn, to change, to do what it takes to be
healed. Faced with such refusals we cannot escape from asking ourselves the fundamental question, "By what right do I ask this change
of another?" From this question the examination of one's will and

that of the other that the limitations of purpose and service and an effective relation to change can be learned.

The Mental Health movement in the exuberance of its youth has not faced this separation sufficiently to find its limits in what it has to offer and its reason for offering it. In saying this it is important to differentiate the carefully defined and limited services of the mental hospital, the psychiatric and child guidance clinics, the counseling services in which professional help is offered, from the generalized mental health or mental hygiene programs which have sprung up under all kinds of auspices.

It is not within the scope of this paper to examine these programs. I intend instead to limit what I write to an examination of the problem of requiring and effecting change in individuals when such change is initiated and carried out under professional limitations and controls in the field of social casework and education for social casework where service, function and process have been clearly defined. In years of working in this field with the psychological nature of the problem always in mind, I have been impressed by the fact that it is the inevitable two-sidedness of change from which one cannot escape but with which one finds it so difficult to deal. I refer to the necessity of the individual to create change for his own needs and to use what is outside himself for this purpose combined with his aversion to any change that is put upon him or demanded of him from the outside. Man's capacity for change, tested it seems to the limit in these times, is far greater even than we can know. For any one individual, I believe, the apparent limitation on his capacity for change lies in his own attitude, in his belief or disbelief in his own autonomy in relation to himself and to what is outside himself.

If this is so, the technical problem of method for those professional groups who are concerned in furthering change and growth in individuals is in finding the clue for touching this fine point of balance in the individual's organization between inner and outer forces, the point where energy is concentrated in refusal, in a conviction of "this is done to me" and where it can become accessible to release in the feeling and belief, "I myself can do something about it." This turning point is the hinge of fate, to borrow Mr. Churchill's phrase. To find it asks that we divorce ourselves from the projection of our own strength and positive will, the more natural way to accomplish change, in favor of trying to find the strength of the other, the point where change can take place in the use of his own will.

1. ATTITUDES: THEIR CAPACITY FOR AND ACCESSIBILITY TO CHANGE

The power to will, the ability to think are priceless possessions of the educated human being. We have experienced them united in the rare individual, at home with himself and his universe. By what processes of natural growth and education this maturity has been achieved we can never fully know. That circumstance alone is now powerful enough to impede this development, the achievements of many successful individuals give evidence. As educators, social workers, professional helpers, we must believe that we can stimulate, facilitate and foster this development by our own contribution, that we can help to bring about change in the individual who is not using himself and his environment to the ends of life and growth. Without this conviction and actual knowledge of our own part in this process and skill in using ourselves effectually, we feel confused and baffled.

Before examining the problem of how one can touch these aspects of the self that we designate as will power and mind, it will be valuable, I believe, to examine the meaning of attitude. It is attitude change to which the effort of professional groups is directed and one must stop to examine what is meant by attitude and how much is intended by those who attempt to bring about change in attitudes. What function do attitudes serve in the organization of the self and in its use in relation to its environment?

We can start this process of exploration for an understanding of the meaning and function of attitude simply and externally by identifying some familiar, common attitudes and asking ourselves what purpose they serve. In relation to food objects and eating, for example, we can name our own characteristic attitudes readily and recognize the positive connection with certain objects: "I like, or I love, or I must have, rare meat or potatoes or milk or ice cream or whatever," and the rejection of other objects in "I cannot eat, or I never eat, fish, or red meat or milk or olives." In the field of personal relationships more significant attitudes can be recognized expressed in, "I love and respect, admire and trust this person; I hate, despise or distrust another." Carried beyond the individual, the attitude may express a relation to a class or category of people, to people who are stupid or intellectual, aristocratic or common, rich or poor, to a racial or minority or majority group. Or we may seek illustration in attitudes towards political theories or parties, towards ideologies, towards art, science, or religion. Most fundamental and determinative in its potential for change or refusal of change is the attitude each individual carries towards himself, of belief and trust in that self, of confidence, of arrogance, of doubt or mistrust.

Out of even a cursory, superficial examination of our own characteristic attitudes, we can see at once that an individual's attitudes grow out of his efforts to relate to what is outside himself, complex and overwhelming as it is in its varied possibilities for response and usefulness, accessible and suitable to his need, or alien and threatening. The "yes" and "no" with which he greets or rejects the opportunities which his world extends to him begin long before speech, in total or partial organic reaction and in gesture. As this "yes" or "no" attaches to an object or groups of objects there begins a process of choice, of definition of the environment in which certain classes of objects, certain areas of external experience, become open and accessible for further exploration and others become firmly, perhaps irrevocably, closed to the child. Many opportunities for experience are necessarily excluded in this process and, for the individual whose necessity to say "no" to what is presented to him is greater than his desire to say "yes," there is indeed an early narrowing of experience which can be deplorable. But except for the negatively organized child, this active process of selecting, choosing and defining the environment is economically valuable as it is necessary for immediate experiencing and for growth and development of the total self. Once acquired, these attitudes provide the child with well-known connections between himself and the objects of his environment. They sustain his relation to what is outside himself and contribute a sense of stability and consistency while his inner strength to choose, to will, to determine his own course is deepening.

By the time an individual reaches adulthood he is possessed of a wide range of attitudes by which, however conflicting and inconsistent they may be among themselves, he is held in stable relationship to the world around him. The passive verb "is held" best expresses the static, already determined, nature of these connections and the function that they serve in a world where so much is constantly presented beyond the individual's capacity for reaction and the definition of new response and attitude. On the other hand, the active nature of the process of attitude formation is obvious to us daily as we see ourselves reacting to news, information, propaganda where we are drawn into a process of defining ourselves, of forming new attitudes towards new information, opinions and events. We are not held static by previously formed attitudes but must, almost in spite of ourselves, respond to the new, engage in examination, exploration, definition of our relation to the world about us, make our attitudes over from day to day.

When we look at attitudes in others, from the point of view of accessibility to change, we can recognize certain attitudes as so loosely held, so flexible in nature that they seem closer to mood and feeling than to the firmer quality of the established attitude. Others seem hard and unyielding, laid down in the very structure of the organism like muscle and bone extending to their objects like bands of steel. Such attitudes may be described in such a way that they characterize the object as unchanging as when the individual says: "To lie or to drink, or to smoke is wrong." On the other hand they may be used to proclaim some characteristic of the self in its inalienable, unchanging nature as when an individual says, "I am the kind of person who cannot bear a lie."

Let us look at the natural process of change in attitudes with which everyone is familiar which comes about often without notice under the influence of new associations, new friends, a change in situation, or in group membership. The child experiences change of this kind as he may move from one neighborhood to another, from one school to another, become a member of a new club in a community house or of a scout group. Depending on the child's own individual makeup and way of reacting to experience, he will eventually change certain of his attitudes as he finds himself in the new situation. An inevitable initial period of strangeness, of felt difference from the others, of fear or resistance to the change, expressed in varying degrees of withdrawal or aggressive assertion of himself in the situation, will break up into something that begins to let him respond to what is present in the new situation, to find elements of likeness with which he can identify or of difference on which he can project his own need. How important a part a teacher can play in the process if he is aware of the child's strangeness and can recognize it sensitively with just the right degree of support given to his efforts to move into the class until he can find his own place on his own strength! This is the skill which all leaders of groups must learn, whether they work with children or adults, in helping individuals move into new groups in a way that will enable each one to experience change of behavior and attitude in the new situation. Such an attitude as the prejudice towards racial or nationality difference can break up and disappear almost overnight in a group where white and colored, Jew and Gentile, meet under skilled leadership to learn to do something together. It may not even require any skill of the leader or teacher beyond the fact that he accepts the members of this group as all alike in the purpose for which they have come together. Just this degree of unity—the common, self-chosen purpose—may be enough to enable the individual members to extend themselves to each other freed of the stereotyped attitude which may have previously prohibited acquaintance. The small town girl or boy who has grown up in a homogeneous provincial community may experience what seems almost revolutionary change of attitude in a first year at the big college or university just through the class or extracurricular experience with all sorts of students united by common interests, purposes and loyalties to "the college." In a change of experience and attitude as complete as this a boy or girl often feels himself to be a different person, and all the old associations of family and friends formed in the home town may seem to be strange, no longer capable of carrying the values of the self. Yet these radical changes of attitude are not unusual but within the natural growth process of the average individual who is free enough to change his situation and use the different objects and persons he finds in the new environment.

In what I have just said about changes in attitude which come about naturally in use of new situations I have purposely ignored the factor of the individual's fundamental readiness for change on which alone depends his capacity to use the new experience in any profitable way. Against his own readiness or beyond it, neither pressure nor skill can be effective in enabling him to use what is offered to him. This unreadiness may be a matter of physical or psychological immaturity which only time and natural organic growth can change, or it may be a problem of deep-seated resistance and refusal which inhibit the natural use of what is offered. Every class and every group provides at least one disturbing refusal of growth and change. Our experience as professional workers with these refusals to change in individuals who seem determined to cut themselves off from the natural processes of living precipitates the problem of change into deeper levels.

Experience with infants and little children shows us how early this refusal manifests itself and how successfully it can maintain itself against all adult efforts to change it. When we feel this negative strength in a child's activity and responses, even more than when we feel his positive strength to find and take from the environment what he needs, we seek for the word that will express the force of this power in him apart from its objects. The word "will" throughout the years in common usage for this purpose still seems to express, as the psychoanalytic terms "aggression" or "ego" do not, the strength and force of the child's effort to grapple with his world, to meet the forces that press upon him from within and without, to control and mould these in some way to his immediate needs and growing purposes. It has firmness and persistency, designed to shape the impulsive and the transitional into the reliable, the stable, the consistent: designed as well to do battle with whatever in the environment opposes its movement, capable of inhibiting and restricting its own life forces as well as opposing the forces and pressure from the environment.

For every individual, the fundamental problem of living, underlying all the specific content of experience, taking precedence over all circumstance in the environment, depends on the way in which will is related to impulse in the pattern of his organization. This pattern is established so early it often seems inborn and may indeed be manifest in birth itself. We have no difficulty in recognizing extreme types, the delinquent who acts, we say, on impulse, whose will does not succeed in bringing impulse into organized relation to his own needs or the environment, who seems lacking in the inhibitory power of the will. In contrast, we point to the admirable man with highly developed will control whose ideal of himself as strong and self-consistent may permit of too little impulsive expression, who must maintain himself in one light, "I am never sick, or weak, or bad, or mistaken." So will can go beyond itself in its search for inner self consistency and external control. Strangely enough, it is this most characteristic inalienable fact about himself, this activity of his own will, which the individual does not know and which professional groups who meet it in others to their own bafflement and defeat, seem bent upon denying. The individual can readily know his own attitudes since he believes them to belong to the object, to identify it as good or bad, right or wrong. It is more difficult to know the attitudes which identify the self; usually they are recognized casually or irresponsibly as partial expressions of a self that can evade being known in its active immediate intention or its total willing capacity.[1]

As the will of the individual develops always in interaction with other wills one must ask, how is it ever possible for the will to know its own intention and power. The degree of separation this would require from the objects of projection and immediate experience would seem impossible of achievement. But the possibility of fundamental change in the impulse-will balance depends upon the possibility of arresting the ongoing will expression in some moment of separation from its object. Out of this moment a new feeling experience, a shift in the impulse-will control and a new responsibility for will may emerge.

There is growing concern in all fields of education, particularly in professional education, with this problem of psychological change in the student but as yet little clarity as to the nature or level of the change required or the process through which it can come about. A first step in clarifying this problem for any field of education is to identify the knowledge or the skill it undertakes to teach and to decide whether change in attitudes and behavior is enough to ask of learners. In the field of professional education for which I speak, education for social work, a more fundamental change, change in the impulse-will organization, has proved to be required by the nature of the professional skill social work renders. In the sections that follow I have undertaken to identify that skill and to describe the process of change through which it is learned.

2. THE CONCERN OF SOCIAL WORK AND SOCIAL WORK EDUCATION WITH CHANGE IN THE WILL ORGANIZATION

Social work, throughout its long development from its beginnings in various lay activities described under the names of charity, philanthropy and correction, to the present in which professional services requiring professional training are recognized, has always been concerned with bringing about change. At what is this desire and intention to bring about change directed: at circumstance or at the individual himself? At the individual's attitudes and behavior or at the will which underlies these expressions of himself? In an early phase of development in social work in these efforts to effect change, the individual was held responsible. Moral judgment operated to indict the individual in need as bad, a ne'er-do-well, a deserter, an alcoholic. Pressure to change his behavior was exerted on him directly: "You must get a job, support your family, stop drinking." In a swing against this moralistic attitude, we see the opposite tendency in a later phase of social work, the tendency to excuse the individual in trouble, to lay the blame on circumstances and try to effect some change in his situation.

Today both tendencies operate in the field of social work, in the field as a whole between different schools of social work, between the emphasis on individual will and present experience of the functional school.

The social worker must take the impact of this problem at every moment of his professional life. People come to social agencies out of desperate need to have something change in the circumstances in which they are caught. They believe the problem lies outside themselves, in the situation or in the other person, the marital partner or the difficult child. The circumstances are always limiting, frustrating, burdensome; their recital is almost unbearable to hear. Whether the social worker can do any more than listen depends on what he can introduce that will momentarily stem the tide of this evil which seems to flow from outside the individual in order to touch something in the individual himself with which he can take hold differently. If the individual, now the client of the social agency, can engage his will with the function of this agency expressed and carried by the will of the worker, there is immediately set in motion a highly dynamic process of change in which the pressure to change the other, or the defeatist attitude that nothing can change that the client brought to the agency, can shift to a constructive will to change those conditions which can be attacked when will moves positively and realistically, step by step into circumstance.

An illustration may help to make this point clearer. A mother had been throughout the years on the record "the client of many social and health agencies." Her predicaments, her problems and her desperate need of help in raising a family single-handed had engaged them all in desire and determination to help her for her sake and for the sake of her miserable neglected children. Nothing seemed to avail to change the persistent recurrent pattern of misfortune and neglect. But here was a mother who seemingly and avowedly wanted something different for herself and her children. Recently the oldest child, the greatest problem to the mother, was admitted to a children's hospital for heart care. The mother was asked to come in for an interview with the medical social worker. This interview was followed by several others and by one with the doctor. In this experience this mother, perhaps for the first time in her life, was treated as the mother of her child and asked to take responsibility for what was happening to her. The total burden of her family and her own inefficiency seemed lifted by what the social worker, the doctor and the hospital offered in care, skill and understanding and within this support she could find some strength in herself to take hold, to begin again, to examine with the social worker what was possible for her child and what she herself wanted. In these few interviews she came to a decision to ask for placement of this child. Now she could choose the plan herself and take the steps necessary to carry it through.

This mother wanted change desperately but despairingly, as she was able to tell the social worker in an ending interview. The burden always seemed too great for her; misfortune seemed to come at her. She had no belief in herself, in her ability to do anything about it. "Somehow you have helped me to believe I have some strength in myself," she told the social worker. An amazing change has taken place in this mother's belief in herself and in her capacity to do something for her child through the use of what social work calls by the simple name of "help." This would have been the word used by others but to the mother what had been extended to her so untiringly felt like the pressure of their own good intent and all her strength was mobilized in resisting.

A student in a school of social work, a college graduate with a good record, articulates a problem similar to this mother's. She had been more aggressive in her resistance to her teacher but had never found the positive strength in herself. She says in a paper to her casework teacher:

> How can one ever know what one thinks, or when one is right or wrong. I read this authority and that one and the other but when they differ how can I decide among them. I never realized it before but it seems to me now that I always read a thing by placing myself in the opposite position, resisting and fighting everything the writer says. At the end I can repeat what he says but I still don't know what I think. I believe I've

been like that with every teacher. As a little child I remember feeling afraid of the teacher, accepting that she was always right and yet underneath I think I was always resisting her and trying to find her wrong. There must be something in myself that feels right but I never get to it. How can one ever get a conviction that one is right, that one can have enough confidence in to act on.

Different as environmental circumstances have been for these two people, the mother and the student, the problem they present from the point of view of how effective change can take place is the same. The social worker must help the mother to find in herself the positive will she has denied that alone has the power to change circumstance; the teacher must be able to offer help that will enable her student to relax the use of her fighting will and its efforts to oppose the other in favor of finding her own positive will, her own opinion and conviction. In either case the change to be effected is not the kind of change in attitudes and behavior which can take place in the natural growth processes which I have illustrated in the preceding section of this paper, rather it necessitates a change in the use of the will in its positive and negative aspects and in its control of impulse and environment.

There is neither time nor space in this paper to describe the process by which change took place in this mother or this student. But it is important that the meaning of help as I am using it here as the effective agent of psychological change be made clear. For that purpose I quote from an unpublished statement of Jessie Taft that I used in "The Dynamics of Supervision Under Functional Controls."[1] It seemed to me then and now, as I go over the literature, the most comprehensive statement of the meaning of help and a helping process.

I would draw a distinction between what might be called 'real' help, by which I mean a realistic meeting of need without hindrance and on its own terms, and psychological help whose meaning and value are registered in the very experience of taking help through the medium of a helping person whose difference from the applicant is maintained and becomes effective in the process. To take help in this sense is, we believe, the deepest, most fundamental form of personality change and of learning because it penetrates to the roots of human relationships as they are developed from the beginning in the manifold forms of giving and taking, of relying upon, yet struggling to control those who supply the answer to urgent need from the mother on. Because the original human need is of necessity placed, not on things but on a person, it sets the pattern of all our later efforts to develop within the self enough integration and self-possession to grant to the 'other' his equal right to a self of his own, a self which is not there just to meet our need in our own terms. Perhaps no human being ever gives up completely that first image of the all-giving one who has no self-interest to consider, no desire beyond that which is attuned to our own changing necessity. But if maturity, as a result of psychological growth, has any meaning surely it must relate to the degree of success which has been attained in that unending struggle to develop a strength and integrity that can accept and bear internal need without assuming the obligation of the other to meet it and without exerting pressure upon him to fulfill our requirements regardless of his own desire or willingness.

When a man is brought to the necessity of asking assistance from an outside source because of his own inadequacy, inability, or failure to manage his own affairs, whatever has been faulty in his way of relating to the other will be brought into focus as he tries to find his role as client of a social agency. While he is free to concentrate on his own need and to try to get it satisfied in exactly the way he has planned, he is met in the person of the caseworker by something that is quite unknown to him out of his experience in purely personal relations. He has no personal claim or hold on this worker or this agency, although he may try to establish one, yet she meets his request with a consideration for him, an understanding of what it costs him to ask, that answers to an unmet hunger of which he has probably been unaware. He finds also that this worker is not there just to meet his need but that she represents an agency which has a character of its own, a defined purpose, a service with limitations as well as resources. This applicant, whose request has been received with such respectful and thoughtful consideration, is now faced with the fact that the agency presents a difference which must be taken into account and that to use its service, he must go beyond the pressure for immediate fulfillment to a reevaluation of his own situation in relation to the service which the agency can give. He may decide that this agency does not have what he requires and go elsewhere but, if he stays, he will have to modify his idea of his need and his determination to have things his way in terms of a new plan or purpose which includes the agency in its difference. This does not take place easily or at once but, if the need is acute, the pressure for fulfillment intense, and the worker skillful in meeting it, the struggle to find a way to use the agency that is right for both can precipitate an experience that goes to the very roots of the client's faulty relationships.

No difference in the other is so painful, so unbearable, as that difference which threatens the satisfaction of a need that seems vital. How then can a client who is forced to ask help, not of a friend but of an impersonal agency, ever find the difference which the agency represents to be anything but intolerable although he may be forced to submit by the urgency of his need? That this experience can be a source of fundamental learning, of actual reorganization of the self with which he comes, is due to the fact that the agency is known, is differentiated, through the medium of his relation to the worker whose human understanding, professional skill, and genuine readiness to help, give to the client increasing awareness and possession of himself as an individual whose right to differ is thoroughly respected. It is this combination of regard for him and his need, together with the worker's affirmation of agency as something which goes beyond her power to alter in his favor, that can break up the client's impulsive or willful presentation of himself and finally permit a true yielding to the reality of the situation, the agency's and his own, not blind submission to superior force or inner need, but a new willingness to let the other have a part in the giving because that other has recognized the true nature of the asker, has not tried to control, although he has refused to be controlled.

This, then, is what I understand to be the essence of the helping process, which can take place as a professionally determined process only when the helper has developed in his own person a professional self to which the personal need is subordinated and by which it is controlled when responsibly engaged with a client as the human representative of an agency whose purpose and raison d'être is to give a service so that it will be truly helpful to the individual who can use it.

It is with the problem of change as it relates to the will and responsibility for its use that education for social work has been concerned in recent years. It has passed through the stage of effecting change in attitude that saw its task as teaching students to identify with their clients in need, to relax their punishing and reforming efforts to make them over. To a great extent these changes in attitude were easily and readily enough accomplished in the school setting in devotion to the task of helping others. But recalcitrant attitudes in certain students continued to baffle teachers and supervisors. Students with "personality problems" were thought to be unsuitable for social work or in need of therapy for themselves before they could give help to others. While this may still be true of individual students it is important for educators in this field to grasp the deeper problem; to accept the fact that they are concerned with change and training of the denied and irresponsible will, not merely with change of attitudes and to admit that this undertaking is one before which the educator may indeed quail.

The only justification for undertaking so fundamental a responsibility is the realization that change in the use and organization of the will is essential for the student who would learn to use himself professionally in helping others rather than in the natural personal ways of give and take.

In the following section I have undertaken to describe a training process where training is understood to require of students a change in the use of the self, in will organization. In this description I do not pretend to speak for the field of social work or education for social work as a whole but limit myself to one school of social work known as the functional school, where I have carried responsibility for the development of the training process for many years and have had the opportunity to observe the results of this process in class after class of students and graduates.

3. THE BEGINNING PHASE OF STUDENT MOVEMENT: POSITIVE AND NEGATIVE ASPECTS OF THE ADMISSIONS AND PLACEMENT PROCESS

The college graduate who makes his vocational choice the profession of social work and applies for admission to a professional school has already committed his will to the learning of something new and different. He admits that this learning may be difficult and that some change in himself will be expected but what this will involve he cannot possibly know in advance of the actual experience.

At the point of application, in his very first contact he is presented with a unique situation in which psychological change, change in the organization and use of the self, is frankly accepted as a requirement in the attainment of an educational goal. The question may well be raised when the goal is stated thus starkly as change in the will, if it is not of the very essence of will that it must oppose this require-ment to change, so that one should expect a mobilization of resist-ance to change at the very beginning of this process. Experience proves that this is the case and that this resistance will persist to the defeat and failure of the student unless his positive will is engaged as well as his resistance in that the choice of this profession is so deeply his own that he cannot leave it but must struggle through resistance to some new acceptance of change for himself.

It is the function of the application process for admission to this school to make sure as far as possible that the sutdent has really chosen this profession. I say as far as possible, for, with all that the school can put into this process in catalogue information, in letters and interview, the applicant cannot fully know what is ahead of him; nor can the admissions secretary, reading what the student has pre-sented in his application of his educational background, his working experience and whatever he has selected out of past or current expe-rience which constitute to his mind the reasons for his choice of this profession and this particular school, know in every case whether the choice is deeply rooted enough to stand the test of struggle the applicant must undergo before it is truly his own. During the depres-sion years when many vocational fields were closed to applicants, the field of social work was open and has continued open to the pres-ent day. The knowledge that there are more jobs in the field than there are trained workers to fill them may influence the choice of this field unduly. Applicants who come admittedly on advice from vocational advisers in college must be worked with, in interview, to disentangle what has been taken on superficially from what is the applicant's own interest and direction. Sometimes in the inter-view with the secretary of admissions the applicant can find his way to a more real choice of this profession and school or to a rejection of one or the other. The very discussion of his choice of this school in face-to-face, arranged interview with the secretary of admissions in whose hands now lies the right to reject or accept the applicant together with the opportunity which is now his to ask questions, to explore further the requirements of this training which he seeks, creates a psychological situation which contains within its brief and limited time span the very essence of the experience which charac-terizes the training in the two-year process. The applicant has given something in writing of himself, to a school which he may know only by its catalogue and by hearsay, he has complied with its re-quirements in filling out its forms and making his appointment. He has organized all his powers, submitted what is his to offer and risks his all in asking to be admitted as a student. In this projection of him-self on the school the will is already actively engaged when he comes for interview. The impact of the actual school as it appears to him in its physical aspects now seen for the first time, in its students who may be crowding the halls, above all, in the person, the questions and responses of its secretary of admissions cannot fail to shake the structure of his own self-created projection in some degree. It is pre-cisely with his reactions to this experience that the secretary of ad-missions must work in the interview, to see if the applicant can let any change take place in his previously conceived idea or expecta-tion, make use in any way of the new information which she may be able to offer him. The area in which this change can be worked on is very limited, realistic and practical, such as future living arrange-ments, fees, possibilities of scholarship, etc. With all students, one common focus where this difference between the student's expecta-tion and the projection and the actuality of the school can be worked on is in relation to the field work assignment. Every applicant with few exceptions comes with an already formed idea in his mind of the field or social agency in which he would like a placement. The secre-tary welcomes his own interests in placement but needs to elicit the reasons for his choice. Some of these reasons are valid guides for the school in deciding on a suitable placement. Where the student lives is one of the important factors which must be examined between applicant and the secretary of admissions as giving indication of what agencies would be possible for him and what agencies, because of travel distance, are too remote to be considered. Race and religious affiliation are other factors which play a valid part in determining suitable placement. The applicant's genuine interest, "I want to work in a child placing agency, or a family agency or a hospital," is given real consideration. But every applicant must be told that placement finally depends on many factors, including what is avail-able in agencies for the whole student body and that the decision must be made by the school. Can he let it be that way and wait to know the result until the school is ready to make its placement definite? Usually he says he can and believes himself able and ready to accept the school's necessities and judgment in this respect. But his reactions rarely become known to him until much later, for the first and more total placement of his will is on the issue of acceptance or rejection of the application. As long as there is real doubt all other issues are minor. Once the decision is made in the affirmative, and frequently this may be decided and made known to him in the admissions interview, he may be able to engage himself more fully in the question of placement. Our experience, however, goes to show that it is very difficult in this early stage of relationship with the applicant to give him actual realization of the extent to which he will react against the responsibility that the school must carry for his placement.

This placement in a social agency in which three-fifths of his time during the entire first year of training will be spent, can become the focus of his whole resistance to the will which is not his own in this training situation. For whatever the placement is, no matter if it would have been his own choice, it is actually made by the school and so is done *to* him. Some students fight the placement at the very beginning and exert their own wills in trying to change it. Others accept the school's placement more readily. When the agency placement is made the student is also assigned to a practice section in the school and knows that the teacher of this practice section will be his adviser throughout the first year of his training. At his first meeting with his adviser, which occurs when he comes to register, if not before, the reaction to his placement will be between them for discussion. His adviser may be able to help him become more aware of his resistance or objections to the assignment and in some instances he may be able with her help to face the fear of the total process ahead of him in which he must risk so much without guarantee of success or even knowledge of where he is going.

4. THE MOVEMENT TOWARD CHANGE IN THE SELF

In emphasizing the will aspects of this admissions and placement process at the beginning of the training experience, it is important not to lose sight of the impulsive life which is released in the student in this new beginning. There can be no doubt that he approaches it with eagerness, excitement, even emotion, as well as with fear, resistance and determination. Anyone can feel, if he will, the quickening in the self of impulsive sources, the stirring of creative energy when one moves from an old anchorage, an outgrown situation, into new self-chosen experience with its infinite as yet undefined possibilities. It is this energy which makes possible new learning or a renewal of creative activity. But for only a fleeting moment is it felt as free, bursting with life, undefined and unlimited. In this beginning state impulse is wholly unreliable, ambivalent, unwilling to be tied down to any pathway or bound by any requirement. Yet in the very moment of exultation over its freedom and spontaneity, it seeks commitment, limitation for its freedom, the form and structure within which it can shape itself. If in this moment one can make the choice, "This I will learn no matter what it takes," then impulse becomes commited to the external task, inner life and external requirement become inextricably and rightly related.

Every good experienced teacher knows how to facilitate the movement of impulsive energy in this first phase of learning by providing the structures and requirements which permit its expression, at the same time setting the needed limits. But in education for social work more is needed, for here the teacher and the professional school have undertaken to teach not only an understanding, but a conscious use, of human relationship, the very process of helping itself. This special psychological skill, the ability to help others bring about change in themselves and their problems, rests on the understanding of the movement of the impulsive forces in the self and of the way in which they use what is outside the self and on the ability of the helping person to facilitate this movement by his own activity and responses in the process. Learning such as this cannot be acquired by the rules in any book but must be wrought out of one's individual experience in this very process of feeling the impulsive life in one's self break through its old willed control of outside objects. Only a new appreciation of outside objects and persons as they are, apart from one's projected needs and controls, and a new acceptance too of one's self and the life forces in that self can bring conviction of the validity of this learning.

However, the student coming into a professional school of social work can scarcely be aware of this movement into training as having an impulsive basis. Having made a decision which has involved the most careful consideration of many factors, separation from former ties, perhaps from a job and sacrifices of all kinds he regards himself as acting wholly responsibly, purposefully and intelligently. If asked, he would no doubt say that the change which would be required of him in the professional school would be in the direction of giving up self-chosen, impulsive experience in favor of greater control of his time and his activities. He has become aware, at the point of his decision to become a social worker and to take training, of a new and firmer organization in himself, more clearly and directly related to a goal. This organization of will operates in each student characteristically to control the impulsive energy released in the separation from old ties and an old self which every one experiences in different degrees in the process of choosing a new profession. However individually each student handles this phase of the experience, all students say in effect, "I must learn to do this right as soon as possible," thus from the very beginning turning will and pressure back on the self and the new impulsive life.

Every student batters at his teachers and his supervisor to find a right way, to be told what to do and how to do it in this situation where everything in him seems set to want the right way and where so little is clear to him about what it is or how to do it. Added to this intense pressure of the student's own will to do right, is a new pressure against the requirments which the learning introduces. As I have indicated earlier, the student begins to feel and to react against this requirement aspect in the school even in the application process. These requirements as they are now defined with clarity and conviction by the school faculty and the agency supervisor may seem to impose more limitation and to ask more in work and responsible performance than any student could bear to face. Actually they are not beyond what students can and do meet. Let us look at these requirements in their tangible external aspect as they are presented to the student at the beginning. First, there is the assignment in the field work agency where the student is required to keep regular hours usually from nine to five, three days a week and carry responsibility for the part of the agency load that is given to him. Small as this part may be—a few cases in a casework agency, a club or two in a group work agency—his responsibility is not slight. For these clients in the student's case load or group will receive the help they seek only if the student discharges his responsibility rightly and fully as a representative of the agency. This he cannot do adequately until he has learned more than superficially the function of the agency he represents. Sensing this as every student must, fear and frustration in the face of this requirement are inevitable reactions, try as he may to deny these feelings and to redouble efforts to do what is expected. The supervisor is there to carry some responsibility for his work in this agency experience. But in spite of the fact that the student knows she is there to help him, in actuality she constitutes an additional responsibility for him. She weighs on his mind, limits his freedom of action, threatens his power to act. He must keep a regular weekly conference with her and submit to her some record of his work on the basis of which she can criticize what he has done.

The school requirements in their external, tangible aspects are: first, regular attendance at classes; second, written papers; third, participation in class discussion. Written papers are of two kinds. One type resembles what has become familiar to the student in college courses, based on a reading list with a date for the paper set well in advance. The other type of paper is in response to assignments made at the close of a class session, requiring an immediate and spontaneous response out of the student's own experience, written within the week and handed in in time for the next class session.

Conformity to these external but essential requirements of attendance at classes and papers is practically one hundred per cent. There is no cut rule for students and no absences except for unavoidable reasons. Curiously enough, illness in students is rare and not infrequently classes go through a semester without absence. Class participation is not so simply within the student's power to control. It expresses the individual's use of himself and his ways of relating to the group and changes and develops throughout the training process. It cannot be handled simply as external requirement or secured by teaching pressure. It is enough for students to know from the beginning that they will be expected to take part in class discussion, to present their own practice material, to talk about, as well as to write about, what they are working on and what they are learning.

Of the two types of assignment for written papers, the longer paper based on a reading list with a due date set well in advance seems to be in a familiar field and within their capacities. They can begin to work on this assignment at once. They take books out of the library and start note-taking. Sometimes a student will write a paper not due until mid-November in the first few weeks and must learn painfully that it is not acceptable but must wait to contain the learning from class and field which the weeks he has skipped over should provide. This is a particularly frustrating experience for the young student, the recent college graduate, who has learned the value of independent study and effort. All students in their first reactions to this assignment reveal how completely they are in new territory. For all, the realization that these papers must grow out of everything that has gone into the six weeks experience in school and agency, out of class discussion and conferences as well as their independent reading, is a first step in understanding the value of process in learning.

Of all the requirements the one on which the greatest fear focuses is the requirement of weekly papers for the class familiarly known as "The Personality Class." They have heard of these papers from graduates before they come to school; they have even inquired about them in the admission interview. They sense in advance that these papers in which they must write out of immediate experience will ask for more of themselves, of the self which is as yet unknown to them but in which change may be expected to take place.

This brief description of the first reactions of the student group to the requirements may be enough, I hope, to indicate that there is in this training process a common experience. Each student individualizes it in his own feeling about it and in his reactions to it although in these first stages few can know their own feelings or claim responsibility for their reactions. But the teachers, whose responsibility it is to know the feelings and reactions which are aroused in this training process, can help the students to recognize them by permitting and encouraging expression of feelings in relation to the situation that calls them forth. The students' reaction to their field placements, for instance, can be helped to honest expression by the adviser in an early class session, and out of as many individual expressions of feeling as there are students in a class a realization of the common base of experience emerges.

A typical reaction which will find expression in an early class when it is permitted and encouraged is protest against some element of the training situation. This protest is valued and used by the teacher, not rejected. A sense of confusion will appear as another reaction with which all students can identify. This, too, must be accepted and valued by the teacher as a necessary phase of learning, not to be denied or skipped over. The teacher's ever present temptation to clarify it, as he can so easily do from her own knowledge and experience, must be resisted by her conviction that it is only the slowly developing readiness of the students to deal with this experience that counts in this process. Her ability to wait for their readiness, to bear with the confusion and the uncertainty counts also and is indeed the support that underlies this whole learning movement.

Confusion as total as this which I am describing and which is inevitable in a process of change where the old patterned use of the will is challenged at the outset by the strangeness of the requirements, can only be broken up individual by individual. For this reason it is essential that each student have access to his adviser in the school and to a supervisor in the agency. From the beginning these two relationships have continuity in time: the relationship with the supervisor carried in weekly conferences throughout the two semesters of the school year; the relationship with the adviser carried in the weekly practice class (where a homogeneous age group of not more than 20 students permits individual knowledge of each student) and in frequent conferences on the student's or adviser's initiative. This degree of individualization constitutes in the beginning an additional burden, threat and source of confusion to the student who feels himself identified as an individual before he is ready to respond to this identification. ("How do you know all our names so soon?" he may say suspiciously in the first class.) While he may quickly begin to see, at any rate superficially, that he must have conferences with a supervisor on his work in the agency, he is at a loss to know what to do with his school adviser. Is it safer to see her often, if so for what purpose? These questions begin to find concrete answers as soon as his papers and teachers' comments begin to show him his problems in specific terms where he can work on them.

Besides the fearful implications of this early recognition of each student as an individual, there is also an equally bewildering but exciting quality in being called by name. The student feels known here in a new way with its fearful possibilities of self-revelation beyond what he can know himself, while at the same moment and in the same breath he is asked to be responsible for his actions in agency and school, for his opinions, for his inner feelings as he has never been before.

In this lies the strange and unique characteristic of this training process out of which change eventuates, in the degree to which it penetrates at the very beginning into the organized structures which these individuals have spent a lifetime in developing, thus laying open the fundamental denied ambivalence which underlies the structure and organization—and this by no more than the expectation put out on each student that he begin to find himself, in his behavior, in his attitudes, in his feelings as the separate individual that he is. It is not surprising that a few students react against what they now feel will be required of them which goes beyond what they had contemplated and may actually leave school by the end of a first semester.

The different class content in the so-called practice unit, the casework class and the "personality" class, focus the two sides of this conflict of individualization and carry them with a different emphasis. At the same time, the steady focus on the training movement and the relation of all teachers and the supervisor to the curriculum as a whole and the training movement insures against a separation of the two sides of the self in that conflict. The practice class to which the students bring records of their own work with clients for class discussion obviously emphasizes the development of responsibility for what the student is doing in his efforts to help his clients. The class known as "The Personality Class," which goes throughout the training under such specific titles as "The Development of the Individual," "The Nature of the Self," "Patterns of Growth," presents the student immediately and frighteningly, if seemingly more permissively than the other courses, with the problem of change in himself. Nothing in the school curriculum arouses more fear than the assignments for this course, of papers, to be written within the week on a topic assigned in the class session and mailed into school in time for it to be read and commented on by the teacher, used by her in the next class session and returned to the student with her brief written comment at the end of class. The first assignment asks the student to examine his own movement in deciding to come to school. What started it? What outside influences, what inner motives? It asks him to think about the moment of final decision, then to describe the process of getting ready to come. The second assignment asks how the School impinged on him in actuality. Where did he feel an impact with it which was different from what he expected?

The students' apprehension about these papers located at first in the question, "What will I write about?" extends at the same time to, "What will the teacher do with them?" This second question the teacher discusses with the class at length in the first session and reassures the group that in using the papers their anonymity will be preserved. Two class discussions are usually enough to reassure them on this score and to give them in addition some appreciation of the serious regard and consideration that are given to each student's contribution. They begin, too, to get hold of a sense of the common experience here as the teacher selects and reads aloud from the papers parts which bring out the universal problem of moving into a new situation, of the projected will to make it be as one desires or conceives it and of the difficulty of taking in anything of the strange, foreign reality outside of the self.

These two assignments, completed in the first three weeks of this class, constitute for the teacher the first unit of content which might be written down in her teaching outline as "movement into a new situation." The 15 to 25 papers of any class of students will provide illustration of every aspect of this problem, of the ever-present two-sidedness of psychological movement in its relation to inner necessity and outer control. Regardless of the teacher's long experience and her own understanding of this problem, this first set of student papers never fails to make the problem come alive again in the vivid human terms in which each class of students recreates it. Her own comprehensive organization of the problem, a true generalization which she must not lose, is broken up for this specific teaching experience by the realization of the different learning needs of these students before her. Each student individualizes this movement in his own way. Some cannot deal with the second assignment in any but the most superficial stereotyped terms, since they are using their old patterns and do not know themselves as clearly as the word "impact" asks of them. The mere word asks that they know more and stirs up new differentiation of feeling and awareness in the self. What a student has managed to get on paper about his reaction is returned to him with a comment which always recognizes what he has done if it is real and sincere but which at the same time gives him a little help to get further by pointing out what he might feel or see differently. As this class proceeds, students begin to be aware of inner experience that they have never faced before, of fear and resistance, of control of both inner and outer reality by will. Their actions, in school or agency, often express the negative aspects of their inner reactions before they can feel them as such or claim them as their own. It is essential that these negative, characteristically denied aspects and expressions of the self be admitted and accepted into the self in a new way if responsible, disciplined behavior is to be achieved. Teachers and supervisors, knowing from experience how hard it is for the individual to admit these unwanted negative feelings, look for specific concrete situations where the student can express his badness to the teacher or supervisor in partial and bearable terms.

The totality of his conception of good and bad will begin to break up once he can find fault with his supervisor for something she has said or done or failed to do or when he is able to criticize any piece of school or agency policy or requirement. There is in this experience, if the teacher or supervisor understands it and can help him with it, not only the relief of expressing his negative feelings but the importance of placing them on a person who carries actual responsibility for what is being asked of him while at the same time she values his feeling and can help him find and acknowledge it as his own. In this experience for the first time, he begins to feel the separation of his own will from that of the other and takes the first step in differentiating his own will and feeling and a beginning of a new relation to self responsibility.

The struggle in the "Personality Class" as it goes on into the semester becomes defined for the student in terms of, "Shall I let myself go? Shall I risk stopping to find out what I feel, will I put this down on paper, impulsive and fragmentary as it seems?" The risk becomes defined then in terms of, can he risk knowing himself and can he risk letting the teacher know, can he risk being bad with all that that risk assails of the student's concept of himself as good and seeking the good in his very decision to become a social worker.

The teaching goal, which is expressed in every assignment in this class and is inherent in the teacher's every attitude and every comment, requires a searching out of what is real and valid for the self. It asks the student to value his experience, to admit inner feelings, to claim them as his own. To the students still holding to goals set up by constructive purpose, the "good" will on which they have come into this profession, the teaching goal feels like pure, outside pressure. Here indeed is a psychological dilemma, that what is *required* is *spontaneity*. This opposition of wills between student and school becomes the fundamental struggle of the first semester of training. The student may feel everything converging upon him to force something from him. What is he *supposed* to feel, what is he *supposed* to know? He indicates some movement towards awareness of what it is and some knowledge of his own resistance to this awareness when he says, "I don't know how to risk myself further." The hard, tight refusal to give to the teacher or the supervisor, or to give in, is at bottom the inhibitory action of will against impulsive forces in the self. This stubborn will often held as wholly virtuous in the past, a prized development of the independent, proud character, feels at first wrongly assailed. If there is to be any change the will must finally feel itself to be wrong not right in some specific instance and it can only come to this as teacher or supervisor holds with an even firmer stronger will to what she is asking of the student. This dramatic moment when will breaks up into feeling, and admission of, "I was wrong," is difficult to describe but well known to all those who deal with children. It must be clearly differentiated from the external effort to adjust to what the teacher says is right on which it is possible to get by in most educational processes where the requirement of learning content or skill is externalized by both teacher and child to a degree that does not involve the total self. In this training process I am describing, where students must learn how to help the other person, the will must be felt as such in its opposition to the other and more and more of the self must be engaged as it moves further into this process.

The admission of being wrong involves in varying degrees in different individuals, depending on the strength and rigidity of the organization of the will, a very fundamental change in relation to the handling of the forces in the will organization and in the way of relating to the other person. The admission, one must recognize at this early stage in the process, is comparatively superficial; there are still questions, reservations, suspicions about what is being asked of me here—where is it taking me? But new feelings are stirred up in any yielding to another out of which new experience grows.

For every student this new yielding constitutes a differentiation of himself in relation to the other, the client, the supervisor, or the teacher. He begins to say now in a way he could not feel or understand before, "The school has something to teach me, to give me. I am a student." It is difficult to believe how long and how hard, in how many ways and on how many levels, the proud, independent, competent self will struggle against this seemingly simple and obvious acceptance of the student role.

In this experience of real yielding and acceptance of the student role, the inhibitory will is softened, and impulse and feeling which had been tied down and denied by the undeviating pressure of the will are released. Inevitably that release moves into some awareness of need and feeling for the oher person.

Here we face a serious problem which has confused training for social work and all undertakings which attempt to bring about psychological change through professionally controlled relationship process. For wherever there is a true will engagement in a relationship process and the client or the counselor, the patient or the student, feels the yielding of will in response to the helper, there is a spontaneous release of need to use the helper in new ways. Instead of the original projection of the will to resist or fight the helper or to make him over in the terms of the one receiving help, there is a need and capacity to give a positive feeling reponse in this relationship and to crave a feeling response from the other. This need for feeling itself can be powerful and overwhelming, frightening indeed to the student who has come to the school for the serious purpose of professional training.

Now the risk may take on an even more fearful shape to the student, the risk of feeling the total need for the other person, so frightening to face in any relationship. This need can not be denied but must be felt deeply if the student is to be able to help his clients in their need. It is made bearable only by the realization, which the student fights at the same time he depends on it, that the other, the teacher or the supervisor, does not need him in the same way that he needs her and will not be drawn into the personal, mutual use of relationship. It is made bearable too, in this educational process by the fact that there is not only one person carrying the helper's role·but several, his teachers and a supervisor. Giving assurance and support under it all, is the knowledge that this is a time-limited training process and that others have come through it successfully with degrees and professional competence. But the essential loneliness of the individual's own need in the early stages of this process cannot take comfort from any comparison with what others have done before him.

Whatever use the students may or may not make of their knowledge of the time limit in this process, there is no doubt of its value for teachers and supervisors in facing the risk in this use of relationship. For the realization of need on its deepest level is frightening to the helper as well as to the one he would help. The need object, be it concrete and tangible, or the unknown and intangible possibilities opened up by the presence of the other person in a professional relationship, is never wholly accessible, never within one's control. From the baby crying for breast or bottle to the adult seeking for the other who can give the needed love or reassurance and restore the lost wholeness, the pain of actually feeling the need of what is outside oneself is terrifying and unassuageable. Most people never let themselves know this need in its total, frightening, lonely nature and it is not necessary that they should if they are able to find and relate to their need objects in the natural ways of living. But it is essential that those who have elected the profession of helping other human beings in need should know this moment in experience and realize to the full the fright and aloneness it provokes. Teachers and supervisors find the courage to live through this experience with their students in the knowledge that this need will move to new levels and to new strength and wholeness in the self within the time structure of the process. I believe it is scarcely possible to overestimate the extent to which this known fact of a definite ending differentiates this educational process from therapy where the time of ending is not known in advance to either the patient or the therapist but must eventuate wholly out of the relationship itself.

What are the manifestations of this feeling of need in students at this first point of yielding to the other person, the teacher or the supervisor, in the relationship process of training? Fear underlies these manifestations in all students, no matter how it is expressed, but now it is fear on a different level from the fear that accompanied the first movement into the school. In the beginning there was fear of the strange, the unknown, of what was still outside the self but the organized successful self was intact and approached the experience with more or less assurance, "I can do this." Now that the self has yielded its organization to some extent and has admitted some small part of the strange outside into itself, it is already related beyond its capacity to extricate itself. The nature of this relationship is new and the old patterns of control do not serve as before.

The desperate effort to establish control is one of the most obvious characteristics of this beginning movement toward a deeper use of relationship. At the same time, students feel the controls inherent in the clearly defined functions of the teacher and supervisor, in the requirements of the agency, in the work they are doing in the agency load, and while they may batter against these limitations, they use with relief the boundaries they provide, within which their own personal individual forces can move.

In this phase of the training process students bring to teacher or supervisor more of themselves in terms of content. Their personal relationship problems of the present or past may come into conference and the teacher or supervisor must hold clearly to her own focus in the training process lest she be drawn into working with the student too realistically in terms of the content the student has presented. She may not be able to discriminate between content which is realistic on which he might be able to use *real* help and content which he is bringing primarily as an expression of his present need and response in this training situation or content which he is using to defend himself from the impact of the present experience but if she can maintain a constantly alert, active, conscious focus through a disciplined use of the teaching self in the training process, the student will be able to handle his own realistic problem.

Realistic problems are no different from those with which students struggle in all professional schools:—financial problems, health problems, housing problems and problems of family relationship. In its realistic aspect the problem is often so serious that it is not easy to know what use the student is making of it in his training process and to help him find his own relation to it. An illness in the student's family may be carried to the adviser as something so serious that the student is considering whether it is not his duty to leave school. Perhaps he feels himself needed to take care of the sick person or to get a job and contribute money to the family situation. An examination of all that is involved for him in this problem when it is focused by the adviser on his training, on what he has undertaken in coming to school and the point he has reached in this process will bring out a new relation to the reality problem. The student will be able to disentangle the realistic need from his own problem whatever it may be. It may be he is using the family situation to escape from the pressure which training puts upon him and if he can face this evasion in himself he may be able to move beyond this block in his training. Or it may be that the depth of his involvement in training and his guilt for the use of it for himself, creates, or at any rate exaggerates, the importance of the reality problem.

Financial difficulties are common to these students and as these are brought to the adviser she may work with the student to help him find borrowing resources if he needs them. But again, the meaning of this difficulty in his training process and the weight he now attaches to it are the main concern of the adviser. The student who finds out in the middle of the semester that he does not have enough money to live on may see that his inability to foresee the cost in economic terms carried a characteristic problem in his way of planning. His realization of his own responsibility in this is more important than his economic predicament with which he is, in most cases, well able to deal realistically once he faces his own part in the problem and deepens his choice of training in this reexamination of its meaning to him in economic terms.

The marital partner, or the boy or girl with whom the unmarried student is involved in relationship, is almost invariably introduced into his conferences with the adviser in this phase of training, if not as problem, at any rate as a part of himself which affects and is affected by the experience he is undergoing. This training experience in its strangeness and in the student's absorption in it can be very alienating to the other partner. For the married student some hint of this problem is felt in the first weeks, created or focused by the assignments for the personality class. "Shall I let my wife read everything I write?" "How will she feel about my sharing so much with another person?" "What meaning will the teacher's comments have for her?" These questions as the student begins to feel them are puzzling ones. He may settle them for himself or in conference with the adviser whose efforts must be directed to helping the student find his own self in relation to what he is writing and experiencing in training and leaving him free to decide how he will share it with his wife. Astonishingly perhaps, our experience shows that it is usual for the student to share fully with the marital partner and many times this partner will come to Commencement to meet the teacher for the first time and to say, "I feel as if I had gone through the school with my husband." This speaks better for the constancy of these marital relationships than does the divorce rate for the population at large.

But there are students who are separating from an unsatisfactory marriage relationship when they come to school and this separation process may continue and become clearer and more decisive in the training movement. Every student is in fact separating from some old relationship which carries the self he is outgrowing and this separation is accentuated by this process of change as the new self moves into more meaningful and responsible relationships in this professional situation. The problems of old outgrown relationships may loom very large, particularly to the young student just out of college who may still live in the family home and be dependent on the father for support. For them, old attitudes and projections operate in daily living and the stress and strain of the student's effort to free himself from these ties, to find his own choices and his own direction, necessarily are involved with his training process. At each step into training, as he deepens and reaffirms his vocational choice, he feels himself to be more of a person, torn apart, it may be, again and again by what is put upon him by the old parental attitudes and equally by his own habitual use of parents, but with increasing strength to affirm his right and necessity to make his own decisions.

Of all the variety of problems in personal relationship which are involved in some way with the training process none is more difficult to handle both for the student and the adviser than the problem presented by the woman student who has a young child to care for. If the husband is dead or she has separated from him the problem of carrying her responsibility for the child along with the training process is almost insuperable. The school will examine this with her in the admissions process and unless she can make a practical plan for the child's care which assures the stability that the child requires the school may have to reject the application. The presence of the grandmother or a related third person in the home has assured this in some situations. But even when the plan seems satisfactory and the school accepts it, the training process is never free from a realistic entanglement for which the school carries some responsibility. When the child is ill, as it may be in reaction to the loss of the mother in the training process, the adviser is not as free to hold the student to the requirements of training as she is to hold the student who has no child.

The Christmas vacation interrupts this training process at the end of eleven weeks. The timing arbitrarily introduced by the calendar is unfortunate. Teachers have no choice but to accept it knowing that in two weeks vacation period students will move out of the pressures they have felt in the process and will have to be brought back after Christmas against great resistance for the four weeks in January that remain and are so important for their learning. On the other hand, teachers themselves are of two minds about this vacation period. They feel in themselves some need to escape from the burden of the process they carry, from the undivided use of the self in behalf of the students. Whatever the individual preference of teachers may be in relation to the time and length of the Christmas vacation, as a faculty they know what they will have to expect in student reaction and behavior. They must open up for students in class discussion the opportunity to consider what obligations they carry for their clients and how they can leave these responsibly when they go on vacation. The written assignments at this point in all the classes give opportunity to the students to bring together what they have learned. They leave for vacation full of a sense of this new learning, eager to try out its meaning in old situations. They return to their homes, meet old friends, see students who are in training in other schools of social work. Students who came into training from previous experience in social work almost invariably return to visit the agency where they were employed before they entered the school.

These diverse experiences of the vacation period can be utilized by the teacher in the first class after vacation to bring the students together in awareness of the change in the self which the training process has introduced. They are full of comparisons and contrasts, of the sense of difference in themselves, of the differences they find in old friends and old working relationships. This sharp consciousness of difference from the old is a common experience uniting the student group in a new identification with change as it occurs in the training process. The teacher utilizes this experience as content to bring out the meaning of inner change and its capacity to differentiate outer experience into past and present, old and new, like and different. The psychological processes of identification and projection begin to have new meaning for the students and they can explore their meaning eagerly in their own experience and in their reading assignments and their professional relationships. They use the last four weeks of the semester to pull together and to deepen their awareness of and belief in the new self as they can affirm its learning in new psychological understanding and in action, in what they can see in themselves and what they can do in their work in the agency differently from what they could see and do in October.

An evaluative process for each student as the final ending of the semester, with the supervisor in conference on his practice and with each teacher expressed in what he puts into his final paper and her full comment, gives further punctuation to this unit of experience and assurance that he has come through something, is on the right track. This ending has the value of a positive separation experience within the total two-year training process and releases new energy for the self in its ongoing movement. This ending is partial, not total, and while it takes the student out of classes and the school process for a two weeks period between semesters, it asks that he move into his agency responsibilities for full time work, with undivided concern. This period leaves great responsibility on the supervisor to help the student to use his time and energy to the fullest extent. It seems often to ask more of the supervisor than she may be ready for—to carry this two weeks process alone with the student, but if too much problem falls on her she knows that the student's adviser is available to help her understand and handle what troubles her.

Even the most experienced teachers who have been through this training process many times are not prepared for the greater serious-ness of purpose and the development of understanding which students bring back to school to the opening classes of the second semester. They have become better integrated into their agencies, more firmly identified with the functions they represent; they have a greater responsibility for the case load or the clubs to which they have been giving undivided time for two weeks. This undivided time, this concentration of effort and concern, is important in this develop-ment but time alone cannot account for the progress of learning, the deepening of understanding with which students now take hold of problems of helping in practice classes. They show an indication of a deeper readiness to use themselves more sensitively and more fully responsibly than at the end of the first semester. Second semester feels like a new beginning but on a new level made more consciously than the beginning in October with what is in the self more clearly known, more fully committed. Students not only feel this change in themselves, they sense it in each other, and in the quality of the rec-ords from their own practice which come in for class discussion. The teacher's selection of material for class use, out of what has been given in their papers, emphasizes their gains in understanding and skill, in ability to represent their functions helpfully with their cli-ents, at the same time it opens up new areas in which the learning of the second semester must move. The assignment of a complete case on which they will write a paper and work in class at a time in the middle of the semester; the request for a fully analyzed record of a piece of work from their own practice due in the second half of the semester; the indication from the teacher that they will be using this piece of work to pull together their first year practice: all of this be-gins to set up a time structure which gives some shape to the second semester, a sense of beginning, middle and end for the class to hold on to.

One other factor not to be ignored which makes for the very constructive positive character of this beginning of second semester arises out of the fact that in the final evaluative process of first semester, students who are not rightly involved in this educational process are asked not to return. In the section of experienced tested students there is often no loss but in the younger sections one, two, three or four students may not have progressed enough to be ready to go on to second semester. Nothing stirs up more fear in a group of students than to have one of their own section "dropped." Frequently the student spreads his reactions, anger, disappointment, blame of the school or whatever, over his classmates and they may be torn in pieces, each one in proportion to the degree of his unsureness of his own relation to his training and to the school that leaves him open to identification with and championship of the student who is not making the grade. Each student has to sort out of this conflict (and frequently he uses the help of his supervisor or teacher to do this), his own difference, affirm again his hold on his own training and his relation to the school. Since he cannot know and evaluate the problem of the failing student himself, he must let the school do it and if he can, it constitutes a new yielding of his own will, a differentiation of himself from the other, that furthers his own individualization process and at the same time deepens his trust of the school that must carry responsibility or evaluation and judgmnet of its students. Teachers can count also on some sensitivity and awareness in students who are rightly in this process to the fact that others are not. While they may have to deny this difference to the end and hold on to the support which identification with each other provides, they are grateful for the results when the class loses a member who is not related rightly to the work of the school by the end of the first semester. The loss of one, or several students on the fringe of the class, whose resistances may have blocked understanding for the other students, gives greater cohesiveness and firmness to the group as a whole in the beginning of the second semester. Their identification with each other is established in common purpose, in progress in learning, in professional rather than personal elements.

This description of the class unity and will-to-learn at the beginning of the second semester must seem too positive and total a condition. Actually this condition is true only for the moment and occasion will arise almost immediately to break into the unity. Each student's continuing individual problem revealed in his practice offers the occasion which the adviser must take hold of. She has more help to offer this semester as she knows the student's practice more specifically and the way he uses himself, the points where he must take more help from her and from the supervisor, if he is to gain skill in the helping process. The point of contact between himself and his adviser has become clear to the student. He has accepted the relationship between his supervisor and his adviser, knowing that they discuss his progress together, share their knowledge of where he is in training and what he needs to learn. This sharing, obscure to the student in the first semester, often protested violently, has become by the second semester the trusted ever-present bedrock of his training movement on which he relies for help that will carry him through the year. Each student individualizes his use of this relationship and of these two people in it while all have in common this growing trust in what the teacher-supervisor connection has to contribute to their learning.

But the other side of this positive trust is always present and the awareness of it and the admission of it in conference and in class must never be omitted in the development of the educational experience. This very trust itself engenders fear of where it leads, of what is expected, in other words that ever-present fear of further change in the self over which the individual does not exercise complete control.

The fear which I have been describing as characteristic of the beginning of second semester, the other side of the deeper trust and confidence which has developed in the school in the training process, is focused particularly in the "Personality Class," where the reading list, the discussion of assignments and content in the first session indicate that a new and deeper incursion into the self will be required. Students often feel, "I have lived through so much in myself, how can I bear to go further," at the same time the craving for deeper experience cannot be denied. Whatever their apprehension and resistance may be they are committed individually and as a group to going further and deeper for they are in a process, the will is engaged, the whole self is involved and the longed-for freedom for the self lies ahead to be achieved only by traversing the road on which their feet are set.

The content of the "Personality Class" which is so powerfully influential in providing the material and the time structure for the next movement in this process of change comes from the early experience and developmental history of the child, from the pre-natal experience and birth through the nursing relation with the mother, to weaning and the movement to a connection with the father or some third person. The later development through adolescence is included in this course content but the first three years of life provide the most significant experience for student use. Students read from the scientific literature in this field in references to Corner, Gesell, Gutmacher, Ribble, Spock and others, together with a few works of fiction that give the feeling side of the mother's relation to child birth or to the young child as Enid Bagnold's "The Door of Life" and Naomi Royde-Smith's "The Mother."

What is the value for students in a graduate professional school of social work of this material, this curious mixture culled from scientific, medical, psychological, psychiatric, psychoanalytic, fictional and biographical sources? Clearly it is not just that the student may know what Gesell, or Freud or Gutmacher or Corner have contributed to the fund of knowledge about human beginnings. When the assignments are made, the teacher's attitude creates the tone, she indicates the direction for the exploration of these materials, anticipating what the reading list has to offer in opportunity to find out how others have approached this most meaningful exploration of the sources of the human being. Gesell, too, sets the tone in the quotation from the Wisdom of Solomon which he places in the frontispiece of his scholarly work, "Embryology of Behavior":

"For no king had any other first beginning.
But all men have one entrance into life,
And a like departure."

The Wisdom of Solomon
The Apocrypha.

Students learn from this reading that with all the facts that have been revealed no final right answer has been discovered. They realize that each writer, psychobiologist or biographer or novelist, is striving to find for himself some understanding of the incomprehensible problem of the origin of the will in human relationship, the beginning of individuation. "Which came first, the egg or the chick?" crude statement of the problem that it is, can still be argued. In this reading and for these students the problem may be stated in terms of separation and movement. Where does responsibility for movement reside—in the foetus or the mother, the carrying organism in which he is conceived and protected? By what impulse, what will to separation does birth take place?

Gesell says to this question:

> We lack a satisfactory theory to explain the onset of the labor which normally results in child birth. . . . Some theories ascribe the initiating role to the mother, others to the foetus.

> One reason for all this variability is the fact that birth depends not upon a single life cycle but upon an accommodation between two life cycles, the maternal and the foetal.

The mystery of life itself greater than man's amazing power to analyze and diagnose it with his intellect is felt throughout these readings and class discussions. To find that science does not know all the answers frees the student to a new willingness to seek in himself for new understanding of his attitudes towards his early experience and relationships.

A quotation from a student's paper brings out this use of the reading assignments:

> I think that the first part of the reading list, on uterine experience and birth, and the early life of the infant, had the most meaning for me. Beyond the content, there was a real psychological value for me, in this reading about birth: I had not read any material like this for many years. Like a good many people, a good deal of my knowledge about birth, and relationships between men and women, originally came from books. It made me remember my childish guilt at obtaining 'forbidden' information—since I got the information myself, without adult sanction, there was always a feeling of reading what I should not read. It was practically therapeutic, to be doing this reading now, as something I *should* be doing—as if I was given freedom to make my own relation to this material, to identify with the life processes as something which should hold meaning for me, personally. It is fascinating to see again, that the relation one makes even to factual material is interwoven with relationships —the feeling that 'Miss____ said to read this,' changes the orientation to the material.

> I think that chiefly in this course, and around the reading in it, I came to an emotional acceptance and sureness about a lot of ideas that I had held only intellectually. I would have been willing to state unequivocally at any time, that all man's creativity,

spiritual experience, intellectual achievement, etc., had a physical basis—that life was rooted in the physical: but it was new to me to get to an emotional conviction that conception, uterine life, birth, nursing, and early experience hold the roots of all human togetherness and separateness. I don't think, oddly enough, that I had really felt that giving birth was a creative experience: if I can grope after my feeling, I would say that I had thought of the mother as being used by the child, of the child having something 'done to' him, as if all this business of birth was arranged by some outside force. To see the life force as there, but to see the highly individualized use to which the mother and child put it, was new. The difference in attitudes, the sense of the will, both of the mother and of the infant, the use of the self going with or against these tremendous experiences, still astonished me.

Throughout the reading about infancy and early childhood, I got a sense both of the way in which the will can mold and use experience for its own ends,and an acceptance that the negative, separating parts of experience, as shown in birth, weaning, toilet training, etc., are intrinsic to life, cannot be avoided, and are also the means of growth and emotional development.

It seemed to me that any of this reading about early childhood and infancy, whatever its point of view, points up human creativity—the child with its need to alter the outside for its own purposes, and in its attempts, discovering itself.

In addition to the reading, students are asked to write weekly papers in which they find their own relationships newly to the moving, changing aspects of this experience—to the uterine experience, the birth process, to nursing, to weaning and to the father or third person as he becomes a factor in the child's situation. A student in beginning one of these papers states in vivid words the change in attitude which is the first and fundamental dynamic for change in this course. She says:

I began to work towards this paper by refusing to let myself beat upon the dead carcass of things that had happened to me.[1]

Throughout the ensuing weeks each student returns in feeling to the earliest sources of experience with the resultant release and gain in new life which this return to source inevitably brings. There is no more fundamental or universal human need than the need to return to source for new life and for this pilgrimage; only relationship, another human being, or a human setting in which this need is acknowledged and given its rights, will serve. This need can be felt and lived through in various experiences and contents, in illness and healing, in pregnancy and birth, in live relationships and creative experiences.

Every student can feel this deep connection with source and this stir of new impulsive life if the supporting human environment is there for his use. The school situation has been created and has been made trustworthy for this purpose through the preceding semester by means of every moment and every part of the process in which the student and the school have been engaged. It constitutes for him now, not the old environment to which he returns to discover this past, but a new environment in which he can find new life and choose himself newly. What is discovered then is never factual, never the truth of the way it was, but a new attitude towards what one has always taken for granted was the way it was between oneself and one's mother or between oneself and the source of life outside oneself. It may be expressed in any terms, "I always thought my mother refused to feed me, now I know I refused to take the breast." A student's paper gives convincing testimony to this new recognition of the power of will over circumstance in these words:

> I once asked my mother about my nursing and it seems strange now that I cannot remember what she told me. It is as if I will not to be influenced by what actually was but want to have it the way I would want it to be.

This new conviction of knowing how it was is no more an ultimate or factual truth than the original projection but it represents an admission of the own will and responsibility. The projection on the external cause has been internalized.

It is important to differentiate this experience which I have called a return to source from the recovery of memories of previous life experiences characteristic of psychoanalytic therapy and diagnostic social casework. For while the student or any individual in an experience of return to source must of necessity use his own patterns of relating, he can never relive the past experience for the obvious reason that it is past. He can only live newly in a new present. The powerful feeling of return that he experiences is due to the break up of denials in the structure of the self, to the rush and surge of released impulse and renewed life like the rush of waters when the ice breaks up in spring. The sense of discovery and of creative power, never the feeling of repetition, is what is inariably voiced by each student.

This sense of discovery, whatever its concrete expression may be in the various contents in which students individualize it, can be generalized in terms of the change in the fundamental attitude toward one's own will and toward compulsion from the outside in these terms: what has been done to me becomes what I have had some part in. There is a shift in the attitude which seeks the cause of the problem or the object on which blame can be placed; there is a new capacity to let both the self and the other each carry some responsibility for evil as well as good. The lifelong protest against compulsion can yield to an affirmation of choice and the assertion of the capacity of the own will to create in part its own experience.

No one has identified this fundamental moment of psychological change more clearly than Kierkegaard from whom I quote the following excerpt which is used as a chapter heading in the last chapter of Rank's *Art and Artist*.[2]

> The invidual becomes conscious of himself as being this particular individual with particular gifts, tendencies, impulses, passions, under the influence of a particular environment, as a particular product of his milieu. He who becomes thus conscious of himself assumes all this as part of his own responsibility. At the moment of choice he is thus in complete isolation, for he withdraws from his surrounding; and yet he is in complete continuity, for he chooses himself as product; and this choice is a free choice, so that we might even say, when he chooses himself as product, that he is producing himself.
>
> Kierkegaard.

This I believe to be the most fundamental change that can take place in the structure of the personality, a change which can choose and affirm the self and its own experience. It is the only change which makes possible a new growth process when the deep projection of blame on the outside, the past, the other, has been lifted.

That this process of return to source will eventuate in new strength in ego separation is guaranteed, it may be unconsciously, to both student and teacher, by the knowledge of the time limited structures and the experience of their use in the first semester. The teacher in addition rests upon her experience with many other classes, upon the tested experience of other teachers and the school as a whole. It is possible and indeed necessary for her to yield to the powerful feelings which this content stirs up with deep and full response knowing always that it is a movement which will carry itself not only to the bottom of organic resonance but that it will move as inevitably upwards and outwards into separation, ego partialization, and truer differentiation of self from other.

Again one must contrast this dynamic growth experience in behalf of an educational goal assured by a time limited structure with the experience of the patient in a typical psychoanalytic process who looks forward to treatment for the sake of his own health in a time structure the end of which is undetermined. In this latter relationship and in the casework treatment processes sustained by workers of the diagnostic, psychoanalytically influenced school, the fear of dependency is well founded since the patient remains involved with the recall of early experiences so long that new patterns of reality relationship to the therapist or caseworker develop. True, in the growth process I have described new patterns must develop, but now the reality of change in relation to new skill in helping takes precedence over the reality use of the other. The experience of change and growth for professional use is the fundamental reliable experience here and the student is freed to use each relationship and experience more fully knowing that he will not be caught in dependency upon it.

In this generalized description of the change in projection from that which places blame outside the self to a new responsibility for the own will, I would not wish to imply that all students feel it to the same degree. There are all kinds of individual differences in the organization and structure of the self, in the actual quality of the impulse life, in spontaneity and creativity on the one hand and in the rigidity with which denials operate on the other. There can be no final solution to this problem of impulse and will control, no adjustment that is "right" or "normal." All one can ask of oneself or the other is a freer use of all that is in the self, a greater acceptance of its badness as well as its goodness, its strength as well as its weakness. The "bottom-nature," the natural self, does not change but its freedom to live, to express itself, to relate, does change and this change can make all the difference in the world.

When one has felt this fundamental shift in an individual's projection upon the other and the new acceptance of responsibility for himself, which accompanies it, he will know that the next movement of this new energy is outward from the two person relationship, the source relationship in which this change was felt to a new person or object in the environment. At this point the introduction into the persoanlity course of material about the father is seized upon as appropriate. Each student writes of his movement to the father or other third person with a new capacity to find its two-sidedness. He can recognize this person as the invader of the intimacy of the mother-child relationship, as well as offering in his very difference the opportunity needed by the growing child for his movement away from the mother. Students amaze themselves as they write of the father by the revelation of new qualities in him, by their feelings about him of which they were not aware before. One student says:

> I have never looked honestly at my relation to my father, a painful admission to make.

Another describes her first reaction to the assignment as:

> One of consternation, almost shame, for despite my many recollections of my early years I could not place my father at all. I still have not managed a vivid picture of him.

Again one can ask where is fact, where truth? What is happening here is reevaluation, a re-creation of experience, through the eyes of the newly enlarged self which can see and bear the two-sidedness of its own feeling and of experience. It is no longer necessary to force the father into the stereotyped picture of the all-bad, authoritative person, or the all-good and giving person. He can be permitted to be himself, to be human, as is the child.

As this process moves on in the semester each student is creating a new self and a new understanding and concept of himself as he takes back old projections and identifications and discovers new attitudes towards himself and the personal objects he has used and is using. These aspects of himself, even the less admirable ones since they are now self-chosen, can be accepted and even enjoyed as they were not in the first semester when they seemed to be discovered by the supervisor or teacher rather than himself. This constitutes also a new-found power in the self to examine and criticize its own work and its own practice without the fear of attack attaching to criticism when it is felt to come at one from the outside.

The practice class and its assignments provide the opportunity for this critical examination of case material and of the student's own work with his clients. The mid-semester assignment of a long case record consisting of a series of interviews from application to an ending interview shows a helping process in which agency function and structure and fine skill on the part of the worker were used most effectively to help the client move from a serious problem in his relation to living to a new attitude towards the problem and new energy to handle all the obstacles that loomed so large before. The interviews in which the client in this record material is helped to express both sides of his conflict, to come through to knowing what he wants for himself in his seemingly desperate situation and to take steps in a new direction, reveal a skill beyond the capacity of first-year students to use in their own practice. But students can understand this work by the middle of the semester when the paper is due and write with amazing perception of the fine points of movement in this process. This understanding would have been impossible for them in the first semester or at any earlier period in the second semester. It grows out of the experience in the "Personality Class" which has given them the clue to the understanding of the two-sidedness of inner experience, of its wanting and not wanting, its fear and resistance to growth along with the amazing capacity of the own will to move into a new creative relation to the environment once it has yielded in its fight to preserve what it has and has taken in that strange intangible substance from the other person known as "help." To be able to see this process of change actually working for a client in need, to read it in a record and analyze its parts is a valuable objectification of experience which identifies and defines the professional elements in this process as a common base for all students who are learning how to give help not merely to take help for themselves.

The last half of the semester is important and necessary in enabling the student to consolidate this professional base in his understanding and his actual work. For purposes of describing this process of change it is not necessary to detail this structure and movement further except to say that by the end of the second semester of this school year, the student feels himself to be a professional person essentially different from the person who entered training ready to make a plan for a second year in which he will, through new and deeper learning, consolidate the changes he feels in himself and realiize new learning and growth.

The thesis, the work of the final semester of training , is the true expression of the ending of the training process in which each student looks back over the way he has come to evaluate his learning in professional terms and to show its eventuation in his own practice.

5. THE RELATION OF TIME STRUCTURE TO CHANGE AND GROWTH

It remains to examine the question of the importance of time structure for the movement I have been describing. As I have indicated throughout, our experience proves that the use of a fixed definite time structure is of fundamental importance in promoting the psychological process of change I have described. Teachers know this time structure in its smaller units, its week-by-week assignments as well as in the larger rhythms of beginning, middle and end which repeat themselves in each semester and operate throughout the two-year experience. Students feel it in the assignments and their own responses, learn to use it, to fight it at times, but yield to it eventually and rely upon its externality, its fixed requirements, its boundaries and its known end set from the beginning.

It is of interest to question whether this particular time structure—built up out of the arbitrary semester units of the educational institution—is particularly adapted to this process of psychological change or whether any time structure would serve the purpose. The experience of the school faculty in developing this structure throws some light on the question. In earlier years and before it understood the value of a time structure in learning, the school operated on the quarter system and gave it up because of its dissatisfaction with the short 12 weeks unit for its courses and with the too rapid change necessitated in changing classes and content three times a year. Once the semester time structure was established its slower speed seems to provide a much more satisfactory pace for the movement of curriculum content and training. Now that all learning processes are set up on the 15-week semester basis it is interesting to note how it seems to fit what is required. In fifteen weeks a beginning can be made, a turning point reached, an end accomplished by the teacher in her handling of her content and by each individual and the class as a whole in use of it. There seems to be a natural organic and psychological basis for this time span.

It is interesting to note in this connection that the Army is using the fifteen week time span in its training of recruits. Meyer Berger reporting this training process for the New York Times Magazine Sunday, February 18, 1951 in an article entitled, "The Making of an American Soldier," describes the change that takes place in these fifteen weeks as, "a miracle of human conversion," one that astonishes the "Army potters" who are responsible for it. "They can't, for example, tell at what period in training a man crosses the psychological line that separates the civilian from the G.I. They know it lies—somewhere around the fifth week in training. Then the indefinable transition subtly happens; the invisible cord that bound the civilian to his immediate past inaudibly snaps. You sense the change in the soldier's physical attitude, in the drift of his small talk, in the ease with which he settles down in an environment that only last night was still a little difficult and uncomfortable. . . . Physical and psychological transition develops so subtly that no man can measure it."

This comparison of time structure in two processes of change as different as that in which the raw recruit becomes a soldier and that in which a lay student becomes a professional social worker may seem forced. But whatever magic or rightness or significance there may or may not be in the fifteen weeks time span there is surely significance in the recognition of a turning point in each of these processes which develops "so subtly that no man can measure it." When one really feels this turning point in student after student, class after class one knows one thing about this process of change wherever and under whatever circumstances it takes place that is of fundamental importance. One knows that the forces which finally move to change are in the individual himself, not in the teacher or the supervisor or the army officer or whoever makes himself responsbile for initiating and seeing this process through to an end result. One can and must be absolutely responsible for setting up the conditions in which the process is initiated, for the time structure, for the expectations, requirements, assignments, at every step of the process and finally for holding firmly to the ending requirements of the process. Here are external controls within which the forces in the individual self can fight and struggle their way through to this amazing moment when these forces come together in themselves in some indescribable miraculous way, in unison with the structured external which holds them. When this point is reached, and it is in the middle between the fifth and eighth week, out of a fifteen-week span that the turning point comes, one knows that the individual is on his own, in a sense, that he is moving under his own steam, with the difference that he has taken in something vital from the situation which at first seems so foreign to him now on the way to being assimilated and possessed as his own. When one comes to terms with this unalterable fact, that one can never produce this moment of change in the other person, one becomes more, not less, responsible for all that one contributes to the process.

So detailed a description of this particular training process in education for social work is hard to follow and tedious to read. There would be no justification for taking the reader through this movement if I did not believe this process to be a typical learning movement which reveals the characteristic phases of learning in any field. In any learning process, whether the learner seeks to acquire additional knowledge, a new skill or the full use of himself in professional service or creative expression, he risks an unknown experience and faces external requirement and compulsion of the other will placed upon him. He may approach it with eagerness, assurance and determination to succeed, but the risk in entering an unknown situation for which he cannot know his capacities entirely in advance is undeniable. His movement into the situation will have in it the ambivalence of wanting and not wanting, of fear, resistance and effort to control in his own terms. Every aspect of the will struggle between his own will and what is outside himself will be present and there can be no peace in this struggle until the learning goal is accomplished and external compulsion becomes inner discipline.

Any learning situation, I believe, contains the essential twosidedness of living and relationship and can be used to precipitate psychological change on any level. The level of change on which movement will be precipitated depends on three factors: first, on the nature of the learning goal; second, inextricably related to the first, on the amount of the self that must be involved in accomplishing the goal; third, on the way in which the teacher who holds in his hands the goal, the content, the requirements and the time structure, conceives of and carries his function.

6. CONCLUSION

The exploration of the problem of psychological growth and change which I have undertaken in this statement rests upon a belief in the individual's capacity for change and growth far greater in degree than is ordinarily realized by any individual in a lifetime. It rests also upon the individual's necessity to refuse opportunity and oppose his own need for change and growth by a powerful resistance and refusal that may even choke out the growth tendency itself. Baffled by the capacity of individuals to deny their own growth potentialities, professional helpers have sought for the explanation in the frustrating or depriving environment. My own conviction in which this statement is rooted is that, while we can always find explanation and excuse for an individual's problem in his environment, we can never find there, or in anything we do there, the effective dynamic for psychological change. Not circumstance but the individual's use of circumstance, the ability to create out of what is given, rather than to fight against or to strive to control circumstance, is of first importance. If we accept this as a basis for our efforts, our relation as professional workers to the problem of growth and change is focused and limited, at the same time the sense of the responsibility we carry is deepened.

As professional helpers or educators, we should know that, if we are to be of help to the individual in his struggle with circumstance in behalf of his capacity to change and grow and create, we must have something new to offer him, something that is important and valuable to us that we would share with him or give to him if he can use it. It may be information, it may be a skill, it may be a service, it may be therapy. It can be offered through a group or individual relationship or in a combination of these. It is essential that we value it greatly so that we will want both to share it and to protect it from encroachment or misuse. As we take responsibility for offering it we must never lose awareness of the problem aroused in the person who enters this situation which is so new to him and which is defined and created in our terms. We must seek to understand his apprehension, his timidity, his aggressiveness, not in terms of his past or his pattern but in terms of his reactions to the new situation, the situation for which we have assumed responsibility. It is in this curious combination of opportunity and limitation, of recognition of the individual's right and necessity to choose within the firm requirements set up by another, that he may find the chance for a new experience in which psychological change can take place. The level on which change will take place depends on the content of the experience, on the amount of self the individual has staked in it and the amount required of him by nature of the goal, and on the way the helper understands and carries his function as helper. In the training required to become a professional helper this change must go deep enough to affect the organization of the self in its impulse-will balance and can be stated as a new acceptance of outer compulsion with a simultaneous freeing of inner impulsive life. This released life is felt to be the own self which now has the power to relate to circumstance with less fear, resistance and fight, to choose what it wants for itself with greater courage and initiative. The more the individual can find in himself the ability to affirm and use, rather than to fight the inevitable in himself and the environment, the more life and growth it is possible for him to experience.

To require change in another, the professional helper must accept the discipline of change in himself, not once but again and again, as he must remake himself in every new situation since every individual and every group one helps is different. In this acceptance of function, of the obligation of the helping task as greater than the individual will, lies the justification and the common humanity of this process. Only when the helper has come to this inescapable acceptance of the compulsion put upon him by his function and developed a new relation to will and compulsion can he trust himself to set up the structures that limit and define the helping process without losing his own spontaneity or that of the process itself.

Notes

THE INFLUENCE OF RANK IN SOCIAL WORK

1. There is no note of this address among Rank's papers—strangely enough, since it was his practice to keep some note of every paper he gave.

2. Two chapters from *Genetic Psychology* were published in the *Journal of the Otto Rank Association* (June, 1968, Vol. 3, No. 1). During the nineteen-twenties some chapters as articles were published in *Psychoanalytic Review* and *Mental Hygiene*.

3. Published in 1942, in *Training for Skill in Social Case Work,* edited by Virginia P. Robinson.

4. Virginia P. Robinson, *The Dynamics of Supervision Under Functional Controls* (1949), pp. 17-18 (this volume, p. 258).

5. *The Nature of Choice in Casework Process,* (1953), p. 17.

6. *Ibid.,* p. 42-49.

7. *Otto Rank: A Biographical Study,* p. 229.

8. *A Comparison of Diagnostic and Functional Casework Concepts.* Report of The Family Service Association of America to Study Basic Concepts in Casework Practice. Cora Kasius, editor. Published by The Family Service Association of America. New York (1950), p. 7-9.

9. *Ibid.,* p. 13.

10. Kenneth L.M. Pray, "The Agency's Role in Service," in *Training for Skill in Social Case Work,* (1942), p. 117-126. Also in pamphlet *Problems of Agency Organization and Administration,* Child Welfare League of America, (1941).

11. Kenneth L.M. Pray, *Social Work in a Revolutionary Age,* p. 260. Paper entitled "A Restatement of the Genetic Principles of Social Casework Practice," (1949).

12. See *Journal of The Otto Rank Association,* December, 1967, for Dr. Pearce Bailey's account of this occasion and Rank's paper, "Psychology and Social Change."

13. Taken from papers on "Activity and Passivity in Social Work." Unpublished.

14. From unpublished papers. For Rank's description and explanation of therapy *Will Therapy* in English translation is available.

A CHANGING PSYCHOLOGY IN SOCIAL CASEWORK

1. EARLY BACKGROUNDS

1. Edward T. Devine, *The Principles of Relief,* p. 315.

2. *Ibid.,* p. 292.

3. *Ibid.,* p. 317. Quoted from *Memorial of Robert M. Hartley,* p. 187.

4. *Fifty Years of Family Social Work 1877-1927,* p. 18.

5. *Ibid.,* p. 20.

6. Frank D. Watson, *The Charity Organization Movement in the United States.*

7. *Proceedings of the Seventh Annual Conference of Charities and Correction,* 1880, p. 127.

8. *Proceedings of the National Conference of Charities and Correction,* 1885, p. 341.

9. *Ibid.,* 1886, pp. 187-88.

10. *Ibid.,* 1895, p. 87.

11. *Ibid.,* p. 115.

12. *Ibid.,* 1897, p. 197.

13. *Hand-Book for Friendly Visitors Among the Poor,* compiled by the Charity Organization Society of the City of New York, 1883.

14. Mary Richmond, *Friendly Visiting Among the Poor,* p. 180.

15. *Proceedings of the National Conference of Charities and Corrections,* 1900, p. 265.

16. *Ibid.,* 1899, pp. 12-13.

17. *Ibid.,* 1901, p. 300.

18. *Ibid.,* 1903, p. 274.

19. *Ibid.,* 1906, p. 3.

20. *Ibid.,* pp. 330, 334.

21. *Ibid.,* 1907, p. 347.

22. *Ibid.*, 1903, pp. 275-78.
23. *Ibid.*, 1911, pp. 1-8.
24. *Ibid.*, p. 261.

2. INFLUENCES FROM SOCIOLOGY AND PSYCHOLOGY

1. *Life and Confessions of a Psychologist*, pp. 400-1.
2. In 1904.
3. *Studies in the Psychology of Sex*, Vol. I, (General Preface), p. vi.
4. *Life and Confessions of a Psychologist*, pp. 408-9.
5. Freud was brought to this country for lectures and conferences by Hall in 1910.
6. *Proceedings of the National Conference of Charities and Correction*, 1911, p. 66.
7. *Feeble-mindedness. Its Causes and Consequences.*
8. *The Individual Delinquent.*
9. *Proceedings of the National Conference of Charities and Corrections*, 1877, p. 81.
10. *Proceedings of the National Conference of Social Work*, 1918, p. 547.
11. Mabel Ruth Fernald, etc., *A Study of Women Delinquents in New York;* Edith R. Spaulding, M.D., *An Experimental Study of Psychopathic Delinquent Women.*
12. *The Individual Delinquent*, p. 22.
13. *Ibid.*, pp. 26, 28.
14. *Ibid.*, p. 31.
15. *Ibid.*, p. 31.
16. *Ibid.*, p. 353.
17. *Mental Conflicts and Misconduct*, Preface.
18. *Ibid.*, p. 20.
19. *Ibid.*, p. 46.
20. *Ibid.*, p. 26.
21. *Ibid.*, p. 36.
22. *Ibid.*, p. 36.
23. *Ibid.*, p. 46.
24. *Ibid.*, p. 58.
25. *Ibid.*, pp. 60-61.
26. *Ibid.*, pp. 61, 66.

27. *The Bearings of Psychology on Social Case Work, Proceedings of the National Conference of Social Work,* 1917, p. 109.

28. *Ibid.,* p. 107.

3. THE STIMULUS OF PSYCHIATRY

1. *The Institutional Care of the Insane in the United States and Canada,* I, 234.

2. *Proceedings of the National Conference of Charities and Correction,* 1910, p. 13.

3. Adolf Meyer, "Where Should We Attack the Problem of the Prevention of Mental Defect and Mental Disease?" *Proceedings of the National Conference of Charities and Correction,* 1915, pp. 298-307.

4. EARLY PSYCHOANALYTIC INFLUENCES

1. "For readers of English we may cite here, as showing something of the broader aspects of mental analysis:

Mental Mechanisms by W.A. White, 1911; *Human Motives,* by J. J. Putnam, 1915; "The Freudian Methods Applied to Anger," an article by Stanley Hall, in *American Journal of Psychology,* July, 1915; *The Freudian Wish,* by E.B. Holt, 1915; "Psychoanalysis and Study of Children," an article by O. Pfister, in *American Journal of Psychology,* 1915, p. 130; *Psychopathology of Every Day Life,* by Freud, and *Psychology of the Unconscious,* by Jung (both of the latter recently translated). Then, lately has appeared *Mechanisms of Character Formation* by W. A. White"—From Wm. A. Healy, *Mental Conflicts and Misconduct,* footnote, p. 35.

2. Sigmund Freud, "Three Contributions to the Theory of Sex," *New York Journal of Mental and Nervous Diseases,* 1910. Monograph.

Adolf Meyer, "A Discussion of Some Fundamental Issues in Freud's Psychoanalysis," *New York State Hospitals Bulletin,* March, 1910, p. 22.

J. J. Putnam, "Comments on Sex Issues from the Freudian Standpoint," *New York Medical Journal,* June 15 and 22, 1912.

3. Pp. 12-13.

4. *Mechanisms of Character Formation,* preface.

5. *Ibid.,* pp. 12, 15, 16.

6. P. 47.

5. "SOCIAL DIAGNOSIS"

1. *Proceedings of the National Conference of Social Work,* 1917, p. 114.

2. Mary E. Richmond, *Social Diagnosis.*

3. *Ibid.,* p. 34.

4. References to psychiatrists in *Social Diagnosis* are as follows: Dubois, Paul, pp. 116, 136, 347; Fernald, William E., pp. 43, 44; Healy, William, pp. 9, 117, 129, 136, 137, 150, 153, 314, 375; Meyer, Adolf, pp. 114, 131, 218, 352, 362, 434; Mitchell, S. Weir, pp. 49, 70; Neff, Irwin H., pp. 147, 430; Putnam, James J., pp. 4, 26, 136.

The words mental hygiene are used once in the book in a reference to the mental hygiene movement on p. 32.

5. *Ibid.* Preface p. 5.

6. *Ibid.,* p. 5.

7. *Ibid.,* p. 4.

8. *Ibid.,* p. 368, quoting from Mrs. Helen Bosanquet, *The Standard of Life and Other Studies,* p. 131.

9. *Ibid.,* p. 369.

10. *Ibid.,* p. 51.

11. *Ibid.,* p. 51.

12. *Ibid.,* p. 43.

13. *Ibid.,* p. 53.

14. *Ibid.,* p. 63.

15. *Ibid.,* p. 54.

16. *Ibid.,* p. 55.

17. *Ibid.,* pp. 55-56.

18. *Ibid.,* pp. 65-79.

19. *Ibid.,* p. 134.

20. *Ibid.,* p. 138.

21. *Ibid.,* p. 139.

22. *Ibid.,* p. 194.

23. *Ibid.,* p. 343.

24. *Ibid.,* p. 56.

25. *Ibid.,* p. 361.

26. *Ibid.,* p. 200.

27. *Ibid.,* p. 114.

28. *Ibid.,* p. 114.

29. *Ibid.,* p. 115.

30. *Ibid.,* p. 115.

31. *Ibid.,* p. 114.

32. *Ibid.,* p. 130.

33. *Ibid.,* p. 123.

34. *Ibid.,* p. 130.

35. *Ibid.,* pp. 130-31.

36. *Ibia.,* p. 131.

37. *Proceedings of the National Conference of Social Work,* 1917, p. 112.

38. *Ibid.,* p. 114.

6. AFTER "SOCIAL DIAGNOSIS"

1. Agnes Murray, "Case Work Above the Poverty Line," *Proceedings of the National Conference of Social Work,* 1918, pp. 340-43.

2. Mary Jarrett, "The Psychiatric Thread Running Through All Social Case Work," *Proceedings of the National Conference of Social Work,* 1919, p. 587.

3. *Ibid.,* p. 591.

4. E. E. Southard and Mary C. Jarrett, *The Kingdom of Evils.*

5. *Proceedings of the National Conference of Social Work,* 1919, p. 587.

6. *Ibid.,* p. 325.

7. "Minimum of Medical Insight Required by Social Service Workers with Delinquents," *Proceedings of the National Conference of Social Work,* 1920, pp. 66-67.

8. *Ibid.,* p. 68.

9. Thomas W. Salmon, "Some of the Tasks of Organized Work in Mental Hygiene," *Proceedings of the National Conference of Social Work,* New Orleans, 1920, p. 65.

10. Ada Eliot Sheffield, *Case-Study Possibilities.*

11. *Ibid.,* p. 10.

12. *Ibid.,* p. 10.

13. *Ibid.,* p. 10.

14. *Ibid.,* p. 14.

15. *Ibid.,* p. 16.

16. *Ibid.,* p. 19.

17. *Ibid.,* p. 49n.

7. THE EMERGENCE OF A COMMON CASEWORK FIELD

1. Medical social service had its origin in 1905 when a social service department was organized in the out-patient department of Massachusetts General Hospital by Dr. Richard C. Cabot.

2. *Bulletin of the New York School of Social Work, 1920-1921.*

3. *Catalogue of the Pennsylvania School for Social Service, 1919-1920,* p. 8.

4. A quotation from the *Vocational Aspects of Medical Social Work* will bear out this point:

"It is clear from the foregoing illustrations that social work within the hospital is most closely related to the carrying out of medical treatment. Since its inception approximately twenty years ago the primary aim of medical social service has been to help doctor and patient carry through a satisfactory plan of treatment, to gather such significant data as may help the physician to discover the contributory causes of the patient's present condition, to interpret to him the patient's resources in such fashion as to open up new avenues of thought which may prompt the modification of the original plan or create a new plan which the patient can undertake. Helping the patient carry through the plan of treatment often means utilizing the resources of the community in new ways, and sometimes the creating of new resources. . . .

"Medical social work has relationships without as well as within the hospital. It occupies a part of the field of social work; its practice is one of the specialized forms of social casework. Its distinguishing features are due primarily to the fact that it is based upon a medical need and is so integrated with the hospital organization and the practice of medicine that it cannot exist of itself as a separate entity. Its method is similar to that of family case work but it must utilize a particular content of medical and social knowledge and it is on a consideration of medical problems that the social plan is initiated." – pp. 23-25.

5. Jessie Taft in an article appearing in *Medicine and Surgery* as early as March, 1918, under the title of "The Limitations of the Psychiatrist," stated the social worker's inalienable right to work towards understanding and control of the human material with which she is dealing. This point of view, radical in 1918, is generally granted in 1930.

6. *Vocational Aspects of Family Social Work,* pp. 12-13.

7. "Psychiatric Social Work, Its Nurture and Nature," *Mental Hygiene,* Vol. XIII, No. 3 (July, 1929), p. 509.

8. "The Essential Similarities in All Fields of Case Work," *Proceedings of the National Conference of Social Work,* Memphis, 1928, pp. 359-60.

9. P. 11.

8. WORKING PSYCHOLOGIES OF SOCIAL CASEWORK, 1920-1930

1. "Understanding Human Nature," *The Family,* Vol. VIII, No. 2 (April, 1927), p. 60.

2. *Interviews. A Study of the Methods of Analyzing and Recording Social Case Work Interviews.*

3. William Healy and Augusta F. Bronner, Edith M.H. Baylor and J. Prentice Murphy, *Reconstructing Behavior in Youth.*

4. An analysis of the "situational" or "behavioristic" approach as it is being used in the study and control of the problems of child behavior in America is given in *The Child In America,* by William I. Thomas and Dorothy Swayne Thomas.

5. "Social Interaction in the Interview: an Experiment" and discussion of this report by Virginia P. Robinson, Helen T. Myrick, G. Eleanor Kimble and E.H. Sutherland, *Social Forces,* Vol. VI, No. 4 (June, 1928), pp. 545-69.

6. The New York School of Social Work, The Pennsylvania School of Social and Health Work, The Smith College School of Social Work, The Simmons College School of Social Work.

7. In *The Family,* Vol. VII, No. 7 (Nov. 1929), pp. 213-23.

8. By Porter Lee and Marion Kenworthy.

9. *Psychoanalytic Concepts in Mental Hygiene,* p. 213.

10. *Ibid.,* p. 216.

11. *Ibid.,* p. 214.

12. *Ibid.*

13. *Ibid.*

14. *Ibid.,* pp. 214-15.

15. *Ibid.,* p. 219.

16. *Ibid.,* p. 220.

17. *Ibid.,* p. 221.

18. *Ibid.,* p. 222.

19. *Ibid.*
20. *Ibid.*
21 *Ibid.*

9. THE SOCIAL CASE HISTORY

1. *Social Diagnosis,* p. 43.

2. In an article on "The Essential Similarities in All Fields of Case Work" given at the National Conference in Memphis in 1928, previously cited, Miss Dawley comments on this decreasing need for outside sources of information, attributing the change directly to the worker's growing knowledge of the dynamics of human behavior. She says: "It was necessary that the worker should have so assimilated her knowledge of human behavior, in its broadest sense, that she could sort out of the early interviews the gist of the real situation. It is perhaps too obvious to mention that as this background becomes more universal there is less routine emphasis than formerly on the detail of investigation, and more on the understanding of the situation, obtained from the individuals directly concerned."—*Proceedngs of the National Conference of Social Work,* 1928, p. 357.

3. Miss Doran in 1919 in discussing the finding of foster homes places great emphasis on the information to be obtained from references. She says: "To find the persons who are best qualified to give the desired information involves the exercise of judgment and often of considerable ingenuity. There is no hard and fast rule as to the number or the kind of independent sources which need be consulted before deciding that a visit shall be made to a home. Sometimes one or two may be enough; again, reports from a half dozen may not give information sufficiently conclusive to justify a decision. Sometimes the essential facts may come from the family physician, or the pastor, a neighbor, or the stage driver may hold the key to the desired information. In each case the worker must probe for information that will give a positive reaction either for or against the home. Eternal vigilance for something definite is the chief safeguard in the work."—Mary S. Doran and Bertha C. Reynolds, *The Selection of Foster Homes for Children,* p. 19.

4. A good statement of the application of this point of view to the study of the foster home may be found in Charlotte Towle's "The Evaluation of Homes in Preparation for Child Placement," *Mental Hygiene,* Vol. XI, No. 3 (July, 1927), pp. 460-81.

5. *Proceedings of the National Conference of Social Work,* Memphis, 1928, p. 112-13.

6. Very recently, in some child guidance clinic work, a change in the treatment interest is modifying the history-taking process and history falls into the chronological record of treatment as in the record of a family society.

7. Pp. 290-99.

8. *Social Case Work Generic and Specific,* p. 22.

9. Interesting confirmation of this point that the social history offers no criterion by which the relevancy of any facts for treatment can be satisfactorily determined grows out of a critical reading of Mrs. Ada Sheffield's treatment of the Social Case History in 1920 published by the Russell Sage Foundation. As the only book on this topic this discussion was highly stimulating in history taking and recording. Mrs. Sheffield's praiseworthy but futile effort to define social concepts and to place facts in reference to their significance in these concepts reveals clearly that the social concept is essentially fluid and cannot serve as a basis for the selection of significant facts of history or treatment determination.

10. TREATMENT IN SOCIAL CASEWORK

1. Karl de Schweinitz, *The Art of Helping People out of Trouble.*

2. See Bibliography for list of Dr. Healy's publications.

3. By Mary B. Sayles—See Bibliography.

4. By Lee and Kenworthy.

5. *Some Aspects of Relief in Family Case Work,* New York Charity Organization Society.

6. Previously cited.

7. *Proceedings of the National Conference of Charities and Correction,* Buffalo, 1888, p. 133.

8. In the last few years a new trend to include process in the record is noticeable.

9. For example—

Frank J. Bruno, "Objective Tests in Case Work." *The Family,* Vol. VII, No. 6 (October, 1926), pp. 183-86.

Sophie Hardy, "What Measures Have We for Growth in Personality?" *The Family,* Vol. No. 8 (December, 1926), pp. 254-58.

Maurice J. Karpf, "Relation of Length of Treatment to Improve-

ment or Adjustment of Social Case Work Problems." *The Family,*
Vol. VIII, No. 5 (July, 1927), pp. 144-48.

Ellen F. Wilcox, "The Measurement of Achievement in Family
Case Work." *The Family,* Vol. VIII, No. 2 (April, 1927), pp. 46-49.

10. See list of Healy's work in Bibliography.

11. Sophie Theis, *How Foster Children Turn Out.*

12. Kate Holladay Claghorn, "The Problem of Measuring Social
Treatment," *The Social Service Review,* Vol. I, No. 2 (June, 1927),
pp. 181-93.

13. Frank J. Bruno, "Objective Tasks in Case Work," *The Family,* Vol. VII, No. 6 (October, 1926), pp. 183-86.

14. *Social Case Work Generic and Specific,* p. 29.

15. *Ibid.,* pp. 29-30.

16. *Ibid.,* p. 30.

11. THE PROBLEM OF RELATIONSHIP

1. "Dieser Wille zur Trennung ist nämlich genau so ein biolo-
gishces und menschliches Lebensprinzip wie der Wille zur Vereinig-
ung" (the will to separate is just as much a biological and human life
principle as the will to unite). From Otto Rank's *Technik der Psychoanalyse,* Vol. II, *Die Analytische Reaktion,* p. 104.

2. Compare the birth and weaning experiences of a primitive
group like the Trobriand Islanders described by Bronislaw Malinowski
in *Sex and Repression in Savage Society.*

3. Jean Piaget, *Language and Thought in the Child; Judgment
and Reasoning in the Child,* pp. 196-97; *The Child's Conception of
the World.*

4. The following statement by Sorokin in *Contemporary Sociological Theories* (pp. 527-28) bears out this point: "In the meth-
odology of contemporary natural science the conception of functional
relation ("variable" and its "function," which may be one and two-
sided) is being substituted for that of one-sided causal relation,
and correlation for that of one-sided and metaphysical determinism.
That is, the scientist asserts only that associated phenomena are in
functional relations or are correlated to a degree indicated by the co-
efficient of correlation of a certain probability. Such substitution
frees us from all anthropomorphic elements in the connection of
cause and determination, and gives the possibility of studying one-
sided and two-sided relations. . . . Such a conception presents the

possibility of treating any "factor" as a variable and trying to find to what extent and with what phenomena it is correlated. . . . For instance, we may take, in one case an "economic factor" as a variable and study to what extent it is correlated with religious phenomena. . . . In the field of social phenomena we almost always deal with relations of interdependence but not with that of one-dependence. The application to such phenomena of the conception of one-sided causal relations leads to a series of logical and factual fallacies."

5. See Bibliography.

5. Otto Rank, *Technik der Psychoanalyse*, Vols. I and II.

6. A similar attitude of acceptance of others is described in Jacob Wasserman's *The World's Illusion* in the character of Christian Wahnshaffe and in Dostoievsky's *The Brothers Karamazov* in the character of Aloysha.

7. Wolfgang Köhler, *Gestalt Psychology*.

8. Kurt Koffka, "On the Structure of the Unconscious," from *The Unconscious, A Symposium*, pp. 60-61.

12. THE SOCIAL CASEWORK RELATIONSHIP

1. *Op. cit.*, p. 200.

2. *Op. cit.*, 547-48.

3. "How Do We Effect Leadership?" *The Family*, Vol. VI, No. 10 (February, 1926), pp. 290-93.

4. Jessie Taft, "The Use of the Transfer Within the Limits of the Office Interview," *The Family*, Vol. V, No. 6 (October, 1924), p. 145.

5. *Psychoanalytic Concepts in Mental Hygiene*.

6. Lawson Lowrey, "Psychiatric Methods and Techniques for Meeting Mental Hygiene Problems in Children of Pre-school Age," *Mental Hygiene*, Vol. XIII, No. 3 (July, 1929), p. 480.

7. William C. Menninger, "The Mental Hygiene Aspect of the Boy Scout Movement," *Mental Hygiene*, Vol. XIII, No. 3 (July, 1929), pp. 501-2.

8. Grace F. Marcus, *Some Aspects of Relief in Family Case Work*.

9. Lucille F. Nichel, "The Role and Aims of the Social Worker in Treatment," *Proceedings of the National Conference of Social Work*, 1929, pp. 432-444.

Elizabeth Dexter, "The Social Case Worker's Attitude and Problems as They Affect her Work," *The Family*, Vol. VII, No. 6 (October, 1926), pp. 177-81.

Alice Leahy, "1926 Emphasis in Psychiatric Social Case Work," *Mental Hygiene*, Vol. X, No. 4 (October, 1926), pp. 743-50.

10. I am ignoring here all the complicating questions of limitation of intake introduced by functions of agencies and their responsibility for social problems.

13. HISTORY-TAKING AND RELATIONSHIP

1. Jacob Wasserman's *The World's Illusion* where Niels Heinrich tells his story to Christian Wajnshaff gives an interesting illustration of this release.

2. An article entitled "Interview" in *The Family*, Vol. X, No.3 (May, 1929), pp. 74-77, describes an interview in which a worker knowing of a particular fact about a woman's history (that the oldest boy was illegitimate) arranges an interview in which the woman has the opportunity to tell it or to accept it as known by the worker in order to relieve the tension of having it between them as an uncertainty.

14. ATTITUDES AND TECHNIQUES

1. For an interesting discussion and illustrations of this point see an article entitled "The Catch in Praise," by Jessie Taft, in *Child Study*, February, 1930.

2. *Interviews.* See Bibliography.

3. Stuart A. Queen, "Social Interaction in the Interview: an Experiment," *Social Forces*, Vol. VI, No. 4 (June, 1928), pp. 545-69.

4. Mary S. Brisley, "An Attempt to Articulate Processes," *The Family*, Vol. V, No. 6 (Oct., 1924), pp. 157-61.

Pearl Salsberry, "Techniques in Case Work," *The Family*, Vol. No. VIII, No. 5 (July, 1927), pp. 153-57.

Joanna C. Colcord, "A Study of the Techniques of the Social Case Work Interview," *Social Forces*, Vol. VII, No. 4 (June, 1929), pp. 519-27.

5. Pearl Salsberry, "Techniques in Case Work," *The Family*, Vol. VIII, No. 5 (July, 1927), pp. 153-57.

6. H. A. Overstreet, *Influencing Human Behavior*.

7. Pearl Salsberry, *op. cit.,* p. 156.

8. It should not be inferred that the Minneapolis group is unique in this point of view. Rather they should be regarded as having rendered unique service in making articulate in extreme form techniques which operate obscurely in a great deal of casework today. It is interesting that even in the Milford Conference Report the same attitude of patronage of the client which we have criticized in the Minneapolis study comes out in much more subtle guise in the definitions of interviewing, participation, etc. (*Social Case Work Generic and Specific,* p. 24.) The same hope of control "through schemes and techniques which will secure adequate control over human behavior" (p. 268) for social sciences appears in Ernest Mowrer's *Family Disorganization.* University of Chicago Press, 1927.

15. THE WORKER AND HER PREPARATION

1. Lucy Wright, "The Worker's Attitude as an Element in Social Case Work," *The Family,* Vol. V, No. 4 (July, 1924), pp. 103-9.

2. I have tried to define the active feeling aspect of "identification" as opposed to its intellectual aspect in a discussion of Dr. Greene's study of the interview published in *Social Forces,* Vol. VI, No. 4 (June, 1928), pp. 545-69.

3. Alice M. Leahy, "Emphases in Psychiatric Social Case Work," *Mental Hygiene,* Vol. X, No. 4 (October, 1926), pp. 743-50.

4. Grace Marcus, "How Case Work Training Can be Adapted to Meet the Worker's Personal Problems," *Mental Hygiene,* Vol. XI, No. 3 (July, 1927), pp. 449-59.

5. The question has been asked whether I mean to imply here that the supervisor requires a professional analysis as part of her technical equipment. I should be sorry to seem so dogmatic in regard to an experience which each individual must accept or reject for himself on personal as well as professional grounds. I can only say that for myself experience in the dynamic controlled relationship offered in an analysis afforded a unique opportunity for a new orientation of the self to the other and for deeper insight into the meanings of attitudes and reactions in relationship to situations.

PSYCHOANALYTIC CONTRIBUTIONS TO SOCIAL CASEWORK TREATMENT

1. This psychology is incorporated into the literature of social work in Dr. Kenworthy's and Mr Lee's book, *Mental Hygiene and Social Work,* and in other articles by Dr. Kenworthy.
2. For a clear exposition of this concept, see Dr. Glueck's paper, *Psychoanalysis and Child Guidance,* read before the First International Congress on Mental Hygiene, Washington, May 7, 1930, and published in *Mental Hygiene,* Vol. 14, pp. 813-27, October, 1930.

SUPERVISION IN SOCIAL CASE WORK

2. THE DYNAMICS OF THE SELF IN EARLY EXPERIENCE

1. William A. White, *Medical Psychology,* p. 26. (New York: Nervous and Mental Disease Publishing Company, 1931.)
2. The concept of the unity and dynamics of the organism in terms of whole and part has been given scientific validity in biology by the discussions of Child, Ritter, Coghill and others.

In the field of psychology, the Gestalt School is working with the concept of whole and part in detailed psychological processes and in larger units of behavior with monkeys and children. Dr. William A. White has extended this concept into psychiatry in his recent books, *Medical Psychology* and *The Meaning of Disease.* Otto Rank has utilized the part-whole concept in his philosophic and psychological analysis of the emotional life and self-consciousness in his *Will Therapy,* Part II.

This concept is essentially philosophic and abstract and I am well aware that for the strictly scientifically minded psychologist such an approach can never seem anything but obscure and metaphysical. Psychology is still clinging to the language of statics and where it begins to be aware of dynamics has not yet evolved an articulate language.

3. Understanding of the problem of self-consciousness and its development of the definition of the self and boundaries between it and the external world, rests upon much careful thinking from various sources. Mach, Baldwin, Cooley, Dewey, Mead, Rank, Piaget, Levy-Bruhl, the Psychoanalytic School and the Gestalt School, have made valuable contributions to this problem. Recent anthropological studies of primitive development such as Benedict's, Malinowski's, Mead's, are adding concrete illustrations of varied types of self development in different milieus.

4. Edward Kempf in *The Autonomic Functions and the Personality* (New York: Nervous and Mental Disease Publishing Company, 1918), presented a brilliant and original analysis of the relation of organic segments and strivings in the total personality.

5. I have used fear consistently throughout this study to describe an organic experience which seems to be an inevitable and recurrent phase in movement and growth. It is the accompaniment of loss of wholeness, of separation over which the organism has not achieved control. It may have its origin in the movement of the self and be projected on to an outside or it may be stimulated by an external threat or attack or loss. It is an inevitable phase in moving into a new, strange situation, before control has been established and in leaving a situation which has contained satisfaction.

3. THE DEVELOPMENT OF A PROFESSIONAL SELF IN SOCIAL CASEWORK TRAINING

1. The proportion of time spent in classes and in the field work differ in different schools. In the Pennsylvania School three days a week are spent in the field work and two days in classes, in the first year. In the second year, the proportion is four days in the field and one in class.

2. Otto Rank, *Truth and Reality.* (New York: Alfred A. Knopf, 1936.)

3. (New York: Alfred A. Knopf, 1936.)

4. For a more detailed discussion of feeling see "Living and Feeling," by Jessie Taft, *Child Study Magazine,* January 1933.

THE DYNAMICS OF SUPERVISION UNDER FUNCTIONAL CONTROLS

1. THE DEVELOPMENT OF SOCIAL CASEWORK FROM A PERSONAL TO A PROFESSIONAL SERVICF

1. For an analysis of the differences in these two psychological theories in their effect on casework, see the following articles: Grace Marcus, "Some Implications for Case Work of Rank's Psychology," *The Family,* June 1938, and "Family Casework in 1948," *Journal of Social Casework,* July 1948; Jessie Taft, "Review of Rank," *Mental Hygiene,* October 1931 (also published in *Psychoanalytic Review,* October 1931), and her Translator's Introduction to *Will Therapy,* 1935 (republished in Otto Rank, *Will Therapy and Truth and Reality;* Alfred Knopf, 1945).

2. Only one member of the faculty constitutes an exception to this statement. Jessie Taft, already a clinical psychologist and a practicing therapist, as well as a supervisor and teacher of social casework practice, made immediate use of her contact with Rank in her own therapeutic practice, but at no time confused the therapeutic function or treatment form with the social casework function and process. No one has done more to clarify the differences between therapy and social casework than she, beginning with her first published work after this contact, *The Dynamics of Therapy* (Macmillan, 1933). In this book she applied the Rankian therapeutic method to the treatment of children and at the same time examined the problems of differentiating casework from therapy. Her later understanding and clarification of these differences are found in all her writings, notably in "Function as the Basis for Development in Social Work Processes," published by the *Newsletter* of the American Association of Psychiatric Social Work, Vol. IX, No. 1, 1939, and in her discussion of Dr. Gomberg's article "Counseling as a Service of the Family Agency" in *Counseling and Protective Service as Family Case Work*

(Pennsylvania School of Social Work, 1946), pp. 83-94. See also revised version in *Family Casework and Counseling: A Functional Approach* (University of Pennsylvania Press, 1948), pp. 262-72.

3. *Journal of Social Work Process* (Pennsylvania School of Social Work), 1937.

4. *Journal of Social Work Process,* 1937.

5. Jessie Taft, "The Relation of Function to Process in Social Case Work," *Journal of Social Work Process,* 1937. Also reprinted in *Training for Skill in Social Case Work,* pp. 100-116.

6. University of North Carolina Press, 1941.

7. "The Possibility of Help for the Prostitute through Functional Case Work in an Authoritative Setting" in Rosa Wessel, Editor, *A Case Work Approach to Sex Delinquents* (Pennsylvania School of Social Work, 1947).

8. "The Specific Nature of the Family Agency" in *Family Casework and Counseling: A Functional Approach.*

9. Published in *Journal of Social Casework,* October 1947. Also in *Social Work in a Revolutionary Age and Other Papers* (University of Pennsylvania Press, 1949).

10. "Counseling as a Service of the Family Agency" in *Family Casework and Counseling: A Functional Approach.*

11. *Family Casework and Counseling: A Functional Approach,* p. 270.

12. "Counseling as a Service of the Family Agency," in *Family Casework and Counseling: A Functional Approach,* pp. 197-98.

3. THE DEVELOPMENT OF SUPERVISION IN SOCIAL CASEWORK

1. For a vivid description of the paternalistic method of inducting young students into the practice of law in the eighties, see George Wharton Pepper's autobiography, *Philadelphia Lawyer* (Lippincott, 1944), pp. 46-47.

2. Steinbeck's account of this in *Bombs Away* (written for the U.S. Army Air Force; Viking Press, 1942) is a classic description of the way in which the service and the situation in which it develops determine supervisory method.

3. For a selected list of published literature and Pennsylvania School of Social Work theses, see Bibliography.

4. *Supervision in Social Case Work,* p. 53.

5. For a fuller description of the meaning of this movement, see Chapter III, "The Development of a Professional Self," in *Supervision in Social Case Work,* and Chapter I, "The Meaning of Skill," in *Training for Skill in Social Case Work.*

6. P. 4.

4. THE SUPERVISORY RELATIONSHIP, ITS PERSONAL SOURCES AND FUNCTIONAL CONTROLS

1. "A Report With the B-29's" by St. Clair McKelway. *The New Yorker,* June 20, 1945, pp. 34-35. Copyright 1945, The F-R. Publishing Corporation. Used by permission.

5. THE DIFFERENTIATION OF ROLES BETWEEN SUPERVISOR AND STUDENT

1. Except when particular individuals are referred to, the masculine pronoun is used arbitrarily to designate the student, and the feminine to designate the supervisor in order to keep the distinction clear throughout the book.

2. Margaret Bishop, *The Selection and Admission of Students in a School of Social Work.*

3. The following catalogue statement indicates the extent to which this decision as to field work assignment rests with the School and makes clear what the student has in writing before he begins this training:

"Field Work—First Year

"The student receives individual attention in the arrangement of his assignment to field work, as well as to class section. The selection of a field work placement rests upon a number of factors, and the final decision in the selection rests with the School. Nevertheless, the student's preference is taken into account and he is notified by his faculty adviser of his assignment as to agency at registration time, or before by letter, whenever possible.

"First Year field work placement does not commit the casework student permanently to a particular functional field. Specialization occurs in the Second Year.

"Throughout the First Year, students devote three full working days a week to field work. These days are Mondays, Thursdays and

Fridays." (Pennsylvania School of Social Work, University of Pennsylvania, *Catalogue Issue,* 1947-48, pp. 22-23.)

6. THE SUPERVISOR'S RESPONSIBILITY FOR BRINGING OUT THE NEGATIVE ELEMENTS IN THE STUDENT'S EARLY REACTION TO SUPERVISION

1. For a detailed account of the "Personality Course" and its function in the curriculum, see the article entitled "The Function of the Personality Course in the Practice Unit" by Jessie Taft in *Training for Skill in Social Case Work.*

2. "Living and Feeling." Mimeographed article copied by permission from *Child Study,* January 1933, p. 4.

7. THE TURNING POINT IN THE PROCESS

1. For a full discussion of the relation between the adviser and the supervisor, see article by Goldie Basch Faith, entitled "Classroom and Field Work: Their Joint Contribution to Skill," in *Training for Skill in Social Case Work.*

9. EVALUATION AT THE END OF FIRST SEMESTER

1. In the setup I am describing, students remain in the same placement with the same supervisor for a year.

11. THE SECOND YEAR OF TRAINING

1. For a description of this second-year placement process, the following statement from the catalogue will serve:
"Admission to Second Year

"Students who have completed the first year in the School are eligible to apply for second year. This group includes students who are currently enrolled in the first year and those who have previously completed the first year. . . .

"Current first-year students discuss plans for a second year with their faculty advisers in April. Former students applying for readmission also file applications in the Spring. In accepting a student for the second year, the School is influenced both by the quality of his work in the first year and by the availability of an appropriate field placement. In general, the second year immediately follows the first For some students, a year or more of paid employment in an agency before completing training is advisable.

"Plans for Second Year

"A student may undertake the second year of study according to one of the following plans:

"1. Agency fellowship. Fellowships covering tuition and minimum living expenses offered by agencies are available for outstanding students. In offering these fellowships, the School and the agencies take into consideration the quality of work done by the student in the first year, and the amount and type of his current and previous experience.

"2. Agency placement without fellowship. Under this arrangement, students bear the total cost of training.

"3. Work-study plan. Students may apply to complete their training as part-time paid members of field-work agency staffs, providing the agency insures the student adequate supervision acceptable to the School, at least one day a week free from job for classes, suitable adjustment of work load, and access to agency material for a thesis." (Pennsylvania School of Social Work, *Catalogue Issue*, 1947-48, pp. 23-24.)

2. I regret exceedingly that I cannot give credit to the supervisor whose work and thinking I am using here. To identify her would be to identify the student, who herself a supervisor now, might well object to the publication of her learning struggle, although she has consented to its use here. I have taken every precaution, therefore, to disguise her identity without in any way altering essential facts or factors in the process.

12. THE THESIS AS THE ENDING PHASE OF THE TWO-YEAR TRAINING PROCESS

1. Pennsylvania School of Social Work, *Catalogue Issue*, 1947-48, p. 25.

THE DYNAMICS OF PSYCHOLOGICAL CHANGE

1. ATTITUDES

1. For the understanding of will on which this thinking rests I would refer to the writings of Otto Rank, particularly to *Will Therapy* and *Truth and Reality,* translated by Jessie Taft. N.Y. Alfred A. Knopf, First Edition 1936, Second Edition 1945.

2. THE CONCERN OF SOCIAL WORK . . .

1. Robinson, Virginia P. *The Dynamics of Supervision under Functional Controls.* University of Pennsylvania Press, 1949. (cf. present volume, p. 360).

4. THE MOVEMENT TOWARD CHANGE IN THE SELF

1. It is an interesting fact that this student had had previous experience of change both in personal therapy and in social work training. In returning to school for advanced training she brgouht a deeper state, a will to use the school and to find herself in what she thought of as "her last chance for change and growth."

2. Rank, Otto, *Art and Artist.* N.Y. Alfred A. Knopf, 32.

Selected Bibliographies

FROM: *A CHANGING PSYCHOLOGY IN SOCIAL CASEWORK*

Beers, Clifford. *A Mind That Found Itself.* New York, Longmans, Green and Company, 1908.

Bosanquet, Helen. *The Standard of Life and Other Studies.* London, Macmillan and Company, Ltd., 1898.

Brisley, Mary S. "An Attempt to Articulate Processes," *The Family,* Vol. VIII, No. 5 (July, 1927), pp. 153-57.

Bruno, Frank J. "Objective Tests in Case Work," *The Family,* Vol. VII, No. 6 (October, 1926), pp. 183-86.

Bruno, Frank J. "Understanding Human Nature," *The Family,* Vol. VIII, No. 2 (April, 1927), p. 60.

Bulletin of the New York School of Social Work, 1920-21.

Campbell, C. Macfie. "Minimum of Medical Insights Required by Social Service Workers with Delinquents," *Proceedings of the National Conference of Social Work, 1920.*

Claghorn, Kate Holladay. "The Problem of Measuring Social Treatment," *Social Service Review,* Vol. I, No. 2 (June, 1927), pp. 181-93.

Colcord, Joanna C. "A Study of the Techniques of the Social Case Work Interview," *Social Forces,* Vol. VII, No. 4 (June, 1929), pp. 519-27.

Dawley, Almena. "The Essential Similarities in All Fields of Case Work," *Proceedings of the National Conference of Social Work, 1928* (Memphis), pp. 359-60.

Devine, Edward T. *The Principles of Relief.* New York, The Macmillan Company, 1904.

Dexter, Elizabeth. "The Social Case Worker's Attitude and Problems as They Affect Her Work," *The Family,* Vol. VII, No. 6 (October, 1926), pp. 177-81.

Doran, Mary S., and Reynolds, Bertha C. *The Selection of Foster Homes for Children* (Studies in Social Work). New York School of Social Work, 1919.

Eddington, A. S. *The Nature of the Physical World.* New York, The Macmillan Company, 1928.

Ellis, Havelock. *Studies in the Psychology of Sex.* Philadelphia, F. A. Davis Company, 1900.

Fernald, Mabel Ruth. *A Study of Women Delinquents in New York State.* New York, The Century Company, 1920.

Fifty Years of Family Social Work, 1877-1927. Buffalo, New York, Charity Organization Society of Buffalo, 1927.

Flügel, J.C. *The Psychoanalytic Study of the Family.* London, The Hogarth Press, 1921.

Freud, Sigmund. *Psychopathology of Every-Day Life.* New York, The Macmillan Company, 1914.

Freud, Sigmund. "Three Contributions to the Theory of Sex," *New York Journal of Mental and Nervous Diseases.* 1910 Monograph.

Goddard, Henry Herbert. *Feeble-mindedness: Its Causes and Consequences.* New York, The Macmillan Company, 1914.

Hall, G. Stanley. *Adolescence.* New York, D. Appleton and Company, 1904.

Hall, G. Stanley. "The Freudian Methods Applied to Anger," *American Journal of Psychology,* July, 1915.

Hall, G. Stanley. *Life and Confessions of a Psychologist.* New York, D. Appleton and Company, 1923.

Hand Book for Friendly Visistors Among the Poor. Compiled by the Charity Organization Society of the City of New York, 1883. New York, G. P. Putnam's Sons.

Hardy, Sophie. "What Measures Have We for Growth in Personality," *The Family,* Vol. VII, No. 8 (December, 1926), pp. 254-58.

Healy, William. "Bearings of Psychology in Social Case Work, The," *Proceedings of the National Council of Social Work, 1917.*

Healy, William. *Case Studies of Mentally and Morally Aberrant Types.* Cambridge, Harvard University Press, 1912.

Healy, William (with A. F. Bronner). *Delinquents and Criminals.* New York, The Macmillan Company, 1926.

Healy, William. *Honesty.* Indianapolis, Bobbs-Merrill Company, 1915.

Healy, William. *Individual Delinquent, The.* Boston, Little, Brown and Company, 1914, 1915.

Healy, William (with A. F. Bronner). *Judge Baker Foundation Case Studies,* Series I. Judge Baker Foundation, 1923.

Healy, William. *Mental Conflicts and Misconduct.* Boston, Little, Brown and Company, 1917.

Healy, William. *Pathological Lying.* Boston, Little, Brown and Company, 1915.

Healy, William. *Practical Value of Scientific Study of Juvenile Delinquency.* Washington, Children's Bureau, 1922.

Healy, William, and others. *Reconstructing Behavior in Youth.* New York, Alfred A. Knopf, 1929.

Holt, Edwin B. *The Freudian Wish.* New York, Henry Holt and Company, 1915.

Institutional Care of the Insane in the United States and Canada. Baltimore, Johns Hopkins Press, 1916.

"Interview," *The Family,* Vol. X, No. 3 (May, 1929), pp. 74-77.

Interviews. A Study of the Method of Analyzing and Recording Social Case Work Interviews (Studies in the Practice of Social Work, No. 1), New York, American Association of Social Workers, 1928-1929.

Jarrett, Mary. "The Psychiatric Thread Running Through All Social Case Work," *Proceedings of the National Conference of Social Work, 1919.*

Jung, Carl G. *Psychology of the Unconscious.* New York, Dodd, Mead and Company, 1916.

Karpf, Maurice J. "Relation of Length of Treatment to Improvement or Adjustment of Social Case Work Problems," *The Family,* Vol. VIII, No. 5 (July, 1927), pp. 144-48.

Kempton, Helen P. "How Do We Effect Leadership?" *The Family,* Vol. VI, No. 10 (February, 1926), pp. 290-93.

Kenworthy, Marion E. "Psychoanalytic Concepts in Mental Hygiene," *The Family,* Vol. VII, No. 7 (November, 1929), pp. 213-23.

Koffka, Kurt. "On the Structure of the Unconscious," *The Unconscious, A Symposium.* New York, Alfred A. Knopf, 1927.

Köhler, Wolfgang. *Gestalt Psychology.* New York, Horace Liveright, 1929.

Lay, Wilfred. *Man's Unconscious Conflict.* New York, Dodd, Mead and Company, 1917.

Leahy, Alice M. "1926 Emphases in Psychiatric Social Case Work," *Mental Hygiene,* Vol. X, No. 4 (October, 1926), pp. 743-50.

Lee, Porter, "The Fabric of the Family," *Proceedings of the National Conference of Social Work, 1919.*

Lee, Porter, and Kenworthy, Marion. *Mental Hygiene and Social Work.* New York, The Commonwealth Fund, Division of Publications, 1929.

Lowell, Josephine Shaw. *Public Relief and Private Charity.* New York, G. P. Putnam's Sons, 1884.

Lowrey, Lawrence. "Psychiatric Methods and Techniques for Meeting Mental Hygiene Problems in Children of Pre-School Age," *Mental Hygiene,* Vol. XIII, No. 3 (July, 1929).

McClain, W.H. "Relations Existing Between Defective Character and Dependency," *Proceedings of the National Conference of Charities and Corrections, 1907.*

McCord, Elizabeth. "The Value of the Psychiatric Approach for All Children's Case Workers," *Proceedings of the National Conference of Social Work, 1928* (Memphis).

Malinowski, Bronislaw. *Sex and Repression in Savage Society.* New York, Harcourt, Brace and Company, 1927.

Marcus, Grace. "How Case Work Training Can Be Adapted to Meet the Worker's Personal Problems," *Mental Hygiene,* Vol. XI, No. 3 (July, 1927), pp. 449-59.

Marcus, Grace. *Some Aspects of Relief in Family Case Work.* New York Charity Organization Society, 1929.

Meyer, Adolf. "Where Should We attack the Problem of the Prevention of Mental Defect and Mental Disease?" *Proceedings of the National Conference of Social Work, 1915.*

Meyer, Adolf. "A Discussion of Some Fundamental Issues in Freud's Psychoanalysis," *New York State Hospitals Bulletin,* March, 1910.

Mowrer, E. R. *Family Disorganization.* Chicago, The University of Chicago Press, 1927.

Murray, Agnes. "Case Work Above the Poverty Line," *Proceedings of the National Conference of Social Work, 1918.*

Myrick, Helen F. "Psychiatric Social Work. Its Nurture and Nature," *Mental Hygiene,* Vol. XIII, No. 3 (July, 1929).

Nichel, Lucille F. "The Rôle and Aims of the Social Worker in Treatment," *Proceedings of the National Conference of Social Work, 1929.*

Odencrantz, Louise C. *The Social Worker.* New York, Harper and Brothers, 1929.

Overstreet, H. A. *Influencing Human Behavior.* New York, W.W. Norton and Company, 1925.

"Personal Element in Charity, The." *Proceedings of the National Conference of Charities and Corrections, 1885.*

Pfister, O. "Psychoanalysis and the Study of Children," *American Journal of Psychology, 1915.*

Piaget, Jean. *Child's Conception of the World, The.* New York, Harcourt, Brace and Company, 1929.

Piaget, Jean. *Judgment and Reasoning in the Child.* New York, Harcourt, Brace and Company, 1928.

Proceedings of the National Conference of Charities and Corrections, 1877, 1885, 1886, 1888, 1895, 1897, 1899, 1901-1903, 1906, 1910, 1911.

Proceedings of the National Council of Social Work, 1918.

Proceedings of the Seventh Annual Conference of Charities and Corrections, 1880.

Putnam, J. J. *Human Motives.* Boston, Little, Brown and Company.

Putnam, J. J. "Comments on Sex Issues from the Freudian Standpoint," *New York Medical Journal,* June 15 and 22, 1912.

Rank, Otto. *Grundzüge einer Genetischen Psychologie,* I Teil. Leipsig und Wien, Franz Deuticke, 1927. (First lecture series given in English, 1926).

Rank, Otto. *Gestaltung und Ausdruck der Persönlichkeit,* II Teil der *Grundzüge einer Genetischen Psychologie.'* Leipsig und Wien, Franz Deuticke, 1928. (Second lecture series given in English, 1927).

Rank, Otto. *Wahrheit und Wirklichkeit.* Leipsig und Wien, Franz Deuticke, 1929. (Third lecture series given in English, 1928).

Rank, Otto. *The Practical Bearing of Psychoanalysis.* The National Committee for Mental Hygiene, 1927.

Rank, Otto. *The Task of Education.* The National Committee for Mental Hygiene, 1927.

Rank, Otto. *Technik der Psychoanalyse,* Leipsig und Wien, Franz Deuticke, 1926, 1928, 1929.

Queen, Stuart A. "Social Interaction in the Interview: An Experiment," *Social Forces,* Vol. VI, No. 4 (June, 1928), pp. 545-69.

Reynolds, Bertha C. See Doran, Mary S.

Richmond, Mary E. "The Social Worker's Task." *Proceedings of the National Conference of Social Work, 1917.*

Richmond, Mary E. *Friendly Visiting Among the Poor.* New York, The Macmillan Company, 1899.

Richmond, Mary E. *Social Diagnosis.* New York, Russell Sage Foundation, 1917.

Salmon, Thomas W. "Some of the Tasks of Organized Work in Mental Hygiene," *Proceedings of the National Conference of Social Work, 1920* (New Orleans).

Salsberry, Pearl. "Techniques in Case Work," *The Family,* Vol. VIII, No. 5 (July, 1927), pp. 153-57.

Sayles, Mary B. *The Problem Child at Home.* New York, The Commonwealth Fund, Division of Publications, 1928.

Sayles, Mary B. *The Problem Child in School.* New York, The Commonwealth Fund, Division of Publications, 1925.

Sayles, Mary B. *Three Problem Children.* New York, The Commonwealth Fund, Division of Publications,1924.

Schweinitz, Karl de. *The Art of Helping People Out of Trouble.* Boston, Houghton Mifflin Company, 1924.

Sheffield, Ada Eliot. *Case Study Possibilities.* Boston, Research Bureau of Social Case Work, 1922.

Sheffield, Ada Eliot. *Social Case History* New York, Russell Sage Foundation, 1920.

Social Case Work Generic and Specific. A Report of the Milford Conference (Studies in the Practice of Social Case Work, No. 2), New York, American Association of Social Workers, 1929.

Sorokin, P. A. *Contemporary Sociological Theories.* New York, Harper and Brothers, 1928.

Southard, E. E., and Jarrett, Mary, C. *The Kingdom of Evils.* New York, The Macmillan Company, 1922.

Spaulding Edith R. *An Experimental Study of Psychopathic Delinquent Women.* New York, Bureau of Social Hygiene, 1923.

Studies in the Practice of Social Work, No. 2. New York, American Association of Social Workers, 1929.

Taft, Jessie. "The Catch in Praise," *Child Study,* February, 1930.

Taft, Jessie. "The Limitations of the Psychiatrist," *Medicine and Surgery,* March, 1918.

Taft, Jessie. "The Use of the Transfer Within the Limits of the Office Interview," *The Family,* Vol. V, No. 6 (October, 1924).

Theis, Sophie. *How Foster Children Turn Out.* New York, State Charities Aid Association, 1924.

Thomas, Wm. I., and Thomas, Dorothy Swayne. *The Child in America.* New York, Alfred A. Knopf, 1928.

Towle, Charlotte. "The Evaluation of Homes in Preparation for Child Placement," *Mental Hygiene,* Vol. XI, No. 3 (July, 1927), pp. 460-81.

Trotter, W. *Instincts of the Herd in Peace and War.* New York, The Macmillan Company, 1915.

Vocational Aspects of Family Social Work. New York, American Association of Social Workers, 1926.

Vocational Aspects of Medical Social Work. New York, American Association of Social Workers, 1927.

Watson, Frank D. *Charity Organization Movement in the United States.* New York, The Macmillan Company, 1922.

White, William A. *Mechanisms of Character Formation,* New York, The Macmillan, Company, 1916.

White, William A. *Mental Mechanisms.* Nervous and Mental Disease Monograph, Series No. 8, 1911.

Wilcox, Ellen F. "The Measurement of Achievement in Family Case Work," *The Family,* Vol. VIII, No. 2 (April, 1927), pp. 46-47.

Wright, Lucy. "The Worker's Attitude as an Element in Social Case Work," *The Family,* Vol. V, No. 4 (July, 1924), pp. 103-9.

FROM: *THE DYNAMICS OF SUPERVISION UNDER FUNCTIONAL CONTROLS*

1. SUPERVISION AND TRAINING

Allen, Frederick H. "Training in Child Psychiatry," *American Journal of Orthopsychiatry,* Vol. XVI, No. 3, July 1946.

Bishop, Margaret E. *The Selection and Admission of Students in a School of Social Work.* University of Pennsylvania School of Social Work, 1948.

Faith, Goldie Basch. "Class Room and Field Work: Their Joint Contribution to Skill" in *Training for Skill in Social Case Work.* University of Pennsylvania Press, 1942.

Lazarus, Esther. "Integration of Supervision with the Total Program of the Agency," *Proceedings* of the National Conference of Social Work, 1947, pp. 251-60.

Levinson, Frances. "The Generics of Supervisory Process," *Jewish Social Service Quarterly,* March 1949.

Reynolds, Bertha. *Learning and Teaching in the Practice of Social Work.* New York: Farrar and Rinehart, 1942.

Reynolds, Rosemary. *Evaluating the Field Work of Students.* Pamphlet. Family Service Association of America, n.d.

Robinson, Virginia P., Editor. *Supervision in Social Case Work.* Chapel Hill: University of North Carolina Press, 1936.

Robinson, Virginia P. *Training for Skill in Social Case Work.* University of Pennsylvania Press, 1942.

Towle, Charlotte. "The Emotional Element in Learning in Professional Education for Social Work," *Professional Education,* American Association of Schools of Social Work, March 1948.

Wessel, Rosa. "Training for Skill in Casework in a School of Social Work," *The Compass,* September 1944.

2. SUPERVISION

[The following are Unpublished Theses, Pennsylvania School of Social Work, 1941-1948]

Baer, Evelyn S. The Specific Aspects of Supervision in a Child Placing Agency. 1943.

Barral, Esther Rosemblum. The Supervisor's Responsibility for the Professional Development of the Untrained Worker in the Public Assistance Agency. 1941.

Burgess, Caroline Bartow. Learning What Is Involved in Helping a Worker Use a Change of Supervisor in Red Cross Hospital Service. 1947.

Clepper, W. Wendell. Training through Supervision in a County Child Welfare Agency. 1943.

Cohen, Frances G. Policy Which Determines Method—Its Validity for the Supervisory Process in a Public Assistance Agency. 1944.

Cole, Jewell. The Significance of Feeling in the Supervisory Process That Is Directed toward the Development of the Public Assistance Worker's Requisite Skill. 1944.

Finkbinder, Roberta. Supervision as the Fundamental Professional Skill in the Administration of Assistance. 1942.

Goldstein, Lillian Isgur. The Role of the Supervisor in Helping a Student Meet Failure in Casework. 1946.

Hayden, Robert Lawrence. Defining the Role of the Case Supervisor in a New Agency. 1947.

Kahn, Margaret. Resolving Worker-Client Impasse within the Supervisory Relationship. 1945.

Kerner, Catherine. An Experiment in Developing Policy in a Public Assistance Agency through Staff Participation. 1944.

King, Julia. Learning to Use the Function of the Supervisor to Help a First Year Student Move through the Anxiety and Resistance Inherent in the Learning Process toward a Responsible Choice of Training for Skill in Social Casework. 1948.

Lankford, Elizabeth. Supervision, the Process Which Determines the Quality of the Service That Agency Extends to Client. 1943.

Logan, Frances Walker. Learning to Work with Others in a Supervisory Relationship. 1946.

Pierce, Marion. The Contribution of Supervision to the Training of Counseling Teachers. 1947.

Rabinowitz, Eve. Relationship: The Third Dimension in Supervision. 1943.

Royer, William E. Learning to Use the Supervisory Relationship to Induct the Untrained Worker. 1947.

Shapiro, Violet R. Helping an Experienced Worker Achieve the Responsibility for Self That Would Enable Her to Move on to Maximum Salary and Student Supervision. 1948.

Sharkey, Harold B. Learning to Use the Supervisory Role in Working with Case Aides in a Private Immigrant Agency. 1948.

Silverman, H. Kay. The Problem Presented to Supervision by the Experienced Worker Who Has Ceased to Develop Professionally. 1944.

Smith, Rebecca C. Some Aspects of Casework and Supervisory Practice in a Family Agency during Wartime. 1944.

Terrell, Harriet Levin. Evaluation as a Clarification of the Place of Worker and Supervisor in Agency. 1941.

Tingley, Ruth. Supervision of a District of a Public Department through the Supervisory Relationship. 1946.

Whitelock, Marjory. The Supervisor's Use of Difference in Initiating Change in the Caseworker. 1943.

Wiggins, Marguerite. Supervision as It Affects Services to Clients in a Public Assistance Agency. 1942.

Wolfe, Lucille. The Use of Probation Period and Status in Supervision of the New Worker in a Family Agency. 1945.

Young, Marechal-Neil. The Contribution of Supervision to the Movement of Junior High School Counselors in Their First Term of School Counseling. 1948.

Zimmerman, Rebecca. The Critical Phases in the Initial Period of Supervising a Worker in a Child Care Agency. 1943.

Index

Acceptance: attitudes of, 109-111; of difference, 138; of self and difference, 140, 155, 156

Addams, Jane, 51

Adler, Alfred, 4

Adviser, School, function of, 366, 371-378

Ambivalence, 105, 129; caseworker's understanding of, 130-132, 290, 328

Analytic situation, as utilized by Rank, 190-211

Anthony, Sarah, 7

Application, process of, 283, 364, 365-366

Approval. *See* Treatment, techniques

Aptekar, Herbert, 259

Attitudes: casework, toward client, 155-156; meaning and function of, 352-353; to negative aspects of studentship and their potential for self-development, 284, 287-294; process of change in, 354-355; relation to mood and feeling, 354

Bagnold, Enid, 385

Beers, Clifford, 51

Beginning, in training: essential elements to be faced in, 302; problems of, 294-301

Behavioristic interpretation, 84

Bevin, Ernest, 174

Bruno, Frank, 83, 101

Bryn Mawr College, 6

Buel, Estelle, 28

Butler, Edmund J., 38

Campbell, C. Macfie, 8, 52, 66, 69, 70, 85

Carson College for Orphan Girls, 11

Catt, Mrs. Carrie Chapman, 7

Causality, in mental life, 89, 168

Change: of attitude, 179, 182, 183, 387; natural reaction to, 324; process of, 184, 357, 358, 379, 392; psychological problems of, 350, 363; psychological, through professionally controlled relationship, 375; readiness for, 355-357; reality of, 350; refusal to, 355; risk of, in self, 344; in use of will, 360, 363; turning point, in process of, 394

Charity Organization Society, 35, 36

Child guidance clinics, 52; changes in history taking process in, 96

Child placing agency: changes in investigating process, 94, 96

Child study, 42, 43, 239

Choice: of profession, 175, 364, 368; process of, 353; choice of school, 364; affirmation of, 389

Claghorn, Kate Holladay, 101

College Association for Women Suffrage, 101

Common casework field, 78, 82

Commonwealth Fund, publications, 98; organization of Committee for Prevention of Delinquency, 100

Constitutionally inferior personality, 48

Constructive and destructive classification of experiences, 86-87

Contact: long-term, 159; nature of, 63-64; one-sided meaning of word, 103-104; substitute terms for, 112-113

Control: arbitrary, 128, 135-137; as exercised by caseworker over client's situation, 127-128; external, 394; as manipulation of client's inner behavior, 135-136; over own circumstances and reactions, 3; will to control, 178; worker's control of own processes, 135, 136, 137, 150

Copp, Owen, 51

Cornell Clinic of Psychopathology, 9

Creativity, as search for form, 188

Davis, Katherine Bement, 8, 43

Dawley, Almena, 81, 258

Denial, 291

De Schweinitz, Karl, 98

Destructive. See Constructive

Determinism, 53, 85, 108

Devine, Edward T., 33

Dewey, John, 6, 83

Dexter, Elizabeth, 114

Diagnosis: as discussed by Healy, 46-49; by Richmond, 56, 57-58; by Sheffield, 71-74. See also Ego-Libido method

Difference, 361, 362, 381-383; dynamics introduced by, 181, 190, 282-286

Dunham, L., 52

Dynamic interaction, in the analytic situation, 109

Education for social work: concern for, 357; early phases, 10; first steps, 266-267; professional education, 209-210; two-year structuralized process of, 269

Ego-libido method of case analysis, 85-88; See also Kenworthy

Ellis, Havelock, 42

Ending: objectifying student's reaction to, 320; as positive separation experience, 381

Eugenics, 44-45

Evaluation, subjective: of casework results, 101; of student's progress, 307-318

Experience: as means of expanding consciousness, 345; positive-negative classification, 86-87; of taking help, 13

Faatz, Anita J., v, 18-20

Falconer, Martha, 43

Family Service Association of America, 21-22

Fear: of ending, 313; of loss of control, 203-204; of loss and separation, 203

Feeblemindedness, 43

Feeling, defined as awareness movement, 218

Ferenczi, Sandor, 13, 14, 15

Fergusson, Harvey, 216

Fernald, Mabel and Walter, 51

Fieldwork: assignment to, 365; as reality opposing student's outgoing energy, 284; selection of, 189; variety of placement situations in, 219-222

Flügel, J.C., 55

Focus: maintaining of, 187; objective, 190, 305, 318, 336, 345, 395; of resistance, 366; in training process, 378

Folks, Homer, 40

Form, in relation to process, 19-20; search for, 188

Frankel, Lee, 38

Freud, Sigmund, 4, 9, 13, 14, 21, 26, 43, 47, 52-54, 86, 88, 108, 257, 385

"Friendly visitor," 36-37

Function: assimilation of agency function in training, 182; as expressed in agency policy, structure, procedures, 258; "functional" and "diagnostic" casework contrasted, 21-22; identification with, 304-305; lack of use, 188; limitations imposed by, 258-264; support it lends caseworker, 182

Gesell, Arnold, 385-386

Gestalt psychology, 111

Giddings, Franklin H.S., 36

Glueck, Bernard, 52, 53, 66, 85

Goddard, Henry E., 43, 51

Gomberg, M. Robert, 259

Graduate School of Jewish Social Work, 4

Green, Rose, 23

Groves, Ernest, 83

Growth: norm of personality growth, 89, 90; process of, 181, 186, 199, 389; process in relationship, 104-108; stimulated, as contrasted to natural, 211

Hall, G. Stanley, 41, 42, 43, 52

Healy, William, 43, 44, 45-49, 52, 56, 98, 101

Help: determining kind needed, 125-126; kinds of, 359-360; in making use of service, 189; real contrasted with psychological, 260-262, 362

Henderson, C.R., 37

Hill, Octavia, 35

History taking: as affected by treatment relationship, 118-120; changes in content, 91-94; decreasing use of outside sources in, 94; distinguished from knowledge of the present, 120; uses in training students, 121

Hoch, August, 8, 49-50

Hodder, Jessie, 43

Holt, Irwin B., 54

Idealization, 27

Identification, 27, 113, 131, 132, 140, 141, 142-145, 148, 178; definition and movement of, 201-202; with agency function and supervisor, 186, 304-305; on physiological level, 204-206; on psychological level, 206-208. See also Projection

Impulse: creative, 176; to give, 178, 180, 356; impulse-will balance, 357; released in new beginning, 366-368; will control of, 357

Individualization, 184, 187; of clients, 189

Intercity Conference on Illegitimacy, 100

Interpretation, to client, 130-131

James, William, 7

Jarrett, Mary, 66

Journal of Social Casework, 250

Journal of Social Work Process, 18, 20, 258

Jung, Carl Gustav, 4

Kempf, Edward, 9

Kempton, Helen, 112

Kenworthy, Marion, 85, 88-89, 96, 113, 114

Kierkegaard, Soren, 389

Koffka, Kurt, 111

Laboratory of Social Hygiene, 8

Langstorth, Lowell, 88

Lawrence, D. H., 30

Lay, Wilfred, 52

Leahy, Alice, 52

Learning: aims, in professional education, 196; areas of student learning needs, 227; common characteristics of all, 197, 198; essential nature of, 226-227; human organism in learning, 197; individual differences in, 228; involvement of self in, 198; levels of learning, in relation to casework functioning, 219-222; levels of learning behavior, 215; as an organic process, 199-200; patterns of, 207, 208, 211; principle of self-determination in, 200-201; stages of, 198

Lee, Porter R., 40, 68, 79, 96
Liggett, Irene, 258
Limits, setting of, 367
Lowrey, Lawson, 113
Lurie, Harry K., 83

McClain, W.H., 39
McCord, Elizabeth, 94
Marcus, Grace, 99, 114, 116, 146
Maturity, as a norm, 90
Mechanisms of behavior, 88
Medical social work, 76, 77
Menninger, Wilhelm C., 114
Mental conflict, 46, 47, 49
Mental Health movement, 351
Mental Hygiene, 9
Meyer, Adolph, 8, 49, 50, 51, 66
Meyerson, Abraham, 85
Milford Conference Report, 81, 96, 102, 104
Minor, Maude and Stella, 43
Moore, Frank, 43
Myrick, Helen, 80

National Conference of Social Work, 6, 15, 31, 153
New York School of Philanthropy, 249
New York School of Social Research, 13

New York School of Social Work, 4, 10, 13, 14, 16, 66, 76, 79, 109
Nickel, Lucille, 114

Objectivity, 95, 132-133
Otto Rank Association, iii, 24, 111
Overstreet, H.A., 135

Passivity in treatment process, 157, 159, 166
Pennsylvania School of Social and Health Work, later the University of Pennsylvania School of Social Work: adaptations of Rankian psychology to "functional" casework, 21; contributions of new concepts of learning and teaching aims and processes, 16-20, 268; curriculum development, 66; initiation of supervisor's meetings, 146; reorganization into five fields of social work, 79; into nine departments, 76-77
Philanthropy, private, 171
Piaget, Jean, 107, 108
Pierce, William, 7
Pleasure Principle, 86
Pragmatism, 7
Pray, Kenneth, L.M., 10, 22-23, 259
Present vs. historical past, 121-126. See also History taking
Progoff, Ira, 21
Projection, 142, 202; of negative attitudes, 81, 304; on physiological level, 206; on psychological level, 206. See also Identification
Psychiatry: courses in, 85; influence on social work, 51, 52, 66, 77-78; psychiatric social work, 76-78

Psychoanalysis: contributions to casework, 154, 162, 167, 168; influence on social work, 108, 153, 167; pioneers in, 4; social worker's contacts with, 257; treatment goals, 160-161

Psychology: as basis for social work, 55, 75; caseworker's development of a genetic psychology, 54; contrast between behavioristic and psychological interpretations, 84; movement of, in relation to function, 189; movement of social work into psychological phase, 148; special psychological knowledge, 191

Putnam, James J., 57

Queen, Stuart O., 85

Rank, Otto, 12, 13, 14, 15, 17, 20, 22, 23, 24, 25, 29, 30, 108, 112, 216, 257, 343, 389; basic principle of therapy, 26; develops new form of therapeutic process, 4; influence on social work, 6-18; lectures, 10, 109

Rappaport, Mazie, 259

Records, case: changes in, 91-97; objectivity in, 95. *See also* History taking

Reformatory for Women, New York State, 8

Relationship: characteristics of, in social casework, 112-118; of client and caseworker, 109; difference between personal and professional, 28; identification with morally right, 131-132; objectivity in, 132-133; particular characteristics of, 252-253; patterns of, 206-208; professional, 190; reaction in, 129-131; relationship psychology, 27, 29-30; of supervisor and student, 142-147

Relativity, concepts of, 108-109

Relief Agencies, 33-34

Resistance, in student, 288, 318

Reynolds, Bertha, 32

Richmond, Mary, exponent of "social diagnosis," 8, 16, 17, 36, 37, 55-65, 66, 68, 89, 96, 112, 147, 249

Royde-Smith, Naomi, 385

Rush, Benjamin, 49-50

Russell Sage Foundation, 8

Sacks, Patricia, 21

St. Clair, McKelway, 275

Salmon, Thomas, 8, 52, 60, 70

Salsberry, Pearl, 135

School, professional: function of, 210; guideposts for training students, 345-347

Selection, of students, 141

Self: acceptance-denial of, 27; commitment of, 176; constant process of defining self, 354; concept of social self, 57; degree of engagement, 176; demands on, in training, 210-211; discipline of, in assuming responsibility, 316; movement of, in projection and identification, 201-202; need in training for recognition of whole, 187; part-whole movement of, 199; professional self, 209-210; reaction of, to education interpreted as pressure, 208; reorganization of structure and functioning of, 196; as tool, 180

Sensitivity: to difference, 17; to injustice and inequality, 17; to other; 189; to wrong, 172

Separation: aspects of, 162; experience, 162-164; principle of, 26

Sex, recognition of, 42

Shaw, Anna Howard, 7
Sheffield, Ada, 71-74
Sheldon, Elinor, 21
Skill: definition of, 175, 179, 182, 190; development of, 174, 176; essential, in supervision, 186, 188, 319, 342-357; generic and specific, 188; meaning of, in single interview, 183; three levels of, 191
Smalley, Ruth, 24
Smallwood, William, 37
Smith College for Psychiatric Social Work, 51, 66, 342
Social Diagnosis, 55-56, 71, 75, 76, 93, 96, 98, 147. *See also* Richmond, Mary
Social Security Act of 1935, 251
Social Service Agency: defined by function, structure, limits, 256; as reality situation standing between worker and client, 179-180
Sociology, influence on casework, 41
Southard, E.E., 51-52, 66, 68, 74, 112
Spaulding, Edith, 51, 56
Specialization in social casework, 76-77
Spock, Benjamin, 385
Supervision: defined as technical process, 265-266, 268; different uses of, 229-231; essential basis of, 319, 342-347; supervisor-advisor coordination, 308

Taft, Jessie, iii, 4, 7, 8, 9, 10, 12-14, 15-16, 17, 18, 20, 45, 66, 113, 258, 260, 289, 293, 360
Theis, Sophie, 101
Thesis, requirement, 339-342
Thomas, W.I., 7
Time structure, relation to change and growth, 393-395
Transference: borrowed from psychiatric terminology, 104;

meaning of, 114; positive-negative aspects, use of, 156
Treatment, in social casework: casework seen as individual therapy through a treatment relationship, 150; contrasted with psychoanalysis, 155-168; of delinquency, 100-101; emphasis on relationship in, 103-104, 112-115, 151-152; of illegitimacy, 100; literature of, 98-99; prescriptions before 1900, 99-100; techniques, 133-137; treatment goals of casework, 90, 102, 149; use of application for social service in, 166; use of function as tool in, 248, 257-259
Trotter, William, 104
Tufts, James, 7
Turning point, in training, 305-310; connection to time structure, 318, 394-395

Understanding, factor in caseworker's attitude, 128-131
University of Chicago, 6
University of Southern California, 23

Vocational pamphlets, published by the American Association of Social Workers, 79

Watson, Frank D., 35
White, William A., 52, 53, 54
Will: Change through will forces, 351; concern of school with student's will organization, 357-363; to create professional self, 191; as expression of self, 215-217; origin of will, 385; positive-negative, 4; power of will over circumstance, 385

Yielding: definition of, 346; as differentiation of self, 375, 383; as potentiality for growth, 337

DATF